World's Great Men of Color

WORLD'S GREAT MEN OF COLOR

VOLUME I

J. A. ROGERS

*Edited with an introduction, commentary,
and new bibliographical notes by*

JOHN HENRIK CLARKE

COLLIER BOOKS
Macmillan Publishing Company
New York

COLLIER MACMILLAN PUBLISHERS
London

Macmillan Publishing Company
866 Third Avenue, New York, N.Y. 10022
Collier Macmillan Canada, Inc.

World's Great Men of Color was originally published
by J. A. Rogers and is reprinted in this revised edition
by arrangement.

Library of Congress Catalog Card Number: 73-180437

ISBN 0-02-081300-7

First Collier Books Edition 1972

15 14 13 12 11 10

Macmillan books are available at special discounts for
bulk purchases for sales promotions, premiums, fund-
raising, or educational use. For details, contact:

Special Sales Director
Macmillan Publishing Company
866 Third Avenue
New York, N.Y. 10022

Printed in the United States of America

Contents

v

AFRICA

Illustrations

Introduction

J. A. ROGERS devoted at least fifty years of his life to researching great black personalities and the roles they played in the development of nations, civilizations, and cultures. This book is his greatest achievement. In his lifetime his books did not reach a large popular reading audience. All of them were privately printed and circulated mainly in the black communities; he died, unfortunately, on the eve of the "Black Studies Revolution." Mr. Rogers had already delivered what some of the radical black students were demanding. He had looked at the history of people of African origin, and had showed how their history is an inseparable part of the history of mankind.

A number of recent books have validated the early claims of J. A. Rogers, who started his research at a time when a large number of black people had some doubts about their contribution to human history. In books like *Blacks in Antiquity* by Frank M. Snowden, Jr. (1970), *The African Genius* by Basil Davidson (1969), *The Prehistory of Africa* by J. Desmond Clark (1970), *Topics in West African History* by A. Adu Boahen (1967), *Introduction to African Civilizations* by John G. Jackson (1970), and *Great Civilizations of Ancient Africa* by Lester Brooks (1971) these doubts are put to rest.

In a recent paper Professor Keith E. Baird calls attention to how and why Africa was lost from the respectful commentary of history. Until quite recently it was rather generally assumed, even among well-educated persons in the West, that the continent of Africa was a great expanse of land, mostly jungle, inhabited by savages and fierce beasts. It was unthought of that great civilizations could have been born in might and wisdom over vast empires. It is true that there were some notions current about the cultural achievement of Egypt, but Egypt was conceived of as a European land rather than as a country of Africa. Even if a look at an atlas or globe showed Egypt to be in Africa, then popular thought immediately saw in the Sahara desert a formidable barrier and a convenient division of Africa into two parts: one, north of the Sahara, was inhabited by a European-like people of high culture and noble history: the other, south of the Sahara, was inhabited by a dark-skinned people who had no culture, and were incapable of having done anything in their dark and distant past that could be dignified by the designation of "history." Such ideas, of course, are far from the truth, as we shall see. But it is not difficult to understand why they persisted, and, unfortunately, still persist in one form or another in the popular mind.

Europeans have long been in contact with Africa, that is, Northern Africa. The names of Esop and Memnon, of Terence and Cleopatra are the names of Africans who have figured in the legend and literature, the arts and history of Greece and Rome. Indeed, the land of Africa was a land of wonders for the ancient Greeks and Romans, and this to such an extent that among them it was a proverb that out of Africa there is always something new. The concept of "darkest Africa" refers to the comparative ignorance of Europeans regarding that continent and its peoples over the last four centuries. An English writer, Jonathan Swift, made a sharp but witty comment on his fellow Europeans' lack of knowledge of Africa when he wrote:

> Geographers in Africa maps
> With savage pictures fill their gaps,
> And o'er uninhabitable downs
> Paint elephants instead of towns.

There is another reason why the people of Africa, with the notable exclusion of Egypt, were depicted as uncivilized and lacking in cultural attainments. A number of pious people in Europe would have been struck with horror if they knew of the cruel and blood acts of their country men in the course of the inhuman slave-trade. Ruthless European adventurers promoted the hunting down of men, women and children like beasts, and the destruction of complete villages in order to capture the inhabitants and sell them like cattle. Therefore, slave-traders would invent fantastic tales of savagery about the Africans so that their capture and their transportation to labor on the plantations of the Americans would appear to be acts of Christian concern and high minded enlightenment.

In the books of J. A. Rogers an attempt has been made to locate Africa's proper place on the maps of human geography. That is what his life and research were about.

The distinguished Afro-American poet Countee Cullen began his poem "Heritage" with the question "What is Africa to me?" This book extends the question by asking, "What is Africa to the Africans?" and "What is Africa to the world?" This book also answers those questions.

In his monograph on *The Significance of African History,* the Caribbean-American writer Richard B. Moore observed:

The significance of African history is shown, though not overtly, in the very effort to deny anything worthy of the name of history to Africa and the African peoples. This widespread, and well nigh successful endeavor, maintained through some five centuries, to erase African history from the general record, is a fact which of itself should be quite conclusive to thinking and open minds. For it is logical and apparent that no such undertaking would ever have been carried on, and at such length, in order to obscure and to bury what is actually of little or no significance.

The prime significance of African history becomes still more manifest when it is realized that this deliberate denial of African history arose out of the European expansion and invasion of Africa which began in the middle of the fifteenth century. The compulsion was thereby felt to attempt to justify such colonialist conquest, domination, enslavement, and plunder. Hence, this brash denial of history and culture to Africa, and, indeed, even of human qualities and capacity for "civilization" to the indigenous peoples of Africa.

According to all of the evidence we now have, mankind started in Africa. In his book *The Progress and Evolution of Man in Africa,* Dr. L. S. B. Leakey states that:

In every country that one visits and where one is drawn into a conversation about Africa, the question is regularly asked, by people who should know better: "But what has Africa contributed to world progress?" The critics of Africa forget that men of science today are, with few exceptions, satisfied that Africa was the birthplace of man himself, and that for many hundreds of centuries thereafter, Africa was in the forefront of all world progress.

The southern origins of North African civilizations have been established; here, I am only alluding to some of the proof.

In his book *Egypt*, Sir E. A. Wallis Budge says, "The prehistoric native of Egypt, both in the old and in the new Stone Ages, was an African, and there is every reason for saying that the earliest settlers came from the South." There are many things in the manners and customs and religions of the historic Egyptians that suggest that the original home of their prehistoric ancestors was in a country in the neighborhood of Uganda and Punt. (The biblical land of Punt was in the area now known as Somalia.)

The civilization of Egypt lasted longer than any other civilization known to man—about 10,000 years. This civilization reached its height and was in decline before Europe was born.

In section one of this book Mr. Rogers calls attention to the great personalities in Africa before the birth of Christ who influenced early Europe and all the known world of their day. In section two he writes about a little-known aspect of history, which has only recently come under investigation by a few scholars, that is, the impact of the African personality on Asia.

In section three, on Africa, the biographies range from the emperors of Ethiopia's last golden age to leaders of the resistance movements against the Europeans in the nineteenth and early twentieth century.

Until near the end of the nineteenth century the African freedom struggle was a military struggle. This aspect of African history has been shamefully neglected. I do not believe the neglect is an accident. Africa's oppressors and Western historians are not ready to concede the fact that Africa has a fighting heritage. The Africans did fight back and they fought exceptionally well. This fight extended throughout the whole of the nineteenth century.

This fight was led, in most cases, by African kings. The Europeans referred to them as chiefs in order to avoid equating them with European kings. But they were kings in the truest sense of the word. Most of them could trace their lineage back more than a thousand years. These revolutionary nationalist African kings are mostly unknown because the white interpreters of Africa still want the world to think that the African waited in darkness for other people to bring the light.

In West Africa the Ashanti Wars started early in the nineteenth century when the British tried to occupy the hinterland of the Gold Coast (now Ghana). There were eleven major wars in this conflict. The Ashanti won all of them, except the last. In these wars Ashanti generals—and we should call them generals, because they were more than equal to the British generals who failed to conquer them—stopped the inland encroachment of the British and commanded respect for the authority of their kings.

In 1844 the Fanti kings of Ghana signed a bond of agreement with the English. This bond brought a short period of peace to the coastal areas of the country.

In the 1860s King Ghartey, the West African reformer, advocated democratic ideas in government at a time when the democratic institutions of Europe were showing signs of deterioration. King Ghartey ruled over the small coastal Kingdom of Winnebah in preindependent Ghana. He was the driving spirit behind the founding of the Fanti Confederation, one of the most important events in the history of West Africa.

There were two freedom struggles in preindependent Ghana. One was led by the Ashanti in the hinterland and the other was led by the Fanti, who lived along the coast. The Ashanti were warriors. The Fanti were petitioners and constitution-makers. The Fanti Constitution, drawn up in conferences between 1865 and 1871, is one of the most important documents produced in Africa in the nineteenth century. In addition to being the constitution of the Fanti Confederation, it was a petition to the British for the independence of the Gold Coast.

In 1896 the British exiled the Ashanti King Prempeh, but still were not able to take over completely the hinterland of the Gold Coast. Fanti nationalists, led by Casley Hayford, started the agitation for the return of King Prempeh and soon converted this agitation into a movement for the independence of the country.

The stubborn British still did not give up their desire to establish their authority in the interior of the country and avenge the many defeats they had suffered at the hands of the Ashanti.

In 1900 the British returned to Kumasi, the capital of Ashanti, and demanded the right to sit on the Golden Stool. Sir Frederick Hodgson, who made the demand on behalf of the British, displayed his complete ignorance of Ashanti folklore, history, and culture. The Ashanti people cherished the Golden Stool as their most sacred possession. To them it was the Ark of the Covenant. Ashanti kings were not permitted to sit on it. The demand for the Stool was an insult to the pride of the Ashanti people and it started the last Ashanti War. This war is known as "The Yaa Asantewa War," since Yaa Asantewa, the reigning queen mother of Ashanti, inspired and was one of the leaders of this effort to save the Ashanti Kingdom from British rule. After nearly a year of heroic struggle Queen Yaa Asantewa was captured along with her chief associates, and at last the British gained control over the hinterland of the Gold Coast. To accomplish this they had had to fight the Ashanti for nearly a hundred years.

In other parts of West Africa resistance to European rule was still strong and persistent. While the drama of Ashanti and other tribal nations was unfolding in the Gold Coast, an Ibo slave rose above his humble origins in Nigeria and vied for commercial power in the marketplaces of that nation. In the years before the British forced him into exile in 1885, he was twice a king and was justifiably called "The Merchant Prince of West Africa." His name was Jaja. The story of Jaja is woven through all of the competently written histories of Nigeria. His strong opposition to British rule in the 1880s makes him the father of Nigerian nationalism.

In the French colonies the two main leaders of revolts were Behanzin Hossu Bowelle of Dahomey and Samory Touré of Guinea. Behanzin was one of the most colorful and the last of the great kings of Dahomey. He was also one of the most powerful West Africans during the closing years of the nineteenth century. After many years of opposition to French rule in his country he was defeated by a French mulatto, General Alfred Dodds. He was sent into exile and died in 1906.

Samory Touré, grandfather of Sékou Touré, President of Guinea, was the last of the great Mandingo warriors. Samory is the best-known personality to emerge from the Mandingoes in the years following the decline of their power and empire in the Western Sudan. Samory defied the power of France for eighteen years and was often referred to by the French who opposed him as "The Black Napoleon of the Sudan." He was defeated and captured in 1898 and died on a small island in the Congo River in 1900.

In the Sudan and in East Africa two men, called dervish warriors, Mohammed Ahmed, known as the Mahdi, and Mohammed Ben Abdullah Hassen, known as the Mad Mullah of Somaliland, were thorns in the side of the British Empire. Mohammed Ahmed freed the Sudan of British rule before his death in 1885, and the country stayed free for eleven years before it was reconquered. Mohammed Ben Abdullah Hassen started his campaigns against the British in Somaliland in 1899 and was not defeated until 1921.

Southern Africa has furnished a more splendid array of warrior kings than any other part of the continent. Chaka, the Zulu king and warlord, is the most famous, the most maligned, and the most misinterpreted. By any fair measurement he was one of the greatest natural warriors of all time. He fought to consolidate South Africa and to save it from European rule. When he died in 1828 he was winning the fight.

Chaka's fight was continued with varying degrees of success and failure under the leadership of kings like Moshesh of the Basutos, Khama of the Bamangwato, Dingaan, Chaka's half-brother and successor, Cetewayo, nephew and disciple of Chaka, Lobenguela, whose father, Mosilekatze, built the second Zulu Empire, and Bambaata, who led the last Zulu uprising in 1906.

What I have been trying to say is this: For a period of more than a hundred years African warrior nationalists, mostly kings, who had never worn a store-bought shoe or heard of a military school, out-maneuvered and out-generaled some of the finest military minds of Europe. They planted the seeds of African independence for another generation to harvest.

The importance of these personalities is in the fact that their agitation against the colonial powers in Africa helped to create the basis for the political emergence of modern Africa.

JOHN HENRIK CLARKE

1972

How and Why This Book Was Written

"A people will never look forward to posterity who never look backward to their ancestors." —EDMUND BURKE

I HAVE OFTEN been asked what led me to begin my researches on what for a better name I will call Negro history. As I look back on it now, I think it really began in my early childhood when it was firmly impressed on me by the ruling classes that black people were inherently inferior and that their sole reason for being was to be servants to white people and the lighter-colored mulattoes. The blacks, I was told, had never accomplished anything in all of history, which, of course, began "with Adam and Eve in the Garden of Eden," and that such signs of civilization they now showed were due to the benevolence of Christian whites who had dragged them from Africa and cannibalism, thereby plucking them as "brands from the burning" of hell and eternal torment.

The Christian blacks themselves said amen to this and joined in spreading the doctrine. My Sunday School teacher, an almost unmixed Negro, told us that black people were cursed by God and doomed to eternal servitude to white people because Ham had laughed at his drunken father, Noah. To clinch his argument he read to us from the Bible, which we were taught was infallible. Doubt but a single word, try to change but a tittle, and you were doomed to burn in hell forever and ever. The slavemasters and kidnappers had indeed done their work well. They had so incorporated their iniquities with the Christian religion that when you doubted their racism you were contradicting the Bible and flying in the face of God Almighty.

As for the devout Christian Negro who taught us, so great an impression did he make on me that I still remember his features and his name though nearly half a century has passed. Of course, it was understood that if one had a mixture of "white blood," which was true in my case, one's future was not so entirely hopeless. Still one could never reach the heights of intelligence and accomplishment of an unmixed white person, for any visible degree of Negro strain immutably consigned one to be "lower than the angels," that is, the whites. This eternal inferiority included me. However, even at the risk of eternal torture I could not swallow what this sincere, but gullible, tool of the master class was telling me. There was a streak of logic in me that prevented it. I had been told that God was good. Why, then, I asked myself, had he doomed millions and millions of people to such an ignominious fate simply because their "ancestor" thousands of years ago had laughed at his father because the father had been acting like a pig. Was God so much in favor of drunken fathers?[1]

I had furthermore noticed that some of the brightest of my schoolmates were unmixed blacks and some of them were more brilliant than some of the white ones. The principal of the school, too, was a mulatto. I also saw around me black physicians and

---

[1] This fable of Ham as it is made to apply to black people does not come from the Bible but from Jewish legends. For its sources see *Sex and Race*, Vol. III, pp. 316–17. For how black Southern mammies taught this Ham story to white children, see Andrews, M. P. *Women of the South*, p. 190, 1920. See also *Century*, Vol. XXVIII, May–Oct. 1884, p. 859.

Incidentally, there was ground for setting in operation a similar fable against the whites by the dark-skinned peoples. Today, as Lord Raglan says, civilization is often thought of as being inherent in "a white skin and it is forgotten that the founders of civilization were brown skinned." Aristotle, whose people had received their culture chiefly from dark-skinned Egyptians, found Nordics intellectually and mechanically inferior (*Politics*, VIII, 7) and that was more than two centuries before Julius Caesar carried the light of civilization to those who now make most use of the Ham legend. Lord Raglan rightly says, "The Whites were, it seems, incapable of civilizing themselves. . . . The savages of today seem to be in the same case as the whites were three or four thousand years ago." ("The Future of Civilization" in *The Rationalist Annual*, p. 40, 1946.) For the manner in which the Romans regarded the Nordics, see *Sex and Race*, Vol. III, pp. 3–5, 251.

lawyers, all graduates of the best English and Scottish universities. If the Negro strain were inherently inferior, why had these black people been able to accomplish these things and be more advanced than some of the barefooted white adults I knew? Still I did not contradict this Sunday School teacher. I was not supposed to. My business was to swallow what I heard. One word of doubt and I would promptly have been dubbed an "infidel," which was at bottom worse than being a criminal because a criminal could be saved and go to heaven while special torment in hell, à la Dante, was reserved for deliberate unbelievers. If you did not swallow all the good things the existing order told you, including the yarn about the whale swallowing Jonah and Moses turning his stick into a snake, you were not only not a good Christian but also not a good citizen. I distinctly recall two individuals I had been especially taught to look down on: one was a man who used to argue with my father about the miracles of the Bible, which he called "rubbish"; the other was a relative, a light mulatto, who had married a black woman. Race prejudice, religion, and good citizenship went together.

Of course, the above will seem an exaggeration to many. Well, we can still find plenty of it in any English-speaking land. Millions of whites in the South, what H. L. Mencken called "the Bible belt," pin their faith on the Ham story. One thing I have learned from my travels, especially in civilized lands, is that stupid beliefs and superstititions never die no matter how mechanical progress advances. Even some of the world's great intellectuals find strength and comfort in the superstitions about race.[2] They remind one of the patient who when asked by a psychiatrist whether any members of his family suffered from insanity, replied, "No, they don't suffer from it; they enjoy it."

Jim Crow and upright Christian living are held to be indivisible by millions of whites, especially in the United States and the Brit-

---

[2] B. Berry (*You and Your Superstitions*, 1940) names many of the stupid beliefs still held even by many educated people. Especially is this so in the matter of physiognomy. You will find, he says, some of those listed in *Who's Who* and *American Men of Science* "who will not balk for a moment at the theory that kinky hair and black skin reveal low intelligence and musical temperament and that blond hair and blue eyes reveal intellectual and spiritual excellence."

ish colonies and dominions. As for the Mormons, their missionaries still teach that Negroes can't go to heaven because of "race."
I ran across some of these Mormon missionaries in Germany in
1927 and a Minnesota white woman recently wrote me about their
teachings in her state. In 1903 when burial services were being
held in a Baptist church in Salt Lake City for Eugene Burns, a
Negro, the grandson of Abel Burns, faithful servant of Joseph
Smith, founder of Mormonism, Patriarch Miner, president of one
of the quorums of the Seventies of the Mormon Church, "walked
up to the pulpit and to the consternation of the mourners began a
highly sensational discourse" to prove that Burns, as a Negro,
"could not reach the state of exaltation necessary to entrance into
heaven" and that "his soul was doomed before birth." The only
Negro who had ever entered heaven, Miner declared, was Burns'
grandfather, and that was because of the latter's fidelity to the
"Prophet." (*New York Sun*, Nov. 15, 1903).[3]

As I grew older I revolted more and more at this asininity
concocted by "the master race" but I had no books at hand to
contradict it, nor knowledge of any kind. To make matters worse I
had from a Negro friend of mine a book in which this alleged
inherent inferiority was stressed, and which, ironically, had been
given to him as first prize for the best essay in which white chil-

---

[3] Prejudice against Negroes is a cardinal tenet of the Mormon religion.
Black people are considered accursed and so are all their offspring with
white people. The Mormon prophet Joseph Smith had the "Lamanites," a
white people, changed to black by God for their sins. The *Book of Mormons*,
II Nephi, Chap. 5, verses 21–23, reads, "And he caused the cursing to come
upon them, yet, even a sore cursing because of their iniquity. For behold
they had hardened their hearts against him that they had become like flint;
wherefore as they were white and exceedingly fair and delightsome that they
might not be enticing unto my people, the Lord God did cause a skin of
blackness to come upon them. . . .

". . . and cursed shall be the seed of him that mixeth with their seed; for
they shall be cursed with the same cursing."

Utah law punishes mixed marriages severely.

Negroes are permitted to attend Mormon services but they are not welcome as devout Mormons do consider them an accursed "race." They are
ineligible for Mormon priesthood and incapable of redemption. Not so the
Japanese, however, thanks to their lighter color. "Several Japanese," says
Carey McWilliams (*Nation*, N.Y. Jan. 26, 1946, p. 98) "are members in
good standing of the Mormon Church and eligible for the priesthood and
are not segregated." Negroes, he says, are treated quite differently in Utah
and in the Mormon Church.

dren had also competed. Years later to make it still worse I read Thomas Dixon's *The Clansman*, a highly emotional novel in which all but the Uncle Toms were painted in a most horrible light and which said that if one had but a "drop" of "Negro blood" he was damned intellectually forever. There were also the books on Africa, "darkest Africa," by Stanley, and works by missionaries in which Africans were painted either as faithful dogs or horrible savages. Occasionally, I heard a newly returned missionary from Africa, who, at a Sunday morning service, would paint a most pitiable picture of what he called "the heathen," and preach how we should all contribute, and put into the collection plate "the feathers that would make the gospel fly." Incidentally, when I did go to Africa I saw natives who lived better than a large number of whites in Europe, especially in England and Italy, and who, unlike the whites, could not even read the Bible. As for the poorer blacks, I venture to say that their huts of grass, sticks, and clay were no worse than the slums I saw in the East End of London.

Up to the time of these "racial" experiences I had been identifying myself with the characters in the books I read. For instance, in my great favorite, Shakespeare's *Julius Caesar*, I saw Brutus, Caesar, Cassius, and the rest not as "white" men but as individuals either to be emulated or shunned. In *Paul and Virginia* my deepest sympathies went out to Virginia because I never thought of her as a "white" woman but as one whose high ideals had brought her suffering and death. But after these experiences I began to search for some world figures that were of Negro ancestry. However, there was not a single one to be found, so carefully had they been expurgated by the masters. Alexandre Dumas was one of my favorites, but not a single word was there of his Negro strain. Literature, religion, education had all been carefully bleached. At last I did hear of one great mulatto whose "race" could not be hid because I knew people who had seen him, and who was then in the world news—General Antonio Maceo, Cuba's greatest military leader. However, it was not until years later that I found in Chicago a friend who introduced me to books in which I found the names of several great men of Negro ancestry, past and present. In my spare time, and with no thought of writing a book, I began to collect some of these names. That was about 1911.

About a year later, however, I had a setback from an entirely different quarter. I belonged then to a radical economic group composed of whites and Negroes. When during a discussion at one meeting I mentioned great Negroes and how I had been collecting their names, there was a general howl of disapproval from the whites and most of the Negroes. They called me a "chauvinist" and said that I was suffering from an inferiority complex.

Who were these great Negroes I was digging up? Tools of the capitalist order or they wouldn't be in capitalist books. In short, I was one of the most despicable of all creatures: a Negro who was a capitalist hero-worshipper. Furthermore, they said, such work as I was engaged in would be useless when "the industrial revolution" came and color differences mattered no more. A true radical would be studying Marx, Engels, and La Fargue, and preparing for the workers' utopia, which was just around the corner. (The economic radical viewpoint has broadened considerably since then.)

With my enthusiasm dampened by this rebuff I allowed much time to pass without doing any research on great Negroes. However, I noticed that books alleging inherent Negro inferiority continued to appear. And Dixon's *Clansman* had now been made into a flaming attack on Negroes in a motion picture, *The Birth of a Nation*. All of these, I felt, should be answered not with sentiment, as I noticed certain white friends of the Negro and Negroes themselves were doing in the Chicago press, but with facts. It seemed to me, too, that if the new order was going to be all that my radical friends said it would be, then one of its aims would be not to exclude or ignore the cultures of minorities but to conserve them, as a knowledge of other peoples and their art, literature, and accomplishments helps to produce that variety necessary for a high state of civilization. I decided also that those who were really interested in righting the Negro's wrongs in a concrete way ought to welcome any knowledge that would equip them with the means of refutation of Negro inferiority.

About this time I also made what was to me an important discovery, namely, that the recital of the deeds of the great or the worthy was instinctive in humanity. I found that all peoples— English, French, Germans, Spaniards, Italians, Americans, Chinese, Jews, Moslems—had lists of their great and noted men. And more than that, even states of the union, cities, and small towns had their list of "greats," as well as doctors, scientists, lawyers, preachers, engineers, and almost every professional group. Why, even the radicals who had called me a chauvinist had their own heroes whom they were forever extolling and whom they worshipped as blindly as the conservatives did theirs. What the radicals really wanted was that I should worship at their own particular shrine, eschewing all others. Moreover, I felt that if I were the victim of an inferiority complex, I certainly had a host of illustrious company dating back to Plutarch with his *Lives of Illustrious Greeks and Romans.*

Another thought that decided me to continue my researches was that man's chief knowledge of himself was what has been done by man; that the good and the evil that others have done were our sole guide through life's wilderness. And was not the recital of great and stirring deeds the most gripping of all dramas?

To bring out the best in ourselves (and at times the worst, too) a study of the lives of the great of all races, ages, and climes is a necessity. Biography will ever be the highest and most civilizing form of literature. That is why Plutarch is still a best seller after two thousand years.

As regards "race," a concept that was thrust upon me (I had never felt otherwise than as a member of the human race), I realize that the further back the Negro's past could be pushed, the more ridiculous would appear the old slave-holding dogma of Negro "inferiority." I saw, also, that the white overlords to inflate the ego of their own group had reached back to claim the coal-black Ethiopian, the mulatto Egyptian, the black Hindu, the Negroid Polynesian, not to mention certain individuals of Negro ancestry such as Aesop, Terence, Cleopatra, and Mohammed, as white. Later, I saw Mussolini trying to prime his people by telling them of their great Roman past; and Hitler puffing up his by calling them Aryans and claiming that the ancient Egyptians were really Teutons. In short, Negro history was only a rebuttal of this braggadocio of the white masters. Let me say here that I feel emphatically that any boasting by Negroes about their history is just as nauseating. Furthermore, those individuals who work themselves up to a state where they talk as if the deeds of an ancestor were actually done by themselves will probably go no further than that in doing something worthy themselves. One of the world's greatest needs has ever been unboastful, unbiased history.

I noticed too that there was an urge not only to delve into national and "racial" history but into individual ancestry also. I thought of the great genealogical societies, of the immense number of books tracing genealogies even here in America, and of the money paid out by the newly-rich and others for a family tree and a coat-of-arms. I was especially struck by one magazine founded in 1899, *The Mayflower Descendants*, that minutely traced living Americans to the *Mayflower*, even though such strain after more than 300 years is extremely attenuated. Yes, it does appear that a past is as necessary to man as roots to a tree.

Of course, it is true that people who boast of their ancestry do so because they realize their own inferiority. Such have been rightly compared to a potato plant whose best part is underground. However, it is undeniable that a knowledge of one's ancestors does have a certain psychological value, especially if such ancestors were worthy. Especially for youths would this be an inspiration. In short, as with almost everything else, ancestry is what you make of it.

I reasoned now that since so many other groups and individuals were tracing their past, why should the objection be so strong when the Negro did so? Was not such objection but another manifestation of the white superiority complex, even in the case of the white economic radicals?

As regards the lives of great Negroes, I felt too that the greater handicaps they had had to overcome because of color ought to prove an inspiration to right-thinking white people with their lesser handicaps. Queen Victoria made her grandchildren read Booker T. Washington's *Up From Slavery*. In view of the foregoing and in spite of the taunts of the economic radicals, white and Negro, I continued my researches on great Negroes, purely as a hobby.

In 1924, however, while I was writing a column of criticism for the *Messenger* magazine, George S. Schuyler, the managing editor, asked me to do instead short sketches of noted Negroes. I complied rather reluctantly, feeling that the public, not only white but

Negro as well, would not be interested. However, the stories seemed to take. A South African magazine carried one of them and *Time* magazine made mention of another.

When the *Messenger* was discontinued about three years later, Schuyler, then editor of a supplement, *The Illustrated Weekly*, that went to some forty Negro newspapers, wrote to me in Paris, where I was then living, asking me to write biographies for it. Still not liking the idea, I did not reply immediately, and he wrote again, urging me to accept. I did and so successful were the biographies that many requests came in asking for the sketches in book form. Finally, in 1931, I published a small paper-bound edition at a dollar, which sold very well. Two other editions had even more success. The last copies of this book were sold in 1938 and are out of print.

Something now about the research itself. That was not easy since the story of the contacts of whites and blacks is usually told from the white angle. To get the material I had to browse through an immense number of books and other printed matter in the libraries of America, Europe, and North Africa, as well as search long and persistently through museums, old bookshops, churches, and private collections. I knew, for instance, that the Negro had been important in Portuguese history but I sought in vain, at least in books of English text, for the name of a single great Portuguese Negro. It was not until I went to Portugal that I did learn of some.

From two works by Negroes I received much perspective and valuable leads. These were George Wells Parker's *Children of the Sun* and William H. Ferris' two-volume work, *The African Abroad*. Later, I found three invaluable books by white authors on the Negro's past: Godfrey Higgins' *Anacalypsis* and Gerald Massey's *A Book of the Beginnings* and *Ancient Egypt, the Light of the World*. From others, such as the late Arthur Schomburg, I also received some rare leads.

With regard to Parker I must make a belated apology. I once disagreed with him in the *Messenger* for saying that Cleopatra and Mohammed were of Negro ancestry. The simple truth is I had never looked into the matter, but having so often heard that Cleopatra was "pure Greek" and knowing that her ancestor, Ptolemy, was Greek, I accepted it as fact, not knowing that the Egyptian Ptolemies were very much mixed, and furthermore that the Greeks were a nationality and not a so-called race, and that even as one can be "pure" American and be of mixed race, so was it with the Greeks. Later, I did find evidence to make me believe that Parker was right about Cleopatra and most certainly about Mohammed.[4]

As a result of these prejudices on my part, I can readily understand how preconceived ideas on the Negro's real past must constitute a barrier to the acceptance of a book such as this. One truth that research has taught me is that however incredible things may sound, there are very, very few situations in the life of humanity that could not be true. This is particularly true of miscegenation and the mixed strain it has brought into the ancestry of peoples and individuals. It is possible for the fairest Nordic to have had a Negro ancestor. This latter, by migrating to Europe and he and his offspring mating only with blonds, would in time produce blonds, who unless records were kept would know nothing of their Negro ancestor. A white migrating to Central Africa and his offspring mating, in like manner, only with blacks would in time produce blacks indistinguishable from his fellows. This process has doubtless taken place innumerable times in human history. There is no doubt in my mind either that even without miscegenation climate alone would effect such a change after fixed habitation over a very long period. Europe was once inhabited by an indigenous Negro people and by tropical animals and plants and might be again. Wherever coal is found was once tropical, including what is now the Arctic Circle. However, many find it impossible to believe that the forces of nature which are able to change black anthracite to a diamond of the purest water would change a coal-black Negro into a white man. There are scientists, too, who find it easier to believe that they had an ape for an ancestor than a Negro.

In 1945, when the New York Public Library carried an exhibit intended to prove the equality of "races," a Southerner who is

---

[4] Al-Jahiz, Arab writer of the ninth century, says that Mohammed's parents were black. See "Al-Jahiz" in this volume.

editor of an atheist magazine and is very well read in science but who, while he has been able to throw off religion, has not been able to throw off his racial superstitions, denounced the exhibit, calling it "side-show science . . . a disgraceful exhibit, farcical in its presentation" and an attempt to "Barnumize" science.[5]

This brings me to what is usually meant by "Negro" ancestry. What most scientists and sociologists call a "Negro" (when achievements are being spoken of) is a highly specialized and very primitive type that has been isolated in Central Africa or New Guinea for thousands of years, as isolated as were the savages Julius Caesar saw in Britain. Of this type there are, at most, but a million and a half, too few in number to have built up a civilization at any time. When, however, it is a question of what is not very creditable, the Negro variety is made to include hundreds of millions of individuals, some of whom are more Nordic in color and features than many whites.

The scientists are as divided on who is a Negro as the theologians are on who is God. The ethnologists certainly cannot say because ethnology is but a mass of conflicting opinions based on the opinions of observers who were subject to many influences and made pronouncements according to their personal likes and dislikes of this or that people. What ethnology has to say on the alleged inferiority of certain people reminds one of the Haitian proverb, "When the rooster and the cockroach come to court, you don't have to guess which will win." What ethnology needs most is emancipation from an exploiting capitalism—a complete divorce from the slavemaster's legend of Ham.

As certain individuals who I know positively are of Negro ancestry but are fair enough to pass for something else will say that they are of Indian, Spanish, or South American ancestry, so do certain anthropologists in the case of evidently Negroid peoples as the Egyptians, Moors, Ethiopians, and some Asiatic and Polynesian peoples, the entire idea in both cases being to duck admission of Negro ancestry. Even in the case of those paleolithic men whose Negro characters were evident they use such phrases as "proto-Negroid."

[5] *The Truth Seeker*, April, 1945, p. 60. I discussed a similar attitude on the part of certain world-famed scientists in *Sex and Race*, Vol. III, Chap. 25.

These anthropologists, while pretending to scorn the biblical story of the origin of man and his distribution over the earth, continue to use such terms as "Hamitic" for the Ethiopians and "Semitic" for the Jews. These terms, if they have any meaning at all, designate only language groups, precisely as Latin, Anglo-Saxon, Arab. It is as nonsensical to talk of a Jewish race as it is to talk of a Christian one.

As to who is a Negro in the United States, I have come to the conclusion after long and careful thought that to be an expert on that subject the first qualification is to be crazy. Only those who are able to throw all logic, all reasoning to the winds, can ever hope to be authorities on that matter. I have more than once witnessed the amazing spectacle of one American calling another American fairer and more Nordic in features than himself a "nigger" and relegating him to the Jim Crow car. Again, one can be very visibly a Negro and because he speaks broken English with a foreign accent, or doesn't speak English at all, become legally white. I recall the case of a friend of mine, an unmixed Negro, who once lived in Sweden and speaks Swedish fluently. When he was traveling in the South, the conductor tried to send him off to the Jim Crow car. Pretending not to understand English, he replied in Swedish. Finally an interpreter was found, and when the conductor learned that the Negro, who is a native of the British West Indies, could speak Swedish in support of his statement that he was a Swede, he was allowed to remain in the white coach.

I know several West Indians and South Americans, visibly Negroes, who were drafted into the white army and navy while other Americans who were fairer than many whites were placed in the Negro regiments. I recall the case of a Harlem newspaper photographer, who is as white as any of the Nordics, but is of Negro ancestry. He was drafted into a Negro regiment, but when he was taken South and went into the Negro quarters, he was arrested by the white M.P.'s as whites were forbidden there. Thereafter, to save arrest, he carried a paper stating that he was a Negro. Had he permitted himself to be drafted as "white," however, he would probably have been punished. Many times, too, I myself have taken "white" for "colored" and the reverse.

Congressman Adam Clayton Powell was fairer than some of the

anti-Negro Southerners in Congress yet to them he is of another "race."[6] Even some of the cleverest whites don't know their own. In 1939 a chain of moving-picture theatres—the RKO—offered a prize for the American who looked most like Abraham Lincoln and who should win it but a Negro! Of course, the judges discovered that too late.[7] Several of the Southern states and some of the Northern ones have their own particular definition of what is a Negro, and as I have shown in *Sex and Race,* in certain Southern states even the state constitution and the state laws differ on the subject. As for the United States Bureau of the Census, it has its own ruling, which is that if one has a "drop" of "Negro" blood, he is a Negro. Someone has defined a "Negro" as one who, regardless of complexion, is not entitled by his ancestry to ride in a white coach in the Southern United States. *This definition would be true of every personage in this book.* Of course, such a definition is idiotic. I use it only by way of argument.

The persons who hold to the above doctrine happen to be also the ones who will usually attribute ability in those of mixed blood to their white strain. To avoid this I have included no one with less than an eighth of Negro strain with the exception of Dom Pedro II, who was about one-sixteenth, or perhaps one-thirty-second, Negro. I have given him as an example chiefly to show what would have happened to him had he lived, say, in Virginia, where the law provides that the remotest trace of Negro ancestry makes one a Negro. Dom Pedro married a white woman and that would have brought him five years' imprisonment in Virginia. Dom Pedro was no fairer or more Nordic in features than thousands of Virginia Negroes. I recall, too, the case of Jean Toomer, the novelist, a grandson of Governor Pinchback of Louisiana, whose Negro ancestry is a matter of record. When Toomer, who was fairer than millions of American whites, married a white woman in 1931 it was reported in both the Negro and the white press as the marriage of a Negro to a white woman. Toomer has since

---

[6] When Congressman Powell married Hazel Scott, whose Negro strain is evident, an irate Southerner who saw their pictures in *Life,* wrote him, "Dear Senator Scott [*sic*]: I simply want to tell you that you are an eternal disgrace to the white race." (*Afro-American,* Feb. 23, 1946.)

[7] See account and this man's portrait in *Sex and Race,* Vol. II, pp. 377–378.

ceased to be a "Negro," which, I think, is logical. My contention is that those who look white are white, and those who look mixed, are mixed, no matter on what side of the fence a fantastic American dogma places them. If we see a Negro with evidence of white train, we'll say unhesitatingly that he is mixed. I carry my logic all the way and when I see a white person with evidence of what my eyes tell me, after fifty years of experience, is a Negro strain, I attribute the same to that person no matter in what society or in what part of the world he is. One's ancestry does not come out of the air. Though invisible, it is as real as anything else on this planet. Every "atom" of our ancestry could be accounted for. Many, many millions of individuals over vast centuries—individuals who lived and breathed even as ourselves—built it up as surely as insects build up a coral reef. Had there been the tiniest break in our ancestral line we could not be the individuals we now are. In fact, we might never have been born at all.

No matter how proud one may be of his ancestry, no matter how far back he may trace it to great kings and chiefs who lived, he reaches inevitably a point of obscurity as dark as the darkest depths of the ocean. To talk, therefore, of a "pure" race or a "pure" ancestral line is abysmal ignorance.

Certain difficulties in research might also be noted. In lands where there is no color discrimination, color is rarely mentioned, except in the case of "pure" blacks, who were generally aliens. This is particularly true of ancient and modern Egypt and Arabia.

Outside the United States a mulatto is not a "Negro," and still less so is a quadroon or octoroon. If Pushkin's great-grandfather and Alexandre Dumas' father had not been so prominent we would have lost knowledge of their Negro strain as we have in the case of hundreds of thousands of other Europeans. For instance, the English people between 1440 and 1834 absorbed the Negro slaves who had been brought into England at the rate of thousands annually. What do we know of the descendants of these Negroes and where there strain is now to be found, high or low, in the English population? Practically nothing.[8]

----

[8] See *Sex and Race*, Vol. I, Chap. 18. (1941) and Vol. III, p. 15.
Let's take a concrete case: that of Charles Morett, a Negro child belonging to Lady Hillsborow of North Aston, Oxfordshire, who was baptized

António Vieira, Portugal's grandest personage, is an instance of how Negro ancestry could be lost to history. We should probably never have known of Vieira's Negro strain if the Spanish Inquisition, failing to suppress him in other ways, had not finally pounced on his dark skin and frizzly hair, hoping to prove through these features that he was of Jewish or Islamic strain, and therefore "heretic," which would have called for his expulsion from the priesthood.

Discovering great men of color in Central and South America is not easy either because the white strain in the mixed-bloods is emphasized and the Negro one suppressed. What Sir Richard Burton said of Brazil is, on the whole, true of Latin America: "Here all free men who are not black, are white, and often a man is officially white but naturally almost a Negro. This is directly opposed to the system of the United States, where all men who are not unmixed white, are black." Indian strain, also, was considered higher caste than Negro, hence Negro strain is often called "Indian" and even "West Indian." Take the case of Thomas Mann,

---

there on July 20, 1722. In the same parish register is a record of the baptism of his daughter, Eleanor, May 13, 1744. (*Notes & Queries*, 5 ser. Dec. 7, 1878.) Morett's wife was very likely white, as Negro women were, and are, few in England. What became of Morett's descendants as well as those of hundreds of thousands of similar Negroes during the centuries—as, say, those of Francis Barber, servant of Dr. Samuel Johnson? In present-day England I saw the process of the absorption of blacks and mulattoes by whites. Coleridge-Taylor's descendants will doubtlessly disappear into the white "race" as did those of Dumas. My researches lead me to believe that the marriage, or mating, of the Negroes in the sixteenth, seventeenth, and eighteenth centuries with white women was the usual thing and that their mulatto offspring usually married white, until the Negro strain disappeared.

As regards names and surnames, the Negro children were baptized with ones characteristic of their color, as Morett (little Moor), Moorish (later shortened to Morris), Moore, Moor, Blackman, Blackie, Blackamore, Blackmur, Blackmuir, Blackmore. (See British Museum catalogue for list of authors with similar names.) The Duke of Queensbury's ten-year-old blackamoor was christened "Blackmore." (*Notes & Queries*, 3 ser., Vol. VII, p. 198. Mar. 11, 1865.) Is it not likely that certain white people who bore the names above-mentioned were descendants of these Negroes, as say, Sir Richard Blackmore, knighted by William III? David McRitchie, noted archaeologist, holds to this theory and gives a long list of British names derived from the black people who lived in England and Scotland even before William the Conqueror. (See his *Ancient and Modern Britons*. Sources from him are given in *Sex and Race*, Vol. I, pp. 198–200, 1941.)

the great German writer and Nobel Prize winner. Mann's mother was a Brazilian creole who was sent to study in Germany. Now I am not saying that she was of Negro strain since I have not investigated that, but because she was colored, or at least not white, it was inevitable that she should be said to be part "Indian" or part "West Indian" by his biographers.[9]

In Cuba quadroons and even mulattoes are considered white, hence the census reports list the bulk of the population as white. The same is true of Puerto Rico. The result is a looking-down on Negro strain by such individuals.

In the United States an individual who is more Caucasian than some of the whites is rarely offended if called a Negro. The reason is that the white colonists of America, thanks chiefly to continued and fairly large immigration, did not need the mulatto to help them keep the blacks in check and thus did not elevate him to a caste superior to the blacks but generally lumped blacks and mulattoes together. South of the Rio Grande, however, especially in Haiti and the British West Indies, the whites there erected the mulattoes into a caste above the blacks and taught them to regard the blacks as inferior. The result is that today the mixed-bloods of Central and South America and the West Indies are generally offended when classed with blacks. In the British West Indies the census reports still list them separately.

Some of these near-whites are probably more sensitive of their Negro ancestry than they would be of a police record. Mention of it is more distressing to some than would be a large boil on the face of a movie star.

A case in point is José María de Heredia, a Cuban, who was a member of the French Academy. Heredia was usually taken as "colored" by both white and Negroes in France.[10] Ordinarily no mention might have been made of his color but it happened at the

[9] J. Cleugh (*Thomas Mann*, p. 12, 1933), says she was of German, Portuguese and West Indian ancestry and that her mother, that is Mann's grandmother, was "a Brazilian creole." See also Prof. Phelps on this subject. (*New York Herald-Tribune*, June 23, 1938.)

[10] V. Thompson, a white, writing on American artists in Paris, shows clearly that de Heredia was regarded as colored. He says, "There is no artist more talked of than Mr. H. O. Tanner. Perhaps this is because he is a mulatto and in spite of the example of Dumas and De Heredia, we are still

time that France's most prominent writer was one whose Negro strain was widely known because of his illustrious parentage, namely, Alexandre Dumas, fils, who was president of the French Academy, or Forty Immortals. Heredia, to make matters worse for him, was darker than Dumas.

When Heredia was elected to the Academy some of the Negro intellectuals of Paris, accepting the popular belief that he was colored, called on him to congratulate him. Heredia snubbed them and told them that he was not of Negro but of "conquistador" ancestry. Dumas, fils, on the other hand, was not only not sensitive about his Negro ancestry, but mentioned it in his first address to the Academy. The difference is that Dumas had not been taught to despise the pigment in his skin, while Heredia had.

Pushkin was so proud of his Negro strain that he credited himself with more of it than he had. Colette, France's leading woman writer and Officer of the Legion of Honor, mentions her Negro strain too, though one would hardly guess it. "The idealistic temperament of the Latin American, his pretension to a high civilization and to the status of caballero, creates a natural yearning for a white skin," says García Calderón. Europe is the Latin American's model. The first colonists taught even the whites born in the colonies to look down on themselves and to worship things European. The tradition still remains.

---

surprised when the artist reveals himself under a dark skin." (*Cosmopolitan*, p. 19, May, 1900.)

Heredia's snubbing of Negroes seems to have caused more than a little stir in Paris at the time, and while I was there I discussed the affair with several persons well informed about it, as Professor Cenac-Thaly, physicist, of the Sorbonne, and Louis Beaudza, chief editor of the Secretariat of the Grand Chancellery of the Legion of Honor, and all confirmed the belief that Heredia was colored and gave me additional stories regarding him. As late as 1935 I saw Negroes paying homage to Heredia's bust in the Luxembourg Gardens. Heredia might, or might not, have been of Negro ancestry; I have never looked into it. What I did learn, however, is that talk of his alleged Negro ancestry galled him.

Heredia, by all accounts, was about the color of W. E. B. Du Bois and resembled him somewhat and had a mustache like his. Heredia's portraits do not show a Negro strain nor do several of Du Bois' that I have seen. Again, take Paul La Fargue, socialist writer and distinguished contemporary of Heredia's. La Fargue's portrait looks like that of a Nordic, yet he was certainly a colored man, a native of Cuba. La Fargue married Laura, second

The United States as a part of its good neighbor policy caters to this Latin American yearning to be white. The 1940 United States census lists Mexicans as white, which, of course, will make anyone who has been to Mexico and seen the bulk of its population laugh.

Touchiness about Negro ancestry is, of course, still more characteristic of whites in the Southern United States. Southerners with dark skins or Negroid faces will assert that they are of Indian ancestry, as if the Indian were not also very much mixed with the Negro.

A study of Latin American portraits helps little in discovering Negro ancestry. It is almost the usual thing to find Negroes, even unmixed, whose portraits have been doctored to make them look like whites. For instance, General Laurencio Silva, who from an incident in his domestic life we know positively was a Negro.[11] In the case of General Vicente Guerrero, President of Mexico, who was very definitely a mulatto, I defy anyone to tell from the pictures most current of him that he was not a European. It was only after long research that I found two pictures of him which bore out what is said of his ancestry. General Antonio Sucre of Venezuela, President of Bolivia, is painted up to look like a white movie star though he was a dark mixed-blood. The same is true of Sam Martín, liberator of Argentina.

The second and the third dictators of Paraguay, the Lópezes, were of Negro ancestry but you would never know it from their portraits. And even General Antonio Maceo of Cuba was doc-

---

daughter of Karl Marx, and Marx in a letter dated Sept. 5, 1866, refers twice affectionately to La Fargue as the "Negrillo," that is, little Negro. (Private letters of Karl Marx. *Socialist Review*, Sept., 1929, p. 45.) Portraits, especially etchings and woodcuts, I have discovered, are often deceptive.

As regards Heredia's statement that he was of "conquistador ancestry" and therefore white, this would be poor proof. Many of the first Spaniards who came to the New World had a Moorish or Negro strain. There were also mixed-blood conquistadors, as Francisco Fajaro, Juan de Urquijo, and Alonzo Ruiz Vallejo. As for Nuffo de Olano, who went with Balboa to the Pacific, he was an unmixed Negro. Moreover, not a few conquistador descendants undoubtedly ended their lives in jail or on the gallows.

[11] See his portrait in *Sex and Race*, Vol. II, p. 26, and read what was said of his Negro ancestry on p. 25.

tored up to look less and less like the dark mulatto he was. Thus, while noted men of Negro strain are not infrequent in Latin America, it is a great task to locate them. I happened to know of Dom Pedro's Negro strain only because I ran across a description of his grandfather, John VI of Portugal.

In South Africa a condition even worse than that in Latin America exists. The number of eminent South Africans who have a Negro strain must be considerable because the older the South African family, the more likely it is to have one. Very few white women existed in the colony as late as the end of the seventeenth century. In 1633 there were only thirteen.

The same is true of Australia, where the first mothers of the white colony were aborigines, who were coal-black with Negro features and with hair not wooly but frizzly. In Tasmania the aborigines were definitely Negro with peppercorn hair. Their women became the mothers of the first native Tasmanian whites.

As regards Islamic lands, locating Negroes was most difficult of all there. Not only is there no color line in Islam but portraiture of any kind was absent until recent years, having been forbidden by Mohammed. As a rule, the only great Negroes who are mentioned as such in Islamic literature are "pure" blacks, the Zends or Zenghs, who were brought chiefly from Central Africa as slaves and were later converted to Islam, as Lokman and Kafur. Negroes born of a free Islamic father and a slave mother from the land of the Zenghs may sometimes be distinguished also since the birthplaces of slave mothers were mentioned. For instance, we know that Ibrahim Al-Mahdi, half-brother of the famous Haroun Al-Raschid, was of Negro ancestry since his mother, though also of royal ancestry, was a slave. However, there was a heavy Negro strain in some of the highest Islam-born families, as the Abbasides, rulers of the Mohammedan empire at the height of its power. If the Caliph Al-Mahdi, father of Haroun Al-Raschid, were not almost black himself, is it likely that Ibrahim would have been so dark as to be called a Negro by his nephew, Caliph Mamoun? Caliph Al-Muktafi also had a Negro mother. Ibn Khallikan mentions several distinguished Negroes in his *Biographical Dictionary*, but no mulattoes, the inference being that these were regarded as "white."

As regards great men in the Far East, I have done almost no research on them. I have come across certain names in China and Japan such as Sakonouye Tamuramaro, the first *shogun* of Japan, but I did not follow them up. In India I did little on the Negroes among the Mohammedans there, while in Turkey I did no intensive research, though the number of great Turkish Negroes, some of whom were virtual rulers of the empire, is considerable. I have given the names of some of them in *Sex and Race*.[12]

As regards the evaluation of the personages in this book there will be, naturally, differences of opinion. Some might even go so far as to dismiss most of them. For instance, the late Professor Edward M. East of Harvard University said that among the "15,000 or 20,000 Great Ones of the Earth,"[13] there was only one of Negro strain: Alexandre Dumas, père. Toussaint L'Ouverture he dismisses as being of only "fair calibre."

Now if we take East seriously it is necessary to know what was his standard of greatness? And did he arrive as it by some methods other than haphazard? Where did he find his 15,000 to 20,000 great men? Evidently in the encyclopedias. It would have taken him a lifetime to read up on each one and compile his own list.

Did he check on his 15,000 to 20,000 great names to see whether his opinion differed with those of the editors of the encyclopedias? And did he go to the trouble of picking out the Negro names in these encyclopedias; or did he classify Negroes only by hearsay? All of the leading encyclopedias have the names of several Negroes. This is true of the *Encyclopaedia Britannica, Larousse, La Grande Encyclopédie, Biographie Universelle, The Dictionary of National Biography*, the *Dictionary of American Biography, Enciclopedia Universal Ilustrada*, the *Encyclopedia of Islam, Who's Who, Who's Who in America*, and *American Men of Science*. In these last eight Negroes were mentioned with each. In the seventh edition there are seventy-seven Negroes.

Furthermore, what constitutes greatness is largely a matter of opinion. East's 15,000 to 20,000 could be whittled down to three

[12] See Vol. I, "The Negro in Turkey," pp. 286–287, 1941.
[13] *Heredity and Human Affairs*, pp. 199–200. 1927.

or four or expanded to a million, depending on the appraiser. Victor Hugo in his *William Shakespeare* narrowed down the world's greatest writers, poets, and artists to six and placed Shakespeare first. But Voltaire, who was as great as Hugo, ridicules Shakespeare and calls him a "ninny" and a "charlatan with occasional outbursts of ability." Shakespeare's tragedies he called "monstrous farces that ruined the English theatre."[14] Also, Tolstoy, another immortal, says that Shakespeare was "inartistic," "trivial and positively bad," and that any praise of him is "false adulation."[15]

Again, do we consider a man great because of the degree to which his life and actions affected humanity? If this be so, then how many biographers really endeavor to trace and to check up such for themselves? If they did, they would find that some men of "fair calibre" who received only a few lines in an encyclopedia, and some who were not even mentioned, have affected mankind more than some who were ranked "great."

How many persons, for instance, have heard of Fernandès and Ni-cot who introduced tobacco into Europe, thereby causing a greater effect on Europe, America, and Africa than Shakespeare? Or of Hargreaves who discovered gold in Australia? The men who discovered gold in California or diamonds in South Africa probably had a more profound influence on world conditions today than any of Carlyle's heroes.

Suppose for the sake of argument that Toussaint was not "great," yet did he not set in motion events that have had the most far-reaching effects on humanity today? His success against the French was chiefly instrumental in causing Napoleon to sell the Louisiana territory for a ridiculously small sum, without which the great America of today would not have been possible.

Had East been informed on Toussaint he would have found noted scholars who ranked him among the great. I will mention only three: Lamartine, who placed him above Napoleon; Wendell Phillips, who called him greater than Washington; and Auguste Comte, French philosopher and sociologist, who ranked him with

[14] *Lettre de M. de Voltaire a l'Académie Française,* Aug. 25, 1776.
[15] *Shakespeare and the Drama.* New York, 1928.

Charles V, Coligny, Gustavus Adolphus, Walpole, Franklin, Washington, and Jefferson in statesmanship.[16]

Finally, it will be interesting, I think, to see how East came to say that there was only one great man of Negro ancestry. In 1918 E. B. Reuter wrote *The Mulatto*,[17] which was intended to show the superiority of mulattoes over blacks, and gave several thousand names of prominent Negroes compiled by Negro writers and organizations including 139 given by W. E. B. Du Bois in his *Who's Who in Colored America* (1916). Now the Negroes who compiled the lists said little or nothing about Negroes outside of the United States, and Reuter, whether he knew of them or not, gave only what the Negroes had given. In nearly all of these lists there appeared many who had made only a trifling success, and nearly all, it is safe to say, were mediocre and would probably have risen but little higher had there been no color prejudice against them. Such is the source from which East speaks so authoritatively. It is clear he knew nothing of his subject himself, and could go only as far as Reuter took him.

It seems to me that out of sheer competence those who declare that such and such individuals were greater than others ought to be informed on the lives of the persons compared.

Another important factor in the true evaluation of a person's capabilities is the degree of opportunity afforded by his environment. For instance, had Napoleon been forced to remain on the island of Corsica, we should have known no more about him than we do about one of the bandit chiefs of that island despite the fact that he had within him all the potentialities of the Emperor Napoleon. He would have been but one of the innumerable flowers "born to blush unseen and waste its sweetness on the desert air." Similarly, certain personages in this book such as Queen Nzingha, Rabah Zobeir, and Nat Turner might be ranked as insignificant, but the test is how well did they play on the small stage on which destiny had placed them?

In estimating greatness one should consider the intensity, sincerity, and capability with which an individual plays his role,

---

[16] *Calendrier Positiviste* (Douzieme Mois). Paris, 1852.
[17] See pp. 217–314.

whether that role be large or small. To exclude a great "small" man because life gave him a small role and include one whom it appointed to play a larger role seems to me to be idealizing the stage and not the individual. Snobbery, pure and simple. Had Napoleon been born black and a slave in Haiti, he could not possibly have been other than a Toussaint. Every character in this book has caused repercussions of greater or lesser world importance; every one is of sufficient merit to have brought their inclusion in one or more encyclopedias.

I have also been asked not to include such figures as Chaka, Dessalines, and Samory, since "they reflected no great credit on the Negro race." But while I dislike conquerors, tyrants, and dictators, whatever their color, I am endeavoring to write not "Negro" history but history in which people of a certain color played a prominent part—in which case, genius and ability must be presented regardless of the manner in which these were employed. We must remember, as Lord Acton said, that great men are sometimes bad men. Furthermore, there are great men of whom much good has been said and yet I do not consider them worthy of imitation, as St. Benedict the Moor, here included, who reached greatness through a subhuman humility that was, in reality, pride.

As regards living persons, I have been advised not to include any, as certain of those left out might be offended. Rivalry of any kind is not the spirit of this book. Certainly there are living people who ought to be included and are not, but had I named 10,000 instead of only 200, the favorites of some would still have been omitted. One can only hope that those who have been left out will show that they are worthy of inclusion in a really great book by having no such feelings. The selection was my own and I do not claim to be an authority on who are great and who are not. Moreover, certain of these sketches were written before I had thought of other persons not included. Variety of occupation also had to be considered to avoid monotony.

As regards my sources, I have given those I thought the most important. And I have checked them as carefully as is humanly possible in a work of this magnitude. I had also to be on guard for overstatement not only by Negro writers but also by noted white ones. For instance, H. G. Wells says, "In the eighteenth century he [the Negro] was the backbone of the British navy."[18] Even Mr. Wells' broadmindedness on "race" does not make this true. As for the names I received from readers of individuals supposed to be of Negro strain, when I investigated I found that either their statements were too nebulous or too difficult to be proved, or the individuals had too little Negro strain, which fact, as I said, led me to omit all but one. The list of persons who might have been of Negro ancestry but are generally supposed to have been white is a rather large one. I have said more on this matter in the section entitled "Additional Great Men of Color."

In conclusion, let me say that my intention was not to write highly critical and psychoanalytical, or even literary, essays, but rather principally success stories, chiefly for Negro youth. I hope white youth will find some inspiration in them too.

And not only young people but adults too need the encouragement to be had from the lives of the great. Dr. Albert E. Wiggam very rightly says, "The extraordinary and never-ending success of success stories in books, magazines, movies, soap operas, etc., would indicate that even the most obscure persons gain courage from them. In all ages, stories of heroism—success against great odds—have furnished most of the themes for literature and drama. On the other hand, nothing is more discouraging than stories that end in defeat and tragedy."

Of course, it is true that all the personages in this book did not win. Some fell short either through force of circumstances or defects in their character. But all were giants. I have been careful not to claim more for them than did those from whose books I gathered the facts.

[18] *World of Willam Clissold*, Vol. II, p. 614. New York, 1926.

CELEBRITIES
BEFORE CHRIST

Commentary and Notes on References

WHEN MEDITERRANEAN EUROPE became known to history for the first time, Africa was already old and in decline. There is a need to be mindful of this fact while reading the biographies of the great celebrities in Africa before the birth of Christ. The Ghanan writer, the late Dr. Joseph B. Danguah, calls attention to little known facts of history in his introduction to the book *United West Africa (or Africa) at the Bar of the Family of Nations*, by Ladipo Solanke (1927), when he says:

By the time Alexander the Great was sweeping the civilized world with conquest after conquest from Chaeronia to Gaza, from Babylon to Cabul; by the time this first of the Aryan conquerors was learning the rudiments of war and government at the feet of philosophic Aristotle; and by the time Athens was laying down the foundations of modern European civilization, the earliest and greatest Ethiopian culture had already flourished and dominated the civilized world for over four centuries and a half. Imperial Ethiopia had conquered Egypt and founded the XXVth Dynasty, and for a century and a half the central seat of civilization in the known world was held by the ancestors of the modern Negro, maintaining and defending it against the Assyrian and Persian Empires of the East. Thus, at the time when Ethiopia was leading the civilized world in culture and conquest, East was East, but West was not, and the first European (Graecian) Olympiad was as yet to be held. Rome was nowhere to be seen on the map, and sixteen centuries were to pass before Charlemagne would rule in Europe and

Egbert become first King of England. Even then, history was to drag
on for another seven hundred weary years, before Roman Catholic
Europe could see fit to end the Great Schism, soon to be followed by
the news of the discovery of America and by the fateful rebirth of the
youngest of World Civilization.

It is too often forgotten that when the Europeans emerged and
began to extend themselves into the broader world of Africa and
Asia during the fifteenth and sixteenth centuries, they went on to
colonize most of mankind. Later they would colonize world scholarship, mainly the writing of history. History was then written or
rewritten to show or imply that Europeans were the only creators
of what could be called a civilization. In order to accomplish this,
the Europeans had to forget, or pretend to forget, all they previously knew about Africa.

In his booklet *Ancient Greece in African Political Thought*
(1966), Professor Ali A. Mazrui of Makerere University in
Uganda, after reading the book *A History of the Modern World*
by R. R. Palmer and Joel Colton, observes that:

As Africans begin to be given credit for some of their own civilizations, African cultural defensiveness would gradually wane. Not everyone need have the confidence of Leopold Senghor as he asserts that
"Negro blood circulated in the veins of the Egyptians." But it is at
any rate time that it was more openly conceded not only that ancient
Egypt made a contribution to the Greek miracle, but also that she in
turn had been influenced by the Africa which was to the south of her.
To grant all this is, in a sense, to universalise the Greek heritage. It is
to break the European monopoly of identification with ancient
Greece.

And yet this is by no means the only way of breaking Europe's
monopoly. In order to cope with the cultural offensive of the
Graeco-Roman mystique, African cultural defenders have so far
emphasized the Africanness of Egypt's civilization. But a possible
counteroffensive is to demonstrate that ancient Greece was not
European. It is not often remembered how recent the concept of
"Europe" is. In a sense, it is easier to prove that ancient Egypt
was "African" than to prove that ancient Greece was "European."
In the words of Palmer and Colton:

There was really no Europe in ancient times. In the Roman Empire we may see a Mediterranean world, or even a West and an East in the Latin- and Greek-speaking portions. But the West included parts of Africa as well as of Europe, and Europe as we know it was divided by the Rhine-Danube frontier, south and west of which lay the civilized provinces of the Empire, and north and east the "barbarians" of whom the civilized world knew almost nothing.

The two historians go on to say that the word "Europe," since it meant little, was scarcely used by the Romans at all.

Even as late as the seventeenth century the notion that the land mass south of the Mediterranean was an entity distinct from the land mass north of it had yet to be fully accepted. Melville Herskovits has pointed out how the Geographer Royal of France, writing in 1656, described Africa as "a peninsula so large that it comprises the third part, and this the most southerly, of our continent."

In the years when the slave trade was getting effectively under way, some Europeans were claiming parts of Africa—especially Egypt—as an extension of their "continent" and their "culture."

During this period, most history books were written to justify the slave trade and the colonial system that followed. Therefore, any honest writing of African history today must take this fact into consideration and be, at least in part, a restoration project.

Part of this project is to restore great African personalities to their proper place in history. Among the great personalities of the ancient world Imhotep is particularly outstanding. His life is especially important to the Africans and Afro-Americans of today for he was one of the many wise Africans who at the dawn of history gave the world those ideas of enlightenment and wisdom that made what we now call civilization possible. Imhotep was the world's first multigenius. New interest in his life was started early in 1965 when Professor Walter B. Emery of England, one of the world's leading Egyptologists, excavated his tomb.

"When we find the entrance of Imhotep's tomb," Professor Emery said in an interview on the eve of the discovery, "we will know a great deal more about ancient Egypt—its diseases, medicines, surgery and magic." He further stated, "Imhotep was a genius unequaled in ancient times, particularly in these fields, and in these secrets are so far undisclosed." (*The New York Times,* Jan. 10, 1965.)

Additional information on the life of Imhotep was published in the magazine *Mankind,* Vol. I, No. 1 (1967). See article, "Medicine in Ancient Egypt" by George A. Bender, p. 52 and in *MD* magazine, Vol. XIII, No. 3 (March, 1969).

During the rise of the great dynasties in Egypt, Kush, and Ethiopia the role of the African woman was advanced, along with the general society. Some women became heads of state. It was with the emergence of Queen Hatshepsut, about 1500 years before the birth of Christ, that their role in the affairs of state became particularly outstanding. Hatshepsut left a lasting impression on her time that has significance for our day. Her reign was one of the brightest in Egyptian history, and it proves, if proof is needed, that a woman can be a strong and effective head of state and a gracious and beautiful woman at the same time.

On the western banks of the Nile River, opposite the site of what was once the ancient city of Thebes, her temple, the most beautiful in all Egypt, still stands. It is known today as Deir-el-Bahari. In it is the mortuary chapel of Her Royal (and mysterious) Highness, Queen Hatshepsut. She was, according to Egyptologist James Henry Breasted, "The first great woman in history of whom we are informed."

The story of the great Queen Hatshepsut began in tragedy and ended in the same way. Her road to power was not an easy one. Her father, Thotmes I, had four children by his great royal wife. All died in childhood except the little Princess Hatshepsut. King Thotmes had a son by one of his secondary wives, a common custom in that day. In the midst of conquering most of the known ancient world, King Thotmes was stricken with paralysis. Hatshepsut became his chief aide. Through her father she managed the affairs of state, and became, in fact, the co-ruler of Egypt. This fired her ambition to rule Egypt and its empire alone. When her father was sure that he did not have long to live, he married Hatshepsut to her half-brother, his son by the secondary wife. When Thotmes died, this young man became King of Egypt, Thotmes II, and Hatshepsut became Queen of Egypt. She was now in her late teens. Thotmes II had a son by a woman in his harem. When the boy was about nine years old, the court physicians told Thotmes II that he had not long to live. Since the royal family was again without a crown prince, Thotmes married his tiny elder daughter to his son by the harem girl. Upon the death of Thotmes II, this sturdy boy became Thotmes III. This frustrated the ambitions of Hatshepsut, without abating them at all. Now in her early twenties, she was relegated to the role of Dowager Queen Mother, although she had been named one of the group of regents that was to govern Egypt until Thotmes was old enough to rule alone.

During all this time she apparently gathered the reins of government more firmly in her hands and made the allies that she needed in order to seize power. For soon, according to one of the court historians of the day, "Hatshepsut carried on the affairs of the two lands according to her own ideas, Egypt was made to work in her submission and at her will." It was said that, "The Lady of Command, whose plans are excellent, satisfied the two regions when she speaks."

It was not enough for her to govern Egypt in the name of the young Thotmes III. She wanted more and she planned for it.

So one day, after her patience in this matter had worn thin and her plans and allies were ready, she dressed herself in the most sacred of Pharaoh's official costumes, a ceremonial dress that went back to the predynastic Kings of Egypt. With the royal scepter in one hand and the sacred frail, or crook, in the other, she mounted the throne and proclaimed herself Pharaoh of Egypt. And thus the first, and perhaps the greatest, woman ruler of all time came to power in Egypt. (The best new study of her life and reign is in the book *Hatshepsut* by Evelyn Wells [1969].)

Thotmes III came to power after Hatshepsut and consolidated Egypt into a great empire. He was possibly the greatest Pharaoh in the history of Egypt, although he was a man of humble birth whose mother was a harem woman named Isis, or Asnut. In spite of this, he forged ahead of those of nobler birth and became the master of Egypt.

Sometime around 1386 B.C. Queen Tiyi gave birth to a boy who was first named Amenhates after his father. There was great rejoicing in the court and throughout the Nile Valley because he was the king and queen's first son. Very little is known of his childhood except that he was sickly from birth. He developed an interest in art, poetry, and religion. His closest companion was said to be Nefertiti, his beautiful little cousin (some archaeologists believed she was his sister).

When the crown prince was about twenty-one years of age, he and the lovely Nefertiti were married. Three years later his aging father, Amenhotep III, named him co-regent of Egypt and crowned him Amenhotep IV. After the death of his father, he came into full power in Egypt and took the name Akhenaton. In full partnership with his beautiful wife, Nefertiti, he had a profound effect on Egypt and the entire world of his day.

Amenhotep IV, better known as Akhenaton, and often referred to as "the Heretic King," is in some respects one of the most extraordinary monarchs who ever sat on a throne. Centuries before King David he wrote beautiful poems like those of the Judean monarch. Thirteen hundred years before Christ he preached and lived a gospel of love, brotherhood, and truth. He has been called the world's first idealist, the first temporal ruler ever to lead his people toward the worship of a single God.

When Akhenaton came to the throne more than 3000 years ago, Egypt dominated the world. But behind this panoply of power was a cowering citizenry plagued by gods and demons conjured up by a sinister priestcraft, which he swept aside. Then, creating his own priesthood, he proclaimed a new religion—a religion of a single God. This visionary pharaoh, more interested in philosophy than in power, was unlike any other Egyptian ruler. He introduced the concept of monotheism at a historic crossroads, for at that point in time the Hebrews were in Egypt.

The story of Akhenaton is not complete without the story of his extraordinary wife, Nefertiti. She was a woman of fabled beauty and grace. A magnificent treasure remains to remind us of her loveliness, a painted bust which is considered one of the great works of Egyptian art.

Akhenaton and Nefertiti humanized the Egyptian monarchy. The new religion that he introduced into the life of Egypt brought them into conflict with the prevailing priesthood, and subsequently with his mother, the great Queen Tiyi.

Among recent books about Akhenaton and Nefertiti the most readable are *Akhenaton: The Rebel Pharaoh* by Robert Silverberg (1964) and *Nefertiti* by Evelyn Wells (1964).

There are parallels in the lives of Lokman and Aesop. They were both of African origin and they had their greatest influence on people outside of Africa. There has been very little new writing on Lokman and Aesop in recent years. Of course, Aesop is the better known of the two because his sayings and fables are part of universal knowledge. He lived in the sixth century B.C. according to Planudes the Great, a monk in the fourteenth century, to whom we are indebted for Aesop's life and fables in their present form. In the works of Planudes and other writers he is described as being a dark-skinned African. His name is a variant of Ethiop or Ethiopian.

The nation that is now called Ethiopia came back upon the center stage of history around 96 B.C. It was then represented by a queen who in some books is referred to as Makeda, and in others as Belkis. She is better known to the world as the Queen of Sheba.

In the book *Ethiopia, A Cultural History*, the English writer Sylvia Pankhurst tells the story of this journey.

"The Queen of the South shall rise up in the judgment with this generation, and shall condemn it; for she came from the uttermost parts of the earth to hear the wisdom of Solomon; and behold, a greater than Solomon is here . . ." Matthew xii, 42; Luke xi, 31.

The history of the Queen of the South, who undertook a long and arduous journey to Jerusalem, in order to learn of the wisdom of King Solomon, is deeply cherished in Ethiopia, as part of the national heritage, for she is claimed as an Ethiopian Queen, Makeda, "a woman of splendid beauty," who introduced the religion and culture of Israel to her own land.

Her journey to Jerusalem is described in a fine old Ethiopian book, the Kebra Nagast, which means "the Glory of Kings." We are told that the Queen, having communed with Solomon on important themes, was wedded to him, and on returning to Ethiopia, gave birth to their son, David. When this first-born son of Solomon reached manhood, he visited his father, who desired to keep him at his side to succeed him on the Throne of Israel. David, however, insisted that he must return to his mother. King Solomon therefore ordered that the

first-born sons of all the priests and nobles of Jerusalem should accompany David to his home and remain there at his Court when he
ascended the Ethiopian Throne, as Menelik I, the founder of the
Solomon line of Emperors.

One of a large number of magnificent literary works, written in the
ancient Ethiopic or Ge'ez, the Kebra Nagast comprises a wealth of
historical and traditional material, derived from the Old Testament,
the later Rabbinic writings, and from Ethiopian, Egyptian and Arabian sources. It has been ably translated by Sir E. A. Wallis Budge,
under the much too unduly restricted title, "The Queen of Sheba and
Her Only Son, Menyelek."

There is much information on the Ethiopian origin of the
Queen of Sheba, yet she remains one of the intriguing mysteries of
history.

Of the three generals who brought the ancient nation of Kush,
or Ethiopia, to the apex of its last golden age, Piankhy is singu-
larly outstanding. He established Kushite rule over Egypt that
lasted for over a hundred years. In the third of a series of articles
on African history in *Ebony* magazine (Feb., 1965), the distinguished Afro-American historian Dr. William Leo Hansberry says
of Piankhy:

Toward the middle of the eighth century, before the beginning of the
Christian era, and when Greece was young and Rome yet in her
swaddling clothes, a young Nubian prince, later to be known as
Piankhi the Great, was proclaimed King of the already ancient kingdom of Kush. During his reign of approximately thirty-two years (c.
744–712 B.C.) Piankhi expanded greatly the boundaries of his ancestral domain through the force of arms; but he never engaged in
military activity if it could be gracefully avoided, and the national
interests and imperial honor otherwise preserved. In short, Piankhi
was primarily a patron of the pursuits of peace.

In 725 B.C. the warrior-king of Kush, Piankhy, led a Kushite
army north across the sand-and-rock frontiers of Egypt. His soldiers carried bronze and stone-tipped weapons. His cavalry had
been toughened by years of warfare against desert tribesmen.

In the attack on Egypt, the Kushites followed a strict code of
military honor. They always gave the Egyptians advance notice of

an attack. After several years of war Piankhy entered Egypt in triumph.

Of the many books about Piankhy and his times, the most readable are *Piankhy the Great* by Harper E. Johnson and the chapter on Kush in the book *African Glory* by J. C. de Graft-Johnson.

The life of Clitus proves again, if proof is needed, that Africans were part of the armies of southern Europe during the first age of European expansion that started with Alexander the Great. Color was not an important factor in human relationships in this period in history, and very often Africans were on both sides of a conflict. In books about Alexander the Great a number of writers have written about Alexander's companion and cavalry commander Clitus without once mentioning the fact that he was a black man.

The genius of Hannibal is known to the world. But he is not generally known as an African genius. Hollywood and European historians long ago declared this great military genius to be a hero of the white race. He was not. Professor Frank M. Snowden's new book *Blacks in Antiquity* (1970) proves this point both in words and in pictures.

Massinissa, King of Numudia, led a life similar to Hannibal's but he is not as well known to history.

The writings of Publius Terentius Afer, or Terence the African, are still being studied in some Western universities without any reference to his African origin. He was one of a number of African cultural figures whose talent was appreciated both in Africa and in Rome at a time when the Romans were in ascendancy.

There has been more nonsense written about Cleopatra than any other African queen, mainly because it has been the desire of many writers to paint her white. She was not a white woman, she was not a Greek. Let us dispose of this matter before explaining the more important aspects of her life. Until the rise of the doctrine of white superiority, Cleopatra was generally pictured as a distinct African woman, dark in color.

Cleopatra's birth in 69 B.C. marked the last golden age of Egypt. She met Julius Caesar when she was seventeen years old. In 47 B.C. he restored her to power and started their relationship, which was both sexual and political. This maneuver saved Egypt from the worst aspects of Roman domination. In her early twenties Cleopatra met Mark Antony, which started another maneuver. But this was a love affair and her effect on Mark Antony was profound. This noble Roman turned traitor to his own people on behalf of Cleopatra. He attempted to save the country of this black queen whom he loved from Roman domination.

This is a simple telling of the story. To understand Cleopatra's story in greater detail, it is necessary to know something about the culture and customs of her time in history.

In the book *Life Under the Pharaohs* (1960) the writer Leonard Cottrell gives this information about the status of women during Cleopatra's day:

The high status which "respectable" women enjoyed in Ancient Egypt arose in part from the matriarchal system, on which the family was based. All landed property descended in the female line from mother to daughter. When a man married an heiress, he enjoyed her property only as long as his wife lived. On her death, it passed to her daughter and her daughter's husband. This practice was never more strictly observed than in the Royal Family, which explains why so many of the Pharaohs married their sisters, or even their infant daughters. Often these marriages were purely formal affairs. Margaret Murray in "The Splendour That Was Egypt" says: "The marirage laws of Ancient Egypt were never formulated, and knowledge of them can be obtained only by working out the marriages and genealogies. It then became evident that a Pharaoh safeguarded himself from abdication by marrying every heiress without any regard to consanguinity, so that if the chief heiress died, he was already married to the next in succession and thus retained the sovereignty . . . the throne went strictly in the female line. The great wife of the king was the heiress; by the right of marriage with her, the king came to the throne. The king's birth was not important. He might be of any rank, but if he married the queen he at once became king; the queen was queen by right of birth, the king by right of marriage."

To continue this explanation from *The Splendor That Was Egypt* (1949; revised edition, 1963):

The custom of matrilineal descent also explains the many marriages of Cleopatra; she was married first to her eldest brother, who reigned by right of that marriage; on his death she was married to the younger brother, a peculiarly vicious youth, who also reigned by right of that marriage. By those two marriages she had no children. When Julius Caesar took Egypt, the only way by which he could be acknowledged as the ruler was by marriage with the queen; and by that marriage there was one son, Caesarion. When Anthony was aiming at the purple his first step was to secure Egypt, the granary of Rome; he took the only course possible in the circumstances, and married the queen. The fact that he already had a wife in Rome would mean nothing to the Egyptians; the queen would be the Great Wife and her husband would be the king. There were two children of the marriage, a boy and a girl. When Anthony was killed and Octavius entered to take possession of Egypt, he was quite prepared to marry Cleopatra, but she very wisely preferred death.

With the death of Cleopatra Egypt's long Golden Age came to an end. The books about her life and times, good and bad, are numerous.

J. H. C.

Imhotep

GOD OF MEDICINE,
PRINCE OF PEACE, AND THE FIRST CHRIST
(c. 2980 B.C.)

NO INDIVIDUAL of the ancient world has left a deeper impression on history than Imhotep. He was the real Father of Medicine. He is, says Sir William Osler, "The first figure of a Physician to stand out clearly from the mists of antiquity."

Of the details of his life, very little has survived though numerous statues and statuettes of him have been found. He lived at the court of King Zoser of the Third Dynasty, about 2980 B.C., where he established such a reputation as a healer that he was worshipped as a god for the next 3000 years, not only in Egypt but also in Greece and Rome. Even early Christianity worshipped him as the Prince of Peace.

His father was an architect named Kanofer; his mother was Khreduonkh, and his wife, Ronfrenofert. Imhotep appears to have been versatile like Aristotle and Leonardo da Vinci. In addition to being the chief physician to the king, he was sage and scribe, chief lector priest, architect, astronomer, and magician. At that time magic and medicine were allied, as in native Africa and the East today.

He was also a poet and a philosopher. He preached cheerfulness and urged contentment. His proverbs, embodying a philosophy of life, caught popular fancy, and were handed down from generation to generation. One of his best-known sayings is: "Eat, drink, and be merry for tomorrow we shall die."

There is evidence that the Egyptians, and perhaps Imhotep also, diagnosed and treated more than 200 diseases, among them 15 diseases of the abdomen, 11 of the bladder, 10 of the rectum, 29 of the eyes, and 18 of the skin. They knew how to detect disease by the shape, color, or condition of the visible parts of the body, as the skin, hair, nails, tongue. They treated spinal tuberculosis, gallstones, appendicitis, gout, rheumatoid arthritis, mastoid diseases, and dental caries. They practiced surgery, knew of auscultation, and extracted medicine from plants.

They were also familiar with the position and functions of the stomach, the lungs, and other vital organs. Imhotep, it is said, knew of the circulation of the blood, which is 4000 years before it was known in Europe. This could be true because Egyptian civilization lasted for 6000 years, which was sufficiently long for its thinkers and scientists to have carried research along most lines to a high degree. That Egypt excelled in architecture we know, and as regards medicine, Homer said in the *Odyssey*, "In Egypt the men are more skilled in medicine than any of human kind." The Greeks sent their young men to be educated in Egypt, as today students from Egypt go to Europe.

Imhotep's fame increased with his death. He was worshipped as a medical demi-god from 2850 B.C. to 525 B.C., and as a full deity from 525 B.C. to A.D. 550. Kings and queens bowed at his shrine. Later he was jointly worshipped with the great conqueror Amenophis III, and still later as the Son of Ptah, Father of the Gods. "Turn thy face towards me, My Lord Imhotep, Son of Ptah. It is thou who dost work miracles and who are beneficient in all thy deeds" were the words of supplication addressed to him.

The great temple of Amen (Karnak) contains two bas-reliefs of him. On the island of Philae there is a temple in his honor. The inscription to him there reads: "Chancellor of the King of Lower Egypt; Chief under the King of Upper Egypt; Administrator of the Great Mansion; Hereditary Noble, Heliopolitan High Priest, Imhotep."

When Egyptian civilization crossed the Mediterranean to become the foundation of Greek culture, the teachings of Imhotep were also absorbed there. But as the Greeks were wont to assert that they were the originators of everything, Imhotep was forgotten for thousands of years and Hippocrates, a legendary figure who lived 2000 years after him, became known as the Father of Medicine.

The *Encyclopaedia Britannica* says, "The evidence afforded by Egyptian and Greek texts support the view that Imhotep's reputation was respected in very early times. . . . His prestige increased with the lapse of centuries and his temples in Greek times were the centres of medical teaching."

Breasted says of Imhotep:

In priestly wisdom, in magic, in the formulation of wise proverbs; in medicine and architecture; this remarkable figure of Zoser's reign left so notable a reputation that his name was never forgotten. He was the patron spirit of the later scribes, to whom they regularly poured out a libation from the water-jug of their writing outfit before beginning their work. The people sang of his proverbs centuries later, and 2,500 years after his death, he had become a god of medicine in whom the Greeks, who call him Imouthes, recognized their own Asklepios. A temple was erected to him near the Serapeum at Memphis, and at the present day every museum possesses a bronze statue or two of the apotheosized wise man, the proverb-maker, physician, and architect of Zoser.

As regards Imhotep's influence in Rome, Gerald Massey, noted poet, archaeologist, and philologist, says that the early Christians worshipped him as one with Christ. The early Christians, it will be recalled, adapted to their use those pagan forms and personages whose influence through the ages had woven itself so powerfully into tradition that they could not omit them. Thus, says Massey:

The child-Christ remained a starrily-bejewelled blackamoor as the typical healer in Rome. Jesus, the divine healer, does not retain the black complexion of Iu-em-hotep [Imhotep] in the canonical gospels but he does in the Church of Rome when represented as a little black bambino. A jewelled image of the child-Christ as a blackamoor is sacredly preserved at the headquarters of the Franciscan order, and true to its typical character as a symbolical likeness of Iusa, the healer, the little black figure is taken out in state with its regalia on to visit the sick and demonstrate the supposed healing power of this Egyptian Esculapius, thus Christianized. The virgin mother, who was also black, survived in Italy as in Egypt. At Oropa, near Bietta, the Madonna and her child-Christ are not white but black, as they so often were in Italy of old and as the child is yet conditioned in the little black Jesus of the Eternal City.

He adds as regards the worship of Imhotep in Rome, "Surely the profoundest sigh of an ever-warring world went up to Heaven in the cult of Iu-em-hotep, who is worshipped as the giver of rest, the Kamite prince of peace."

REFERENCES

Garry, T. G., *Egypt, Home of the Occult Sciences*. London, 1931.

Hurry, J. B., *Imhotep*. Oxford, 1928.

Osler, Sir W., *Evolution of Modern Medicine*, p. 10. London, 1921.

Sethe, K., *Der Asklepios der Aegypter*. Leipzig, 1902.

Breasted, J. H. *History of Egypt*, pp. 113. 1911.

Bryan, C. P., tr., *The Papyrus Ebers*. London, 1930.

Massey, Gerald, *A Book of the Beginnings*, Vol. II, p. 754.

ADDITIONAL REFERENCES

Aldred, Cyril, *The Egyptians*, pp. 83–84. New York, Praeger, 1961.

Bender, George A., "Medicine in Ancient Egypt." *Mankind*, Vol. I, No. 1, p. 52. Los Angeles, Cal., Mann King Publishing Company.

Bratton, Fred Gladstone, *A History in Aegyptian Archaeology*, pp. 21–22, 96. New York, Crowell, 1961.

Breasted, James Henry, *Development of Religion and Thought in Ancient Egypt*, pp. 182–84. New York and Evanston, Harper and Row, Publishers, 1959.

Cormack, Mariabelle, *Imhotep, Builder in Stone*. New York, F. Watts, 1965.

Gardiner, Sir Alan, *Egypt of the Pharaohs*, pp. 72–73, 76. New York, Oxford University Press, 1966.

Hawkes, Jacquette, *Pharaohs of Egypt*, pp. 23–24, 79. New York, American Heritage Publishing Company, Inc., 1965.

Osei, G. K., *The Forgotten Great Africans 3000 B.C. to 1959 A.D.*, pp. 7–8. London, G. K. Osei, 1965.

Payne, Elizabeth, *The Pharaohs of Ancient Egypt*, p. 87. New York, Random House, 1964.

Sullivan, Walter, "Historic Find." *The New York Times*, Jan. 10, 1965.

"Imhotep's Tomb: A Scholar's Lure." *The New York Times*, Jan. 10, 1965.

"Search for the First Intellectual." *Time*, Jan. 15, 1965.

The New York Times, Jan. 6, 1965, p. 1.

Hatshepsut

THE ABLEST QUEEN OF FAR ANTIQUITY
(c. 1500 B.C.)

HATSHEPSUT of ancient Egypt was the greatest female ruler of all time, according to some Egyptologists. Among those whom she dominated was her brother, Thotmes III, "The Napoleon of Far Antiquity."

She is also said to have been the first woman in history to challenge the supremacy of the male, though arrayed against her were more than 3000 years of masculine tradition. There was no word for "queen" or "empress" in the language of her day—but she fought her way to power and held the throne of the world's then leading empire for thirty-three years.

Hatshepsut lived 150 years before Tutankhamen, or 3500 years ago. Her father, Thotmes I, was the conqueror of the known world, and when he was stricken with paralysis, Hatshepsut became his chief aide. So efficient did she prove that Thotmes in time entrusted her with the management of the kingdom and made her co-ruler.

When Thotmes called the nobles together, he said to them, "This daughter, Khummit Amen Hatshepsitou, the Loving One, I put in my place . . . henceforth she shall guide you. Listen to her words and submit unanimously to her commands. Whoever adores her, I will adore, but he who speaks evil against Her Majesty will die."

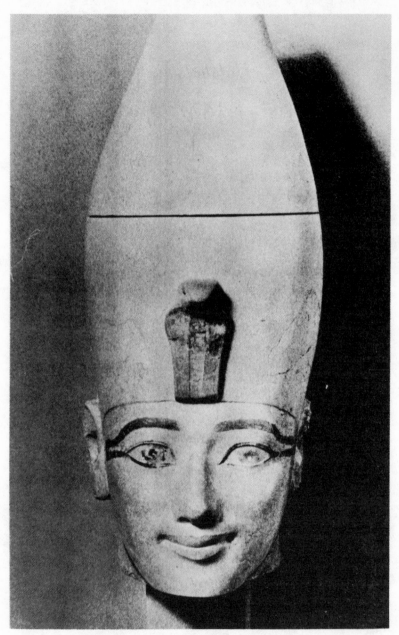

Hatshepsut

Together father and daughter traveled over the empire, receiving homage, offering sacrifice in the temples, erecting monuments and buildings, improving industry and agriculture.

But Hatshepsut had several rivals, principally the two sons of Thotmes, one of whom, later Thotmes II, was born of a wife not of royal birth, and was a minor. The other, later Thotmes III, was the son of a slave named Asnut.

Thotmes III, hoping to oust Hatshepsut, staged a trick in the Temple of Amen to demonstrate that it was he, not she, who was the elect of God. Whilst he was at prayer one day in a secluded part of the temple, he had a priestly procession which bore a glittering image of the supreme God, Amen-Ra, swerve suddenly into the main aisle, as if drawn by some unseen power, and come toward him, whereupon he fell prostrate to the ground as if in a trance. It was then, the priests declared, that the God himself stepped out of his shrine, raised Thotmes to his feet, conducted him to the innermost altar where only the Pharaoh could tread, and bade him rule over Egypt.

This plot was extremely effective and Hatshepsut was faced with the alternatives of war or compromise with Thotmes. She ended by marrying him. The two now put their father off the throne but the old lion reasserted himself, drove them both out, and made Thotmes II, the real heir, ruler. The latter, however, was by all accounts a weakling and died, it is believed, by assassination.

At this period much of the record is lost and there is a gap in the story of Hatshepsut. When we next hear of her, she is again on the throne with Thotmes III, who is now so strong that he is able to restrict her to the position of chief royal wife. However, by skillful intrigues she not only restores herself as co-ruler but finally thrusts him into the background as a mere husband, who is inferior to her prime minister, Nehusi, which name in Egyptian means "full-blooded Negro."

Hatshepsut had yet another handicap besides that of sex, namely, ancestry. On her father's side, she was not of pure Theban stock, though her mother was. Her enemies, the priests of Amen, now seized on this "taint" in her lineage and plotted to dethrone her. To offset this, she began to publicize herself in the most sensational manner of that time: by the building of temples, pyramids, and obelisks, the size and grandeur of which were regarded by the popular mind as a gauge of the ruler's power. Accordingly Hatshepsut decided to build a temple the like of which the world had never seen, and sent for her chief architect, Senmut, who to all appearances was a full-blooded Negro. Together, they chose a site which was not only appropriate but strategic. This was on an elevation three miles away from the stronghold of her opponents, the Temple of Amen-Ra. From this site her temple looked down on theirs.

Under Senmut's genius, Hatshepsut's temple developed into what is still one of the world's most remarkable specimens of architecture. It had a frontage of 800 feet and was for the most part hollowed out of the great cliff that overlooked it. Double and triple rows of columns lined the entrance, and the approach was marked by innumerable statues, wonderful terraces, and paradisical gardens. Colorful inscriptions decorated the interior, which abounded in architectural novelties.

Not content with this, Hatshepsut decided to carry her triumph into the very camp of her detractors. She ordered to be made two obelisks, taller than any others in Egypt. Each was hewn from mighty blocks of rose granite and when completed took two great rafts, each manned by 900 men, to transport down the Nile. Hatshepsut intended these as a gift to the Temple of Amen-Ra but very astutely she had ordered them made so tall that they were higher than the temple, whose ruins, now known as Karnak, reveal it to be one of the most colossal structures made by man. Accordingly, to make the obelisks fit, the roof of the temple was opened, and from this Hatshepsut's obelisks reared their heads as chimneys over a roof.

But that was not all. To make the obelisks still more conspicuous she had their tops encased in electrum, a metal costlier than gold. (Electrum was a composition of silver and gold. Silver being rarer than gold in ancient Egypt, it was more precious.)

In the bright sunlight of that rainless land the obelisks shone like glittering peaks. Their brilliancy, in the queen's own words, lit up the two lands of Egypt. Whenever a resident of Thebes or a visitor looked out on the city, the most dazzling sight he saw was no longer the temple of Amen-Ra but her obelisks.

When the people entered the temple, they read on them this engraving:

O ye people, who shall see my monument in the ages to come, beware of saying, "I know not, I know not why this was made and a mountain fashioned entirely from gold." These two obelisks My Majesty hath wrought that MY name may abide, enduring in this temple for ever and ever.

The queen's popularity increased and she became firmly established. Great prosperity came to the land and gold was so plentiful it was no longer weighed but was measured in bushel baskets. She wrote in her own praise, "It came to pass that Her Majesty was increased above all things; was beautiful to look at above all things; her voice was that of a god; her frame was that of a god; her spirit was like a god. It came to pass that she was a beautiful maiden."

But in spite of all this, she was still a woman with masculine prejudice against her. To overcome it she boldly announced that she was really a man. Whether Egypt was startled we do not know, but this step crushed all further opposition. She donned male garb, changed her name from Hatshepsitu to Hatshepsut, its male equivalent, and announced that she was of virgin birth. Her father, she declared, was not Thotmes I, but the great God Amen himself. The latter had appeared to her mother "in a flood of light and perfume."

The whole story in its most intimate bedroom details was painted on the walls of her temple and may still be seen. The child shown as being born of this union is a boy. Thereafter her sculptured portraits showed her with a man's chest and beard. She also took the title "King of the North and South; Ka-Ma-Ra; the Horus of Gold; Bestower of Years; Conqueror of all Lands; Vivifier of Hearts; Chief Spouse of Amen; the Mighty One."

But the feminine in her cropped up when she wrote of herself:

His Majesty, herself, put with her own hands oil of ani on all her limbs. Her fragrance was like a divine breath; her scent reached as far as the land of Punt; her skin is that of pure gold; it shines like the stars in the hall of festival in view of the whole land . . . she has no equal among the Gods who were before since the world was. She is

living Ra, eternally. He hath selected her for protecting Egypt, for
rousing bravery among men. . . .

"I rule over this land like the son of Isis; I am mighty like the son
of Nu. I shall be forever like the stars which changeth not. . . .

Hatshepsut sent expeditions to distant lands, one of which, to
Punt, merits special attention. Punt was the traditional home of
the earliest Egyptians and was located somewhere in East Africa.
The mission was entrusted to her three favorites: Nehusi, the
unmixed Negro who is spoken of in her inscriptions as "Prince
Chancellor, First Friend, Wearing the Collar"; Senmut, the architect, who is depicted as holding the Queen's infant daughter,
Nefruara, on his knees; and Thutiy, her treasurer. They left with
five vessels of about 300 tons each, and returned with gold, myrrh,
incense, incense-bearing trees, strange animals, and other products
of that region. The full story of this expedition may be read on the
walls of her temple at Deir-el-Bahari.

In the fifteenth year of her reign, and the thirtieth of her rule,
she held a jubilee. Her husband, Thotmes III, was permitted to
burn a little incense to Amen-Ra as he joined the procession. She
wrote triumphantly, "I have no enemy in all the land; all countries
are my subjects: He [Amen-Ra] hath made my boundaries to the
extremities of heaven; the circuit of the sun hath labored for
me."

At last she died, her end hastened, perhaps, by Thotmes III.
Succeeding to the throne, he killed off her friends, defaced her
inscriptions, chipped her features from her portraits, and walled in
her obelisks, doing all with such thoroughness that she was forgotten for 300 years.

In 1906, however, an American excavator, Theodore Davis,
discovered her tomb and amazed the world with the story of this
remarkable woman, a worthy predecessor of Elizabeth, Joan of
Arc, and Catherine the Great.

Hatshepsut's grandmother, Nefertari-Aahmes, was Ethiopian,
and is shown in her portraits as being very black. In addition,
Hatshepsut was of southern Egyptian ancestry, which was and still
is very much mixed with the pure Negroes of the Sudan, whose
territory adjoined Egypt.

Of Hatshepsut and her temple, Robert Hickens says:

To me most feminine she seemed when I saw her temple at Deir-el-Bahari with its brightness and its suavity; pretty shallowness and sunshine; its white and blue and yellow and red and green and orange all very trim and fanciful, all very smart and delicate; full of finesse and laughter breathing out to me of the twentieth century the coquetry of a woman in 1500 B.C.

After the terrific masculinity of Medinet-Abou; after the great freedom of the Ramasseum and the grandeur of its colossus, the manhood of the ages concentrated in granite, the temple of Deir-el-Bahari came upon me like a delicate woman perfumed and arranged, clothed in a creation of white and blue and orange standing ever so knowingly against a background of orange and pink, of red and brown, a smiling coquette of the mountains, a gay and sweet enchantress who knew her pretty powers and meant to exercise them. . . .

A radiant queen reigns here, a queen of fantasy and splendor and of that divine shallowness, refined frivolity, literally cut into a mountain. . . . Instead of being uplifted or overawed by form, we are rejoiced by color, by the high vivacity of arrested movement; by the story that color and movement tell, and over all there is a bright, blue painted sky, studded, almost distractedly studded, with a plethora of the yellow stars of the Egyptians made like starfish. . . . Through this most characteristic temple one roves in a gaily attentive mood feeling all the time Hatshepsut's fascination.

One thing seems certain: Hatshepsut held her own until the last. Her tomb was discovered in the Valley of the Kings, where only the lordly males were buried. The queens had a burial place of their own.

Hatshepsut's dearest wish was to live in the memory of mankind. To the Egyptian, that was true immortality. And she has achieved this, for graven in imperishable granite, her story is as fresh and fascinating now as when it was written thirty-five centuries ago.

REFERENCES

Sir John Garstang, noted archaeologist, thinks that Hatshepsut was the princess who reared Moses (*The New York Times,* Jan. 27, 1932).

Theodore Davis says as regards the leader of the expedition to Punt: "Having once made the decision the queen had to choose the chief to lead her ships to the land of Punt. We have preserved the name of this chief, whom we see appearing before the queen with other high officials at a ceremony in the year IX. His name is Nehusi, 'The Negro.' He is entrusted with the transport of soldiers to Punt. It is not impossible that he was a real Negro. The Egyptians felt no aversion towards Negroes. We know that a king of the XIVth Dynasty, of whom the base of a statue remains, was called 'The Negro' and we have every reason to believe that King Taharka of the XXIVth Dynasty was one also . . . nevertheless, at the time of the XVIIIth Dynasty when a native race occupied the throne, it would be surprising if so important a command had been entrusted to a Negro and also that he should have such high titles for it is said he was 'prince, chancellor, first friend, wearing the collar,' he, therefore, belonged to one of the highest ranks of the administrative hierarchy."

This statement sounds contradictory. It is true that there was a social difference between the unmixed Negro who was not a native Egyptian and the unmixed Negro who was—the former was an alien. But the bulk of the Egyptian army was composed of these foreign-born Negroes, who were known as Matoi. We have pictures of them as commanders-in-chief of the Egyptian army. All through the East these Negroes from the Sudan held high posts. For 700 years, and as late as 1906, the most trusted man of the sultans of Turkey was the Daroussada-Aghassi, or head eunuch, who by tradition was an unmixed Negro from the Sudan. He bore the title of Prince, Marshal, and was ruler of the holy city of Mecca. (*Bull. et Mem. Soc. d'Anthrop. de Paris*, March 14, 1901, p. 237. See also "Eunuchs" in index of *Sex and Race*.)

As regards Punt, it was known, says Davis, as "the divine land." The name, he says, "seems to indicate that it had played an important part in ancient Egyptian tradition." (p. 26) "It cannot be doubted that the fauna [of Punt] is of an African country so the five ships of Hatshopsitu landed in Africa."

Davis, Theodore, *Tomb of Hatshopsitu*. London, 1906.

Maspero, G., *Histoire Ancienne des Peuples de l'Orient*, Vol. II, p. 245.

Breasted, *Ancient Records of Egypt*, Vol. II, pp. 119, 144. Chicago, 1906.

Rawlinson, G., *Ancient Egypt*, Vol. II, pp. 215–216. 1880.

ADDITIONAL REFERENCES

Hawkes, Jacquetta, *Pharaohs of Egypt*, pp. 17, 56–65, 71, 121, 131. New York, American Heritage Publishing Company, Inc., 1965.

Massey, Gerald, *Ancient Egypt: The Light of the World*, Vol. I, p. 262. New York, Samuel Weiser, Inc., 1970.

Montet, Pierre, *Lives of the Pharaohs*, pp. 80–86, 90–100. London, Weidenfeld, 1968.

Payne, Elizabeth, *The Pharaohs of Ancient Egypt*, pp. 87–103. New York, Random House, 1964.

Wells, Evelyn, *Hatshepsut*. Garden City, N.Y., Doubleday and Company, 1969.

Thotmes III

Thotmes III

THOTMES III (or Thutmose), mightiest conqueror and administrator of Far Antiquity, was the son of Thotmes I and a slave woman named Isis, or Asnut. In spite of this handicap of birth, he forged ahead of those nobler born and won supreme power not only in Egypt but in the then known world.

Thotmes began his career as an ordinary priest in the temple of Amen at Thebes. His early bid for power failed in the long contest for the throne with Hatshepsut, his sister, for whom he proved no match.

But upon her death, he emerged from the background to inaugurate a reign even more dazzling than hers. On ascending the throne, he continued the conquests begun by his mighty ancestor, Aahmes, who had ousted the Hyksos, or Shepherd Kings. Leading the way at the head of his army, "mighty like a flame of fire," Thotmes III brought back to Egypt the kings of other nations to grace his triumphs, and such wealth of golden thrones, royal chariots, gold, jewels, gold and silver vessels, and cattle as had never fallen to Egypt before. It is on record that in his seventieth year the envoys from "Nubia of the Negroes" brought him a tribute of 1570 pounds of gold from Waiwat alone.

Utterly fearless, he once attacked an elephant in battle single-handed. The beast was about to seize him when his general,

Amenenhab, struck off its trunk with a blow of his sword and saved his life.

Unlike most conquerors of antiquity, Thotmes, it seems, was merciful, and spared the conquered instead of putting the old and the decrepit to the sword. Says Breasted:

His character stands forth with more color and individuality than that of any other king of early Egypt save Ikhnaton. We see the man of tireless energy unknown in any Pharaoh before or since; the man of versatility designing exquisite vases in a moment of leisure; the lynx-eyed administrator who launched his armies upon Asia with one hand and with the other crushed the extortionate tax-gatherer. . . . While he was proud to leave a record of his unparalleled achievements, Thotmes protests more than once his deep respect for the truth in so doing. . . . His reign marks an epoch not only in Egypt but in the whole east as we know it in his age. Never before in history had a single brain wielded the resources of so great a nation and wrought them into such centralized permanence and at the same time mobile efficiency, that for years they could be brought to bear with incessant impact as a skilled artisan manipulates a 100-ton forge hammer. Although the figure is inadequate unless we remember that Thotmes forged his own hammer. The genius which rose from an obscure priestly office to accomplish this for the first time in history reminds us of an Alexander or a Napoleon. He built the first real empire and is thus the first character possessed of universal aspects, the first world hero. From the fastnesses of Asia Minor, the marshes of the Upper Euphrates, the islands of the sea, the swamps of Babylonia, the distant shores of Libya, the oases of the Sahara, the terraces of the Somali coast and the upper cataracts of the Nile, the princes of his time rendered tribute to his greatness. He thus made not only a world-wide impression upon his age, but an impression of a new order. His commanding figure, towering like an embodiment of righteous penalty among the trivial plots of the petty Syrian dynasts, must have clarified the atmosphere of oriental politics as a strong wind drives away miasmic vapors. The inevitable chastisement of his strong arm was held in awed remembrance by the men of Naharin for three generations. His name was one to conjure with for centuries after his empire had crumbled to pieces. It was placed on amulets as a word of power.

Thotmes died at the age of eighty-two. He built many temples. One of his obelisks was taken to Central Park, New York City; another was set up on the Thames Embankment in London.

REFERENCES

Breasted, James Henry, *Ancient Records of Egypt*, Vol. II, p. 166. Chicago, 1906–07.
———, *History of Egypt*, p. 319–321. New York, 1921.

ADDITIONAL REFERENCES

Hawkes, Jacquetta, *Pharaohs of Egypt*, pp. 43–44, 53–58, 63–72. New York, American Heritage Publishing Company, Inc., 1965.
Kenrick, John, *Ancient Egypt under the Pharaohs*, Vol. II, pp. 181–196. New York, Redfield, Clinton Hall, 1852.
Montet, Pierre, *Lives of the Pharaohs*, pp. 92–99, 100–117. London, Weidenfeld, 1968.
Payne, Elizabeth, *The Pharaohs of Ancient Egypt*, pp. 90–120. New York, Random House, 1964.

Akhenaton

Akhenaton

THE FIRST MESSIAH AND
MOST REMARKABLE OF THE PHARAOHS
(c. 1350 B.C.)

AMENOPHIS IV, better known as "Akhenaton, the Heretic King," is, in some respects, the most extraordinay monarch who ever sat on a throne. Lord Supreme of the then civilized world, with the mightiest army at his command, he preached the gospel of peace and preached it so consistently that when subject nations rebelled he refused to attack them.

Living centuries before King David, he wrote psalms as beautiful as those of the Judean monarch. Thirteen hundred years before Christ he preached and lived a gospel of perfect love, brotherhood, and truth. Two thousand years before Mohammed he taught the doctrine of the One God. Three thousand years before Darwin, he sensed the unity that runs through all living things.

Akhenaton, too, was the richest man on earth. The entire empire of Egypt was his personal property, and with it the lives of his subjects. It is impossible to convey an idea of his wealth. Only those who have visited the museum in Cairo and seen the immense treasure taken out of the tomb of his son, Tutankhamen, will have an idea of it.

Akhenaton's great-grandfather, Thotmes III, and his father, Amenophis III, were among the world's mightiest conquerors and had extended their kingdoms over the then civilized world, and

even into savage Europe. Their armies raided the adjoining islands
of Europe for slaves, as later Europe raided Africa for them.

Weigall says:

Egypt was at the height of power to which the military skill of
Thotmes III, had raised her, when Akhenaton came to the throne.
The kings of Palestine and Syria were tributaries to the young Pharaoh; the Princes of the sea-coast cities, sent their yearly impost to
Thebes; Cyprus, Crete, and even the Greek islands were Egyptianized;
Sinai and the Red Sea coast as far as Somaliland were included in the
Pharaoh's dominion; and the Negro tribes of the Sudan were his
slaves. Egypt was indeed the greatest state in the world and Thebes
was a metropolis at which the merchants, the ambassadors, and the
artisans from the various countries met together. Here they could look
upon buildings undreamed of in their own land and could participate
in luxuries unknown even in Babylon. The wealth of Egypt was so
enormous that a foreign sovereign who wrote to the Pharaoh asking
for gold, mentioned that it could not be considered as anything more
valuable than so much dust by an Egyptian. Gold vases in vast quantities adorned the tables of the King and his nobles, and hundreds of
golden vessels of different kinds were used in the temples.

The rulers of the then known world bowed before Akhenaton.
Inscriptions of his time read:

Year 12, the second month of winter, the eighth day . . . the King
and the Queen . . . living forever and ever, made a public appearance
on the great palanquin of gold to receive the tribute of Syria and
Ethiopia and of the West and of the East. All the countries were
collectd at one time, and also the islands in the midst of the seas,
bringing offering to the King when he was on the great throne of the
city of Akhenaton, in order to receive the imposts of every land, and
granting them in return the breath of life.

And the King rested upon his great throne with which he is well
pleased and which uplifts all his beauties."

And His Majesty said: "Bring me the companions of the King, the
great ones and the mighty ones, the captains of the soldiers, and the
nobles of the land in entirety." And they were conducted to him
straightaway and they lay on their bellies before His Majesty, kissing
the ground.

But Akhenaton was little interested in these displays because within him there burned the spirit of truth and beauty, and the desire to spread the knowledge of the One God.

He saw his people worshipping bulls, hippopotami, lions, cats, and a multitude of other gods. The priests of Amen, firmly rooted in the great city of Karnak, disseminated these superstitions, suppressed free thought, and upheld ignorance.

This grieved him for he held that there was but a single Force running through all life—a Force of which all other forces were but a part. That Power, he held, was the One God. Belief in that God made him happy, and with absolute power at his command he wished to create conditions under which his subjects would also be happy.

Moreover, his people loved war and conquest, which he despised. The sight of burnt sacrifices also disgusted his esthetic soul. Later he forbade them and banished the sacred bull, Apis. God, to him, was a formless deity. A thousand years before Moses wrote the Second Commandment banishing graven images of God, Akhenaton did so.

But realizing that it would be necessary to have a symbol of his new God—something that the less enlightened could see—Akhenaton selected the sun, source of all life. God to him was the unseen and yet ever-present Father of Mankind made manifest in sunshine, the Creator of the Universe and the Bestower of all Good.

And his God, unlike that of Moses, was not a jealous God, but a God of Perfect Love, a God who was compassionate even toward the chicken that "crieth in the eggshell," a God who gives the manchild a mother "to soothe him so that he may not weep." Nowhere in his writings does Akhenaton make mention of an avenging God.

In order to have his religion better developed and understood, he moved his court from the magnificent city of Thebes, home of his ancestors, and, descending the Nile, built the beautiful city of Akhenaton (now Tell el'Amarna)—a city "great in loveliness, mistress of pleasant ceremonies. . . . At the sight of her beauty there is rejoicing. She is lovely and beautiful; when one sees her, it is like a glimpse of heaven."

Here he erected beautiful temples dedicated to religion, art, and music. He taught his poets to write what they felt, and his artists to paint what they saw. The temples of his new God were unlike any that had been built before. In the place of gloomy, mystifying, terror-inspiring structures, he constructed halls, resplendent with light and beauty. No oracles, no stage effects, no tricks of priest-craft to terrify the ignorant. "He gave," says Breasted, "the first signal of the religion that the West upholds today."

In his Dream City, he abolished pose and pretense by setting the example. Other Pharaohs had taught that they were of heavenly origin. Their persons were held so sacred that no one dared to look at them. They could be depicted only in certain conventional attitudes. But Akhenaton showed himself to the people, and when he drove through the streets his guard was unarmed.

He allowed himself to be painted in all manner of poses, thus being, perhaps, the first Pharaoh of whom we have a true likeness. (His earliest pictures, however, are of the conventional type.) In his pictures he is seen in such familiar scenes as playing with his daughters, resting in his garden, eating a roasted pigeon, or putting his teeth into the neatly trimmed meat adhering to a large bone which he holds in his hand. Of jewels, he wore none, and his crown was used only for state occasions.

In all things he attempted to teach naturalness. Truth, to him, was the daily facts of life.

He also encouraged respect for women by setting an example. He is portrayed in many affectionate poses with his wife, the beautiful Queen Nefertiti, who is said by several authorities to have been his own sister. (It was the practice of the Pharaoh, like that of the Inca ruler, to marry his own sister in order to preserve the purity of the royal strain.) Although she presented him with seven daughters and he longed for a son, he did not take another wife as was the custom. He seemed never to tire of posing with the members of his family for the artists. As for his mother, the great Queen Tiyi, a coal-black woman, his affection for her stands out as one of the great examples of filial love.

As his religion was one of happiness and joy, he loved the good things of life—the flowers, the beautiful gardens, the charms of music, the tonic of a good bowl of wine or a well-cooked meal. Hating cruelty, he abolished the use of the lash. The art of his time shows no slaves burdened with chains.

Intoxicated with the artistic passion that burned within him, his mind was ever at work. "His brain," says Weigall, "was so active that he could not submit to be idle, and even when he reclined amidst the flowers in his gardens, his whole soul was straining upwards in the attempt to pierce the barrier which lay between him and the God which caused the flower to bloom."

But alas! the young Dreamer-King—he was only fourteen when he came to the throne—was to learn, like all others who try to create perfection, that mankind was not ready for it. The soldiers, who had fought under his mighty father in Lebanon, Tyre, Sidon, and Ethiopia, conquering city after city, and returning laden with loot and wives, were chafing with inaction. The commander-in-chief of his army, mighty Horemheb, was urging him to conquest. The people, too, wanted to see the stolen wealth from other nations flowing into the empire as of yore.

Troubles multiplied. The priests of Amen, seeing the wealth that had formerly come to them going to the worship of the new God, began to conspire against the Pharaoh. Thereupon Akhenaton, who up to now had been tolerant, showed the weight of his hand. He repressed them and ordered the name of Amen to be hammered out of every monument in his empire, and that of the new God inscribed in his place. He went so far as to have it removed from the tomb of his father, and to banish the word "Gods" from the vocabulary.

As for the subject nations, he endeavored to impress upon them also his gospel of love; but designing leaders threw insults at him and rebelled. He consistently refused, however, to attack vassal nations, saying that they had been brought under his rule by force and were now free to go.

As these subject nations seceded, the rich tribute they used to bring in fell off. Egypt, from a mighty nation, was falling to the rank of a petty state. But Akhenaton held firmly to his principles, amid all trials, till his death at the age of thirty-one.

He left his throne to his chief disciple, Smenkara, who had married his eldest daughter, but Horemheb and Tutankhamen quickly overthrew him. They made war on the rebels, restored all the old injustices, and brought back prosperity to the nation.

The triumphant priests closed over his new religion as hungry waters over the land. They tore down his temples, obliterated his name, and thereafter referred to him as "the criminal."

Akhenaton's conduct has been denounced as obstinate and fanatical by some historians. It was certainly an excess of zeal that caused him to enter even his father's tomb and strike the "Amen" from his name, but it was the custom of the time to disfigure the monuments of a predecessor whose teachings were considered undesirable.

Several leading Egyptologists have spoken in highest praise of him. Breasted calls him "the most remarkable of the Pharaohs," with whom "there died a spirit such as the world had never seen before . . . a brave soul undauntedly facing the momentum of immemorial tradition, and thereby stepping out from the long line of conventional and colorless Pharaohs that he might disseminate ideas far beyond and above the capacity of his age to understand . . . the modern world has yet adequately to value or even acquaint itself with this man who in an age so remote and conditions so remote became the world's first idealist."

"No such grand theology had ever before appeared in the world so far as we know," says Petrie.

Arthur Weigall says:

When the world reverberated with the noise of war he preached the first known doctrine of peace; when the glory of martial power swelled the hearts of his subjects, he deliberately turned his back upon heroics. He was the first man to preach simplicity, honesty, frankness, and sincerity, and he preached it from a throne.

He was the first Pharaoh to be a humanitarian, the first man in whose heart there was no trace of barbarism. He has given us an example three thousand years ago that might be followed at the present day—an example of what a husband and father should be; of what an honest man should be; of what a poet should feel; of what a preacher should teach; of what a scientist should believe; of what a philosopher should think.

Like all other great teachers, he sacrificed all to his principles and his life plainly shows, alas! the impracticability of his doctrine; yet there can be no question that his ideals will hold good 'till the swan turns black, and the crow turns white, 'till the hills rise up to travel, and the deeps rush into the rivers.

His poems, as was said, bear a striking resemblance to certain of those of David, who came five centuries later:

How manifold are Thy works. Thou didst create the earth according to Thy desires—men, all cattle—all upon the earth.

The world is in darkness like the dead. Every lion cometh forth from his den, all serpents sting. Darkness reigns. When Thou riseth in the horizon the darkness is banished. Then all the world do Thy work.

David speaks of God as a "tower of defense"; Akhenaton speaks of him as a "wall of brass of a million cubits."

All of Akhenaton's psalms reflect joy:

O Lord, how manifold are Thy works. The whole land is in joy and holiday because of Thee: They shout to the height of heaven; they receive joy and gladness when they see Thee.

All that Thou hast made leaps before Thee. Thou makest the beauty of form through Thyself alone.

This first Messiah of the West of whom there is any record uttered the words "The kingdom of God is within you," long before Christ did.

On his golden coffin he had engraved:

I breathe the sweet breath which comes forth from Thy mouth: behold Thy beauty every day. It is my desire that I may hear Thy sweet voice, even the north wind that my limbs may be rejuvenated with life through love of Thee. Give me Thy hands, holding Thy spirit, that I may receive it and live by it. Call Thou upon my name, and it shall never fail.

His bust in the Louvre shows a face of extraordinary sweetness, gentleness, and refinement. It strongly resembles that of Toussaint L'Ouverture's, seen in profile.

Judged by prevailing standards, Akhenaton was not handsome. His skull, which has been preserved, is what some scientists call that of a typical Negro. The jaw is exceedinly prognathous. His lips, as seen in profile, are so thick that they seem swollen. His father Amenophis was Negroid, and his mother Tiyi a full-blooded African. That his wife Nefertiti was a Negro cannot be denied.

Howard Carter, discoverer of the tomb of Tutankhamen, says that he was especially struck by the resemblance that Tutankhamen bore to Akhenaton, and the latter's mother, Queen Tiyi. Several leading Egyptologists are inclined to believe that Tutankhamen, whose earlier name was Tutankhaton, was both the son and the son-in-law of Akhenaton. Tutankhamen addressed him as "father."

Arthur Weigall has written a very fine life of Akhenaton, and both he and Professor Breasted have included a number of his poems in their works. Akhenaton's "Hymn to the Sun" is one of the most majestic and moving compositions of its kind. This is the first verse:

> Thy dawning is beautiful in the horizon of heaven,
> O living Aton, beginning of life.
> When Thou risest in the eastern horizon of the heavens
> Thou fillest every land with Thy beauty,
> For Thou art beautiful, great, glittering high over the earth,
> Thy rays they encompass the lands even all Thou hast made.
> Thou art Ra, and Thou hast carried them all away captive;
> Thou blindest them by Thy love.
> Though Thou art afar, Thy rays are on earth;
> Though Thou art on high, Thy footprints are the day.

REFERENCES

Sir J. G. Wilkinson says, "The era of Amenophis III [father of Akhenaton], was noted for the great spirit and beauty of its sculptures . . . the features of this monarch cannot fail to strike every one who examines the portraits of the Egyptian kings, as having more in common with the Negro than those of any other Pharaoh." (*The Ancient Egyptians*, Vol. I, p. 42. London, 1878.)

Pure-blooded Negroes sometimes sat on the throne of both Upper and Lower Egypt. At least there are records of three of them. (See "Taharka" and "Piankhy.") Budge says, "In the year 1860 the natives of Tell-Mukdam in the Delta discovered among the ruins of an old house the base of a black granite colossal seated figure of a king. . . . It was first thought to be a Hyskos king but on examination it was found to be that of the king, Nehsi, or Ra-Nehsi. . . . The word, Nehsi, means Negro, and it is possible that this king was a veritable Negro who by some means made good his claim to the throne of Egypt as in an inscription at Tanis he calls himself, 'royal son, first-born Nehsi,' he seems to have been entitled by law thereto. He was certainly a man of alien race." (*History of Egypt*, Vol. III, p. 104. New York, 1902.)

Peet, T. E., *City of Akhenaton*. Boston, 1922–33.
Breasted, J. H., *History of Egypt*. New York, 1905.
Carter, H., *Tomb of Tut-Ankh-Amen.*, Vol. II, pp. 144, 182. 1922–33.
Weigall, A., *Life and Times of Akhenaton*. New York, 1923.

ADDITIONAL REFERENCES

Aldred, Cyril, *Akhenaten, Pharaoh of Egypt*. New York, McGraw-Hill, 1969 and 1968.

Bille-de Mot, Elenore, *The Age of Akhenaten*. New York, McGraw-Hill, 1966.

Bratton, Fred Gladston, *A History in Aegyptian Archaeology*, pp. 28–29, 141–43, 214–16, 264. London, Crowell, 1961.

Breasted, J. H., *Development of Religion and Thought in Ancient Egypt*, pp. 322, 344–345. New York and Evanston, Harper and Row, Publishers, 1959.

Desroches-Noblecourt, Christiane, *Tutankhamen: Life and Death of a Pharaoh*. New York, New York Graphic Society, 1963.

Gosse, A. Bothwell, *The Civilization of the Ancient Egyptians*, pp. 92, 139–143. London, T. C. and E. C. Jack, Ltd., 1923.

Hawkes, Jacquetta, *Pharaohs of Egypt*, pp. 73–98, 134–138. New York, American Heritage Publishing Company, Inc., 1965.

Mahmoud, Zaki Naguib, *The Land and People of Egypt*, pp. 27–29. Philadelphia and New York, J. B. Lippincott, 1959.

Montet, Pierre, *Lives of the Pharaohs*, pp. 134–145. London, Weidenfeld, 1968.

Myres, J. L., *The Dawn of History*, pp. 77–78, 129, 130, 131, 306. New York, Henry Holt.

Payne, Elizabeth, *The Pharaohs of Ancient Egypt*, pp. 138–151, 153–158, 162–167. New York, Random House, 1964.

Prideaux, Tom, "Ancient Egypt." *Life*, May 31, 1968.

Silverberg, Robert, *Akhnaten: The Rebel Pharaoh*. Philadelphia and New York, Chilton Books, 1964.

Smith, William Stevenson, *Ancient Egypt*, pp. 108–114, 126–132. Boston, Beacon Press, 1960.

Velikovsky, Immanuel, *From the Exodus to Akhnaton*. Garden City, N.Y., Doubleday, 1952.

————, *Oedipus and Akhanton*. Garden City, N.Y., Doubleday, 1960.
Wells, Evelyn, *Nefertiti*. Garden City, N.Y., Doubleday, 1964.
Egyptology and Medicine, Vol. XIII, No. 3, March, 1969, pp. 167–169.
New York, M.D. Publications.

Lokman

LOKMAN IS THE MOST celebrated sage of the East. So great is his fame there that there is still a saying, "To teach wisdom to Lokman," which is the equivalent of "Carrying coals to Newcastle." In Islam his fame equals that of Solomon in the Christian-Jewish world. Mohammed quoted him as an authority and named the thirty-first chapter of the Koran after him.

Much that is said about him is legendary. The Arabs say that he lived about 1100 B.C., was a coal-black Ethiopian with woolly hair, and was the son of Baura, who was a son or a grandson of a sister of Job. Lokman is often confused with Aesop, who was also a Negro, and who, it appears, adapted some of Lokman's fables to his own use. Aesop lived about 500 years later than Lokman.

Of Lokman's intimate life all we know are what may be deduced from his proverbs and from the anecdotes about him. The following are some of them:

Some choice fruit was missing from the master's garden and Lokman was accused by his fellow slaves of being the thief. To prove his innocence Lokman took an emetic and threw up his food. At his request the master forced his accusers to do likewise, whereupon it was proved that they were the guilty ones.

On another occasion the caravan with which he was traveling was held up by brigands. Unmoved by the tears and lamentations

67

of the merchants and their wives, the robbers were taking everything when one of the victims, as a last resort, told Lokman that he ought to give the thieves lessons in good conduct and wisdom. He felt sure, he said, that Lokman by his eloquence could make them return at least a part of their goods, to which Lokman replied, "It would be a greater pity to prostitute lessons of wisdom to rascals incapable of understanding and appreciating them; there is no file that can clean iron of its rust after the rust has eaten through."

When asked how he came to possess such great wisdom, Lokman replied, "It is in seeing the actions of vicious and wicked people and comparing them with what my conscience tells me regarding such actions that I have learnt what I ought to avoid and what I ought to do. The wise and prudent man will draw a useful lesson even from poison itself, whilst the precepts of the wisest man mean nothing to the thoughtless."

Given a bitter melon by his owner, Lokman ate it with apparent relish. Astonished at his act of obedience, the master asked him how he had been able to eat such a distasteful fruit. Lokman replied, "I have received so often of your kindness that it is not astonishing I have eaten the single bitter fruit that you have given me in my life." His master, touched by this reply, set him free.

One of the most beautiful of Lokman's fables is the following:

A drop of water escaping from a cloud was falling into the sea. Ashamed and confused in seeing itself about to be lost in that vast immensity it said, "What am I in comparison with this vast ocean. Certainly my existence is less than nothing in this abyss without limit."

But as it dropped into the ocean it was swallowed by an oyster and in time it became a magnificent pearl. The oyster was caught and the pearl was found and sold to a great king who wore it in the center of his crown, where, on state occasions, its beauty held the attention of the noblest in the land.

Among his best-known fables are the following:

A hare meeting a lioness one day said reproachfully, "I have always a great number of children while you have but one or two now and then."

The lioness replied, "It is true but my one child is a lion."

A fly buzzing around full of its own importance finally lit on the horns of the bull and said, "Let me know if I am too heavy for you and I will take myself off."

The bull replied, "Who are you? I did not know when you came, nor shall I know when you leave."

A Negro one day took off his clothes and began rubbing his skin with snow. When asked why he did it he replied, "Perhaps I will whiten myself."

A wise man passing said, "Cease tormenting yourself because your body will rather blacken the snow than lose its own color."

To illustrate that some persons are deaf to all appeals save those involving their own interests. Lokman related the following fable:

A blacksmith had a dog that slept soundly while he was hammering on the forge, but as soon as he began eating the dog awoke. The master said, "O wicked dog, why does the sound of the hammer whose noise shakes the earth not trouble your sleep while the little noise I make in eating does?"

Those who strive for high office and attain it should not complain if they encounter difficulties, Lokman said, illustrating with the fable of the flag and the carpet. The first, in a dispute with the second, complained that although both were in the service of the same master, it was he who always did the harder work. "I am carried," said the flag, "by valets in front of the battle to be shot at, always bearing the heat and the brunt of the day, while you are never exposed to fatigue. You rest in a palace among beautiful slaves; you enjoy luxuries; you are as brilliant as noon, and perfumed like the jasmine."

The carpet replied, "It is true, but I repose humbly on the floor never rearing my head to the sky as you. Whoever wishes to enjoy glory ought to know that in return he must expose himself to a thousand pains and dangers."

* * *

Lokman is also credited with the Fables of the Sun and the Wind, and of the Peacock and the Jackdaw.

According to tradition, David, King of Israel, wished to name him his heir, but Lokman refused, preferring to be known as a simple *hakim,* or wise man.

The prestige of this Negro slave who lived 3000 years ago is still great in the East. His influence on the philosophy and morality of the West is hardly less potent. That Lokman served as a model for all the fabulists who came after him is incontestable.

REFERENCES

NOTES ON LOKMAN AND HIS CONFUSION WITH AESOP

Marcel says:

"If it is really true that Esop was only a fictitious personage and of pure invention, he existed at least a long time after Lokman. Plutarch, Suydas and Pausanius agree in placing Esop in the time of Croesus, King of Lydia, and of Solon, legislator of the Athenians, that is to say, in the interval between the 46th and the 59th Olympiad; now all the Oriental writers, whether Arab or Persian, unite in agreeing that Lokman existed more than five centuries before the time of Esop at the epoch where they place the reign of David among the Hebrews. . . . In that case Lokman would have been the original with regard to Esop, who in that case, would only have been the translator of the former. Esop could have learned of Lokman in the sojourn that he is said to have made at the courts of the different princes of Asia.

"An opinion more generally received and which has, in effect, greater probability and appearance of truth is that Lokman is the same wise man made known to us by the Greeks under the name of Esop; this name in the Greek being none other than the word Ethiop, altered by the changing a letter which often occurs in the passage of a word from one language into another.

"In effect, Lokman was Habechy, that is, an Abyssinian or Ethiopian slave, and the Oriental writers attribute to him nearly all the same physical characteristics that they give to Esop as well as the stories that we have of the life of this last-named famous fabulist. An accurate comparison of these characteristics drawn from the writings of the Orientals would establish the identity of Esop and Lokman.

"Lokman was, as was just said, of the race of black slaves with thick lips and wooly hair, who were drawn from the interior of Africa and sold into the countries where this kind of commerce existed. Lokman was thus transported and sold among the Jews during the reign of David and Solomon. His ordinary employment was to guard the flocks of his master and this occupation permitted him abundant leisure for meditation. Having received from God, as the Oriental writers say, the gift of wisdom, he composed has apologues, his parables and his proverbs, which are said to number 10,000. . . .

"Of this prodigious quantity of instructive works, which has been used as a base of morals, tradition has conserved but the small number that the destructive hand of time has wished to spare. This small portion which has crossed the abyss of the centuries serves but to make us regret all the more what has been lost.

"The wisdom of Lokman is regarded by the Mohammedans as a point of belief, the more incontestable as it is founded upon the witness of the book of their religion. The 31st Chapter of the Koran is entitled Sourat Lokman (Chapter of Lokman) and in the 11th verse of this chapter Mohamet makes God speak in these words:

'And certainly we have bestowed the gift of wisdom on Lokman,' followed by several other maxims from Lokman.

"Mohamet used Lokman in support of his own teachings, which has increased Lokman's fame to such an extent in the Mohammedan world that some Moslem writers call Lokman, Saint and Prophet."

Savary says, "Most of the Arab writers agree that Lokman was a shepherd and that he was black with thick lips. The sky had given him eloquence and his precepts carried with them persuasion. They give to Lokman the same ingenious responses that are attributed to Esop, and describe him as having the same physical traits. If one adds to these points of resemblance those that are found in their works, one is led to believe that Esop and Lokman are one. Indeed the fables of Esop appear to be but a copy of Lokman." From the Arabic they have been translated into Greek, then into Latin, into French, and so on, into English. As each translator has added to the original something of his own personality and his own nation, it is in bringing together the four that one sees the shades of the character of the different peoples. In the Arab, the truth simple and nude speaks to men; the Greeks have added some ornament; the Latins have lent it finesse; and the French, gaiety.

De Bellegarde, however, doubts that Lokman and Aesop were one. He says:

"Lokman has been confounded with Aesop because of the nature of his own works, which were composed like those of Solomon and called in Arab, Amthal, as the proverbs of this king.

"The name of Aesop signifies nothing else but Ethiopian. . . . Lokman and Aesop are two different men although there is an astonishing resemblance of feature in what history has given us regarding them both."

Universal History thinks that the Greeks stole Lokman's fables. It says:

"There is a strong resemblance between the history of Lokman as reported by the Eastern writers and that of Esop as we find it written by the Greeks. Both were mean in their origin; both delivered their maxims in the same manner, that is, by apologue. But there is a wide difference between the times in which the Oriental writers placed Esop. As to the first, it is generally allowed that Lokman lived in the reign of Solomon; whereas Esop is said to have been the contemporary of Croesus and Solon, the Athenian legislator. From the history of their lives and the comparison of their fables there is all the reason in the world to believe that Lokman and Esop were the same person. The difficulty seems to lie here: whether the Orientals took him from the Greeks [or vice versa]. It seems most natural to believe the former since in such cases the Greeks are found to have been notorious thieves."

Sale thinks that "Planudes borrowed part of his life of Esop from the traditions he met in the East concerning Lokman, and that he thought they were the same persons because they were both slaves."

Masudi, Arab historian (A.D. 956), says he was a Nubian, slave of Lokain, son of Djesr, and was born in the tenth year of David's reign. (*Prairies d'Or*, Vol. I, p. 111. 1861.)

Sale, G., *The Koran*, p. 307. New York, 1898.
Marcel, J. L., *Fables de Loqman*. Cairo, 1799.
Savary, *The Koran*, Chap. XXXI, pp. 178–179.
Hanauer, J. E. *Folk-Lore of the Holy Land*, pp. 19–22. London, 1907.
De Bellegarde, *Les Cinq Fabulistes*. Paris, 1802.
Also see "Aesop."

ADDITIONAL REFERENCES

Lokman, *Fables de Lokman surnommé le Sage*. Paris, T. Barrois, 1847.

Aesop

INSPIRER OF THE WORLD'S GREATEST MINDS
(c. 560 B.C.)

THE INFLUENCE OF AESOP on Western thought and morals is profound. Plato, Socrates, Aristophanes, Aristotle, Solon, Cicero, Julius Caesar, Caxton, Shakespeare, La Fontaine, and the other great thinkers found inspiration in his words of wisdom. Socrates spent his last days putting his fables into verse.

The books that have been written about him and his works would fill an immense library. His writings have been translated into almost every language of the civilized world.

According to some writers, he is supposed to have been Lokman, another Negro slave, who was the wisest man of the East, and who was used as an authority by Mohammed in the Koran. But the manner of his death, as told by the Greeks, gives so living a touch to Aesop that it is not difficult to believe he was distinct from Lokman.

Of Aesop's early life nothing definite is known. He lived in the sixth century B.C. According to Planudes the Great, a monk of the fourteenth century to whom we are indebted for Aesop's life and fables in its present form, he was a native of Phrygia, in Asia Minor, and a Negro slave, "flat-nosed . . . with lips, thick and pendulous and a black skin from which he contracted his name (Esop being the same with Ethiop)."

Camerarius, Osborn, Baudoin, Bellegarde, and almost every writer agrees with Planudes.

Aesopus Phrix genere, scriptor fabular
floruit Olymp. 54.

Aesop

Aesop's first master was Xanthus, who saw him in a market where he was for sale with two other slaves, a musician and an orator. Xanthus asked the musician what he could do. He replied, "Anything." The orator, to the same question, replied, "Everything." Turning next to Aesop, Xanthus asked, "And what can you do?" "Nothing," was the reply.

"Nothing!" repeated Xanthus, at which Aesop replied, "One of my companions says he can do anything and the other asserts that he can do everything. That leaves me nothing."

Struck by the reply, Xanthus said, "If I buy you, will you promise to be good and honest?"

"I'll be that whether you buy me or not," retorted Aesop.

"Will you promise not to run away?"

"Did you ever hear a bird in a cage tell his master that he intended making his escape?" demanded Aesop.

Xanthus, pleased at Aesop's wit, was strongly tempted to buy him, but hesitated because of his black and ungainly form. He said, "That unlucky shape of yours will set people hooting and gaping at us wherever we go."

"A philosopher," replied Aesop calmly, "should value a man for his mind and not for his body."

The purchase was made. Xanthus' wife made the same objection and chided her husband for having bought him, but Aesop's cleverness soon won her over too.

A few days later Xanthus went on a journey accompanied by slaves to carry the luggage. When Aesop chose the heaviest load, the others laughed at him. That, however, contained the food, and grew lighter and ligher as the days went on until nothing was left.

One day Xanthus' gardener asked Xanthus why it was that weeds grew so much better than cultivated plants. Xanthus could find no better reply than to say that Providence had ordered it so, but Aesop said, "Nature is a mother to the weeds, but only a stepmother to the cultivated plants."

One day, after a quarrel, Xanthus' wife left him. Aesop promised his master that he would have her back before many days. Going to the market he bought meat, fish, cake, flowers, wine, the best of everything. At each shop and to each acquaintance he said that the reason for the purchases was that his master was going to get married. The news soon reached the ears of the recalcitrant wife, who came running back. "Don't you ever flatter yourself with the hope of having another wife while I am alive," she screamed.

To celebrate her return Xanthus decided to give a feast and invited the leading philosophers of Greece. Aesop was entrusted with its preparation. When the guests sat down to eat, however, each dish was found to be tongue of some sort. When Xanthus angrily demanded an explanation, Aesop replied with assumed naïveté, "You ordered me to make the best provision that I could think of for the entertainment of these excellent persons. As the tongue is the key that leads to all knowledge, what could be more suitable than a feast of tongues for philosophers?"

Xanthus, mollified by the laughter of his guests, said, "I invite you all to dine with me tomorrow. Since my slave seems set on contradictions, I am ordering him to prepare a feast of the worst. We shall see what that shall be."

But again only tongue was served. To the angry Xanthus Aesop explained, "Was it not an evil tongue that caused a break in your family? Was it not a soft tongue that healed the breach? The tongue is at once the best and the worst entertainment."

Aesop also had the better of an encounter with Croesus, King of Lydia, the richest man of antiquity. Croesus threatened war upon Samos if its inhabitants did not pay him tribute. They decided to submit, but finally asked Aesop's advice. He replied, "There are two ways before you: the way of liberty, which is narrow and rugged at the entrance but plainer and smoother the further you travel; the second is the way of servitude that seems easy at first but which is afterwards full of intolerable difficulties. You must choose."

The Samians chose the first, which meant war. When Croesus learned that it was a few words from one man that had made the Samians change their mind, he was anxious to see the one who could so powerfully influence others and promised peace on condition that he be sent to him. The Samians urged Aesop to go. He agreed but told them the following fable:

"There was a war between the wolves and the sheep. The latter, aided by the dogs, had the better of it. Finally the wolves agreed to make peace on condition that the dogs be sent to them. The sheep agreed. As for the rest of that story, you do not need to hear it, I am sure."

The Samians now begged Aesop not to go but he went, feeling that he was able to protect himself.

When Croesus saw him, he looked at him in scorn. "Is this ill-favored slave one to hinder me, the king of Lydia, from being the master of Samos?" he asked. But Aesop, bowing low in the Lydian manner, replied gently that he had come of his own free will, and told Croesus the following fable:

"A boy hunting locusts had the fortune to take a grasshopper. Seeing that he was about to kill her, she pleaded for her life, saying, 'I have never done ill to anyone, having had it neither in my will nor in my power. All my business is my song. Will you be the better for my death?' The youth relented and he let the grasshopper go.

"Your majesty has now that innocent creature before you. There is nothing I can pretend to but my voice, which I have ever employed, so far as I could, for the service of mankind."

When Croesus, touched by his modesty, bade him ask for anything he wanted, Aesop asked that Samos be left in peace.

With this bloodless victory attained, he returned in triumph to his countrymen. Croesus, however, made him promise to return to him, and Aesop kept his word. He spent several years in Lydia writing his fables.

Aesop finally expressed a wish to travel and Croesus gave him a large sum of money and letters of introduction to the leading rulers of the East. He visited Greece, Babylon, Egypt, Asia, and at Corinth met the Seven Wise Men of Greece at a banquet given by Perimander in honor of the occasion. "The encounter was to the common satisfaction of the whole company; the entertainment philosophical and agreeable; among other discourses they had some controversy upon the subject of government. Aesop being for a monarchy; the rest for a commonwealth."

Aesop was skilled in playing on the vanity of mankind. He realized that it was necessary to sugar-coat the truth, especially in dealing with the great. This won him success where others of higher prestige had failed.

Once Solon, the great Athenian law-maker, visited Croesus. The latter displayed his enormous wealth, hoping to impress Solon. But Solon, unmoved, said frankly that riches did not bring happiness, and that he knew several heroes who had suffered glorious death for their country whom he considered more fortunate than his very rich host. This frankness caused Solon's abrupt dismissal.

When Aesop was shown this same treasure, he replied, "Croesus is to other men as the sea is to the rivers that flow into it." After this he then declared in his own way that he considered honor superior to riches.

His sharp wit and ready tongue were, however, to be the cause of his death: When he visited Delphi, he was so disappointed at the place which had such a worldwide reputation for piety, learning, and wisdom that in an unguarded moment he told the following fable to some acquaintances:

"Some persons standing at the seaside saw an object on the ocean coming toward them a great way off, which had all the appearances of being something of importance, but when it came close enough to be discernible they found it to be a great mass of weeds and rubbish. Such, I find, to be the curiosity that brought me to Delphi."

When the remark came to the ears of the authorities they decided that Aesop should not leave alive. His opinion, if broadcast, would ruin Delphi, whose principal wealth came from its visitors. Accordingly, as soon as he had left the town they sent soldiers after him who accused him of stealing a sacred cup from the temple, which had been planted in his bag.

Aesop readily permitted a search of his effects. The cup was found. Pronounced guilty of sacrilege, he was sentenced to be thrown from a precipice into the sea. He succeeded, however, in breaking away from the guard and fled into the temple where he took refuge. But he was wrenched away. Hoping to save his life, he told his captors fable after fable in vain.

As a parting shot he told them the fable of the Asses:

"An old man who had spent his whole life in the country without ever seeing the town decided that nothing would please him better than to see it before he died. His friends were too busy to take him, but they had some asses which knew the way to the town and decided to let the animals guide him there.

"On the way a storm arose and in the darkness the beasts lost their way and tumbled with the old man into a deep pit where he said with his last breath, 'Miserable wretch that I am to be destroyed, since I must, among the basest of all animals, asses.'"

The Delphians, whipped to fury, threw him from the cliff to his death. But they greatly regretted it later, for their action brought universal condemnation down upon them.

Among the most noted sayings attributed to Aesop are the following:

"The world is like a true play of wheels, turn by turn one mounts and one descends."

"Prometheus, in making man, did not use water to mix the clay; he used tears."

One of his most impressive fables is the following:

A wolf, peeping through a window, saw a company of shepherds eating a joint of lamb. "Lord," he exclaimed, "what a fuss they would have raised had they caught me doing that."

Another striking one is that of the fly who buzzed about a lion's nose, forcing the king of beasts to notice him; but even while he was gloating over his triumph, the fly fell into a spider's web.

The most famous of all these fables—one that has profoundly influenced politics through the centuries—is that of the frogs who wanted a king.

Finding life in their pond too quiet, these frogs prayed to Jupiter for a king. He threw them a log, which after the first splash, lay still. Finding this king not noisy and spectacular enough they leaped on him with contempt and again begged Jupiter for a ruler —a real one this time. He now sent them a stork, which made life very exciting because it began to eat them.

REFERENCES

A coin found at Delphi is believed to bear the effigy of Aesop. Champfleury (*Histoire de la caricature antique*, pp. 101–102, Paris, 1867) quotes Zundel: "Among the numismatists it is now accepted that the head of the Negro that one sees upon the medals of the Delphians is the head of Aesop, whom the Greek biographers describe as follows: 'He had a flat nose and everted lips, and he was black, hence his name, which means Ethiop.' " Leaf and Lawson say he was a black slave.

Bellegarde, *Les Cinq Fabulists*, p. xlix. Paris, 1802.
Planudes, *Fables d'Esop*. Paris, 1649.
Barlow, F., *Aesop's Fables*. London, 1666.
Leaf, M., and Lawson, R., *Esop's Fables*. 1944.
See also "Lokman."

ADDITIONAL REFERENCES

Aesop, *Izinsumansumane Zika Aesop*. Durban, P. Davis & Sons, Printers.
————, *Hadithi Za Esopo*. London, Sheldon Press, 1931.
————, *Les Fables d'Esope*. Rouen, R. Lalle Manti Imprimer Ordinaire du Roy, 1764.
Gonzales, Ambrose Elliott, *With Aesop Along the Black Border*. Columbia, S.C., The State Company, 1924.
Seifert, Charles Christopher, *The True Story of Aesop "The Negro"*. Privately published 1947.
Snowden, Frank M., *Blacks in Antiquity*, pp. 5, 6, 7, 188, 197. Cambridge, Mass., Belknap Press of Harvard University Press, 1970.

Makeda

QUEEN OF SHEBA
(c. 960 B.C.)

"I am black but comely,
O ye daughters of Jerusalem,
As the tents of Kedar,
As the curtains of Solomon,
Look not upon me because I am black
Because the sun hath scorched me." (*Song of Solomon*)

OUT OF THE MISTS of three thousand years emerges this beautiful love story of a black queen who, attracted by the fame of a Judean monarch, made a long journey to see him with a goregeous escort and the richest gift on record.

The story is from the *Kebar Nagast,* or the *Glory of Kings,* a chronicle of the rulers of Ethiopia. When Solomon was building the Temple, he sent his messengers to all lands inviting the merchants to come to Jerusalem with their caravans that he might buy of them.

He was particularly anxious to meet a famed Ethiopian merchant, Tamrin, from whom he wished to buy the precious woods, the marble, and the red gold of Ethiopia. He sent for Tamrin, who became so fascinated by Solomon that after disposing of his wares he lingered at Jerusalem until duty called him away.

On his departure Solomon gave him rich presents for the Queen of Sheba, who received him in audience on his return and listened rapturously to his tale of the splendors of Jerusalem and the fascinating personality of Solomon.

"When he speaks, Your Majesty," said Tamrin, "it is with gentleness and humility. He pardons those who commit wrong; the wisdom and fear of God govern his house and his kingdom; proverbs are in his mouth; his voice is as delicious as honey; his beauty excelleth that of other men; and everything about him is surprising."

Queen Makeda was so impressed that she called Tamrin again and again to the court to tell her more of the Hebrew monarch. Her interest increased until she decided to go to Jerusalem herself. Calling her people together she said, "I go in search of knowledge and wisdom. My heart forces me; it is wounded by love of wisdom, which is greater than all the treasures of the earth."

Accordingly she left with a great number of her followers and a caravan of 787 asses, mules, and camels loaded with the choicest treasures of her empire—gold and silver, precious stones, amber, rare woods, perfumes, and myrrh.

Solomon prepared an apartment built of crystal from the floor to the ceiling for her. Under the transparent flooring ran a stream of water which she would have to cross to come to him. He had heard that one of her legs resembled that of a donkey and was as hairy, and this was a ruse to discover if it was true.

Finally Makeda with her train arrived and was conducted into the apartment. As she walked over the flooring of glass, she lifted her dress as if to avoid the water. Solomon's attention, however, was so held by the beauty of her face and the magnificence of her apparel that he forgot to look at her ankles. The truth is that Makeda had been bitten by a jackal on her leg in her youth and limped a little. This had given rise to the tale.

She was overwhelmed by the sight of the marvelous Temple, not then completed, the gardens of the palace, the arsenals, the king's escort, and above all, by himself.

"Your Majesty," she cried, "the half has not been told."

Solomon, on his part, was equally impressed by the size of the caravan and the value of the presents she had brought him.

According to the Scriptures (I Kings 10:10), "She gave the king 120 talents of gold, and of spices very great store and precious stones; there came no more such abundance of spices as these which the Queen of Sheba gave to King Solomon."

The 120 talents of gold alone was worth $3,690,000—a sum of vastly greater value in those days.

Truly a royal present! What must be the power of a queen who could make such a lavish gift?

The dark olive-colored king and the beautiful black queen had fallen in love with each other at first sight. Each was dazzled by the other; each was demanding, "What is this, I behold? A vision or a living creature?"

Solomon had a throne set up for Makeda beside his. It was covered with silken carpets, adorned with fringes of gold and silver, and studded with diamonds and pearls. From this she listened while he delivered judgments.

He gave gorgeous feasts for her in halls so perfumed with myrrh, galbanum, and incense that in entering one almost felt filled by their odor alone!

She accompanied him as he went over the Temple, giving orders to the workmen. She saw him giving the measures to the workmen, balancing the delicate instruments, and directing the carpenters, marble workers, and engravers. "All passed by his word and his orders were as light in the darkness," in the language of the day.

"My Lord," she said, "how happy I am. Would that I could remain here always, if but as the humblest of your workers, so that I could always hear your words and obey you.

"How happy I am when I interrogate you! How happy when you answer me. My whole being is moved with pleasure; my soul is filled; my feet no longer stumble; I thrill with delight."

"Your wisdom and goodness," she continued, "are beyond all measure. They are excellence itself. Under your influence I am placing new values on life. I see light in the darkness; the firefly in the garden reveals itself in newer beauty. I discover added lustre in the pearl; a greater radiance in the morning star; and a softer harmony in the moonlight. Blessed be the God that brought me here; blessed be He who permitted your majestic mind to be revealed to me; blessed be the One who brought me to your house to hear your voice."

Solomon replied, "Beautiful Queen of the South, I am the happiest of men. Wisdom has been awakened in you for my happiness and yours. The wisdom with which you credit me I hold from God alone.

"Wisdom was already yours, for without knowing of the God of Israel, you resolved in your heart to come to visit me. You wish to become the humble servant of my God. See, I have reared here the Tabernacle of the Ark of the Covenant. I stand before it. I serve the Ark of the Covenant of the God of Israel which is Zion, the Holy, the Celestial. I am but the servitor of God. I exist by His will alone. I was dust before he formed me and to dust I shall return."

At that moment a workman was passing. On his head was wood and on his shoulders straw. His sandals hung from his hips and sweat poured down the length of his nude form. Solomon halted him and said to her, "Do you see any difference between this humble worker and myself? Am I not a man like him? Am I not made of dust the same as he and tomorrow shall I not be a worm even as he?

"Are we not both the sons of Man? What hindered God from giving my glory to this man and putting me in his place? But at this hour, this workman has more strength than I to accomplish his particular task, for God comes to the help of the feeble as He sees fit."

Bidding the man continue his work, the king went on: "What good are we if we do not obtain grace by practicing good on this earth? For though we wear magnificent clothing, eat delicious food, and clothe ourselves with perfumed garments, we are already of the dead by our sin and corruption. Happy are those who repent and fear God."

And Makeda replied, "What joy do your words give me! How like to the dropping of dew are they! Teach me, O teach me more. We of the South worship the Sun as our fathers have taught us, because we believe that the Sun is the king of all gods.

"But now I wish to worship no longer the Sun, but the creator of the Sun: the God of Israel. Let the Ark of the Covenant be my guide and that of my descendants and of the multitude who bow before my sceptre forever."

And so they talked.

But Solomon in all his wisdom was human. The daily presence of the beautiful black queen stirred him. But Makeda replied firmly that according to Ethiopian law a queen could rule only as long as she remained chaste.

At last came the eve of her departure. Solomon was resolute but the queen was equally so. Finally he resorted to a ruse. He prepared a splendid feast in his apartment for himself and her alone. Makeda consented to come on condition that the king would swear to respect her.

Solomon replied, "I give you my word on condition that you steal none of my treasure." Makeda thought this a good jest, and laughingly agreed. Why should she, the wealthiest woman on earth, want to steal from anyone?

At the dinner meats were served in abundance, with a profusion of salt and spices washed down with wines and liqueurs. But no water. Feeling a raging thirst, Makeda stole away into the courtyard. Here she saw a spouting jet of water and drank greedily from it.

Solomon who had stealthily followed her, reminded her of her pledge not to steal any of his treasure.

"Why," she laughed, "this is only water."

"And is not water the greatest of my treasures?" retorted the king.

Overcome by love and admiration, the queen showed that she too was only human.

Solomon at that time had 700 wives, all princesses, and 300 concubines. Among the wives were Nitocris, daughter of the King of Egypt; Sulamit, daughter of King Suman; Rachel, daughter of Hiram II, King of Tyre; Terada, daughter of the King of Sidon; and Emmah, daughter of Achbal, King of Ceyon. To the great dismay of all of these, he now made Makeda his favorite queen.

Some of them began to reproach her about the darkness of her skin; hence, it is said, the famous passage: "I am black but comely, ye daughters of Jerusalem."

This meant that she was a pure black, because in the East mulattoes are not regarded as black. Some writers say that it is Solomon himself who is referred to.

Six months later Makeda returned to her people, a mother-to-be. Solomon had made her promise that if it was a son she would send him to visit him, and gave her a ring to give him so that he would know him.

A son was born, later Menelik I. But the queen was loath to part with him. Finally, when he neared manhod, she yielded and sent him to Jerusalem.

Solomon's heart went out to his son. What a striking resemblance did he bear to his grandfather, King David! Renaming him, he chose the name of David, and planned to make him his successor.

Menelik declined, saying that he had sworn to his mother, hand on her breasts, to return. But Solomon strove to keep him.

Then an incident occurred that favored young Menelik. Rehoboam, his half-brother, who had been named heir to the throne before the coming of Menelik, now was threatening to revolt. Solonon thereupon yielded.

Before sending Menelik away, however, Solomon, in a brilliant ceremony, crowned him King of Ethiopia. To add prestige, he sent with him 1000 of the oldest sons from each tribe, 12,000 in all, of which twelve were judges. Among the number was Azariah, son of Zadok, the high priest.

Solomon's plan was to establish the religion of Judah in Ethiopia, and in consequence, he made a duplicate of the Ark of the Covenant for Azariah and his 1000 Levites. But Azariah on leaving is said to have changed it for the real one, thus taking the original Ark to Ethiopia.

Once returned to Ethiopia, Menelik established the religion of Israel, choosing 6000 black virgins as the Daughters of Zion, according to the law.

In the Church of Axum in Ethiopia there is a copy of what is said to be one of the Tables of Law that Solomon gave to Menelik, and also the crown of gold and precious stones that he placed on the Queen of Sheba's head.

Arka in the Tigre and Axum were the principal residences of Makeda. A few years ago her tomb, as well as the ruins of a great temple and twenty-two obelisks of her period, were excavated at Axum.

Makeda possessed all the qualities of a great ruler. She has been mentioned in two holy books: the Bible and the Koran. Her fame extended even into distant parts of savage Europe. The Greeks spoke of her as "the black Minerva" and "The Ethiopian Diana."

REFERENCES

In Arabian writings the Queen of Sheba is called Balkis. This has led some writers to say that there were two queens of Sheba, both consorts of Solomon, one of whom came from Arabia. But at that time Arabia was a part of the Sedan Empire, and thus it is likely that Makeda and Balkis are one. Balkis may have been only one of her names.

Le Roux, Hugues, *Makeda, reine de Saba*. Paris, 1914.

Morie, L. J., *Histoire d'Ethiopie*. Paris, 1904.

Mardrus, J. C., *La Reine de Saba*. Paris, 1918.

Littman, E., *Legend of the Queen of Sheba in the Tradition of Axum*. Leyden, 1904.

Budge, E. A. W., *The Queen of Sheba and Her Only Son, Menyelek*. London, 1923.

ADDITIONAL REFERENCES

Crutch, Phinneas A. (pseud.), *The Queen of Sheba*. New York, Putnam, 1922.

Hill, Norman, *The Intimate Life of the Queen of Sheba*. London, A. E. Marriott, 1930.

Jacoub, Prince, *Makeda, Reine Vièrge*. Paris, J. Teguis, 1940.

Kebra Nagast, trans. by Sir E. A. Wallis Budge. London, Oxford University Press, 1932.

Ormonde, Czenzi, *Solomon and the Queen of Sheba*. New York, Farrar, Straus and Young, 1954.

Phillips, Wendell, *Qataban and Sheba*. New York, Harcourt, Brace, 1955.

Pollera, Alberto, *Storie, Leggende e favole del Paese dei Negus*, pp. 18–25. Firenze, R. Bemporad, 1936.

Weigall, Arthur Edward Pearse Brome, *Personalities of Antiquity*, pp. 9–15. New York, H. W. Wilson, 1932.

Wheeler, Post, *The Golden Legend of Ethiopia.* New York, Appleton-Century, 1936.

Wright, Dudley, *Masonic Legends and Traditions*, pp. 119–131. London, Rider, 1932.

Biographies from *Tuesday* magazine. *Black Heroes in World History*, pp. 1–12. New York, Toronto and London, Bantam Pathfinder Ed., 1966, 1967 and 1968.

Piankhy

🌿🌿

KING PIANKHY of Nubia watched his tribute of gold, cattle, slaves, and fighting men floating down the Nile to his overlord, Osorkon III, king of Egypt. For more than 1800 years his country had been dominated by Egypt, which drew from it much of her gold and most of her fighting men. Now he decided that when tribute was next due he was going to be the receiver not the giver.

During his twenty-five years on the throne, he had been strengthening his power. With his renowned warriors, who had won most of Egypt's battles for her, he was going to march until he reached the mouth of the Nile. King Osorkon and his viceroy, the High Priest of Thebes, would both lick the dust from his feet, and he would return to his capital, Napata, loaded with wealth as no Nubian ruler had ever possessed before. This was in the eighth century B.C.

His plans ready, King Piankhy started out on the conquest of the world's then mightiest power. His fleet and transports were so numerous that they stretched for miles down the river. As he advanced, he captured all the small towns, sacrificing to the gods of Nubia on their altars, until at last he arrived at the first fortress, Hermopolis.

This he besieged and pressed so vigorously that the city was soon at his mercy. The ruler, Namlot, offered to surrender and

sent many gifts including even his crown to win Piankhy's favor;
but nothing availed until Namlot sent his queen to plead with
Piankhy's women. Piankhy then consented to listen.

Throwing himself prostrate at the conqueror's feet, Namlot
cried, "Be appeased, Horus, lord of the palace, it is thy might
which has done it. I am one of the king's slaves, paying impost
into the treasury."

To Piankhy he presented silver, gold, lapis lazuli, malachite,
bronze, and costly stones. He filled Piankhy's treasury with the
tribute, and gave him a magnificent horse and a sistrum of gold
and lapis lazuli.

Namlot's example was followed by his people. Piankhy's inscription says: "Hermopolis threw herself upon her belly and
pleaded before the king. Messengers came forth and descended
bearing everything beautiful to behold; gold, every splendid costly
stone, clothing in a chest, and the diadem which was upon his
head; the uraeus, which inspireth fear of him, without ceasing
during many days."

Piankhy spared their lives. Later when he visited the stables of
Namlot and saw that the horses were famished, he expressed his
pity.

With his mighty fleet, Piankhy captured every city until he came
to Memphis, which was strongly fortified with high walls, a large
garrison, and an abundance of food and supplies.

Landing on the north side of the city, Piankhy, though surprised
at the strength of the place, devised a clever plan of assault. Seeing
that the high walls on the west of the city had been recently raised
still higher, he reasoned that the east side, naturally protected by
waters, was probably being neglected. In the harbor ships floated
so high that their bow ropes were fastened to the houses of the
city. Piankhy, therefore, sent his fleet against the harbor and
speedily captured all shipping; then, taking command in person,
he rapidly ranged the captured craft together with his own fleet
along the eastern walls. This furnished a footing for his assaulting
lines, which he immediately sent over the ramparts, capturing the
city before the western defenses could get into action. Tefnakhte,
the commander, surrendered humbly.

Thus Piankhy won mastery of all the region around Memphis

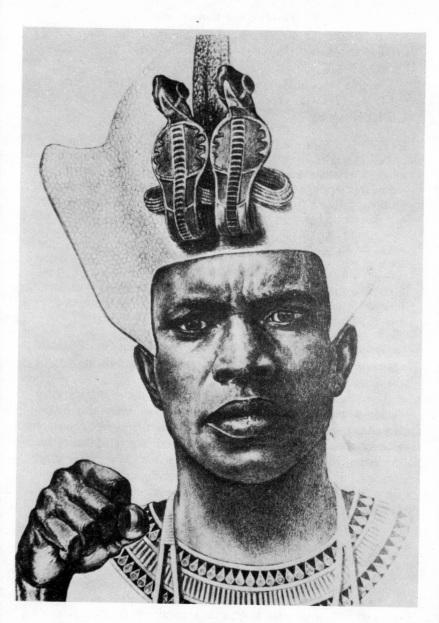

Piankhy

and continued his triumphant march toward Heliopolis; toward the temple of the great god Amen-Ra: toward the palace of Osorkon.

When he reached Heliopolis, King Osorkon and all the lords of the Delta, fifteen in number, surrendered without resistance. An inscription reads:

He came into the house of Ra and entered into the temple with great praise. The chief ritual prayed to the god that the rebels might be repelled from the king. The Dewat chamber was visited that the sedat-garment might be fastened on; he was purified with incense and libations; garlands from the pyramidon-house were presented to him; and flowers were brought to him. He ascended the steps of the front window to behold Ra in the pyramidon-house. The king himself stood alone, he broke through the bolts, opened the double doors, applied the clay and sealed them with the king's own seal. He charged the priests: "I have proved the seal, no other shall enter therein of all the kings who shall arise." They threw themselves upon their bellies before his majesty saying: "To abide, to endure without perishing, O Horus, Beloved of Heliopolis."

By thus entering the holy of holies of the Sun-God, Piankhy symbolized his mastery of Egypt. Ethiopia had become mistress of the then known world!

This done, Piankhy sailed for his home in the south, his ships "laden with silver, gold, copper, clothing, and everything of the Northland; every product of Syria and all the sweet woods of God's Land. His Majesty sailed up-stream with glad heart, the shores on either side were jubilating. West and East . . . singing: 'Oh, mighty ruler Piankhi, thou comest having gained the dominion of the North. . . . Thou art unto eternity, thy might endureth, O Ruler, beloved of Egypt.' "

REFERENCES

What is known of Piankhy comes chiefly from a magnificent granite stele which he caused to be erected in the Temple of Amen and which bears on its four sides the story of the expedition in detail. This is said to be the clearest and most rational account of a military expedition which has survived from ancient Egypt. The ruins of the mighty temples built by the black monarch can be seen at Napata.

He was succeeded by his brother, Sabacon, who pushed Ethiopian dominion as far north as Assyria and Palestine. Sabacon was the founder of the XXVth Dynasty, and according to Manetho, it was he who burned Bocchoris alive. One of his most noted generals was Taharka, a son of Piankhy, who later succeeded to the throne. It was one of the successors of Taharka, King Nastasen, who defeated the great Persian conqueror Cambyses in 525 B.C. But as time went on, Ethiopia receded in importance in world history, to emerge after a thousand years as a Christian kingdom in the fourth century.

Breasted, *Ancient Records of Egypt*, Vol. IV, pp. 406–444. Chicago, The University of Chicago Press, 1906.

Weigall, Arthur, *Personalities of Antiquity*. 1928. (See "The Exploits of the Nigger King.")

ADDITIONAL REFERENCES

De Graft-Johnson, J. C., *African Glory*, p. 12. New York, Walker and Company, 1954.

Gardiner, Sir Alan, *Egypt of the Pharaohs*, pp. 335–340. New York, Oxford University Press, 1966.

Johnson, E. Harper, *Piankhy the Great*. Edinburgh, Toronto and New York, Thomas Nelson Sons, 1962.

Montet, Pierre, *Lives of the Pharaohs*, pp. 243–265. London, Weidenfeld and Nicolson, 1968.

Osei, G. K., *The Forgotten Great Africans 3000 B.C. to 1959 A.D.*, London, G. K. Osei, 1965.

Smith, William Stevenson, *Ancient Egypt*, pp. 151–158, 165, 170, 174. Boston, Beacon Press, 1960.

Snowden, Frank M., *Blacks in Antiquity*, pp. 144–145. Cambridge, Mass., Belknap Press of Harvard University Press, 1970.

Clitus

KING OF BACTRIA AND
CAVALRY LEADER OF ALEXANDER THE GREAT
(c. 300 B.C.)

CLITUS, FOSTER BROTHER of Alexander the Great and commander of Alexander's cavalry, was the son of Dropides and Lanice, the nurse of Alexander. Plutarch, Diodorus Siculus, and Curtius, writers of antiquity, speak of him as Clitus Niger—Niger being Latin for "Negro." In those days one's surname was often given to him because of his color or some physical characteristic. There were other Clituses in Alexander's army and fleet. In any case, Alexander's having a Negro general was not extraordinary. A much later conqueror, Napoleon, had as his favorite cavalry leader a Haitian Negro, the celebrated General Alexandre Dumas.

Clitus was many years older than Alexander and had been a general under Alexander's father, Philip of Macedon. When Alexander succeeded to the throne and started off on his conquests in Asia, Clitus went as his commander of cavalry and so distinguished himself that he was made King of Bactria.

At the great battle of Arbela in which Darius, King of Persia, met the Greeks with 40,000 cavalry, 1,000,000 infantry, and 200 scythe-bearing chariots, Clitus saved the day by saving the life of Alexander.

At the height of the battle, Alexander, who was a conspicuous figure with his golden buckler and helmet's crest and his plumes of unusual size and whiteness, was attacked by a score of the enemy among whom were two Persian generals, Rhoesaces and Spith-radates. Alexander dodged Spithradates and struck at Rhoesaces with his spear, but the weapon snapped in two on the latter's breastplate and Alexander was compelled to draw his sword. "But," says Plutarch, "while he was thus engaged with Rhoesaces, Spithradates rode up, raised himself on his horse, and with all his might came down with a barbarian battle-axe upon Alexander's helmet. Alexander's crest was broken off together with his plumes. Alexander's helmet could barely and with difficulty resist the blow, so that the edge of the battle-axe touched the topmost hair of his head. But while Spithradates was raising his arms for another stroke, Clitus, black Clitus, got the start of him and ran him through the body with his spear."

Alexander and Clitus had, nevertheless, sharp differences of opinion. Clitus was very devout and Spartan in his habits while Alexander was much the opposite, and when in Asia he saw Alexander adapting the luxurious style of living of the rich there instead of adhering to the simpler, more healthful ways of his native land, he was disturbed lest Alexander become as soft as the people he had conquered. Moreover, Alexander, who was surrounded by flatterers, was becoming too boastful. Clitus, out of his deep affection for him, reproached him for these defects and tried to change him. Alexander resented this and a breach developed between the two.

One day while Alexander was at Samarkand, a present of unusually fine and luscious Greek fruits arrived for him and he sent for Clitus to share it with him.

The messenger found Clitus at the temple, sacrificing to Dionysius, and when coming fresh from this shrine he saw Alexander at the banqueting table intoxicated and surrounded by sycophants, he was deeply disturbed, but nevertheless drank the wine Alexander offered him.

When Clitus had entered, the poets were chanting verses lauding Alexander above the gods. One of them now began to ridicule those generals of Alexander who had suffered defeats from the Persians and even to satirize Macedonian skill at arms. This highly displeased the Macedonian commanders but pleased Alexander, who by this deflation of his own people hoped to win over the conquered Asiatics to his support.

The Macedonian commanders, however, not daring or wishing to offend Alexander, pretended to be pleased too. Clitus alone dared to differ. He said, "The defeated Macedonian generals are far superior to those who are mocking them. It is not well, O Alexander, that Macedonians should be ridiculed and made to appear lower than the barbarians."

Alexander laughed in scorn and said sarcastically, "Do not the Greeks appear to walk about among the Macedonians like gods among wild beasts?"

Clitus, raising his voice, replied tartly, "Alexander has permitted himself to be led astray by flatterers until now he deems himself not only superior to his father Philip, but also greater than the gods."

"You must not forget, O Alexander," Clitus continued, "that the Macedonian army has done its part in making you master of the world. You presume yourself to be superior to Castor and Pollux. Aye, even to Hercules. But mortals cannot be compared with the gods."

Stung to the quick, Alexander reached for his sword, but someone had hidden it. He shouted scornfully, "You are pleading your cause, Clitus. You are giving cowardice the name of misfortune."

"Coward!" shouted Clitus in a rage. He stretched out his right arm. "Was it not this cowardice of mine that saved you when you were already turning your back upon Spithradates?"

"Base fellow!" screamed Alexander. Seizing an apple, he threw it at Clitus. "Dost thou think to speak thus at all times of me and to raise antagonistic factions among the Macedonians?"

"Happy are the dead," flung back Clitus, "they cannot see your injustices and cannot see Macedonians being flogged by Median whips with Persians interceding for them."

In high wrath, Alexander bade his trumpeter sound the alarm for his guards. When the man hesitated, Alexander knocked him down, declaring that he found himself reduced to the same position as Darius when he was led about under arrest by Bessus. "I no longer possess the name of king," he shouted.

Springing to his feet, Alexander seized a javelin and was about to throw it at Clitus when friends of the two stepped in between them. Clitus was led out, but consumed with rage, he broke away and rushed back into the hall, shouting, "Alas, in Hellas, what an evil government!"

Alexander, beside himself with rage, threw the javelin. It struck Clitus, piercing his heart. Alexander, instantly repenting what he had done, rushed over to Clitus, picked him up, and begged him to speak. Then, realizing that he had killed his best friend, he pulled out the weapon and aimed it at his own throat but a guard wrenched it out of his hand in time.

Alexander, in remorse, took to his couch and wept aloud, vainly calling on Clitus to return. How would he be able ever to face Lanice again, who had reared him and given her sons to fight for him, all of whom, except Clitus, had been killed in battle. Now with his own hand he had wantonly killed Clitus too.

For three days he refused to touch food and drink, calling himself a murderer and saying that he wanted to die. The Macedonian army passed a resolution declaring that Clitus had been justly slain. But this formal gesture did not ease Alexander's conscience, and he would not be consoled.

Alexander finally drank himself to death, it is said, because he had no more worlds to conquer, but might not remorse at having slain his best friend be the greater reason?

REFERENCES

Diodorus Siculus, XVII, Chap. 8.
Plutarch, *Lives of Illustrious Greeks and Romans*, "Alexander the Great."

Hannibal of Carthage

❧❧

FATHER OF MILITARY STRATEGY
(247–183 B.C.)

HANNIBAL HAS THE REPUTATION of being the greatest military leader and strategist of all time. Napoleon, after selecting the seven supreme military geniuses of the world, ranked him as the first in daring. "And this Hannibal," he said, "the most audacious of all; the most astonishing, perhaps; so bold, so sure, so great in everything; who, at twenty-six conceived what is hardly conceivable, executed what one may truly call the impossible."

Napoleon had also crossed the Alps, but by an easier route, and under much more favorable circumstances.

Hannibal was born in 247 B.C., when Carthage, then the greatest maritime power, was beginning to decline. The Carthaginians were the descendants of the Phoenicians, a Negroid people, who were great merchants. They traded with India, the peoples of the Mediterranean, and the Scilly Isles. Carthage was founded by them as a central base for this commerce.

The Phoenicians, like most commercial peoples, were not warriors. Their immense wealth and their luxurious manner of living had rendered them still softer. It was inevitable that they should inspire plunder in the heart of their powerful neighbor, Rome, which was less than a hundred miles across the Mediterranean.

Rome, then in the prime of her youth, had concentrated on military power. Her fleet also dominated the Mediterranean. Now reaching out for world supremacy, she demanded Sicily from

Carthage as an appetizer. When Carthage refused, the first Punic War followed, in which Carthage lost Corsica and Sardinia to Rome.

Carthage forgot her defeat and continued her commerce. But there was one citizen to whom it was as gall: Hamilcar Barca—the Lightning. Determined on revenge, he aroused his lethargic fellow citizens with his oratory and raised a large force. Attacking the Romans, he won a series of brilliant victories on land and sea.

Then he decided to extend Carthaginian power into Spain. About to leave, he sacrificed to the gods. Among those standing at the altar was his son Hannibal, who though only nine years old had the spirit of a conqueror. For years past he had been imitating in play the battles in which his father had slain the Romans. Now he thought himself old enough to go to war. Throwing his arms about his father's neck, he begged to be taken along. Hamilcar yielded, and Hannibal, kneeling before his father, pledged undying hate to the Romans.

Seventeen years later Hannibal succeeded to supreme command of the peninsula. He defeated all the tribes until only one remained—the Sagentum. The latter were allies of Rome and to attack them meant war with her. But Hannibal, true to his vow, did not hesitate, and after an eight months' siege and a bloody battle, defeated them.

Rome immediately sent her ablest general and foremost counsellor, Fabius the Great, to Carthage to demand the withdrawal of Hannibal. The Carthaginians, who had been receiving loads of plundered treasure from Spain, refused and the second Punic War began.

Rome felt sure of victory. She was impregnable. Her navy, stronger than that of Carthage, would prevent a landing anywhere on the Italian coast. As for the northern approaches, they were guarded by the frozen fortress of the Alps, the crossing of which with an army had long been pronounced impossible.

When the war opened, Hannibal, who was in the northeast of Spain, decided to attack the Roman outpost in Gaul, and marched toward the Pyrenees. He had 80,000 infantry, 12,000 cavalry, and 40 elephants.

When he neared France, Hannibal took leave of his wife, a Spanish princess, and his son. When some of his men took fright at the prospect of the unknown journey, Hannibal sent back 10,000 of them. Then he marched on, defeating the tribes of white savages, who fled in terror at the sight of his dusky legions and his elephants.

Crossing the Pyrenees, he marched eastward until he reached the River Rhone at what is now Avignon, France. The Rhone, at this point, is a deep, swift stream. The problem of crossing was heightened by the masses of the foe on the opposite bank.

With the craftiness of a born general, Hannibal laid his plans. Calling one of his most trusted aides, Hanno, he gave him 10,000 men and bade him cross the river several miles further up. When this was done, he was to make it known by sending up a column of smoke.

Hannibal, in the meantime, had his rafts prepared, and when he saw Hanno's signal, he gave the order to cross. At that the yelling barbarians on the opposite bank pressed forward to repel him but Hanno attacked them in the rear, throwing them into such confusion that Hannibal crossed over and won an easy victory.

After this he marched south until he reached Massillia, now Marseilles, which he captured from the Romans. He was now on the seacoast, and only a few days' march from Italy. But Rome blocked him with her fleet. There was but one course: to retreat northward. When the Romans saw this they grew even more confident. Hannibal retraced his steps until he reached what is now Tarascon, France. From here he must either return to Spain or strike at Rome over the formidable snow-capped peaks of the Alps. Unhesitatingly, he chose the latter.

Then began the most painful, arduous, and terrifying march in the history of war. Hannibal himself had never seen the Alps before and knew nothing of their dangers.

His soldiers, most of them from the tropics, saw snow and felt the cold of winter for the first time. Above them were mountains of ice; below them, precipices. Skirting the narrow edges of these, numbers were swept to death on the jagged rocks below by snowstorms and avalanches, or by rocks let loose on them by unseen savages above. Small wonder if some of them quailed, but their young general, undismayed alike by the forces of nature or of man, urged them on and bade them think of the loot and the triumphs that awaited them when they captured Rome.

But their greatest test was yet to come. They came to a narrow pass which was so well guarded by the Allbrogos, allies of the Romans, that retreat seemed the only course. The defenders had but to loosen a few rocks and the whole army, elephants and all, would be swept to death.

Valor and numbers counted for naught. Strategy was the only weapon. Once again Hannibal's fertile brain came to the rescue. After studying the situation for days, he noticed that the guardians of the pass retired each night, feeling sure that no one would ever be able to scale the frozen heights in the darkness. Spending the nights in their warm huts, they would return early in the morning.

Accordingly, Hannibal with a number of men left early one morning for the heights and reaching them before the Allbrogos did, signaled for his men to come on. Unknown to him, however, another body of the enemy lower down had come forward to ambush them and now attacked his men as they came up.

Great confusion followed. Hannibal, seeing his men and horses being swept to death over the cliffs by stones let loose by the foe, left some of his men to guard the heights, and hastening down, rallied his men to turn what seemed certain defeat into victory.

Continuing up the mountain he met still another tribe, which, pretending to be friendly, led him into an ambush in which he lost many more men. Nine days later he reached the summit and glimpsed the rich plains of Italy far below. But his difficulties were not over. The descent was equally hard and during a snowstorm thousands of his men died. At last on November 15, 218 B.C., six days later, his army reached the plains, emaciated, starved, ragged.

The fifteen days coming over the Alps had taken a heavy toll. Polybius, a historian of the times, says that of Hannibal's original 70,000 infantry only 20,000 remained. Of his 12,000 cavalry half had been lost. But happily for him, all his elephants were safe.

With this ridiculously small force he was now to face the mightiest military power of that age. Rome, according to Polybius, had more than a million fighting men, of which 250,000 were infantry, 25,000 cavalry, and auxiliaries of 770,000 infantry and cavalry.

The news threw Rome into consternation. To cross the Alps with an army! What supermen these Africans must be! But when the weakened state of the attackers became known, fear quickly changed to ridicule.

Rome put into the field the largest army in its history—80,000 men, or more than double Hannibal's. Scipio, its commander, felt certain of victory, that Hannibal had no recourse but to go back the way he had come or be annihilated.

He said to his men, "These Africans are but the resemblances, nay, rather, the shadows of men, being worn-out with hunger, cold, dirt, and filth, and bruised and enfeebled among stones and rocks. Their joints are frost-bitten; their sinews stiffened with the snow; their limbs withered by the frost; their armour battered and shivered; their horses, lame and powerless. With such cavalry, with such infantry you will have to fight; indeed you will not have enemies in reality, but rather their last remains.

"Moreover, we have beaten these miserable Carthaginians by land and sea often before. Now they have had the temerity to cross the Alps. But they won't be strong enough to return over it. We have them in a trap. What I do fear is that victory is going to be so cheap that the world is not going to give us credit for it."

Hannibal really was in a desperate position. Courage and initiative were his sole hopes. Assembling his men, he told them that he had promised to lead them to plunder such as no army had ever seen before and that it was up to them to seize it or die in the attempt.

To impress them with the critical nature of their position, he dramatized in the following manner: He had the enemy prisoners taken in the Alps brought before his men, and throwing down before the captives the weapons with which they usually fought, he said to them, "Each of you who is willing to fight a duel to the death with one of his own tribe let it be known. The winners will be set free and given horses, arms, and money to take them to their homes again in honor."

Every captive volunteered. Friend turned against friend until he slew him or was slain. Hannibal, true to his word, rewarded the victors.

To his men, he said, "You are like these captives, shut in on every side. Behind you are the Alps; before you, the Romans and the river. Your only hope is battle and victory.

"And victory will not be difficult. Think of the splendid and prosperous career before you. It will conduct you to Rome, second in wealth only to Carthage. There are great treasures to be divided amongst us, if we win. If we lose we are lost, for there is no place of safety we can reach by flight. We must win."

Scipio reached Hannibal at Ticino, and confident of victory, hurled his entire force at him. But Hannibal, who had carefully studied the ground, so arranged his men that the Romans would attack him in a body, and when they were bunched together, he let loose his armored elephants on them, trampling them and throwing them into disorder. Behind the elephants came his terrible African swordsmen to complete the slaughter.

The Romans, panic-stricken, fled. The Carthaginians, in pursuit, cut them down ruthlessly. Scipio, badly wounded, was saved from capture by his son, later the famous Scipio Africanus the Elder.

Rome, thunderstruck, gathered a larger army and sent it the same year against Hannibal at Trebia. Hannibal, though still greatly outnumbered, was in a better position now. Moreover, some of the Italian tribes had come over to him. In this battle, he drew the Romans into a marsh, and when they were bogged down in that, killed the greater part of them. Among the slain was their commander, Sempronius. This victory gave Hannibal all of northern Italy.

His next exploit was to cross the Apennines, a feat second only to crossing the Alps. By this time, however, he had lost all of the elephants, except the one on which he rode. Hannibal had also lost one eye.

All that summer he ravaged the coast of the northern Adriatic, and was returning loaded with stores of supplies for the winter when he found himself trapped in a narrow pass by a large Roman army.

The Roman commander was so sure of victory that he placed his men in battle formation to attack the next morning. But once again Hannibal's ingenuity saved him. Assembling a thousand head of the captured cattle, he tied faggots on their horns, set them ablaze and turned them loose. The animals stampeded with terrific noise through the night.

The Romans, thinking that it was Hannibal who was trying to escape over the hills, abandoned their posts, after which Hannibal easily broke through and went off to take up his winter quarters in peace.

Rome, in desperation, now dispatched her ablest general, Flaminius, with a still larger army. Hannibal, knowing that Flaminius had but one road to take—that via Lake Trasimeno—decided to ambush him there. When the armies met, his agile Numidians closed in on the Roman rear and cut off its retreat, while his Africans, Spaniards, and Gauls, suddenly issuing from nowhere as it were, burst on the enemy's flank. A horrible massacre followed. The combat was so violent that though an earthquake shook the region, the fighters were unaware of it. In this battle the Romans lost 25,000 men; Hannibal, 1500.

This victory opened the road to Rome. Livy, the Roman historian, describes in detail the panic that ensued in that city at the news. The Romans, as a last hope, gave complete control of their state to Fabius, he whose decision had started the war with Carthage.

Fabius, wily and cautious, decided as the best means of defense never to accept battle when it was offered by Hannibal, never to attack him in his camp or on familiar ground, but to wear him down by delay. As a result, Fabius became known as "The Cunctator," or delayer. His name is still proverbial as a procrastinator.

Hannibal, in the meantime, was asking Carthage for support. He had sent back bushels of gold rings and other plunder as proof of his success but his commercially-minded countrymen, engaged in bickering at home, took little notice of him. Some reinforcement did reach him over the Alps but it was inadequate.

However, the delaying tactics of Fabius were entirely to Hannibal's liking, and he continued to ravage Italy. At last, the Romans, weary of Fabius, ousted him, and gave command to two new generals, Varro and Emilius, each of whom was to command on alternate days. With 90,000 men they started north, certain of victory.

Hannibal, with only 50,000 men, retreated at their approach. Most of his original army had perished. His famous Numidian cavalry was still largely intact, however.

Varro and Emilius caught up with Hannibal at Cannae on the Aufidius River. Hannibal's back was to the river, making further retreat very difficult. His position seemed hopeless.

Shortly before the battle Hannibal with some of his generals rode up near the Roman camp to survey the vast array of the enemy. One of his generals, named Giscon, at seeing the Romans, made a discouraging remark. But Hannibal laughed. "Ah," he jeered, "there's something you haven't thought of. There's not a single man in all that army named Gisco." Everyone laughed and confidence was restored.

The battle that followed is still the most renowned in the annals of military strategy. Hannibal, knowing that he could not hope to win by main force, placed the weakest part of his army in the center, contrary to the best military rules, with his veterans and his cavalry on both wings.

The battle began on a bright June morning in 216 B.C. The Romans, driving down on the Carthaginians, struck them full in the center as Hannibal had anticipated. Finding little resistance there, they pushed on inwards, sure of victory. But their ranks were broken. The effect was precisely that of one who hurls himself against a door he believes is locked to find that it isn't.

When the Romans had thus penetrated far enough, Hannibal sent his African infantry in solid formation to attack them on both flanks while his cavalry galloped to the rear to attack them there.

The Romans, thus surrounded, were slaughtered like sheep. Their blood changed the water of the Aufidius to crimson. Emilius was slain and with him 80 Roman senators and 70,000 men.

Hannibal was now master of all Italy, except the capital, and that in only two years. Rome was frantic. Was Hannibal coming to attack the city? Maharbal, one of his generals, urged him to do it without delay. But Hannibal, unequipped with siege artillery and with no regular base of supplies, refused, on which Maharbal exclaimed, "Hannibal, you know how to win victories, but not how to use them."

For the next thirteen years Hannibal roamed over Italy almost at will, with little support from Carthage. Many tribes continued to join him, among them the Capuans. Rome, to punish them, besieged their city, whereupon Hannibal decided to frighten the capital again. With his army he marched to within three miles of the city, where, as Frazer says in *The Golden Bough,* he "hung with his dusky army like a storm-cloud about to break, within sight of the sentinels of Rome."

Suddenly he advanced and at the cry "Hannibal at the gates!" the Romans peered nervously over the walls, thinking he was about to strike. They saw him ride slowly around the city with a few thousands of his cavalry, his African war drums beating ominously, then rise in his stirrups, hurl a javelin at the gates and ride slowly away.

Scipio, son of the general whom Hannibal had first beaten, and who was later surnamed "Africanus" for his brilliant victories, had, in the meantime, been undermining Hannibal elsewhere. In Spain, by using Hannibal's own tactics, he had been defeating the Carthaginians and preventing any reinforcements from reaching Hannibal. His next move was to attack Carthage as one way of forcing Hannibal to return there. The Carthaginians, beaten, begged Hannibal to return and he did so.

Hannibal sailed from southern Italy and reached Africa safely despite the lurking Roman fleet. He had maintained himself in Italy for fifteen exciting years.

Back in Carthage, he whipped into shape such fighting material as was available. He took the field with 55,000 men, mostly raw recruits, and 80 elephants.

Scipio attacked him at Zama. He was aided by Massinissa, a former ally of Carthage. Hannibal, though tactically as brilliant as ever, was beaten. His elephants, not sufficiently seasoned for war, ran amuck among his own troops, turning the tide of battle against him.

Carthage now became a vassal of Rome, and was made to pay a staggering indemnity. But Hannibal, who was as able a statesman as he was a warrior, reorganized Carthage on such a sound basis that she was not long in regaining her prosperity, on which she offered to pay off the indemnity in a lump sum. This so alarmed Rome that she found a pretext for accusing Hannibal of conspiracy and demanded that he give himself up.

Hannibal fled to Bithynia and found refuge with the king there. But the Romans demanded his surrender and Hannibal, now sixty-one and worn with fifty years of warfare, knew that the end had come. In a ring on his finger was poison he had always carried for such an emergency. The Romans found him dead.

Hannibal's fame increased with his death. Polybius, Greek historian, and therefore his enemy, said of him, "Who would not be seized with admiration for a general who accomplished such prodigies. . . . All that happened at Rome, as well as at Carthage, depended on a single man. I speak of Hannibal."

As to his conduct, it was irreproachable, so much so that Justin, the Roman historian who had a strong prejudice against Africans, demanded whether it was really possible that Africa could have been his birthplace.

Hannibal, like Napoleon, towers over all the figures of war in an age of war. Through the mists of the centuries we still see the form of his gigantic figure, the greatest of the great in the art of war. As one writer says:

Seldom in the history of the world, has the decisive influence of an individual genius in war been so grandly and so conspicuously made manifest. Here was Rome dreaming of an easy descent on Africa and listlessly making ready for an easy conquest, when Hannibal baffles her by the originality and greatness of his plan. He annihilates her army in battle after battle, showing throughout all, supreme excellence, resource, skill, daring, the heroic spirit, the faculty of command in the very highest degree, caution, sound judgment, extraordinary craft, and last, but not least, a watchful care in providing for the requirements of his men.

Hannibal's tactics are still taught in leading military academies. His strategy at Cannae was successfully imitated by Hitler in his attack on Belgium.

That Carthage is remembered today is due almost entirely to Hannibal.

REFERENCES

There are no less than eight supposed portraits of Hannibal, none of which resemble another. Colonel Hennebert, a leading authority on

Hannibal, says, "There exists no really authentic portrait of Hannibal." (*Histoire d'Annibal*, Vol. I, p. 495. 1870.)

A bust found at Capua 2000 years later is believed to be his, but as Hennebert says, there were several Hannibals in the Carthaginian army and navy at various periods. As for the most widely accepted portrait of him, Francis Pulzky, noted iconographer, says that it was not of him at all but of "the ideal representation of a hero" from the silver coins of Dernes of Phoenicia and Pharnabazus of Phrygia and Lydia. (Nott and Gliddon's *Indigenous Races of Mankind*, pp. 93, 94. 1857). On the other hand, coins issued by Hannibal after the battle of Trasimene show a Negro on one side and an elephant on the other. Hannibal before that battle had lost all his elephants except one, and on that he rode. (*Polybius*, Book III, 79, 82.)

Of these coins, Ernest Babélon, noted numismatist, says:

"The Negro of the coins in question has a definite characteristic which leaves no doubt of the ethnographic intention of the engraver; he has rings in his ears, a flat nose, thick lips, and hair arranged in rows of knots.

"Hannibal, who had lost an eye—commanded his troops on the single elephant that remained to him. . . . Hannibal was victorious on the spot where the money was struck, and it was contemporaneous with the battle. . . . It seems to me, then, it is difficult not to recognize in the type of the head of the Negro and the elephant, pieces struck in honor of the victory of Hannibal, perhaps to pay his troops. . . . Thus, one ought not to accuse me of giving a picturesque twist to a conclusion rigorously scientific when I propose to recognize in these little coins of bronze the elephant that carried Hannibal and his Negro driver."

I go further and suggest that the effigy on the coins was that of Hannibal himself. The coin would very likely be struck in honor of an important person, and was not Hannibal the most important? Take, for instance, the case of General Eisenhower and his chauffeur. Which of the two would more likely be selected for commemoration on a coin? And finally, what proof have we that the mahout of Hannibal's elephant was a Negro?

Furthermore, Hannibal was an African, and therefore, why not a Negro? In fact, until the rise of the doctrine of white supremacy, Hannibal was traditionally known as a black man. Peter the Great so christened his Negro favorite, later a general. On the origin of the racial origins of the Carthaginians, see *Sex and Race*, Vol. I, Chap. 8, 1941.

Polybius, Book III.

Livy, XXI–XXIV.

Mommsen, *History of Rome*, Vol. III, pp. 238–482. 1894.

Abbott, J., *History of Hannibal*, 1876.

See also footnotes in "Massinissa."

ADDITIONAL REFERENCES

Baker, George Philip, *Hannibal*. New York, Dodd, Mead, 1929.

Charles-Picard, Gilbert, *The Life and Death of Carthage*. New York, Taplinger, 1968.

De Beer, Sir Gavin Rylands, *Hannibal*. New York, Viking Press, 1969.

De Graft-Johnson, J. C., *African Glory*, pp. 20–21, 130–131, 184–185. New York, Walker and Company, 1954.

Dodge, Theodore Ayrault, *Hannibal*. Boston and New York, Houghton Mifflin and Company, 1891.

Fonvielle, Wilfrid de, *Comment Périssent les Républiques*, pp. 41–54. Paris, C. Bayle, 1888.

Gsell, Stephan, *Histoire Ancienne de l'Afrique du Nord*. Paris, H. Achette, 1920.

Lamb, Harold, *Hannibal: One Man Against Rome*. Garden City, N.Y., Doubleday, 1958.

Snowden, Frank M., *Blacks in Antiquity*, pp. 130–131, 184–185. Cambridge, Mass., Belknap Press of Harvard University Press, 1970.

Thompson, L., and J. Ferguson, eds., *Africa in Classical Antiquity*, pp. 85, 89–90. Ibadan, Ibadan University Press, 1969.

Biographies from *Tuesday* Magazine, *Black Heroes in World History*, pp. 13–23. New York, Toronto and London, Bantam Pathfinder Ed., 1966, 1967 and 1968.

Massinissa

❧

MASSINISSA, King of Numidia, may be compared to the feather that tipped the scale. When two great nations were struggling for the mastery of the world, he threw himself on one side and it won. There seems nothing extraordinary in that. But at the time he was a fugitive with only five followers. And all for the love of a woman. Massinissa's love affair is one of the most poignant in history.

The leading figures of this mighty drama are:

Hannibal, the Carthaginian, renowned military genius, and himself an African.

Scipio, foremost Roman general of his day, calm in judgment, cultured, ruled by his head.

Syphax, king of Numidia, the kingpin of the situation—both Rome and Carthage were trying hard to win him over.

Sophonisba, the most beautiful woman of her time, the daughter of Hasdrubal, Carthaginian general, and niece of Hannibal.

Massinissa, son of Gala, king of Massylia, a petty kingdom in southern Numidia, Africa.

The Numidians were of mixed Berber and Ethiopian ancestry. The Berbers claimed descent from the Mazoi, the Negro soldiers of ancient Egypt. Their numbers, like others of the peoples of northern Africa, were continually reinforced by Negro peoples from the south brought in as captives and slaves. The great strength of both Carthage and Numidia was the renowned Numidian cavalry.

As a lad Massinissa had been sent to Carthage to study military tactics and while there had fallen in love with Sophonisba. Hasdrubal, her father, disliked Numidians but had consented largely because of Massinissa's exceptional ability. A giant in size and strength, none could equal him on horseback or with the sword. At the lyceum he excelled in Latin, Greek, and military tactics.

At the age of seventeen Massinissa was so greatly in love with Sophonisba that he felt he must do something to impress her and the world. Accordingly he induced her father to declare war on Syphax, and marching against the latter, defeated him in two battles after which he went with Hasdrubal to Spain where Carthage was fighting Rome for mastery of that land. This was at the time when Hannibal had overrun Italy and was winning brilliant battles not far from the walls of Rome.

Arriving in Spain, Massinissa, not yet eighteen, attacked Scipio, Rome's foremost leader, and defeated him. Another Roman general, Gneus, sent against him met the same fate. With his black cavalry, Massinissa seemed invincible.

But while Massinissa was trying to distinguish himself in the eyes of Sophonisba, events at home were shaping themselves against him. Syphax, an old ally of Rome, had rallied his forces and was threatening Carthage. To make peace, the Carthaginians forced Sophonisba to marry Syphax.

Massinissa heard the news in Spain. In a great rage he went to the tent of Hasdrubal, her father, to demand an explanation. The latter, indignant at the thought that his daughter was being forced by the state to marry, found himself having to choose between the national welfare and his private feelings. He finally decided in favor of Syphax.

Massinissa thereupon resigned his command to return to his own country. Before leaving Spain, however, he went secretly to Scipio's camp and pledged himself to Rome. Henceforth Carthage would find him an implacable foe.

Syphax now invaded Massinissa's country and ravaged it. Badly wounded, Massinissa was forced to hide in a cave and to give out that he was dead. Hearing that Scipio had landed in Africa, he joined him with all that remained of his army: five men.

Aided by the Romans, he now rallied his people, and joining his forces with those of Scipio, marched to meet the allied Numidian and Carthaginian armies under Hasdrubal.

Finding themselves greatly outnumbered, Massinissa and Scipio resorted to strategy. Camping not far from the Numidian army, they sent Hasdrubal an offer of peace, and while this was being considered, stole in at night and set the Numidian camp afire. The Numidians, suddenly awakened, thought the fire was accidental and ran out unarmed to fight it, on which Scipio and Massinissa cut them down with great slaughter.

Not far away was the Carthaginian camp, and there too, the men, seeing the fire and hearing the cries, thought it an accident and rushed out to the Numidian camp unarmed. Their camp also was now set ablaze, and caught between their own fire and the foe, they were easily massacred. Forty-five thousand were killed and wounded and 17,000 Numidian horses and six elephants were captured. Hasdrubal and Syphax, utterly routed, took refuge behind the walls of Carthage.

Syphax consoled himself by saying that he had been beaten not by skill and valor but by stratagem. "One is inferior," he said, "only when beaten by arms." Gathering another army, he attacked the Romans but was beaten again.

In this battle Massinissa beat down Syphax with his own hand and made him prisoner. Taking him with a guard, he pushed on to Cirta, Syphax's capital, within whose walls there reposed a prize greater than any military conquest of which he had ever dreamed: his beloved Sophonisba. It was four years since he had seen her— four tortured years.

Reaching the city, he displayed Syphax in chains to the inhabitants and they surrendered.

As soon as the gates were opened, Massinissa in all the ardor of his one and twenty years rode at full speed to Syphax's palace, where Sophonisba, who had heard the news, awaited him with her maidens. Reaching the palace, he sprang from his horse and ran up the steps to meet her, but she, thinking he had come as a conqueror, threw herself at his feet, begging him not to let her fall as a prize to the Romans. "The gods," she said, "thy courage and thy fortune hath given thee power over us. If it is permitted to a captive to embrace the knees and touch the hand of a conqueror, I pray thee by the royal majesty with which we ourselves were invested but yesterday not to hand me over to the caprice of some cruel Roman. Dispose of me thyself."

Massinissa, overcome with love for her, was speechless. Sophonisba went on: "I love better to depend on a Numidian than a Roman. I prefer those born as I, under the skies of Africa. Let death take me rather than a Roman."

Massinissa tenderly lifted her to her feet and led her into the palace where he embraced her and assured her that he still loved her and would save her. But he had to think quickly. Sophonisba, he knew, was really a Roman prize and Lelius, the Roman commander, with his army was approaching. Not far behind the latter was Scipio, the supreme commander.

Massinissa saw but one possibility and even that was risky, for it might offend the Romans: he would marry her at once. He had the ceremony performed without delay.

When Lelius arrived and heard what had been done he was very angry and wished to snatch Sophonisba from the marriage bed and send her off with the other capitves but thought it more prudent to await Scipio.

As fate would have it, Scipio saw Syphax first, and when he reproached Syphax for his desertion of Rome, Syphax, who preferred to see Sophonisba dead rather than married to Massinissa, placed the blame on her. He said, "Yes, I have committed a great fault. It is a folly for which I am extremely sorry now. But the moment I took arms against Rome was the end, not the beginning, of my folly.

"It began when I fell in love with Sophonisba. She was so bewitching and so devoted to her country that though I was your friend, she made me the friend of her country. It was her beauty, her charm that was responsible for all that I have done." He added, "Now I am ruined. But I have one consolation. She has passed into the hands of my enemy, Massinissa, who has already shown himself no wiser than I."

Scipio, who when he had heard from Lelius of the marriage had been disposed to let Massinissa have her, now saw it in a different light. Sending for Massinissa, he said to him affectionately, "I believe, Massinissa, you found in me qualities that you admire when first you came to seek my friendship in Spain and again in Africa. Of all these my qualities the one I am most proud of is my continence—the empire I wield over my passions. This virtue, Massinissa, I would also like to see crown your distinguished services because, believe me well, at your age we have less to fear from the arms of the enemy than from the passions which besiege us."

Telling Massinissa that a victory over himself would be greater than one over Syphax, he continued: "Now I shall leave you to your reflections rather than speak in a manner to hurt your pride. But permit me to say this: Syphax, his throne, his country, lands, and people, his all, are now the property of the Roman Republic. Their fate is in the hands of the Roman Senate.

"Is not his wife a part of all this? Is she not accused of having alienated our ancient ally and thrown him into the war against us?

"Now I urge you to be victorious over yourself. Do not tarnish all your virtues by a single vice. Do not efface all the services you have rendered Rome by one step, the effect of which will be to nullify all that you have done."

Massinissa heard him with leaden heart. He pleaded with tears but Scipio sent him to his tent to think it over. Alone there he spent several hours uttering groans that could be heard on the outside. To keep Sophonisba would be the ruin of his people and himself. Without her life would be empty.

He shuddered too at the thought of seeing her led in triumph through the streets of Rome. There was only one thing for him to do. He took a small package from the folds of his robe, emptied its contents into a cup of wine, and bade his favorite slave take it to Sophonisba. "Say to her," he said, "I would have been happy to keep my first promise but a superior force has made it impossible. Now the only thing left me is to keep my second one not to let her fall into the hands of the Romans. May the remembrance of her father, the illustrious general, and the thoughts of her country dictate her conduct."

Sophonisba received the fearful present calmly. "Tell him," she said, "that I accept the wedding present without regret, if it be true that my husband can do no more for his wife. Tell him that I would have died more willingly if more time had elapsed between the wedding and the funeral." A few minutes later she was dead.

When Scipio heard the news, he was troubled lest the fiery Massinissa take some extreme step; for then and only then had he learned the story of their early love. Sending for Massinissa, he presented him to the assembled army in the most glowing words, proclaimed him king of Numidia, and conferred on him the highest honor possible to an alien: Roman citizenship of senatorial rank. Taking a toga bordered with purple, he draped it about the shoulders of Massinissa. "You are," he said, "the first stranger that Rome has ever deemed worthy of wearing it."

Massinissa, grief-stricken, heard all as in a dream. He blamed the Carthaginians as being the cause of all his sorrow and took a great oath to be further revenged against them.

Rome rejoiced greatly at the news that Hasdrubal had been killed and Syphax was a prisoner. It was also much stirred by Massinissa's sacrifice, and when his envoys arrived in Rome, they were treated like kings.

But Carthage was still very powerful. Hannibal, the terror of Rome for fifteen years, had returned to Carthage and was preparing for a fight to the finish.

Hannibal sent an offer of alliance to Massinissa but the latter refused it and joined Scipio. The rival armies met at Zama in 202 B.C. Hannibal had 55,000 men and the allied Romans and Numidians, 40,000. Outnumbered, Massinissa and Scipio once again resorted to strategy. In the forefront of Hannibal's army were eighty armored elephants which were to be used to trample the foes. Massinissa, assembling his trumpeters, had them make such a noise that the elephants, not sufficiently trained for battle, turned and ran amuck into Hannibal's army, completely disorganizing his ranks, at which Massinissa let loose his famous cavalry on Hannibal's left wing, cutting it to pieces. Scipio at the same time attacked the right one, completing the rout. Thus ended the long fight between Rome and Carthage for mastery of the world.

Following this Massinissa had sixty years of peace during which he devoted himself to the development of his kingdom. From being robbers and marauders, the Numidians became one of the wealthiest and most cultured people of the times. But he had never ceased to remember Sophonisba and the oath he had taken against Carthage for having given her to Syphax. He now resolved as the final act of his career to attack Carthage, which had grown prosperous again, and deliberately provoked her into a war.

Though eighty-eight years old, he had not lost his cunning, and when the Carthaginians came to attack him, he pretended to flee and drew off their forces into a desert region, surrounded by mountains and lacking in food and water. There he made a stand, occupying the plains, while the Carthaginians seized the heights, thinking them the more advantageous. Surrounding them in that position, Massinissa besieged them.

Appian, ancient Roman writer, says of this fight, "Day came and Massinissa, eighty-eight years old, but still a young and vigorous soldier, was mounted on horseback without saddle or other covering as is the custom of the country, equally acting in the capacity of general and soldier, for the Numidians are the lustiest of all the people of Africa."

The Carthaginians, after eating their horses and even the leather of their saddles, finally surrendered. This was Massinissa's last exploit. He died two years later.

Livy, Polybius, Appian, Justin, and all the historians of the period speak in highest terms of him. Polybius says:

Massinissa was the greatest and the happiest sovereign of our epoch. He reigned more than sixty years in perfect health.

Physically he was the strongest and the most robust man of his time.

Thanks to the harmony that reigned in his family, his kingdom was never troubled by intrigue or domestic strife. But this was his greatest merit, his most admirable work; before him, Numidia was wild, uncultivated, and alien to all culture. He was the first to show that it could produce all kinds of fruit like any other country. He has, therefore, more title and rights than anyone that his memory should be honored. A short time before his death he inflicted a great defeat on the Carthaginians. The day after the battle he was to be seen before his tent eating wholewheat bread.

REFERENCES

All of this portion of ancient North Africa was very much more Negroid during the time of Hannibal and Massinissa than it is now—a fact borne out by both anthropological research and history. Bertholon and Chantre tell of the "marked Negro traits" of the skulls of important personages found in the ancient Carthaginian graves and elsewhere. (For sources and discussion of this, see *Sex and Race*, Vol. I, pp. 88–89. 1941.) The original inhabitants of this region were known as Moors, which in ancient Greek, Latin, and Gallic meant "The Black People." (For discussion of this, see Atgier: *Bull. Soc. D'Anthrop. de Paris*, Feb. 4, 1910, p. 110. Also M. d'Avezac, *Afrique*, p. 4, 1842, who shows that the original name of Carthage was "Africa.") Procopius, Byzantine historian of the fifth century, speaks very clearly of "the black-skinned Moors" who inhabited Numidia and Carthage and dominated them for centuries. And what's more, he also distinctly mentions some white people who inhabited the mountains beyond them (*History of the Wars*, trans. by Dewing. Book 4, xiii, pp. 29–36; also IV, x, 24.) See also Sallust: *The Jugurthine Wars*, trans. by William Cooke, Pt. 1, p. 89, 1746. There was a great inflow of whites from Rome into Carthage (now Tunis) and other parts of North Africa, such as present Algeria, after they became parts of the Roman Empire. There was also another influx of whites in the fifth century, namely, the Vandals, Teutonic barbarians who overran Rome.

Interest in Massinissa was revived by Gabriel D'Annuzio's famous love story *Cabiria*, in which the hero is Massinissa. In this Italian motion picture, he is shown as a Negro, the part being played by one. The picture was shown extensively over the United States in 1914, and was seen by this writer. (See motion picture magazines of that year and *The Crisis*, Sept., 1914, p. 233.)

Livy, XXIV, 49; XXVIII, 11, 35, 42 *et seq.*
Polybius, III, 5; IX, 42 *et seq.*
Appian, *Hisp.* 37; *Punica*, 11, 27, 105.
Justin, XXXIII, 1.
Encyclopaedia Britannica, "Massinissa."

Terence

OF THE PERSONAL DETAILS of the life of Publius Terentius Afer (Terence), the greatest of Latin stylists, all that is known are a few lines written by Suetonius, Roman writer, in his *De viris illustribus.*

Terence was born about 190 B.C. and was a native of Africa, as the "Afer" in his surname showed. Suetonius says he was "dusky" in color (*colore fusco*), and that he was a slave brought to Rome and purchased by Terentius Lucanus. He was so fond of learning and possessed such aptitude, that his master set him free and gave him his name—a rare honor.

As a poet and a comedian, Terence soon won a reputation. It is said that he once went to the home of Caecilus, a leading citizen, to read his verses to him. Caecilius, on seeing the shabbily dressed youth, was rude to him; he inhospitably pushed a stool toward him and told him gruffly to commence. But as soon as he heard the first lines, he treated him as an honored guest and invited him to stay for supper.

It is believed that Terence died about 159 B.C., at or near Leucadia in Arcadia, some say in a shipwreck, others of grief at having lost some of the finest productions of his art among his baggage in this catastrophe. It is also believed that he died a poor man, but according to Suetonius, he left twenty acres of land on the Appian Way to his daughter, who was married to a Roman gentleman. Terence was an intimate friend of Scipio Africanus, who saved Rome from Hannibal.

Terence left to posterity six comedies, which have since served as models of Latin composition. He was a supreme master of the elegant style. Although he wrote in verse, his choice of words was perfect and the form in which they were arranged flawless.

Julius Caesar, Cicero, and Horace were among those who used him as a model. Caesar said that his comedies lacked humor, but spoke of him as being "placed among the highest—and deservedly —lovers of pure speech."

In the British Isles and on the Continent Terence is still studied in the leading universities. The works of no other Latin classicist have been reproduced in as many editions as his. *Biographie Universelle* says that up to 1779 there were 395 of them worthy of notice, among them being those of Erasmus and Melanchthon. At present, editions in various languages, manuals, extracts, and other works of his are innumerable. Terence's imitators have been many and include Sir Richard Steele, Sedley, La Fontaine, and Molière.

The six comedies are: *Andria; The Mother-in-Law; The Self-Avenger; The Eunuch; Phormio; The Brothers.*

Terence is immortal, not alone for the purity of his language and the flawlessness of his verse. He is also regarded as one of the greatest humanists of all time. There is one line of his which, if all else had been lost, would have been sufficient to assure his immortality, a line that will remain the criterion of the truly cultured individual as long as breadth of knowledge is valued. It is: "Homo sum, humani nihil a me alienum puto" (I am a man and nothing human is alien to me).

REFERENCES

Terence is named here as a Negro for the following reasons: he was from Africa; he was a slave; and Suetonius (A.D. 98–138) describes his color as *"fusco"* (dusky, very dark). Had he been, say, of a mulatto color, Suetonius might have said he was "subfusco." For instance, Ammianus, fourth century historian, says of the Egyptians of his time,

"Homines autem Aegyptii plerique *subfusculi* sunt et atrati" (The men of Egypt are, as a rule, somewhat swarthy and dark of complexion).

Terence was also called "Afer." The *Century Dictionary* says of this, "The ordinary terms for African Negro or Africans were Ethiops and Afer." *L'Encyclopédie Française* says similarly, "The Latin, Afer, which was both ethnic and geographical, sufficed at a time when Africa was little known to designate its inhabitants by that characteristic which was almost typical of them and most apparent, namely color." (Vol. VII, 1, 46, 6.)

ADDITIONAL REFERENCES

Osei, G. K., *The Forgotten Great Africans 3000 B.C. to 1959 A.D.*, p. 8. London, G. K. Osei, 1965.

Terentius Afer, Publius, *Terence's Comedies*. London, D. Midwinter, 1741.

———, *The Phornio of Terence*, trans. by M. H. Morgan. Cambridge, Mass., Harvard University Press, 1903.

———, *Comoediae Sex*. Hagae-Comitum, Petrum Gosse, 1726.

Cleopatra

EXEMPLAR OF FEMININE FASCINATION
THROUGHOUT THE AGES
(69–30 B.C.)

CLEOPATRA VII, Queen of Egypt, has come down to us through twenty centuries as the perfect example of the seductive art in woman. With her beauty, learning, and culture she fascinated and held two successive masters of the world.

The first, Julius Caesar, was debonair, elegant in manners and movement, a great swimmer, a swordsman, a beloved ruler, and able orator, and one of the world's greatest writers.

In the arts of love, he was unique, excelling in licentiousness whether his amour was a woman or a young man. For any woman to hold him longer than a day was exceedingly difficult.

The second, Caesar's friend and successor, Mark Antony, was tall, well built, and with the muscles of a gladiator. Generous, impulsive, and a bon vivant, he was a matchless orator of whom it was said, "There was no man of his time like him for addressing a multitude or for carrying soldiers with him by the force of his words."

Irresistible to women, he made full use of his powers. He had no intention, he would say, of confining his hopes of progeny to any one woman, but like his ancestor Hercules, he intended to let nature have her will with him. This, he thought, was the best way of circulating noble blood throughout the world and thus begetting personally in every country a new line of kings.

Such were the two giants Cleopatra held enslaved. She on her side, if not the most beautiful woman of her time, was perhaps the most captivating, the most learned, and the most witty. It is said that she spoke Greek, Egyptian, Latin, Ethiopian, Hebrew, Arabic, and Syrian fluently, as well as several African dialects.

Dion Cassius, wrote of her, "She was splendid to see, and was capable of conquering the hearts which had resisted more obstinately the influence of love, and those which had been frozen by age. Her charm of speech was such that she won all who listened to her."

Plutarch, who lived a century after her, said, "She had an irresistible charm, and her presence, combined with the persuasiveness of her discourse and her character, which was somewhat diffused in her behavior towards others, had something stimulating about it. There was a sweetness, also, in the tones of her voice and her tongue, like an instrument of many strings, she could really turn to whatever language she pleaded. She talked to her many subjects in all their languages, not needing an interpreter."

Ambitious to save her country, this girl of seventeen planned to lift Egypt up again to its past grandeur and be a ruler of which history would ever speak. As the first step she decided to get rid of her nine-year-old brother Ptolemy, who, according to the custom of the times, was her husband and shared the throne with her.

She was opposed by her brother's three counsellors: Photion, the eunuch; Theodosius, the regent; and Achillas, commander of the army. They stirred up the people against her and forced her to take refuge with her sister Arsinoe, Queen of Syria.

With an army gathering in Syria, she was returning to Alexandria to give battle when she heard startling news. Pompey, her father's friend, had been defeated by Julius Caesar at Pharsalia and had come to Alexandria to seek her brother's protection, with Caesar in pursuit.

When she reached Alexandria, Caesar, who had arrived with a large army, ordered both Cleopatra and Ptolemy to yield. Ptolemy obeyed; Cleopatra thought the matter over. She had heard much of Caesar. He was undoubtedly a very great man but to her and her people Rome was a land of barbarians. Still she could use him to further her ambitions. He had an army.

She decided to call on him. But how to do so? He had made his headquarters in a palace on the Lochias Promontory. To reach this she would have to pass through her brother's lines, and Photion, his general, would make a bloody finish of her if he caught her. Then an idea occurred to her. Calling a trusted slave, she bade him wrap her in a silken covering, place a magnificent carpet over that, wrap the whole in an ordinary covering, and take it as a present to Caesar.

Caesar received the bearer with his usual politeness but with ordinary interest. Since his arrival he had been deluged with presents—vases, statues, and hundreds of objects for which he had no use. He bade the slaves undo the bundle. Then he gasped as the silken covering stirred and a laughing brown-skinned girl with crinkly hair and voluptuous figure, nude to the waist, stood before him.

In her eyes was a gleam that made him forget his fifty-four years. When, to crown all, she addressed him in flawless Latin a voice full of music, instinct told him that into his surfeited life had come at last the one woman. He ordered his attendants from the room and from then on began to leave the gayest of lives with her.

But she, unscrupulous and calculating, began at once to use him. The next morning when her brother and his counsellors were summoned before Caesar, they saw her on a throne beside Caesar and were informed that she was again co-ruler of Egypt.

Her next move was to lure her brother into plotting against Caesar and to besiege Caesar in his palace. Then with her soldiers she helped Caesar defeat her brother, who jumped into the Nile and drowned himself.

With Pompey killed and Egypt punished for having harbored him, Caesar's mission to Egypt was ended. Pressing business was calling him back, not to mention his wife, Calpurnia, who sent messengers pleading with him to return. But this roué to whom women had hitherto been but as the seeds of a fruit to be spat out after the fruit had been enjoyed lingered on in Alexandria.

And there was good reason for his delay. He was expecting from Cleopatra the heir that Calpurnia had not given him. He had married Cleopatra according to Egyptian rites, but the marriage would be illegal in Rome. No Roman could marry a non-Roman.

To give the prospective heir the greatest possible prestige, Caesar was declared the reincarnation of the great God Amen, thus making him equal in the eyes of the Egyptians with Cleopatra, who was worshipped as the greatest of all goddesses, the Virgin Mother Isis. When a son was born, Cleopatra thought herself the most fortunate of women. The boy was called Caesarion. Caesar now went back to Rome alone but promised to send for her.

He was as good as his word. Cleopatra came with the infant Caesar, and with them came a cortege of such dazzling wealth that Rome had never seen its like, not even in the triumphal march of its conquerors. Caesar, who did nothing by halves, left his wife to live with Cleopatra.

Cleopatra, ambitious for the improvement of her new country, had brought with her hundreds of scientists, artists, architects, astronomers, and financial experts, who revised the Roman calendar, reformed the public accounting, and generally helped to raise the standard of Roman culture.

But these reforms were opposed by the Roman aristocracy, who resented the influence of a foreigner. Cicero, greatest orator of the day, was her most outspoken opponent. He denounced her as vain and arrogant, and complained that she was trying to make of Rome an absolute monarchy with Caesar as its god. In vain Cleopatra tried to placate Cicero with presents of rare books.

Cicero had cause for complaint. Though Rome was a republic, Caesar, under Cleopatra's influence, was acting like a king. He had an eighth royal statue, which bore his likeness, put up beside the statues of the seven earlier kings of Rome. This new statue wore a golden crown with the title "To the Immortal God." It was clear that Caesar intended to proclaim himself king.

Cassius, Casca, Cinna, and Brutus, Caesar's supposed son, thereupon plotted against him and stabbed Caesar to death.

Rome was horrified and Cleopatra most of all. Caesar's death meant the death of all her dreams. She was now no longer Queen of the Earth but only Queen of Egypt. She decided to return home but talk of making her son ruler in Caesar's place delayed her for a while. When this fell through she left secretly.

At this point history repeats itself. Once more a master of the world came east in pursuit of a fugitive. This time it was Mark Antony after Brutus. Having defeated Brutus at Philippi, and having learned that one of Cleopatra's generals had aided Brutus, he demanded that Cleopatra appear before him to give an explanation.

Cleopatra laughed at that. She knew it was only a pretext. Antony was in love with her. He had tried to win her after Caesar's death but she had refused him. She ignored his order now.

Antony sent other orders, with no better results. "She so despised and laughed the man to scorn," says Plutarch, "as to sail up the River Cydnus in a barge with gilded poop; its sails spread purple; its rowers urging it on with oars to the sound of the flute blended with pipes and lutes. She herself reclined beneath a canopy spangled with gold, adorned like Venus, in a painting, while boys, like Cupids, stood on either side of her and fanned her. About her were the fairest of her serving maidens attired like Nereids and Graces, with others at the rudder sweeps and at the reefing-ropes. Wondrous odors from countless incense-offerings on her ship diffused themselves along the banks."

Antony, in delight, hastened to receive her. But Cleopatra, coming near enough only to give him a glimpse of her, ordered her rowers to turn about. The next day she bade the lovesick Antony to come to her.

He obeyed.

She received him on her barge, dressed in a shimmering robe of the goddess Isis, through which one could see her matchless figure in all the glory of its five and twenty years. Antony, the Don Juan of his time, was hypnotized.

Cleopatra, ever a schemer, exerted all her charm on him. She meant to put her son on a throne in Rome. She entertained him on a barge with a feast the like of which he had never seen before. The richness of the food, the music, the golden dishes inlaid with gems, the tablecloth of purple and gold, the flower-strewn floor, and the divinely beautiful woman beside him made Antony feel that he was indeed master of the world.

When Antony marveled, she gave him an even more gorgeous feast the next day, following that with two others, till on the fourth day she gave one for his generals. On this occasion the floor was strewn two feet deep with roses, and after the dinner she gave the guests all the golden dishes and even the golden couch on which she reclined.

When Antony said that she could give no costlier feast, Cleopatra wagered an enormous sum that she could. This was the occasion on which, it is said, she dissolved one of her two famous pearls in a goblet as a drink for Antony.

As for the other pearl, she was about to dissolve that too when Placus held back her hand and told her she had won. Years later this other pearl was sawed in two and a half placed in each ear of the goddess Venus at Rome.

Antony now abandoned himself completely to her, feasting and indulging in the delights of love. At night both went out disguised on the streets of Alexandria to revel in the life of the populace. Like a child, Cleopatra would knock at people's doors, and run away before they could answer.

Together they went fishing. Antony once wagered that he would catch a certain number of fish within an hour. He had a slave swim under the water and place live fish on his hook. Cleopatra, discovering the trick, had one of her slaves put on a salted fish. Then to the discomfited Antony, she said, "Never mind, general. Your game is cities, provinces, and kingdoms. Leave the fishing-rod to us, poor sovereigns of Pharos and Canopus."

Later she gave him the Pergamum Library of 200,000 volumes, the greatest collection of books in the then known world.

Like Caesar, Antony also had urgent affairs in Rome but he dallied with her, while she on her part laid her plans for dispensing justice from the Capitol at Rome. She intended making Rome and Egypt into one vast empire ruled over by herself and Antony, whom she had now learned to love.

This bond was strengthened by the birth of a son, Alexander Helios, and later by twins, a boy and a girl, Ptolemy and Cleopatra Silene.

In the meantime Antony's affairs in Rome grew more pressing. After Caesar's death power had been divided between himself, Lepidus, and Octavius, Caesar's nephew. These two now sent to tell him that he would be ousted if he did not return at once. He did so, promising Cleopatra to return as soon as possible. But once again in Rome, he found himself forced to marry Octavia, sister of Octavius.

For the next four years he remained in Rome, but unable to forget Cleopatra, he seized the opportunity to return to the east when there was a revolt in Parthia.

Once again with Cleopatra, he decided to renounce allegiance to Rome. When he went there again it would be as a conqueror with Cleopatra at his side. He donned Egyptian garments, renounced his wife, married Cleopatra, and took other steps that made him an outlaw in Rome.

To his sons by Cleopatra he gave rich provinces and made his daughter by her Queen of Mauritania. Caesarion, Caesar's son, was made co-ruler of Egypt. To avoid offense to the Egyptians he merely called himself "Autocrat of the East."

For the next thirteen years he and Cleopatra laid their plans for the conquest of Rome. Octavius, in the meanwhile, was planning to strike at Antony in Egypt.

As a pretext for doing so, he sent his sister, Antony's deserted wife, to him. She was accompanied by the family counsellor, a man named Niger (from Niger, and evidently of that race). Antony refused to receive Octavia.

War to the death was now on between the East and the West. Aided by his vassal kings, Antony assembled a vast army, and went with his fleet and transports to await Octavius at Actium, off the coast of Greece, where Cleopatra joined him with 200 warships. Soon afterward more than 400 Roman senators deserted Octavius and joined Antony in Athens, where he and Cleopatra had set up their court.

All seemed favorable for Antony when dissension arose in his camp. The Romans once again were jealous of Cleopatra and objected to the influence she wielded over their leader. In the disunion that followed there was a slight quarrel between the two lovers.

Octavius arrived with his fleet. The destiny of Rome, of the world, hung in the balance. If Octavius failed, Rome, the octopus, would be absorbed by Egypt. The rising West would see an Eastern empress on its throne.

The battle began. The right wing led by Antony was winning

against Octavius, while the left was being beaten. Cleopatra, viewing the battle from afar, thought that Antony was losing. Believing that all was lost, she decided to take advantage of the wind and gave orders to turn about and sail for home.

The effect of this on the battle was unexpected and decisive. Sixty of the Egyptian ships, seeing their queen leaving the battle, followed her. Antony, bewildered, and wondering whether their quarrel of the morning had anything to do with her flight, ordered his ship to follow her's. And thus the battle was lost.

The West had triumphed. Rome was now sole mistress of the world. Egypt's sun had set.

Reaching Cleopatra, Antony fell into her arms. Then learning that the battle had been lost, he threw himself down near the helm, his head bowed in grief, and for three days spoke to no one.

The victorious Octavius pursued him to Alexandria. Cleopatra, feeling that the end had come, prepared for death and entered her mausoleum. Antony, hearing that she had killed herself, stabbed himself mortally, then learning that she was still alive, wished to die in her arms. But since Cleopatra's tomb was already sealed with her in it, there was no means of reaching her except by having himself lowered into it through a window. This was done and he breathed his last in her arms.

Octavius entered Alexandria in triumph. His great wish was to take Cleopatra to Rome and there exhibit her. Accordingly one of his generals entered the tomb by a ruse and stopped her just as she was about to kill herself by telling her that Octavius meant her no harm, but that if she killed herself, her children would be slain.

Octavius treated her mildly. He permitted her to bury Antony. She gave him a magnificent funeral and followed the body to the grave, a pitiful figure.

Soon afterwards she fell ill. When she was convalescent, Octavius called to see her. Unannounced, he marched into her bedroom without giving her time to dress

She was in bed when he entered. Forgetting all but the safety of her children, she arose, and in the single garment she had on, dishevelled and worn with sickness and anxiety, she threw herself at his feet. Once again she had met a master of the world. But under what a change!

What did Octavius, a cold, unsentimental youth of twenty-seven, lacking the chivalry of Caesar and Antony, think of this forlorn widow of thirty-eight? Had he, fearing her witchery, planned this abrupt entrance in order to take her off guard?

He tried to reassure her but she realized that all was lost. For her children's sake she promised not to kill herself. Then news came that Octavius was planning to take her to Rome. This meant the end. She had herself taken to Antony's tomb, bade him a last farewell, and returned to her palace.

Octavius had ordered a strict watch over her, but when a slave arrived with a basket of figs for her, the guards saw nothing suspicious and permitted him to pass.

Underneath the luscious fruit, however, lay an asp, whose bite was certain and painless death. Bidding her maids dress her more royally than ever, she placed the snake to her breast.

When the alarm was given, the doctors rushed in and tried to suck the poison from the wound but it was too late. Octavius arrived to find her stretched in death on her bed, clad in her jewels, a crown on her head, a sceptre in her hand. A picture of her, carried by a slave, was all of her that appeared in his triumphal procession in Rome.

As for her eldest son, Caesarion, Octavius, fearing that the Romans might want to make him king out of the great love they bore his father, had him put to death. Her children by Antony were spared.

REFERENCES

Until the rise of the doctrine of white superiority Cleopatra was generally pictured as colored. Shakespeare in the opening lines of his *Antony and Cleopatra* calls her "tawny." In his day, mulattoes were called "Tawny-Moors," and Captain John Smith, governor of Virginia, a contemporary of Shakespeare's, uses "tawny" as synonymous with "mulatto." Writing of a ruler of Morocco, he says, "King Mully Hamlet was not black, as many suppose, but mulatto, or tawny, as many of his subjects." (*True Travels*, Vol. I, p. 45.)

Also in *Antony and Cleopatra*, Act I, Sc. 5, Cleopatra calls herself "black," made so by the sun (Phoebus).

Robert Ripley, who says he has proof of all his facts, calls Cleopatra "fat and black." (*Believe It or Not*, p. 83, 6th printing. 1934.)

As late as the sixteenth century Cleopatra was regarded as a Negro woman. C. W. King says, "The same age was a little later extremely fruitful in the heads of Negroes and Negresses, the latter often in the character of Cleopatra holding to her breast the asp." (*Antique Gems and Rings*, p. 326. London, 1872.)

Cleopatra's father, Ptolemy XIII, was the illegitimate offspring of Ptolemy XI (Soter II). The legitimate line ended with Ptolemy XII. Those who say that Cleopatra was "pure" Greek evidently forget this fact. Moreover, her father, Ptolemy XIII, shows pronounced Negro traits. As for Cleopatra, there is no bonafide portrait of her.

See "Ptolemy XI," "Ptolemy XIII" and "Cleopatra" in *Encyclopaedia Britannica*.

The best factual account of Cleopatra is to be found in Plutarch's *Lives*, "Antony." See also S. Rapoport, *History of Egypt*, Vol. I, pp. 280–365. 1904.

ADDITIONAL REFERENCES

Abbott, Jacob, *Cleopatra*. New York, John D. Morris and Company, 1904.

Hawkes, Jacquetta, *Pharaohs of Egypt*, pp. 17, 118, 124. New York, American Heritage Publishing Company, Inc., 1965.

Murray, Margaret A., *The Splendor That Was Egypt*, pp. 54, 72, 102, 103, 177. New York, Hawthorn Books, Inc., 1963.

Weigall, Arthur Edwards Pearse Brome, *Personalities of Antiquity*. New York, H. W. Wilson, 1932.

———, *The Life and Times of Cleopatra*. New York and London, G. P. Putnam's Sons, 1924.

ASIA

Commentary and Notes
on References

THE INFLUENCE OF AFRICAN PEOPLE on the Middle East and
Asia was not generally considered by scholars until recent years.
Professor Joseph Harris of Williams College in Williamstown,
Massachusetts, is among the few present-day scholars who have
devoted considerable time to this neglected aspect of history.

The African was a major factor in the ancient world of the
Middle East and Asia. Until recent times there was a land bridge
connecting Africa with Asia, and there was nothing to obstruct the
movement of people back and forth between North and East Africa and the vast land mass of Asia.

With the rise of Islam the influence of Africans in the Middle
East became a more noticeable feature of the religious and cultural transition in this part of the world.

The African Antar is one of the many black heroes who
emerged at the time a new and dynamic religion, Islam, was challenging the social order of the day. He became, and remains, one
of the great heroes of his religion. In recent years there has been
new interest in his career as warrior, romantic figure, and defender
of his faith. The following articles about the life of Antar are most
revealing: "The Black Night," parts one and two, by Cedric
Dover, *Plylon* magazine, first and second quarters, 1945; and
"Antar the Lion," by Philip St. Laurent, *Tuesday* magazine,
March, 1970.

Hadzrat Bilal ibn Rahab, a tall, gaunt, bushy-haired black Ethiopian, was the first high priest and treasurer of the empire of Islam. After Mohammed himself, he was the most important creator of this great religion, which today influences a large part of mankind. He is considered to have been the Prophet's first convert. Bilal was one of the many Africans who participated in the establishment of Islam and later made proud names for themselves in the Islamic wars of expansion.

The lives of Ibrahim Al-Mahdi and Al-Jahiz show a continuation of the African influence on the cultural development of Islam. This influence would last through the long Moorish occupation of Spain and would spread into the Western Sudan (West Africa), then eastward into Asia.

The extraordinary career of Eugene Chen still begs for an astute biographer who can see the significance of the life of this statesman, born in the West, who settled in the East and became a foe of Western colonialism. Western journalists who were attracted to Eugene Chen and believed that a remarkable story could be written about him rarely, if ever, alluded to the fact that he was of mixed African and Chinese descent.

The Life of Ibn-Saud, the late King of Saudi Arabia, calls attention to the different levels of the African presence in this country. In the past, and in the present, Africans have held positions that range from slaves to ministers of state, and there has not been a royal family in Saudi Arabia in the last 500 years that was without some African blood.

J. H. C.

Zenobia

BEAUTIFUL WARRIOR QUEEN OF THE EAST
(d. A.D. 272)

NEXT TO CLEOPATRA, Zenobia was the most famous woman of antiquity. Her empire, Palmyra, stretched from the Euphrates almost to the Golden Horn and included Egypt and Syria.

Palmyra, according to tradition, was founded by Solomon, the Jewish ruler, and was one of the richest cities of the ancient world. It lay on the trade route between the East and the West. Caravans laden with silk, perfumes, gold, jewels, spices, and other products of China, India, Persia, and the East came there to meet the buyers from Greece, Rome, and the West. In wealth and culture it was not far behind Rome, abundant proof of which may be seen in the ruins of its broad streets, mighty arches and temples, extensive gardens, and many villas.

Zenobia took the throne on the death of her husband, Odenathus, who had been a vassal of Rome. One of Zenobia's first acts was to throw off this allegiance and rule in her own right. According to Trebellius Pollio, the Roman writer:

She lived with royal pomp after the Persian manner, received adulation like the kings of Persia, and banqueted like the Roman emperors.

She went in state to the assemblies of the people in a helmet with a purple band fringed with jewels. Her robe was clasped with a diamond buckle and she often wore her arm bare.

Her complexion was dusky, or dark brown [*fusci coloris*], her eyes black, and of uncommon fire. Her countenance was divinely expressive; her person graceful in form and her motion beyond imagination; her teeth were as white as pearls and her voice clear and strong. She displayed the severity of a tyrant when severity was called for, and the clemency of a good prince when justice required it.

She was generous with prudence but a husbandress of wealth more than is the custom with women. Sometimes she used a chariot but more frequently rode on horseback. She would march great distances on foot at the head of her infantry and would drink deeply with her officers, the Armenians, and the Persians, but with sobriety, using at her banquets golden goblets set with pearls such as Cleopatra was wont to use. In her service she employed eunuchs advanced in years and very few damsels.

She ordered her sons to be instructed in the Latin language as befitting the imperial purple in which she had arrayed them. She was herself acquainted with the Greek tongue and was not ignorant of Latin though from diffidence she spoke it seldom. She spoke Egyptian perfectly and was so versed in the history of Alexandria and the East that she made an abridgement of Oriental history.

Other Roman writers, such as Cornelius Capitolinus, have spoken in high praise of her beauty and of the darkness of her skin. Zenobia claimed descent from Cleopatra.

Invading Egypt, she conquered it and added it to her empire. This aroused the fears of Aurelian, Roman emperor, and he invaded Syria. Zenobia met him at Emesa with a powerful army composed of heavy cavalry, light infantry, and the famous Palmyrene archers, who had helped Rome in the conquest of Britain.

"Armed like Diana and beautiful as Venus," Zenobia rode at the head of her heavy cavalry in an onslaught against Aurelian. She swept all before her. But Aurelian skillfully kept his infantry and light cavalry out of the reach of her armored cavalry until the latter was exhausted, and then he attacked her in full force.

Forced to retreat, Zenobia made another stand. When she was beaten again, she fled on a swift camel to seek the aid of the King of Persia, but the Romans, overtaking her, captured her while she was crossing the Euphrates and took her prisoner to Rome. Here, in fetters of gold, she was forced to walk behind the chariot of Aurelian in one of the most magnificent triumphal processions ever held there.

Some historians say that she was later well treated by Aurelian, who gave her a splendid villa in Rome, and that she spent her last days quietly in a certain degree of contentment. But one historian, Zosimus, says that she mourned the destruction of her empire, and refusing all food, languished and died about 272 A.D.

Zenobia's tutor and counsellor was Longinus, author of the immortal *Treatise on the Sublime*. Zenobia, even more than Cleopatra, has been a source of feminine inspiration. Catherine the Great admired her so much that she called her own capital "The Palmyra of the North."

REFERENCES

Trebellius Pollio, *Historia Augustae Scriptores*, pp. 293–294. Paris, 1603.

Gibbon, E., *Decline and Fall of the Roman Empire*, Bury ed., Vol. I, pp. 371–381.

Masudi, *Prairies d'Or*, Vol. III, pp. 181–198. Paris, Berbier de Meynard, 1861.

ADDITIONAL REFERENCES

Hitti, Philip, *The Arabs*, pp. 20, 23. Chicago, Gateway Edition, 1943, 1949 and 1970.

Osei, G. K., *The Forgotten Great Africans 3000 B.C. to 1959 A.D.*, pp. 11–12. London, G. K. Osei, 1965.

Antar

POET, SOLDIER, AND
GREAT CHIVALROUS FIGURE OF THE EAST
(d. A.D. 615)

THE MOST RENOWNED WARRIOR among the Greeks was Achilles; the greatest poet, Homer. Antar is the Achilles and the Homer of the East combined. What Roland is to the French, what Siegfried is to the Germans, what St. George is to the English, that Antar is to 335,000,000 souls of the Mohammedan world. In the literature of the East he is known as "Abul Fouaris" (the Father of Heroes).

Gottheil says, "Even in the cities of the Orient today, the loungers over their cups can never weary of following the exploits of this black son of the desert, who in his person unites the great virtues of his people, magnanimity and bravery with the gift of poetic speech."

Few started lower in life than Antar; few, if any, have risen higher in the esteem and affection of those who once despised them. He was born of a slave mother in the midst of one of the proudest of all peoples—the Bedouins, horsemen and plunderers of the desert, who pride themselves to this day on the purity of their descent from Ishmael, son of Abraham and Hagar, and on their famous Arabian horses.

Moreover Antar was extraordinarily ugly. He was "flat-nosed, bleary-eyed, harsh-featured, and had long, drooping ears." He was also hairlipped and black.

But his eyes! Ah! From them flashed "sparks of fire."

His father, wealthy Shaddad, chief of the Abs tribe, ignored him completely, while his mother hated him and sent him off to mind the cattle to get him out of her sight.

But, like David of the Scriptures, Antar was destined to flash into fame. One day, when he was only fifteen, war broke out between his tribe and a neighboring one over the possession of a famous mare named Jirwet. Antar entered the battle as a common soldier; he emerged from it the hero of the day. Thanks to his skill, the enemy was signally defeated. His father, proud of him now, set him free. He became the protector of his tribe, its mainstay and leader.

When other tribes reproached the Abs because they had a Negro as their chief, Antar declared that he had a sword that was ready to prove that though he was lowly born his ancestry was as good as theirs.

From this point onwards his life, like that of the Seven Champions of Christendom, is so much interwoven with chivalry and romance that it reads more like fable than fact.

According to this record one of his most thrilling encounters was with his rival, Abooddeji, for the love of Ibla, daughter of his wealthy uncle, Malik. Antar was returning from his conquests in distant parts of Asia, loaded with spoils, when Abooddeji, surnamed "The Invincible," in jealous rage marched to attack him.

Challenging this redoubtable warrior to single combat, Antar "pressed on him, wearied him, and terrified him . . . then, extending his sword, pierced him between the breasts, and forced the barb through his shoulders."

Antar's love for Ibla was long opposed by her family, which opposition evoked many of Antar's finest poems. At last, however, thanks to his great wealth and his conquests he was able to overcome all objections. It was in this manner, according to the chronicle, that he came for his bride:

At daybreak, Antar ordered the slaves to prepare for departure. Six hundred was their number. When the mules and camels were loaded and the female slaves, Grecians, Persians, Georgians, and Franks, were mounted on them, Antar presented to Ibla three variegated robes, studded with precious metals and jewels; he clothed her in them and placed on her head the diadem that the king of Persia had given him.

He also ordered forth for her the magnificent silver litter, the supports of which were of burnished gold. At the sight of this mass of splendor, Ibla was stupefied and amazed. Her father, Malik, as he surveyed it, was in the greatest consternation and surprise, but as to her mother, her tongue was tied up in her mouth. Antar cared not for any of them, so entirely was he devoted to Ibla, producing article after article in succession until she was bewildered. He raised her into the litter with her mother and commanded the slaves to go forward.

As regards Antar's poetic skill, we are on surer ground. His poems are of the most exalted nature, combining the spirit of war with sublime devotion and ecstasy. One of them was accorded the highest honor possible to a Moslem writer—it was hung up at the entrance to the great temple at Mecca. There were only six other poems so honored. These seven poems are known as the Moallakat.

Several European critics, among them Ernest Renan, have warmly praised Antar's verses. Lamartine says of his poem in the Moallakat, "It is one of the finest lyrical chants in any language. In many places it equals the best in Homer, Virgil, and Tasso."

Antar's love poems are no less renowned. It is thus he sings the praise of his beloved Ibla:

The logs of aloe sparkle in the fire and the flames rise high in the air; the sweetness of its vapor refreshes my heart when it is wafted with a northerly wind; its brilliancy and flames are the fame of my beauteous Ibla. But, O fire, burn not, blaze not, for in my heart is a flame more furious than thee.

Again:

Slimly made is she and the magic influence of her eye preserves the bones of a corpse from entering the tomb.

The sun, as it sets, turns towards her and says: Darkness obscures the land, do thou rise in my absence; and the brilliant moon calls to her: Come forth for they face is like me when I am at the full and in all my glory.

The tamarisk trees complain of her to the moon and say: Away thou waning beauty, thou form of the laurel. She turns away abashed and throws aside her veil and the roses are scattered from her soft, fresh cheeks.

She draws her sword from the glances of her eyelashes, sharp and penetrating as the blade of her forefathers, and with it her eyes commit murder though it be sheathed. Is it not surprising that a sheathed sword should be so sharp against its victims?

Graceful is her every limb, slender her waist, love-beaming are her glances, waving is her form. The damsel passes the night with musk under her veil and its fragrance is increased by the still fresher essence of her breath. The lustre of day sparkles from her forehead and by the dark shades of her curling ringlets night itself is driven away.

When she smiles, between her teeth is a moisture composed of wine, of rain, and of honey. Her throat complains of the darkness of her necklaces. Alas! the effect of that throat and that necklace. Will fortune ever, O daughter of Malik, bless me with the embrace that would cure my heart of all the sorrows of love? If my eye could see her baggage camels, I would rub my cheeks on their hooves. I will kiss the earth, where thou art; mayhap the fire of my love may be quenched.

The following is a portion of Antar's poem from the Moallakat:

As soon as I beheld the legions of our enemies advancing and animating one another to battle, I, too, rushed forward and acted without reproach.

The troops called out, Antar! while javelins long as the cords of a well were forcibly thrust against the chest of my dark steed.

I ceased not to charge the foe with the neck and breath of my horse until he was mantled in blood.

My steed, bent aside with the strokes of the lances in his forehead, complained to me with gushing tears and tender sobbing.

In the midst of the black dust the horses were impetuously rushing with disfiguring countenance every robust stallion and every strong-limbed mare.

Then my soul was healed and all my anguish was dispersed by the cry of the warriors: 'Well done, Antar, charge again!'

Some of Antar's finest poems extolled the beauty of a black skin: In blackness there is great virtue, if you will but observe its beauty . . . Black ambergris has the purest fragrance. . . .

Antar aided Moundhir, Arab ruler, to defeat Chosroes, King of

Persia. He was killed in A.D. 615, while making one of his dashing headlong charges against the enemy.

Larousse says of him:

From his infancy he gave proof of extraordinary force and courage. By the brilliance of his acts he redeemed his extraction and won his freedom. Like most Arab chiefs, he was as skilled in the poetic art as in the use of the sword. . . .

Deprived of the advantages of good looks and birth, he won merit by force of soul, by the power of his spirit, and the indomitable energy of his character, occupying the foremost rank among men.

Mohammed, who lived at that time, declared that Antar was the only Bedouin he ever admired.

REFERENCES

Hamilton, T., *Antar*, 4 vols. London, 1880.

Thorbecke, H., *Antar*. Leipzig, 1867.

Lamartine, A. de, *Vie de Grands Hommes*, Vol. I, pp. 267–345. 1856.

Gottheil, R., *Warner's Library of the World's Best Literature*, Vol. II, p. 674. 1897.

Palmer, E. H., "An Ancient Arabic Prize Poem." *Eagle*, No. 38. London, 1870.

Huart, C., *Litterature arabe*. 1902.

In 1889 Antar's works were published in thirty-two volumes in Cairo. One of Rimski-Korsakov's best symphonies is based on the life of Antar and bears that name.

ADDITIONAL REFERENCES

Antar, *A Bedoueen Romance*, trans. by Terrick Hamilton, 4 vols. London, J. Murrary, 1820.

Du Bois, W. E. B., *The World and Africa*, p. 190. New York, International Publishers, 1965.

Fleming, B. J., and Pryde, M. J., *Distinguished Negroes Abroad*, pp. 10–20. Washington, D.C., The Associated Publishers, 1946.

Tietjens, Eunice (Hammond), *The Romance of Antar*, trans. by Samuel Glanckoff. New York, Coward-McCann, Inc., 1929.

Le Roman d'Antar. Paris, L'Edition d'Art, 1923.

Bilal

THE FIRST MUEZZIN AND TREASURER OF ISLAM
(c. a.d. 600)

Hadzrat Bilal ibn Rahab, a tall, gaunt, bushy-haired black Ethiopian slave, was the first high priest and treasurer of the Mohammedan empire. After Mohammed himself, that great religion which today numbers upwards of 300,000,000 souls, may be said to have begun with Bilal. He was said to be the Prophet's first convert.

Mohammed was then only a camel-driver but in his soul flamed a great vision. His people, the Koreish, worshipped idols, and he yearned to teach them belief in the One God. But when he talked only the poor folk and the slaves would listen. From among these came his first converts.

The masters, alarmed at the spread of the new religion, began to suppress it by force. The converts were horribly tortured.

Sir William Muir says:

They were seized and imprisoned or they were exposed to the scorching gravel of the valley, to the intense glare of the midday sun. The torment was increased by intolerable thirst until the wretched sufferers hardly knew what was said. If under the torture they reviled Mohamet and acknowledged the idols of Mecca, they were refreshed with draughts of water and taken to their homes. Bilal alone escaped the shame of recantation. He would not yield. In the depths of his anguish the persecutors could force from him but one cry: "Abad! Abad!" (One, only one God).

Persecution of this kind later forced Mohammed to take up the sword, and he ended by becoming one of the world's great conquerors.

Mohammed furnished the executive ability and generalship for the new faith while Bilal provided much of the inspiration. Prayer was its great strength and Bilal could exhort more fervently than anyone else. Whenever he prayed, the crowds sobbed aloud. After listening to him the soldiers of Mohammed, whipped to frenzy, were ready to hurl themselves against any foe.

Bilal also helped Mohammed to create his picture of paradise, which became far more alluring than the Christian one, of which it was an elaboration. Not only were there milk and honey, but also sumptuous palaces of pure gold, with great banquet tables to which thousands of attendants bore the choicest food on golden plates. Each had 300 dishes put before him at once, and he could eat of all of them without becoming sated or being subject to the usual demands of nature.

Paradise also contained Taba, the wonderful Tree of Life, so vast that the swiftest horse would take 150 years to cross its shade. The boughs of this wonderful tree were laden with every kind of good thing to eat, and they bent down toward one at the slightest wish.

But above all they were the houris, or black-eyed daughters of paradise. They had beautiful, well-rounded bodies, fresh with eternal youth and ever-renewed virginity. Seventy-two of these beautiful creatures were given to every believer, who himself possessed eternal youth and vigor.

If a believer died in battle he went straight into the midst of all this. If he did not die there was the prospect of the spoils of battle. No matter what happened, the believer felt that he could not lose.

Each morning at six Bilal would call the faithful to worship with the words: "Great is the Lord! Great is the Lord! I bear witness that there is no God but the Lord! I bear witness that Mohammed is the Prophet of God! Come unto prayer! Come unto salvation! God is great! God is great! There is no God but the Lord! Prayer is better than sleep! Prayer is better than sleep!"

This is the Azan, or Call to Prayer, and to this day it is the most impressive of Moslem rites.

After waking Mohammed each morning with the words: "To prayer, O Apostle of God!" Bilal would lead the followers in prayer. He continued to do this even after Mohammed had become the foremost figure in the world. The two were inseparable. In addition to being the high priest and treasurer, Bilal received and entertained the diplomats and the high guests.

Bilal held prayer no matter what was about to happen. At the battle of Bedr, while the enemy was advancing and all seemed lost, he made the soldiers kneel and pray. Inspired by his impassioned zeal, they swept upon the foe, turning what seemed certain defeat into victory.

Bilal had sworn revenge on his former master, Omeyya, who had tortured him so cruelly. After the battle of Bedr, Omeyya, wishing to save his life and that of his son, surrendered to Rhaman, who, on learning of the prisoner's rank was anxious to take him to Mohammed. But Bilal, spying his old enemy and knowing Mohammed's merciful disposition, shouted to the soldiers, "Slay him! Slay him! That man is the chief of the unbelievers! If he lives I am lost! Kill him! Kill him!" And Omeyya and his son were killed.

At another time, after a great victory over the Jews, Mohammed sent Bilal to fetch the beautiful Safla (fiancée of the slain Jewish general), whom Mohammed intended taking as a wife. Bilal, in his fierce dislike of the foe, purposely led her across the battlefield with its heaps of slain and showed her the frightfully mutilated body of her lover. When the bereaved girl reached Mohammed she was in such a state of hysteria that Mohammed was about to send her away, when Bilal boasted of what he had done. Mohammed kept the girl after rebuking Bilal for his excess of zeal.

Mohammed thought so much of Bilal's loyalty that he granted him precedence in heaven. "What shoes were those you wore last night?" he once asked Bilal. "Verily, as I journeyed in paradise and was mounting the stairs of God I heard your footsteps before me though I could not see them."

When he neared death, Mohammed named Bilal as his successor, but Bilal yielded in favor of the great general, Abu Bekr. The latter continued Bilal in power and so did Omar the Great, Abu Bekr's successor.

After the capture of Jerusalem, Bilal rode through the streets on the right of Omar. Entering the Temple there, he threw out the Christian images and prepared it for the worship of Islam.

His power lasted until his death. On one occasion when Khobab, another devoted follower of Mohammed, called on Omar and showed his wounds and told of the battle in which he had fought, Omar rose from the throne, seated Khobab thereon, and said, "There is but one man in all the empire more worthy of the honor than you, Khobab, and that is Bilal." At another time he called Bilal "the third part of Islam."

Bilal was insulted because of his color at least once, and that was by Prince Constantine, Christian general and head of the Syrian army. Amru, the Mohammedan general, was about to capture Syria and a Christian priest was sent to ask for terms. Bilal was sent back by Amru with the priest to arrange the surrender, but the priest, knowing that Prince Constantine would object to Bilal, hesitated to take him. His fears were justified, for when the Christian prince saw Bilal, he haughtily said, "I will have nothing to do with this black slave!" Constantine paid dearly for this insult, for Bilal imposed drastic terms which met Amru's full approval.

Bilal lived to a ripe old age and amassed an immense fortune. He advanced his family and for his slave brother he secured the rare privilege of marrying a freeborn Arab wife.

Lafcadio Hearn pictures Bilal's last days thus:

Bilal, the black Abyssinian, whose voice was the mightiest and sweetest in Islam. In those first days Bilal was persecuted as the slave of the persecuted Prophet of God. And in the "Gulistan" it is told how he suffered. But after our Lord had departed into the chamber of Allah and the tawny horsemen of the desert had ridden from Mecca even to the gates of India, conquering and to conquer, and the young crescent of Islam, slender as a sword, had waxed into a vast moon of glory that filled the world, Bilal still lived with a wonderful health of years given unto the people of his race. But he sang only for the Caliph. And the Caliph was Omar. So one day it came to pass that the people of Damascus whither Omar had travelled on a visit begged the Caliph saying: 'O Commander of the Faithful, we pray thee that thou ask Bilal to sing the call to prayer for us even as it was taught him by our Lord Mohammed." Now Bilal was nearly a century old, but his voice was deep and sweet as ever. And they aided him to ascend the minaret. Then into the midst of the great silence burst once more the mighty African voice of Bilal—singing the Adzan as it has still been sung for more than 1200 years from all the minarets of Islam. . . . And Omar wept and all the people with him.

Bilal was buried at Damascus, where his tomb was one of the principal sights for centuries.

REFERENCES

Muir, W., *Life of Mohamet*. London, 1894.
Koelle, W. *Muhammad*, pp. 125, 364, 422. London, 1889.
Syed, Ameer Ali, *Life and Teaching of Mohammed*. London, 1891.
Bisland, *Life and Letters of Lafcadio Hearn*, Vol. I, p. 281. Boston, 1923.

ADDITIONAL REFERENCES

Atterbury, Anson P., *Islam in Africa*, pp. 80–81. New York, Negro Universities Press, 1899 and 1969.
Huggins, Willis N., *An Introduction to African Civilizations*, pp. 71, 97. New York, Avon House, 1937.
Fleming, B. J., and Pryde, M. J., *Distinguished Negroes Abroad*, pp. 21–30. Washington, D.C., The Associated Publishers, 1946.

Ibrahim Al-Mahdi

♨

ISLAM'S GREATEST SONGSTER AND
CALIPH OF BAGDAD
(c. A.D. 790)

WITH THE STORY of Ibrahim Al-Mahdi, we enter the enchanted atmosphere of the *Arabian Nights' Entertainments*. Ibrahim was Islam's greatest singer of love songs and its most bohemian spirit at the time these extraordinarily splendid tales were being told.

Fortune smiled on Ibrahim's birth. Paradise could scarcely have possessed greater allurements for the most ardent Moslem than earth lavished upon Ibrahim. In fact, he was the next thing to a god himself. His father, Al-Mahdi, was caliph, which in itself implied divinity. But most impressive of all, he belonged to the father tree that had borne Mohammed, the Prophet. The latter's grandfather was the brother of Ibrahim's great-great-grandfather. This relation to Mohammed, though distant, sufficed to set Ibrahim and his kin above all others.

Ibn Khallika, Arab historian (A.D. 1211-1282), says of Ibrahim:

This prince had great talent as a singer and an able hand on musical instruments; he was also an agreeable companion at parties of pleasure. Being of dark complexion, which he inherited from his mother, Shikla, or Shakla—who was a Negro—he receive the name At-Thinnin (the Dragon).

Ibrahim was a man of great merit and a perfect scholar, with an open heart and a generous hand; his like had never been seen among the sons of the Caliphs, none of whom spoke with more propriety and elegance, or composed verses with greater ability. . . .

He was proclaimed Caliph at Bagdad . . . under the title of Al-Mubarak—the Blessed.

When Ibrahim was born, the Mohammedan Empire was the greatest on earth. It stretched from India to Spain on the Atlantic and included most of the territory on both shores of the Mediterranean. The wealth and the magnificence of its rulers, the caliphs, were fabulous.

An example of this was Caliph Moktader's reception of the Greek ambassador as described by Abdul Feda, Arab historian:

The Caliph's entire army, horse and foot, was under arms—160,-000 men. His state-officers and favorite slaves stood near him in glorious apparel, their belts glittering with gold and gems. Nearby stood 7,000 eunuchs, 4,000 of whom were white and 3,000 black. The porters, or doorkeepers, of the imperial palace numbered 700. Barges and boats, extraordinarily magnificent in decoration, floated on the Tigris.

No less splendid was the palace. It was hung about with 38,000 pieces of tapestry, 12,000 whereof were silk, embroidered with gold. Twenty-two thousand carpets adorned the floors; a hundred lions were led forth, a keeper beside each.

Among other rarities was a tree of gold and silver spreading itself in eighteen branches, whereon and upon the twigs of which sat birds wrought of the same precious metal as were the leaves of the tree. When machinery was put in motion, the birds warbled as though they were alive.

Add to this spectacle such details as halls of rarest marble and woodwork of handsomest inlay; courts with gorgeous flowers and spraying fountains; secret pavillions and perfumed retreats; harems with the most beautiful women of the vast empire; throngs of noblemen, minstrels, poets, and scholars—and you have a picture of an event that in its day was probably just average entertainment.

To indicate the lavishness of the times one need say no more than that Ibrahim's brother, on his father's side, was the renowned Haroun Al-Raschid, whose name is immortalized in the gorgeousness and splendor of the *Arabian Nights' Entertainments.*

Ibrahim's mother was Shikla, daughter of Shah Efrend, a king in southern Persia. Now, as then, this region is largely Negroid. We have Abou'l Mahasin's word for it that Shikla was a Negro. In the course of a war on Efrend, Mansour, the caliph, carried off Shikla, putting her in his harem as an attendant to his favorite wife, Monayyah.

One evening at an entertainment given for members of the royal family, Al-Mahdi, heir to the throne, noticed her, and was so captivated by her that he begged his father's permission to make her his favorite wife, which was granted.

Soon after Ibrahim was born, his father came to the throne. The young prince was carefully tutored in science, poetry, dialectics, and other branches of Moslem culture. Music and especially singing were Ibrahim's chief delight. But these, alas, were considered far beneath the dignity of the high-born. Slaves were chiefly the singers of those days.

But genius, as is so often the case, won against conventions and prejudice. Ibrahim sang privately until tales of the wonderful young singer in the royal palace were carried into all parts of the empire and people became eager to hear him. His father too was won over and gave him consent to sing at concerts, provided only members of the royal family and the caliph's most intimate friends were present.

With immense wealth at his command, Ibrahim lived befittingly. Spirited and irrepressible, he was "the life of the party." A prodigal at heart, he was temperamental, being by turns gentle and cruel, sensitive and cynical, serious and flippant. He took only his art seriously. Believing himself supreme in this, he was as spiteful toward rivals as a jealous woman.

With his favorite companion Haroun Al-Raschid, he wandered through the streets of Bagdad in all manner of disguises, making many strange friends. Though only half-brothers, the two were dearer to each other than are many full brothers. So close was the bond between the two that later when Ibrahim was made ruler of Syria, Haroun could not support his absence, and recalling him, made a pilgrimage with him to Mecca. There was but one point of disagreement between the two and that was Ibrahim's extravagance. Haroun, himself a model of Oriental munificence, hated waste.

Ibrahim in his autobiography tells how he was once reproved by Haroun Al-Raschid because of this. "One day," he says, "the caliph, my brother, deigned to accept an invitation to dine at my home. I ordered the repast served. Raschid had the habit of eating first the warm meats and then the hors d'oeuvres and other cold delicacies. Now, at the second service, there was a dish that resembled a ragout of fish. Raschid asked me why the chef had prepared the fish in such small pieces. I replied, 'Commander of the Faithful, what you take for pieces of fish are but so many fish tongues.' "

Haroun, astonished, asked how many tongues it had taken to make up the dish. Ibrahim says about a thousand but the chef said 1500.

"And the cost?" demanded Haroun. The chef named an extravagant sum—the fish was a rare kind—on which Haroun pushed his plate aside and refused to eat any more until a sum of money equal to the cost of the fish was placed before him to distribute among the poor.

Further to teach Ibrahim a lesson, he ordered a servant to take the jeweled platter on which the fish tongues had been served and give it to the first beggar he saw outside the palace gates.

Ibrahim, hoping to save the dish, whispered to a domestic to follow the bearer and buy back the dish from the one to whom it would be given, but Haroun, divining his intention, called back the bearer, and bade him tell the beggar to whom he would give it not to accept less than 20,000 dirhems (about $5,000), for it.

Ibrahim's prodigality was incurable, however. When he was ruler of Syria and Haroun instructed him to pay 30,000 dirhems to Hakem-El-Wahdi, a popular singer, Ibrahim, in admiration of the singer, added out of his own pocket 299,990 dirhems—ten less so that his generosity should not equal that of the caliph's.

When Ibrahim was thirty-six Haroun died and his son Emin came to the throne. Emin was also a bohemian at heart. Many were the feasts he and Ibrahim gave in the splendid palace gardens on nights when the moon shone brilliantly and the fragrance of jasmine filled the air.

Lighthearted Emin was not to enjoy these pleasures for long. His learned and more serious brother Mamoun killed him and seized the throne. Mamoun took a step that was to bring Ibrahim to the throne eventually: he married the daughter of Riza, head of a faction that was hostile to the Abbasids, and named Riza as his successor.

The wedding was one of the most splendid and costly in history. About $6,000,000 was spent on it. By way of presents to Mamoun's generals, Riza wrote out the names of some of his estates on slips of paper and threw them among the generals. Those who caught the slips received the estates written thereon. Buran, mother of the bride, gave Mamoun 1000 large pearls, together with a candle of ambergris weighing eighty pounds. Instead of rice, seed pearls were throne at the bride. These were left to the mob.

Several months after the wedding Mamoun went away on a military expedition. The Abbasids, foreseeing a visitation of vengeance should Riza's faction ever come to power, took advantage of Mamoun's absence to seize control. They offered the throne to Mansour, Ibrahim's brother, but recalling Emin's fate, he refused, whereupon they offered it to Ibrahim, who accepted it reluctantly.

It would have been difficult to find one less fitted for rulership than Ibrahim. Preoccupied with his singing and his poetry, he turned the government over to his favorites, who abused their powers and pilaged the treasury. Ibrahim soon found himself without money to pay his soldiers. However, he was so much loved by them that instead of revolting they called for him to sing for them. "Since he cannot pay us," they cried, "bring him to us and let him sing for us." Accordingly Ibrahim sang three songs for the soldiers on the left bank of the Tigris, and three for those on the right, leaving them content.

Ibrahim ruled with great kindness. When Sehl, one of his leading generals, revolted and was captured and brought before him, Ibrahim, not having the heart to pass the death sentence on him, turned him over to a friend for safekeeping with instructions to treat him well.

Mamoun, to recover his throne, started for Bagdad with a large army, on which most of Ibrahim's friends deserted him, forcing Ibrahim to seek safety in flight.

Ibrahim remained in hiding for several years. Mamoun knew where he was but made no effort to arrest him because of Ibrahim's great popularity. It was only when the rebels made another attempt to put Ibrahim back on the throne that Mamoun sent to take him. Unable to find him then, he offered a reward for his capture.

Ibrahim, who was in the city, tried to escape early one morning disguised as a woman with two women companions. Wanting to take some food with him, he wakened a shopkeeper to sell him some. The latter, surprised at the request, became suspicious, and demanded the names of the party. One of the women, panic-stricken, offered the shopkeeper a splendid ruby, which only increased his suspicions. When the latter refused the bribe, the three tried to escape and in the scuffle Ibrahim's veil fell off, revealing his beard. A slave who was in the shop, guessing Ibrahim's identity and eager for the reward, ran off to call the police.

Ibrahim was arrested and thrown into prison. But Mamoun was in a quandary about what to do with him. He was too popular to be put to death. Besides, to kill an uncle after he had already killed a brother would be too much. Furthermore, he was very fond of Ibrahim's voice and wanted to hear it again at his concerts.

For several weeks he deliberated, and though adamant against all pleas to save Ibrahim's life, he seemed in no haste himself to take it. Then he let it be known that if he were properly persuaded, he might yield. On this, one of Ibrahim's wives appeared before Mamoun and his court and after a great show of humiliation won consent to let Ibrahim appear to plead for his own life.

Ibrahim, heavily chained, was brought into the throne room before Mamoun. Kneeling to him, he said, after a dramatic pause, "Prince of Believers, may Allah grant thee His mercy and his benedictions!"

"I reject thy salutation as Allah will reject and excommunicate all traitors as thou," replied Mamoun angrily.

"Gentle sire," answered Ibrahim, "sovereign power excludes hate. Those who pardon approach near to Allah."

Mamoun bowed his head, as if torn with emotion. Pointing to his two sons, Abbas and Moutassen, he said, "Here are two in whose rights I must condemn thee."

"Commander of the Faithful," replied Ibrahim, "if it were only a question of politics or the state, this step would be wise, but Allah permits your majesty to be merciful without danger because he has given to thee power that defies all attacks."

Turning to his grand vizier, Mamoun said, "Verily, here are words more precious than pearls; more powerful than magic." Turning to Ibrahim, he said, "My dear uncle, may Allah forgive thee as freely as I have forgiven thee."

Mamoun, kneeling, turned his face toward Mecca and prayed. Then he ordered the chains to be struck off Ibrahim and the royal garb placed on him.

"Henceforth, uncle," said Mamoun, "we shall be the dearest of friends."

An escort of royalty was ordered to accompany Ibrahim to his palace; twelve gift-laden camels were sent along. The next day Ibrahim sent Mamoun a handsome satin screen on which was embroidered eighteen verses of Ibrahim's own composition.

Mamoun's show of forgiveness went further. He ordered all who had been kind to Ibrahim during his adversity to be well rewarded, and those who had been unkind to be punished. Among the latter were the shopkeeper and the slave woman who had called the police. The slave was given, instead of the promised reward, one hundred lashes and sent to prison for life.

"You had neither child nor husband," said Mamoun sternly to her, "hence need was not your excuse."

All of this show of magnanimity, however, was intended by Mamoun to increase his own reputation, especially among the admirers of Ibrahim, because in private life he was everything but the dear friend he had promised to be. He sent spies to follow Ibrahim everywhere and greeted him with sarcastic remarks, reminding Ibrahim that he had spared his life.

"Art thou the Negro caliph?" he once demanded of Ibrahim.

Ibrahim, quoting the words of another poet, replied, "Though I be a slave, my soul, through its noble nature, is free; though my body be black, my mind is fair."

"Uncle," Mamoun replied piously, "a jest of mine has put you in a serious mood. Blackness of skin cannot degrade an ingenious mind, or lessen the worth of the scholar and the wit. Let darkness claim the color of your body; I claim as mine your fair and candid soul."

This persecution continued until in desperation Ibrahim decided on a step which he hoped would put an end to Mamoun's suspicions forever. He applied for the post of court singer, which was equivalent to a renunciation of all claims to the throne. Court singers were held in low social repute because they entertained at feasts and sang in praise of wine, women, and love. To most religious folk they were an especial abomination. Mamoun was greatly pleased at the request but pretended to be horrified, saying the position was far beneath one of Ibrahim's birth. He finally gave his consent after much seemly hesitation.

The change from monarch to public singer was indeed a comedown. But to Ibrahim it was joy. At last he was free to appear from behind the curtain which his royal blood had long drawn around him. He was free to go and sing whenever and wherever he chose. A true artist, he had meant it when he said that he preferred his art to all the empires on earth.

But even this extreme step was not to bring him peace.

Mamoun, still suspicious, continued his spying until his chief spy, himself, took steps to stop it. Captivated by Ibrahim's voice, he took one of Ibrahim's poems to Prince Munoter, the chief of police, and asked him to intercede with Mamoun. The poem, written in a melancholy vein, conveyed the nature of Ibrahim's position. It read, roughly translated:

Stream, flowing lightly and freely, someone has hindered thy course, and thy waters no longer flow free;
Bird, which once flew freely in air, thou art a captive afar from the path that leads to the source.

When this verse came to Mamoun's attention, he was so touched by the discreet manner in which Ibrahim had referred to his surveillance, that he gave him full freedom.

A master of the art of improvising, Ibrahim was admired by friend and foe alike. The astronomer Mohammed said, "For several years I have been one of those privileged to attend the private affairs of the Caliphs Mamoun and Moutassem, and this is what I have noticed: as soon as the voice of Ibrahim was heard, the people in the palace, and especially the valets, slaves, and laborers, would drop their work to listen to him. As soon as another commenced to sing they would resume their tasks without wishing to listen."

Ahmed Daoud, a stern religious noble, said similarly, "Up to the time of hearing Prince Ibrahim I had denied the effect that song could produce and more than once I had expressed this opinion before the caliph himself, but after hearing him, I felt myself forced to stop any criticism."

Of the many anecdotes told about Ibrahim, perhaps the most remarkable is that related by his brother Mansour. The latter says that one day Mamoun sent for Ibrahim to sing but in spite of repeated messages he did not go. The next day, however, Ibrahim, somewhat alarmed, decided to make amends, and hearing that Mamoun was in the menagerie, set off to see him. Stopping to pick up a lyre, he tuned it and hit it under his robe. Arriving there, he was told that the caliph had not yet recovered from the effects of the wine he had imbibed freely at the feast the night before.

Tiptoeing in, Ibrahim saw Mamoun, his back turned, looking at some newly-captured lions. Taking out his lyre, he struck it up and sang:

> I emptied a cup of wine for my pleasure.
> Then I drank a second to correct the effect of the first.

Mamoun was delighted. "Well done, uncle," he said, "you've brought back gaiety again." Mamoun ordered more wine and drank it while listening to the rest of the song.

"What struck me," says Mansour, "was this: My brother that day, held himself constantly to the higher octave of the instrument without showing the least sign of fatigue. He did ever more, which I will refrain from telling lest I be charged with falsehood. Nevertheless, I cannot help but add that as soon as Ibrahim commenced to sing, the ferocious beasts stretched their necks in his direction and approached little by little. They ended by resting their heads on the bars of the cage until the song was finished, when they went away."

"The Caliph," he adds, "was so impressed that he forgot to chide Ibrahim for his neglect of the day before."

Ibrahim's singing sometimes cast such a spell over his listeners that they completely forgot themselves. Once while he was singing for Mamoun, Djar-far, the Barmecide, forgetting that he was in the royal presence, arose and paced back and forth, drawing his silken train after him, while uttering rapturous exclamations. This breach of etiquette could have cost Djar-far his life. The song, Ibrahim's own composition, is roughly translated thus:

In describing the beauty of my beloved, I dream of the pure gold
    in the coins of the ancient Egyptians,
Of the pearl in its shell in the depths of the sea, which is the
    despair of the fisher,
Or of the exquisite fineness of the gold that the gilder puts
    on the leaves of a book.

At another time the aide-de camp of Taber, the leading general, was so affected that he went over to Ibrahim and kissed the hem of his jeweled robe.

Once Ibrahim happened to arrive at the palace while a song contest was in progress. As prizes, the caliph had before him three cups: one of silver, full of gold pieces; another of gold, full of silver pieces; a third of pure crystal, full of amber. Rivalry was intense, each singer hoping for a prize.

Ibrahim joined in and won the first. He sang again and won the second. At the end of his third song the caliph was so delighted that he not only awarded him the crystal cup but also rose, praised him publicly, and showered other presents on him.

The other contestants were much put out. Moussoli, one of them, whispered to Djami, a colleague. "This royal prince in making his living like us is taking the bread out of our mouths."

Ibrahim, overhearing the remark, took the three prizes and handing them to his rivals said, "Take the salary which is your due and leave to me what is but a pastime."

It was a pastime that he took seriously—so seriously that he delved into higher mathematics in order to develop his sense of rhythm and analyzed all the sounds made by animate and inanimate nature in order to acquire greater lyric sweetness and flexibility. It is said of him that he cultivated the human voice to a degree never before reached in the East, which, of course, meant the West too. He blazed the way for the long generations of singers that were to follow. After his day objections to public singers were invariably met with the reminder: "Was not Prince Ibrahim, son of Al-Mahdi and a descendant of the Prophet, the first singer of his day?" Like so many other heritages of Moslem civilization, that of the concert singer was passed on to the European. Ibrahim, therefore, must be remembered in this connection.

Ibrahim did not have the field entirely to himself, however. He had several powerful rivals, the chief of which was Ishak, who with his father Moussoli also sang at the court. The rivalry between the two created great excitement. But for it Ibrahim's name might not be so vivid to us after 1100 years.

Ishak was also a first-rate composer, but he wrote and sang strictly according to the traditional style. Ibrahim, on the other hand, was creative, giving his spirit free rein and never hesitating to introduce innovations that he considered artistic. Believing that his royal birth permitted him this freedom, he had said while caliph:

> I am the king and the son of a king
> What it pleases me to sing, I sing.

Ibrahim and Ishak were as jealous of each other as prima donnas. Ibrahim, though very generous in most respects, had such supreme confidence that he was superior to all others that he once said, "Were it not for the handicap of my noble brith, I would accomplish such feats of voice that all would be obliged to agree that I have never had, and never could have, an equal on this earth."

Always eager to demonstrate his superiority, he once made a wager with Ishak, before the caliph, that he could outsing Ishak in range. Picking up an instrument, he sang first in unison with it, then in a higher octave, next in a chord grave, finishing up in a bass octave. In other words, he covered four octaves, or three registers—tenor, baritone, and bass.

At another time, Ishak sang a composition of his own that pleased Mamoun greatly. Ibrahim, who felt that his laurels were menaced, sought out Ishak during the entr'acte and asked him to repeat his songs. While Ishak refused, Ibrahim pulled off his jeweled vest and offered it to him, whereupon Ishak repeated his song twice in a low voice.

Mamoun, learning that Ibrahim was going to repeat Ishak's song, hurried back to his seat. Ibrahim, in his version of this song, embellished it with grace notes of such beauty that the enraptured Mamoun gave him six purses of gold, all of which Ibrahim impulsively tossed over to his rival.

Not always did Ibrahim win, however. At one concert while twenty singers were performing before Mamoun, ten to the right and ten to the left, Ishak suddenly exclaimed that one of the singers had made a mistake. Ibrahim, taken by surprise, ridiculed Ishak.

The latter, to prove his contention, ordered those on the right to stop and those on the left to continue. After listening a while, he pointed to the eighth singer from the right, declaring he was responsible. Taking him out from the ranks, Ishak made him sing alone, and thus discovered the mistake, which so impressed Mamoun that he said to Ibrahim, "Uncle, cease henceforth making fun of Ishak. A man capable of detecting a single error amid twenty throats which are singing, and eighty-four chords which are vibrating, deserves respect."

Ibrahim did not hesitate to use underhanded methods to maintain his supremacy. One day, while passing Ishak's home, he heard the latter's father going over an original composition which was to be sung before the caliph. Moussoli kept repeating the difficult passages while his slaves kept time. Ibrahim, who was in disguise, hid under the balcony and memorized it all. That night, after Ishak and Moussoli had scored a triumph at the palace, Ibrahim rose and charged the two with plagiarism and as proof offered to sing the song note for note, which he did so much better than they that the caliph rebuked them. Later, however, Ibrahim confessed to the caliph and sent Ishak a rich present.

Ibrahim was even less gallant with his feminine rivals. One of the latter named Dinak, who was very beautiful and had a host of artistic admirers, received such acclaim that Ibrahim singled her out for abuse and composed the following song:

> Cursed creature, thou art the mistress of the human race.
> Wouldst thou have all the men in the world as lovers?
> In mixing thou the fat with the lean, dost not thy soul
> rise with disgust?

Dinak resorted to a rather unusual method of revenge. She sent a friend of hers named Bedl, a woman of uncommon beauty with "a complexion of gold" and a voice of exquisite sweetness, to Ibrahim's palace with instructions to sing for him but on no account to let him see her. Arriving there early one morning while Ibrahim was still in bed, she hid behind a curtain and sang her repertoire of amorous songs for him. Ibrahim, his passion aroused, and eager to see the one who could sing so bewitchingly, hastened toward the curtain but Bedl, giving him just one glimpse of her face, dropped her veil and hurried out of the palace. Later he spent a fortune trying to find her but never did.

Once, however, he saved the life of a beautiful slave girl. The caliph, after listening to one of Ibrahim's songs about a camel, ordered him to teach it to the girl. The song was difficult, and the girl hesitated several times when she came to an intricate passage that she could not master. Mamoun, angered by what he held to be a display of unwarranted obstinacy or stupidity, swore to have the girl thrown into the Tigris from the palace windows if she did not succeed in three more attempts. Ibrahim, to save her life, changed the melody to fit the girl's error.

Ibrahim's musical triumphs continued until his fiftieth year, when he became involved in a religious dispute as to whether the Koran, or Holy Book, "was created, or existed before the Creation." Mamoun insisted that it was the handiwork of man and was torturing and putting to death all who did not agree with him. Ibrahim, as a member of the old Arab party and one of the learned men of the kingdom, sat as one of the judges, and he with several others, anxious to please both sides, gave evasive decisions, which so vexed Mamoun that he ordered them to be put to death, but before sentence could be carried out on Ibrahim, Mamoun died. His son and successor, Moutassem, spared Ibrahim's life but carried on the dispute.

For six years this dragged on, forcing Ibrahim to abandon his music. Then suddenly one day Moutassem ordered him to appear at court with his singers. Ibrahim was greatly disturbed. He had no money to buy suitable dresses for his singers.

At the concert the poor clothes of his choir looked very shabby against the rich ones of the caliph's wives. Ibrahim's voice, how-

ever, had lost none of its magic and so pleased the caliph that he
not only forgot past disagreements with Ibrahim but gave him a
large sum of money, which hereafter permitted his troupe to appear in style.

In his sixtieth year Ibrahim, who up till then had dealt only
with profane themes as love and feasting, turned his attention to
patriotic odes. The change was inspired by the invasion of Syria
by Theophilus, King of Greece. When Ibrahim saw the havoc
being caused among his countrymen he appeared before the caliph
with a fiery war poem in which he urged the people to rally against
the Greeks. He sang:

> Oh, anger of God, thou hast seen this horrible spectacle,
> Avenge, therefore the female victims.
> As to the men, they have found a glorious death,
>   perhaps a just punishment for their sins.
> But what of the innocent women and children?

His patriotic cry aroused the nation, stirring it to such frenzy
that it arose and swept out the Greeks. This was his swan song; he
never appeared in public again.

Troubled by religious scruples, he spoke contemptuously of his
career as a singer in his last days. He was distressed, too, by the
disrespectful manner of some of those who had once saluted him
as caliph. One had written a satire about him which he took much
to heart, and in which he was called "The Dragon" in reference to
his huge frame and his dark skin.

On his death bed he regretted leaving behind so many monuments to his worldly taste. When, however, one of his religious
friends advised him to burn his poems and his music manuscripts,
he replied, "Fool thou art, what should I do with Charayah?
Ought I to burn her too? She knows all my songs by heart."
Charayah was his favorite disciple.

Many of Ibrahim's love songs are preserved in Isfahani's *Book
of Songs*. Isfahani says, "In the art of sound, Ibrahim was one of
the most instructed men of his time. In singing, in rhythm, and in
playing the stringed instrument, he excelled at all. The religious
prejudices of his day and his royal birth at no time left him free to
develop his rare gifts."

REFERENCES

Preceding Ibrahim was another celebrated singer and poet. Ibn Suraidj, or Soreyj. He introduced the Persian lute into Mecca, was a composer of elegies, and a boon companion of the caliph. G. Palgrave says of him, "Ebn Soreyj, the Mario of Hejaz singers; his dusky and irregular features half-hidden by a veil betray his mulatto origin; he is known everywhere as the first musician; the sprightliest born-singer; and the ugliest face of the day." (*Essays of the Eastern Question*, pp. 292–296. London, 1872.) Soreyj died in A.D. 724. (See also *The Encyclopedia of Islam*, Vol. II, Pt. 1, p. 423.)

Masudi. *Praires d'Or*, Vol. VII, pp. 62–72. Barbier de Meynard, 1861.

Ibn Khallikan, *Biographical Dictionary*, trans. by Baron MacGuckin de Slane, Vol. I, p. 17 *et seq.*

Zotenberg, *Works of Tabari*, Vol. IV, pp. 511–519.

Barbier de Meynard, *Journal Asiatique*, March–April, 1869.

Harun Mustapha Leon, *Islamic Culture*, Vol. III, pp. 249–272.

Palmer, H. H., *Haroun Al-Raschid*, pp. 206–210. London, 1881.

Al-Jahiz

LORD OF THE GOLDEN AGE OF ARAB LITERATURE
(A.D. 778–868)

FOR AN APPRAISAL of Al-Jahiz, let us turn to the eulogies of three savants.

"The most genial writer of the age, if not of Arabic literature, and the founder of the Arab prose style, was the grandson of a Negro slave, Amr ben Bahr, known as Al-Jahiz, 'The Goggle-Eyed'," says Gibbs, Arabic scholar.

"Al-Jahiz," says Christopher Dawson, "was the greatest scholar and stylist of the ninth century."

P. K. Hitti says, "An early representative of the zoological and anthropological sciences was Abu-Uthman Amr ibn Bahr al-Jahiz ... whose Kitab-al-Hawaya ... contains germs of later theories of evolution, adaptation, and animal psychology. Al-Jahiz knew how to obtain ammonia from animal offal by dry distillation. His influence over later zoologists ... is manifest. But the influence of Al-Jahiz as a radical theologian and a man of letters if greater. He ... was one of the most productive and frequently quoted scholars in Arabic literature. His originality, wit, satire, and learning, made him widely known."

Al-Jahiz, who seems to have been a very dark Negro, started life in most humble surroundings but by studiousness, a prodigious memory, remarkable powers of assimilation, and unruffled good nature, he reached the highest rank of scholarship and esteem.

Born at Basra in Asia Minor, he studied philology, philosophy, and science there under the noted Mu'tazlite teacher an-Nassam. Of an independent spirit, he was not long in striking out on an intellectual path of his own, and founded his own school of thought, known as the Jahizite. Such was his good-natured wit, his breadth of mind, and his impartiality, that he was beloved even by members of the fanatical religious sects that normally would have treated him as a heretic.

An indefatigable reader, Al-Jahiz would hire the shops of book-sellers outright so that he could spend the whole night reading in them. His works are voluminous. Few writers were as industrious as he, and still fewer wrote over such a long period of time. He was prolific until he died in A.D. 868 at the age of ninety.

He wrote, as Gibbs says, "with a careless loquacity, alternately grave and gay, exalted and extravagant. His wit was ready and his industry was immense."

Al-Jahiz' masterpiece is *The Book of Animals,* in seven volumes. Among his other works are *The Merit of the Turks, In Praise of Merchants and Dispraise of Officials, The Superiority of Speech to Silence, The Superiority in Glory of the Black Race over the White,* and *The Book of Eloquence and Rhetoric.*

In his works, which contain the most varied and curious kinds of information, he presents all sides of the story. Thus in his *Book of Animals* we find him discussing animals pro and con, as, for instance, the good and the bad qualities of the dog.

In personal appearance Al-Jahiz was unprepossessing. His eyes seemed as if they were about to pop out of his head. It is related that Caliph Al-Mutawakkil engaged him to teach his son, but when he saw him, he was so repelled by his looks that he paid him a large sum and dismissed him. Later, however, he re-called him and placed the young prince under his tutorship, al-though he strongly disagreed with Al-Jahiz' religions beliefs.

During the closing years of his long life, Al-Jahiz suffered greatly from ill health. "The maladies of nature," he complained, "have conspired against my body. If I eat something cold, it at-tacks me in my feet, and if I take anything warm, it attacks me in the head. The heaviest weight I am called on to bear is my age." Nonetheless, he let nothing interfere with his literary labors. Yaqut lists over 120 books by him.

In his *Kitab al-Sudan wa l'-Bidan*, or *The Superiority in Glory of the Black Race over the White*, Jahiz begins by naming certain Zengh (Negro) writers as "Loqman, whose writings are well-known and who was called "The Wise" by Mohamet in the Koran." He adds:

There were also Said ibn Jubair, a very pious man, highly esteemed for his profound knowledge of the traditions of the Prophet Mohamet; the Ethiopian, Bilal, of whom Caliph Omar said that he alone was worth a third of all Islam; Afga, the first to die in the holy wars of the Prophet; El-Migdad, the first to fight in the holy war as a horseman; El Wanshi, who killed the false prophet, Musailima; and Julaibib, who died in battle after valiantly killing seven men, and who was buried with the Prophet's own hand.

There were also Faraj, the barber-surgeon, who was so just that he was often called by the judges for counsel; and El-Haiqutan, the poet. When the white poet, Jarir, saw El-Haiqutan in a white robe on a feast day, he remarked, "He looks like the penis of a donkey wrapped in white paper." El-Haiqutan replied to him in a poem in which he said, "Though my hair is wooly and my skin black as coal I am generous and my honor shines. My color does not prevent my being valiant with my sword in battle. Know, you who would boast of your petty glory, that the race of Negroes is more glorious than your race because the Ethiopian Emperor, after meeting the whites, accepted Islam instead. . . .

Jahiz here recites a poem by the celebrated poet Nusaib ibn Riah, a Negro, who says, "If ever you met the Negroes in battle you found them valiant and strong. Ask Ibn Amr who fought against them if he did not find their lances were long. Ask Ibn Jaifar what he got when he made war against us." Jahiz in his commentary adds that Nusaib says that the mulatto children of the Negro women are fully as brave as the blacks.

Jahiz goes on to enumerate other noted Negroes as "El-Ghandaf, the most courageous man in the world, who attacked caravans single-handed; El-Maglul and his sons, who though slaves were very generous and wise and were renowned among the people of the desert; Aflah, who attacked caravans in Khorassan single-handed and who was finally killed only because he was unarmed and drunk."

We, said the Blacks, have conquered the country of the Arabs as far as Mecca and have governed them. We defeated Dhu Nowas [Jewish ruler of Yemen] and killed all the Himyarite princes, but you, white people, have never conquered our country. Our people, the Zenghs [Negroes], revolted forty times in the Euphrates, driving the inhabitants from their homes and making Obollah a bath of blood.

Everyone knows that the Negroes are amongst the most generous of mortals—a quality that is found only among noble characters. Negroes are distinguished amongst other peoples by their natural gift for rhythmic dancing and the best artists on the drum, all of this without any special training. They are also the best singers.

Their language is the easiest to pronounce. They are eloquent, are able to express themselves in a lively manner, and have no stutterers. It happens sometimes that Negro orators speak before their kings from morning till sunset without need for a pause.

Negroes are physically stronger than no matter what other people. A single one of them can lift stones of great weight and carry burdens such as several Whites could not lift nor carry between them.

They are brave, strong, and generous as witness their nobility and general lack of wickedness. They are always gay, smiling, and optimistic, all of which are signs of their honesty and frank nature. There are, however, those who interpret these qualities as marks of a feeble mind or a calculating one. But this would be equivalent to saying that the most intelligent people and the most gifted are the most avaricious and the most callous. Nevertheless the Slavs, for example, are greedier than the Greeks and are, at the same time, less intelligent. Women and children, also, are less intelligent than men and are greedier. This proves that all the above-mentioned good traits are the gift of God, intelligence as well as goodness, generosity as well as bravery.

The Negroes say to the Arabs, "A sign of your barbarity is that when you were pagans you considered us your equals as regards the women of your race. After your conversion to Islam, however, you thought otherwise. Despite this the deserts swarm with the number of our men who married your women and who became chiefs and defended you against your enemies."

You even have sayings in your language which vaunt the deeds of our kings—deeds which you often placed above your own; this you would not have done had you not considered them superior to your own.

Here Jahiz cites verses to prove this assertion and adds:

The Ethiopian, Akym ibn Akym, was more eloquent than Eli-Ajjaj. It is from him that the Syrians learnt the sciences and also from El Montagi ibn Nabhan, who was a native of Negroland and had a pierced ear. He had come to the Arabian desert as a child and left it with a complete knowledge of Arabic.

Akym ibn Akym said in a poem, "On the day of the battle of Ghumdun we were like lions and on the Day of Yathrib we were the stallions of the Arabs. On the fearful Day of the Elephant the hearts of the Arabs deserted them and they fled on their camels."

Jahiz comments on this poem, and gives several extracts, and quotes an Arab poet, Labid, who in speaking of the battle said, "The very clouds seemed as if they were Ethiopians armed with lances." "Labid," he says, "used this imagery because when the Ethiopians, splendid in the blackness of their skins and in the vigor and strength of their superb bodies, attacked with their spears, bows, and arrows they spread an unimaginable terror around them."

For the expression, "We were the stallions of the Arabs," Jahiz explains that the general gave the conquered city over to the troops for pillage and the Negroes cohabited with the captured women, which are mentioned in the following Arab verses:

Ask Musrif El Mwirri [the general in question] about the morning when he gave the captured virgins over to his weather-beaten Negro soldiers.

On this occasion the Negroes fought you, Whites, in spite of your rage. Wahrig defended you with his Perisans, whilst the Ethiopian general commanded in the midst of the destruction. It was then the women of your race were enjoyed by a Negro, whose phallus was the size of a donkey's.

The Negroes can also be proud of the fact that the single dead person over whom the Prophet ever prayed was their ruler, the Emperior of Ethiopia. And this whilst the Prophet was in Medina and the tomb of the Emperor in Ethiopia. It was also this Ethiopian ruler who married Omm Habiba, daughter of Abu Sofyan, to the Prophet.

We, say the Negroes, frighten the enemy by our blackness even as night is more fearful than day. Wooly hair, too, is the finest and strongest. Black is superior. Black cows are considered the best and to have the most durable hides for leather. The same is equally true of black donkeys. Black sheep give the creamiest milk. Mountains and stones are harder the blacker they are. The black lion is irresistible.

Black dates are the sweetest. . . . Black ebony is the most solid and most durable of woods. The blackest hair is the most beautiful and in Paradise everyone will have black hair. The pupils of the eye, too, are black and are they not the most precious part of the human body?

. . . The most exciting spot of a woman's body are the lips of her parts and the blacker these are the more beautiful. . . . Under every comparison, say the Blacks, we are like the night. . . .

No other color is as durable as black. When it is said that such a one is of "white, noble, and distinguished breed" it is not whiteness of skin that is being praised but spotlessness of character. The men of the tribe of Beni Moghira pride themselves on their dark color. The Beni Moghira are a dark-skinned clan amongst the Beni Makhsoum. One of them, Omar ibn Abdallah said, "I am black and I am famous, I belong to a family celebrated in Arabia. Whoever crosses swords with me will find one who is noble and strong."

The ten sons of Abd el Mottalib [the grandfather of Mohammed] were all black and strong; so was Abdallah ibn Abbas, Mohamet's cousin. The members of the family of Abu Talib [a relation of Mohammed and the father of the Sultan Ali] were all more or less Negroid in color.

The Negroes, Jahiz goes on to say, exceed the whites in numbers. The greater portion of the earth is peopled by blacks. This includes not only Africa but all of southern Asia as far as China. As for that greatest of all God's gifts, children, Negro women exceed white ones in fertility.

"Negro men and women haven't many children with peoples of other races. Black women have very little liking for men not of their race. . . ." He also finds that the Negroes are superior in what is very highly prized by the Arabs—sexual competence.

The blacks above all men have the greatest sexual desire—the man for the women and the woman for the man. Black women are the most agreeable sexually of all women. We have some historic data and poems on this and we have taught you and other peoples on this matter. The Arab poet, Ferazdag, the greatest connoisseur of women who had experimented with the women of all races, did he not find their equal among the black women and married Umm Mekkive, a Negro woman, for whom he abandoned all other women, so much did she know how to satisfy him. He has said, "How many young girls are there not among the Negroes with sexual passions flaming like a furnace and like a goblet of khalani wood . . . ?"

The Negroes also have the sweetest breath and the greatest amount of saliva being in this respect like the dog as compared with other animals. As we said the Blacks are more numerous than the Whites since they are made up of the Ethiopians, the Fezzans, Berbers, Copts, Nubians, Faghwans, the people of Meroe, Ceylon, India, Quamar and Indo-China.

. . . The isles between Africa and China are all peopled with Blacks, that is Ceylon, Kalah, Zabig. Most of the Arabs also are as black as we, the Negroes are, and cannot be counted amongst the Whites. As for the Hindus they are even darker than the Arabs. . . .

The Copts [natives of Egypt] are also a black race. Abraham wished to have a child by one of their race and thus Ishmael, the ancestor of the Arabs, was born. The Prophet Mohammet also had a child by Mary the Copt.

If a black skin is thought unsightly what then must be said of the French, the Greeks, and the Slavs with their thin, red, straight hair and beard? The paleness of their eyelids and their lips appear to us, Negroes, very ugly. . . . God did not make us black in order that we should be ugly; our color comes from the sun. The proof of this is that among the Arabs are also black tribes as the Beni Solaim ibn Mansour. . . . [These have] Greek slaves whose offsprings in the third generation become as black as the Beni Solaim because of the climate.

Jahiz goes on to tell how the sun affects the color of even the animals, after which he speaks of the cleverness of the Hindus in mathematics, the arts, and the sciences, and cites a Negro poet in praise of Irar, an intelligent, broad-shouldered Negro. The Negroes, he adds, are fine singers and have a natural gift for cooking. As for trustworthiness, they excel all others. The bankers confide their money and their businesses to them because they have found them more experienced and worthy of trust.

One hardly ever finds a Greek or a Khorassan in a position of trust in a bank. When the bankers of Basra [Jahiz' birthplace] saw the excellent affairs that Faraj Abu Kub, a Negro, had negotiated for his master, each of them took a Negro assistant. Caliph [Sultan] Abdelmalik ibn Merwan often said, "El Adgham is a master among all the Orientals." This El Adgham is also mentioned by Abdullar ibn Khazim, who calls him, "An Ethiopian, a black son of Ethiopia."

This concludes our essay on the Glory of the Black Race.

REFERENCES

The above excerpts from Al-Jahiz are from the Arab edition of this work by G. van Vloten, tria opposcula auctore, *Abu Othman Amr ibn Bahr AlDjahiz*. Basrensi, Leyden, 1903.

To the best of my knowledge there is no translation of this work in any Western language, and the above is but a brief résumé with only such quotations as serve to highlight the title. Much historical matter concerning Negroes has been left out in my résumé and it is to be hoped that a full translation with the poems included will be made some time.

What Jahiz says about the Negro strain in certain great Arabs is supported by other writers, European as well as Arab. For instance, he says that the sons of Abd el-Mottalib, the grandfather of Mohammed, were Negroes, which in turn would make Mohammed a Negro. (See also *Sex and Race*, Vol. I, pp. 95, 96, 284. 1941.)

It must also be noted that when Jahiz refers to "Negroes" he is speaking principally of those in Africa and the first generation of Africans living in Arabia, and that when he speaks of "whites" he is also including Arabian-born mulattoes. An Arab, near-white or mulatto, and even black, was inclined to look down on the incoming blacks from Africa and to consider them inferior, much as a Northern Negro is inclined to consider himself superior to a Southern one or a white or a black city dweller does to someone from the country—that is, in the East it has never been so much a question of color as culture. Therefore, what Jahiz refers to here is not to be confused with Western color prejudice.

The testimony of Jahiz on certain great Negroes among the Arabs is important also because he wrote at the time, or near the time, they lived. What he says about the color of the Ethiopian, (now that the latter are claimed to be white) is very important also. He wrote partly in the eighth and partly in the ninth century, which was long before the coming in of the Portuguese and other Europeans to admixture, and to whom is due the lighter color and straighter features of a small percentage of Ethiopians of our time.

As regards the revolts of the blacks in the Euphrates to which Jahiz refers, one greater than all occurred shortly after his death. Under their leader, Al-Burkhui, they seized Bagdad, capital of the world's then greatest empire, and held it for thirteen years, 870–883. (P. K. Hitti, *History of the Arabs*, p. 382. 1937.)

Among other noted Negro writers of that period were: Abu Dulama
Zend, poet, clown, court jester, and the Rabelais of his age; Khair
an-Nassaj, noted ascetic and Sufi doctor who died in A.D. 934 at the
age of over one hundred; Zu-N-Nun Al-Misri, son of a Nubian slave,
"and the first person of his age for his learning, devotion, communion
with the divinity, and acquaintance with literature," who died in A.D.
860; Abu'l Hassan Ibn Ismael, Al-Kanimi, Ibn Kalakis, Al-Khadi ar
Raschid, all poets; famed Nusaib Ibn Riar, poet and Negro slave, who
for valor at the battle of Al-Kadisiya was liberated by the caliph. (Ibn
Khallikan, *Biographical Dictionary*, Vol. I, pp. 293, 513, 534; Vol. III,
pp. 615, 626; Vol. IV, p. 345. Huart, C., *Litterature Arabe*, p. 65.
Paris, 1902.)

For still others, such as Soleyk, the pre-Islamic Robin Hood, a poet,
see G. Palgrave, who says of this interesting character:

"Nor is the estimation in which Arab annalists and litterateurs hold
him, impaired by his semi-African descent, for intermarriages between
Arabs and Negroes, especially in the midland and southern provinces
of the Peninsula, have been at no period rare or abnormal; to such
admixtures the East owes not a few of her best celebrities, as Noseyyeb,
the poet, Ebn Soreyj, the musician, and Antarah, the warrior, which
are well-known examples each in his type." (*Essays on the Eastern
Question*, pp. 349–377. London, 1872.)

Gibb, H. A. R., *Arabic Literature*, pp. 47–48. London, 1926.
Hitti, P. K. *History of the Arabs*, p. 282. London, 1937.
Ibn Khallikan, *Biographical Dictionary*, trans. by Baron MacGuckin
de Slane, Vol. II, pp. 405–410.
Huart, C., *Litterature Arabe*, p. 212. Paris, 1902.
Margoliouth, D. S., *Yaqut's Dictionary of Learned Men*. Leyden, 1907.
Jour. Roy. Asiat. Soc., pp. 629–697. 1915.
Dawson, C., *The Making of Europe*, p. 152. New York, 1932.
Masudi, *Les Prairies d'Or*, trans. by C. Barbier de Meynard, Vol. I,
pp. 11, 167, 206, 387–388; Vol. II, p. 52; Vol. III, p. 4. Paris, 1861.
Encyclopedia of Islam (see "Djahiz").

ADDITIONAL REFERENCES

Osei, G. K. *The Forgotten Great Africans, 3000 B.C. to 1959 A.D.*,
pp. 12–16. London, G. K. Osei, 1965.

Malik Ambar

BRILLIANT MILITARY LEADER AND
STATESMAN OF INDIA
(1548–1628)

WHEN MOHAMMEDAN RULE was at the height of its spendor in India there was a considerable influx of Ethiopians, some coming as traders, but the majority as mercenaries and slaves. In time they emerged from the mass to become prime ministers, great military and naval commanders, hereditary admirals, and in several instances, sultans. As late as 1833 three of the ruling princes of India were Negroes.

These Ethiopians, or Sidis, as they are better known, first appeared in India about 1300, when a force of them seized the island-fort of Janjira, the site of Bombay. Legend has it that one of their number, disguised as a merchant, obtained permission to land 300 boxes supposed to contain imported wares but in which armed soldiers were actually concealed. Once ashore, the soldiers took the garrison by surprise and captured the island.

Finding commerce unprofitable, the Ethiopians engaged themselves as soldiers in the armies of the Brahmans. They brought tens of thousands of their women and their slaves to settle there, and in time they became the backbone of the armies. Under their own commander, they eventually became the source of central power, as did the Mazois under the Pharaohs, the Zenghs under the caliphs, and the Bokkharas in Morrocco.

Ethiopian industry, skill, and statesmanship helped greatly in

172

making India the rich and prosperous country which the Portuguese, English, and French later found it. The principal regions in
which they settled were Bombay, Gujarat, and the Deccan to the
west and Bengal to the east.

The most distinguished of the Negro rulers of western India was
Malik Ambar, who, beginning as a slave under Queen Chand Bibi,
the Queen Elizabeth of India, rose to the top, becoming commander-in-chief of the armies of the Bombay empire.

When Queen Chand was slain by rebels in her palace in July,
1600, Malik Ambar remained loyal to the ruling dynasty. By a
brilliant coup he captured Ahmadnagar, the principal fort, from
the rebels, and proceeding to the city of Aurangabad, which he
himself had built, he proclaimed Mustaza II, grandson of Nizan
Shah, ruler with himself as regent. Seven years later, however,
Malik Ambar deposed the king and seized the throne.

Malik Ambar's kingdom lay in the vast tableland of the Deccan, which lies to the east of Bombay. His nominal overlord was
Jahangir, the great Mogul emperor. Soon after he took the
throne, however, there was an outburst of dissension among the
Moguls, and Malik Ambar, taking advantage of it, took much of
their territory and even threatened Jahangir's power.

In a long war between Malik Ambar and Jahangir, fortunes
shifted. Now one was victorious, then the other. Jahangir's wrath
was not confined to military operations—he even took up the pen
against Malik Ambar. In his writings he calls Malik Ambar many
hard names, among them "black-faced wretch."

Sometimes Malik Ambar, beaten, was forced to pay large sums
in tribute; at other times Jahangir's throne hung by a thread. His
Ethiopian compatriots stood behind Malik Ambar to a man. On
one occasion he defeated, by sheer strategy, Jahangir's force of
40,000, against which he moved with only 10,000 men. Invading
the coast, Malik Ambar seized the ships of the emperor and forced
the city of Bijapur, in which he started his career as a slave, to pay
him tribute. Golconda, a city whose name was once synonymous
all over the world with wealth, was similarly dealt with.

When in 1628 the English came to India their first contact was
with Malik Ambar. He was then master of the island of Janjira,
which the English, like the Ethiopians of three centuries before,

wanted as a base for commerce with the interior. With gifts, promises, and flattery they tried to gain a foothold on the island, but Malik Ambar would not succumb to their blandishments.

When they tried to oust him by a conspiracy, Malik Ambar retaliated by seizing one of their caravans valued at 200,000 rupees. The English took one of his ships and demanded the return of their money. With characteristic humor, Malik Ambar sent word to the British asking if they were so absentminded as to have forgotten that they had his ship.

With rockets, cannon, and armed elephants Malik Ambar defeated Abdullah, an ally of Jahangir's, in a decisive battle in 1628, and it seemed as if Jahangir were doomed. But then Malik Ambar died, at the age of eighty.

Motamid Khan, an Indian historian, says of Malik Ambar:

This Ambar was a slave, but an able man. In warfare, in command, in sound judgment, in administration, he had no rival or equal. He well understood that predatory warfare which in the language of the Deccan, is called bargi-giru. He kept down the turbulent tribes and maintained his exalted position to the end of his life and closed his career in honor. History records no other instance of an Abyssinian slave at such eminence."

Relics of this great ruler are still to be found in his city of Aurungabad. Ferishta, another Mohammedan, historian, says of him:

Such is the esteem in which his character is held that notwithstanding the lands dedicated to the support of the attendants of his tomb, are yet left incorporated for that purpose. He was the first general, politician, and financier of his age, and his country was the best cultivated and his subjects the happiest of any in the Deccan. He founded Ghurkeh, now called Aurungabad, and ornamented it with a magnificent palace, gardens, and noble bodies of water, lined with stones, which yet remain. His charities and his justice are yet celebrated, and he was also eminent for pieties.

Nawaz Khan, another Arab historian, says similarly, "In military acts and in statesmanship and right judgment, Malik Ambar was unique."

A poet of the times compared him with Bilal, another Negro, who was Mohammed's companion and inspiration. He said:

> There was Bilal, the servant of the Apostle of God
> After one thousand years, there came Malik Ambar.

REFERENCES

Slavery was never a barrier to an ambitious slave, black or white, under Mohammedan rule. Mahmud of Ghazni, the greatest of the Mohammedan rulers of India, was born of slave parentage.

The first of the Indian rulers to use Ethiopian soldiers was Barbek Shah, according to Stewart, who says that Barbek Shah, "finding them faithful, promoted them to high rank and important situations."

"His example," Stewart continues, "was afterwards followed by the sovereigns of Guzerat and Deccan; and many of these people, who, if they had fallen into the hands of Europeans, would have been condemned to servile drudgery became the associates of princes and governors of provinces."

Among other Negroes who distinguished themselves in this region of India were Mawla, who was thrown under the feet of an elephant by Sultan Jalalu-Din because the people wanted to make him sultan; Admiral Sambal, who defeated the Portuguese in several naval battles: Admirals Masud and Ali Kasam; Generals Kafur, Abudullah, Rahim Khan, Abdul Rahman, Battal, Belal, Forts, Hillol, Ibrahim Khan, Jauhar, Johar, Kasim Sabaun, Sambal, Sat, and the eminent military commander, Yakut Khan. Ekhaz Khan was a noted prime minister.

Whenever these people were called Abyssians (Habish), what are known to us as Negroes was really meant, according to E. C. Bayley and others.

Another Negroid people who played a prominent role in India were the Moors. The latter practically dominated Indian trade until 1600.

Banaji, D. R., *Bombay and the Sidis*. London, 1932.
Gribble, J. D. B., *History of the Deccan*, Vol. I, p. 256. London, 1896.
Elliot, H. M., *History of India*, Vol. VI, see Index. London, 1875.
Nawaz Khan, *Maaser-ul-Amara*, pp. 534–536, Bibliotheca Indica. Calcutta, 1911.
Scott, J., *Ferishta's History of the Deccan*, Vol. I, pp. 400–403. Shrewsbury, 1794.
Jackson, A. V. W., *History of India*, Vol. III, p. 119. London, 1896.

Morie, L. J. *Histoire d'Ethiopie*, Vol. II, p. 33. Paris, 1904.

Stewart, C., *History of Bengal*, pp. 100–108. London, 1813.

Bayley, E. C., *Gujerat*, p. 136. London, 1886.

Elphinstone, M., *History of India*, pp. 386–393, 538–560. London, 1911.

Campos, J. J. A., *The Portuguese in Bengal*, pp. 13, 25. London, 1919.

Malik Andeel

BENEVOLENT SULTAN OF BENGAL, INDIA
(d. 1494)

AMONG THE MANY ETHIOPIANS who attained to high power in eastern India was Malik Andeel, possibly the greatest of their number. Born a slave, he ultimately became commander-in-chief of the armies of the rich and potent kingdom of Bengal under the rule of Sultan Futteh Khan, and was later sultan himself.

In the course of a rebellion in 1473 Futteh Khan was killed. The throne was seized by Bareek, chief eunuch, who compelled Malik Andeel to take an oath of allegiance promising that he would never attack him "whilst he was on the throne."

Malik Andeel, however, cherished plans of becoming sultan. Ingratiating himself into the favor of Bareek until he had won his complete confidence and was permitted to come and go in the palace at will, he conspired with Bareek's attendant, another Negro eunuch.

The plan was to get Bareek thoroughly drunk, and when this was achieved, Malik Andeel was called. Malik found the intoxicated Bareek lolling on a chair, not upon the throne, and taking advantage of the occasion he construed this as a condition not covered by his oath, and stabbed the sultan. Bareek, however, was large and powerfully built, and in the rough and tumble fight that followed might have beaten Malik Andeel had not the latter's attendants come to his rescue. Even then they did not know where to strike as the room was pitch dark, the lights having been extinguished in the scuffle, but Malik Andeel, who was underneath and covered by the sultan's huge body, ordered them to stab. Bareek was hacked to pieces and Malik Andeel emerged unhurt.

Malik Andeel was then elected sultan by the people of Bengal with the official title of Feroze Shah. He was an able ruler. His Ethiopian compatriots backed him so effectively that none of the white Turkish or Afghan chiefs dared to rebel against him.

Malik Andeel was noted for his generosity. On one occasion he ordered that a sum of money be distributed among the poor which his ministers thought to be far too much. To impress this upon him they heaped up the money in a room through which the sultan was bound to pass. Learning of the intent, Malik Andeel said when he saw it, "Is that all? Double it!"

After a peaceful reign of thirteen years Malik Andeel died in 1494. He was succeeded by his son Mahmud. The remains of a mosque, a minaret, and a reservoir built by Malik Andeel were still in evidence in 1813, according to Stewart, who commented that Malik Andeel governed with "strict justice and munificent liberality."

REFERENCES

Ferishta, *Rise of Mohammedan Power in India*, Vol. IV, pp. 341 *et seq.*

Stewart, C. *History of Bengal*, pp. 100–108. London, 1813.

See also the bibliography of "Malik Ambar."

Eugene Chen

CHINA'S DYNAMIC STATESMAN
(1878–1944)

EUGENE CHEN, four times Foreign Minister of Chinese governments and one of the most dynamic political figures of the twentieth century, was born of Negro-Chinese-Spanish parentage in Trinidad, British West Indies. His family name was Akam.

Educated for the law in England, he returned to Trinidad where he practiced, but because of minor disagreements with the island government he decided to cast his lot with the Chinese and left for Peking, where he became legal adviser to the Ministry of Communications in 1912.

Two years later he founded *The Peking Gazette*, and being a born polemist and fighter who knew but one tactic, a vigorous and bold attack, he selected as his chief target the strongest foe possible: the *North China Daily News*, chief spokesman of British imperialist interests in the Far East, the defender of capital, and the prestige and power Britain had built up in that region. At that time Chinese commerce was centered in Shanghai, then a so-called international settlement, but this commerce was chiefly for Britain's advantage and to some extent that of Japan, then an ally of Britain. Financial power was centered in the British Hong Kong and Shanghai Bank. As a result of his onslaughts, Chen was arrested in 1916 and thrown into a narrow cell with five lice-covered assassins. However, because he was still a British subject and because extraterritoriality yet existed in China, he asserted that he was being illegally held and was released, apparently because of this, in 1917.

Undaunted, he now entered the enemy's stronghold, Shanghai, where he joined Dr. Sun Yat-sen, founder of Nationalist China, and became his personal adviser and private secretary, a position he held until Sun Yat-sen's death in 1925. He also founded *The Shanghai Gazette*, in which he renewed his attacks on British interests and was again thrown into prison, but was later freed.

In 1919 he was a delegate to the Versailles Conference where he formulated China's demands in clear, unmistakable terms. He demanded, among other things, the abolition of concession territories, insisting that all such be placed under a mixed Chinese and foreign administration with Chinese predominant. This demand later paved the way for China's victory over the extraterritorial powers formerly held by the white governments.

In 1922 he founded the *Ming Pao*, or *People's Tribune*, and became chief adviser to the Southern Government of China. In an effort to build up Chinese commerce, not for the benefit of the whites and the Japanese, but the Chinese, he led a strike and a boycott principally against British interests. He asked the Chinese not to speak English and not to use English ships nor to buy and sell British-made goods. This had such effect that in 1926 the British yielded and asked for a conference in which most of Chen's demands were granted and out of which came the Chen-O'Malley Agreement in which Britain returned to China the rich port of Hankow.

In 1927, while Foreign Minister, he was instrumental in preventing war between China on one hand and Britain and the United States on the other. White people had been mobbed by the Chinese in Nanking and from southern China had come terrible rumors of the violation of white women. The result was a great outcry for military intervention and the world "stood at the eve of a war in which the Russian-Asiatic and the capitalistic-western powers would clash." President Coolidge had already dispatched American marines to the scene, but Chen stepped into the breach and in an eloquent note to the white powers expressed China's willingness for peace. He said that he was willing to have the disturbances thoroughly investigated, asking only that the verdict, whether it be for or against China, be just. This frankness had such an effect on President Coolidge that he recalled the marines and in a public address declared for peace to the great discontent of the interests who wanted war in order to gain greater power in China.

The same year, however, due largely to European intrigue there was a split between the Nanking and the Wuhan governments and Chen retired to France, but returned in 1931 to become Foreign Minister of the Canton Government.

While in China Chen married Miss Chang Tsing-ying, daughter of Chang Chen-kiang, head of the Cheking Provincial Government.

The New York Times in its obituary of Chen (May 21, 1944) says:

Eugene Chen, British-born Chinese publisher and politician, was four times Foreign Minister in various Chinese Governments and twice was a refugee when his political fortunes were at low ebb.

An early member of the Kuomintang and one of the first to support Sun Yat Sen, Mr. Chen was at times a bitter enemy of Generalissimo Chiang Kai-shek and on other occasions was outwardly his ally. However, since 1941 he had been in Shanghai, apparently harbored by the Japanese, with whom he had on several occasions in the Nineteen Twenties and Nineteen Thirties conducted involved negotiations.

When Chiang Kai-shek was friendly with the Soviet Union Mr. Chen was Foreign Minister of the Russian-dominated Hankow Government, unofficially run by Borodin and Bluecher. In 1927, after the collapse of the Hankow Government, Mr. Chen fled to Russia when Borodin staged his famous "retreat across the Gobi Desert," and with him went other Chinese leaders with left-wing tendencies.

SIGNED PACT WITH BRITAIN

In 1927, shortly before he fled to Russia, Mr. Chen wrote his name into Chinese history by attaching it to the Chen-O'Malley agreement which legalized the de facto situation created by the Chinese people when they rose and took back the British concession in Hankow, a sixty-year holding in the center of a Chinese industrial region.

The pact, the first diplomatic triumph for the Chinese nationalists, dissolved British rule in favor of a new Chinese administration in which Britons obtained only minority representation.

For a while he lived in Paris and then in 1931 returned to Canton, China, became Foreign Minister of the Canton insurgent government and in December of 1931 was named Foreign Minister of the National Government when Lin Sen succeeded Chiang Kai-shek as titular President. Chiang's downfall was due to his failure to get the League of Nations to drive the Japanese from Manchuria.

Soon thereafter Chiang regained power and Mr. Chen fled to Fukien Province and helped form another insurgent government there. With the aid of the powerful and famous Chinese Nineteenth Route Army the rebel government made a clean sweep of Nanking officials in the province and then tried to overthrow the national regime. The attempt ended in failure and the leaders fled to Hong Kong. That virtually ended Mr. Chen's political career in China, although between 1937 and 1941 he and Chiang were outwardly on good terms.

As early as 1933 Mr. Chen warned that the Japanese campaign for the subjugation of China was the forerunner of eventual war with the United States. In 1939 he advocated a Chinese declaration favoring the Allies in the European war and asserted it would forestall any secret British-Japanese agreement.

As an editor and owner of *The Peking Gazette* and as editor of *The Shanghai Gazette*, Mr. Chen had deep influence in China, and that was instrumental in his political rise—and fall.

As regards Eugene Chen's ability, there is high praise from those who knew him. Arthur Ransome, correspondent of the *Manchester Guardian*, said, "I never heard a single word against his character. The only accusation made against him was that he had the misfortune to be born in Trinidad." Of his dynamic power, Ransome said, "After my first meeting with him which lasted four and a half hours I left him with the sort of feeling a man might have if he had spent that time with his head under Niagara."

Vincent Sheean, author and newspaper correspondent, says, similarly, "The Foreign Minister was a remarkable man. . . . Physically and in some ways of speech, Mr. Chen reminded me of the French politician, Malvy; his complacency was like that of Austen Chamberlain; his delight in his own language and the care he took to see that it was written down in its baroque magnificence suggested Mussolini. He was theatrical as Briand without the old fox's charm; he was as ingratiating as Streseman, as bitter as Poincaré. In short, Mr. Chen was a politician."

The Trans-Pacific, Tokyo, described him as "a subtle progressive mind that will control China."

Who's Who in China, says, "He prepared some of the principal documents of the delegation to the Versailles Conference, including an important memorandum which set forth China's case for the abrogation of the treaties and notes connected with Japan's twenty-one demands. It was the ablest state paper which the Chinese delegation submitted to the Peace Conference."

Gustav Amann says, "He was a gentleman of the very best education, a clever writer with a politically brilliant training."

REFERENCES

As regards Chen's racial origin, a French writer who interviewed him (*La Revue Hebdomadaire*, Vol. XI, Nov., 1927, pp. 141–162) says, "His color is too dark, too warm; his lips too thick; and the trinity of mulatto, African and Spanish is too noticeable in him for him to be pure Chinese." Vincent Sheean says also, "He was of mixed race, part Chinese, part Negro. . . . He had chosen his wife from the Negro race and in his four charming children the Chinese strain seemed almost to have vanished."

Sheean, Vincent, *Personal History*, pp. 205–207. 1935.
Gunther, John, *Inside Asia*, pp. 259–260, 264, 269. 1939.
Amann, G., *Legacy of Sun Yat Sen*, pp. 127, 149. 1929.
Restarick, H. B., *Sun Yat Sen*, pp. 144–145. 1931.
Who's Who in China, Vol. IV, p. 66. 1931 and later dates.
Who's Who in China contains the following sketch of Percy Chen, brilliant son of Eugene Chen:

"Journalist and business man; born at Trinidad, West Indies, 1901; eldest son of Eugene Chen, former Minister of Foreign Affairs of the Nationalist Government; studied law in England and was made a member of the Middle Temple; called to the English Bar at the age of 21 in 1922 and later practiced law for several years in Trinidad; returned to China in the fall of 1926; was appointed a member of the staff of the Foreign Office of the Nationalist Government and followed the Nationalist Armies to Hankow during their Northern Punitive Expedition; in 1927, he was commissioned by the Nationalist Government to conduct Borodin and other Russian advisors to their own country; he is now advisor to the General Motors Corporation in their negotiations with the Soviet Commissariat of Heavy Industry; he was invited to fill this position on account of his wide knowledge of conditions in the Soviet Union, where he studied the situation during the past six years; he is probably the first Chinese employed by a great foreign Corporation as its advisor in a foreign country; he is now also correspondent of the *Ta Kung Pao* at Tientsin; he believes that Sino-Soviet friendship should be one of the corner stones of Chinese political policy and is working to further that policy. . . ."

Ibn-Saud

KING OF SAUDI ARABIA AND LEADER OF ISLAM
(1880–1953)

IBN-SAUD WAS THE FOREMOST MAN in the Arab world of his time. An upstanding muscular figure, six feet four inches tall, he was as big mentally as he was physically. He was an able and very successful soldier; an astute diplomat who was more than a match for the British and the Germans; and a most generous, amiable, and good-natured ruler, who loved a good joke. No one throughout the length and breadth of the Moslem world had a finer reputation.

Success to Ibn-Saud came the hard way. While a child he was forced into exile with his father, Abd ur Rahman, who was driven from the throne by his rival, Ibn-Raschid, a satellite of the Turks.

At the age of seventeen Ibn-Saud decided to recover his father's throne and gathering the desert tribes attacked Raschid's capital, Riyadh, but without money to buy arms he was beaten again and again for the next three years. Finally in 1901, with only twenty followers, he captured the city by a ruse and made the governor prisoner.

This success brought the people flocking to him and in another brilliant coup he defeated Raschid at Artawiya in 1902 and proclaimed himself ruler. The Turks thereupon sent a powerful army to aid Raschid, but Ibn-Saud meeting them at Bukairiya in 1904 defeated them signally after a long and bloody battle. This marked the end of long centuries of Turkish domination of Arabia. Ibn-

Saud had accomplished what many generations of Arab rulers had attempted in vain.

In the First World War Ibn-Saud outsmarted the far-famed Lawrence of Arabia. The latter, in his attempts to overcome German and Turkish influence in Arabia, backed Husain, King of Hedjaz, a rival of Ibn-Saud, with British gold and guns, on which Husain set out to make himself master of all Arabia. But Ibn-Saud, meeting him at Turaba, defeated him and invaded his kingdom, crushing him and forcing him to abdicate. Later Ibn-Saud captured Mecca after a short siege and had himself crowned king in the famous temple there on January 15, 1926. Thus he became undisputed master of nearly all of Arabia, which is called Saudi Arabia in his honor.

Ibn-Saud also subdued the fierce Bedouins who since Bible days had been preying on caravans. He built motor routes, put the finances of his kingdom in order, established modern hospitals, and installed modern irrigation machinery. When his people oppressed modern improvements, preferring the old ways of biblical times, he used diplomacy to win them over. Beside an old hand pump he would install an electric pumping plant, a labor-saving device that promptly overcame all prejudices. When they opposed the radio, calling it an instrument of the devil, he had passages from the Koran broadcast through it. The people felt that surely the devil would not speak the Holy Scriptures and so accepted it. Ibn-Saud, however, did prohibit Western motion pictures, which he considered demoralizing.

Ibn-Saud was considered by all who met him to be the embodiment of the far-famed Arab hospitality. He established guest houses where strangers might stay free of charge. His people regarded him as a father. The humblest of them were free to bring their grievances to him.

A fluent speaker, he was the greatest champion of Islam of his time. H. C. Armstrong says of him, "An immense man, tremendous, vital, dominant, a giant thrown up out of the chaos and agony of the desert. . . . He is inspired by a driving Belief—the Belief that he has been entrusted by God with a mission to knit all Arabs into one People to lead them back to the greatness of their forefathers and make the word of God supreme." Kenneth

Williams says, "Is there a ruler in all the Orient today like Ibn Saud? . . . Certainly he has no parallel in the Islamic world . . . a successful soldier, an original reformer. The subjects of no land converse more freely, respect him more utterly, would follow him more devotedly. . . ."

REFERENCES

Rihani, A., *Maker of Modern Arabia.* 1928. (See p. 42 for picture of Negro bodyguard of Ibn-Saud.)
William, K., *Ibn Saud.* 1933.
Ikbal Ali Shah, *Controlling Minds of Asia.* 1937.
Crain, M., *Rulers of the World.* 1940.

ADDITIONAL REFERENCES

Armstrong, H. C., *Lord of Arabia, A Biography of Abdul Aziz Ibn-Saud.* Beirut, Lebanon, Kyayat's College Book Cooperative, 1967.

AFRICA

Commentary and Notes
on References

✃✃

THE LIVES OF ABRAHA, Emperor of Ethiopia (A.D. 350), and Abraha Al-Arsham, Emperor of Ethiopia and Yemen (A.D. 569), show the interrelation of Northeast Africa and the Middle East. Their lives also show the extensive influence of Africans during the formative development of both Christianity and Islam. These were the years before the Ethiopians isolated themselves behind their mountains and let the rest of the world move ahead of them. There is no shortage of literature on this subject; unfortunately, present-day scholars have not made the best use of this literature.

It is generally assumed that the dark-skinned Africans only had influence and ruled nations in the part of Africa that is south of the Sahara. This, of course, is not true. The life of Kafur the Magnificent is only one of the many cases that proves this point. At the time he became Lord of Egypt, Islam was still in ascendancy in influence and in the conquest of new territories. That combination of Africans collectively called "Moors" by the Europeans was still ruling Spain and there was no force in the world that could successfully challenge them. In the midst of this atmosphere Kafur the Magnificent, from a humble birth and circumstances, rose to power.

There is still some debate about who the Almoravids were, though honest scholars who have objectively examined the documents, old and new, relating to the eleventh-century rise of this African religious and military force do not believe there really should be any debate. The Almoravids rose up at a time when Islam, which had entered the Western Sudan in the eighth century, was having a revival in this part of Africa. The Almoravids were mainly black Africans. Yusuf ben Tachfin stood at the head of the emerging force. He became, and still is, one of the great heroes of Islam. His biography is a part of most of the major books on the history of North Africa.

The lives of Yakub Al-Mansur (1147-1199) and Abu Hassan Ali (d. 1350) show to what extent black African rulers were the masters of Morocco and Spain during the period when African power was supreme in the Mediterranean, and Europe had not begun to stir from the lethargy of the Middle Ages. Soon after the decline of these rulers the first rumblings of discontent, which would create the emotional basis for the Crusades, were being heard. This did not mean the end of African Mediterranean power —it would last intact for another 300 years. At the time the European slave trade was getting slowly under way along the west coast of Africa, two men—Sonni Ali, whose reign was from 1464 to 1492, and Askia the Great, whose reign was from 1493 to 1528—guided inner West Africa (referred to as the Western Sudan) to the apex of its last Age of Grandeur. Some historians consider these rulers the greatest African heads of state in the last 2000 years. Their lives have been the basis for a number of books. The German writer Heinrich Barth tells about their life and times in great detail in his three-volume work, *Travels and Discoveries in North and in Central Africa* (reprinted 1965). The most readable recent work on this subject is, *Great Rulers of the African Past* by Lavinia Dobler and William A. Brown (1965).

In the sixteenth century the Portuguese position in the slave trade was threatened by England, France, and some of the smaller European nations. This caused the Portuguese to move their slave-trading activities southward to the Congo and Southwest Africa. Their most stubborn and colorful opposition as they entered the final phase of the conquest of Angola came from a queen who was a great head of state and a military leader with few peers in her time. The following important facts about her life were extracted from a forthcoming book, *Queen Nzingha and the Mbundu Resistance to the Portuguese Slave Trade* by Professor Roy A. Glasgow of Bowie State College, Bowie, Maryland.

In the year 1583 one of the most extraordinary and romantic figures in African history was born. She is referred to as Jinga, or Ginga, but more often as Nzingha or Ann Zingha. She was the sister of the then-reigning King of Ndongo, Ngola Mbondi. His country was later called Angola. Nzingha was one of a long line of African women freedom fighters that dates back to the reign of Queen Hatshepsut in Egypt, 1500 years before the birth of Christ. She belonged to an ethnic group called the Jagas. The Jagas were an extremely militant group, particularly when they were led by their determined and capable Queen Nzingha. Together they formed a human shield against the Portuguese slave trade. Nzingha never accepted the Portuguese conquest of her country and was always on the military offensive. As part of her excellent strategy against the invaders, she formed an alliance with the Dutch, intending to use them to defeat the Portuguese slave trade. At her request, she was given the body of Dutch soldiers. The officer commanding this detachment in 1646 said this of her: "A cunning and prudent virago, so much addicted to arms that she hardly uses other exercises and withal so generously valiant that she never hurt a Portuguese after quarter was given and commanded all her servants and soldiers alike."

She believed that after defeating the Portuguese it would be easy to surprise the Dutch and expel them from her country. Consequently, she maintaied a good relationship with the Dutch and waited for the appropriate time to move against them. Her ambition extended beyond the task of freeing her country from European control. In addition to being Queen of Ndongo, she hoped to extend her domain from Matamba in the east to the Atlantic Ocean. To this end she was an astute agitator-propagandist who could easily summon large groups of her fellow countrymen to hear her. In convincing her people of the evil effects of the Portuguese, she would single out slaves and "slave soldiers" who were under Portuguese control and direct intensive political and patriotic messages in their direction, appealing to their pride in being Africans. She offered them land and freedom. This resulted in the desertion of thousands of these "slave soldiers" who joined her forces and presented a serious security problem for the Portuguese. Politically foresighted, competent, self-sacrificing, and devoted to the resistance movement, she attempted to draw many kings and heads of families to her cause in order that they might capture the allegiance of their people and recruit them for the defense of her revolution against the presence of the Portuguese.

Most of her life was involved in a war to keep the Portuguese out of what is now Angola. On December 17, 1663, this great African woman died. Her death marked the end of one epoch and the beginning of another.

Osei Tutu was the first great King of the Ashanti (or Asante) people. In fact, he opened the door to their modern history and helped to lay the basis for the political history of Ghana. His people and his reign have been a natural attraction for many writers. A recent book, *Ashanti under the Prempehs* by William Tordoff (1965), has some new information that has not previously appeared in book form. *A History of the Gold Coast and Asante* (by Carl Christian Reindorf, 1889; republished 1966 by Ghana University Press) is especially valuable in furnishing chronological charts and histories of the kings, royal houses, and various dynasites of the Gold Coast (now Ghana) up to 1865.

During the last years of the seventeenth century and the early years of the eighteenth century, Mulai Ismael was the African personality best known to the people of Europe. Knowing of his accomplishments—good and bad—they spoke his name with fear and reverence. He was the Sultan of Morocco for fifty-five years. During his long reign he defied Europe and kept his country free of its domination. He unified Morocco, gave it a strong and efficient administration and a permanent army. His biography is woven through the history of North Africa. The best short biography of Mulai Ismael can be found in the book *Realm of the Evening Star* by Eleanor Hoffmann (1965).

South Africa has furnished a more splendid array of outstanding kings and warriors than any other part of Africa. Chaka, the Zulu king and warlord, is the most famous, the most maligned, and the most misinterpreted of all South African resistance leaders, although some books published in the last few years have toned down the list of undeserved sins that European writers have been attributing to Chaka for over a hundred years. A different view of the life and times of Chaka can be found in two books by the black South African writer, Thomas Mofalo. These are: *Chaka: An Historical Romance* (1931) and *Chaka, the Zulu* (1949). A recent book, *Zulu Aftermath* by J. D. Omer-Cooper (1966), contains some up-to-date information on this very important South African personality.

When Chaka was assassinated in 1828 the great Basuto king, Moshesh (or Moshoeshal), was about thirty years old and his most trying days of trouble and glory were ahead of him. To the people of Basutoland (now Lesotho) he has a position of respect and endearment similar to that of George Washington in the United States. He was literally the father of their country. Moshesh is one of the few South African kings who is generally treated with respect by all writers. No attempt has been made to depict him as a bloodthirsty savage. He more than earned this respect. The most humane treatment of his life can be found in the books of Georgina Gollack, mainly *Sons of Africa* (1928). The best short biography of Moshesh is *Moshesh, the Man on the Mountain* by J. Grenfell Williams (1959).

After the banishment and death of Dingaan, successor to Chaka, the Zulu people lived through thirty-two years of misrule and decline. The colonies of the Zulus broke away and declared their autonomy. This was during the reign of the weakling puppet, Mpanda, who, like Dingaan, was a half-brother of Chaka. By 1870 the strong son of this weakling had usurped the power of his father and was leading the Zulus back to strength and glory. Mpanda's son was the nephew and disciple of Chaka. He deposed his father and became the greatest Zulu since Chaka. His name was Cetywayo. In the history of South Africa he commands almost as much attention as his famous uncle. The best new treatment of his life and wars is in the book *The Washing of the Spears* by Donald R. Morris (1965).

Among the outstanding personalities in the anticolonial uprisings in Northeast Africa, the Sudan in particular, none stands higher than Mohammed Ahmed, called the Mahdi. He was the most stubborn and troublesome of the so-called dervish warriors that the British encountered while building their East African empire. He defeated some of Britain's most able generals and became a legend in his own time. Books and papers on his life are abundant. Among older books about this warrior-nationalist, *The Mahdi of Allah* by Richard A. Bermann (1932) is particularly good. A comparatively recent book, *A Short History of the Sudan* (1965), written by one of his distant relatives, Mandour El Mahdi, is more up to date in its information.

Paul Belloni Du Chaillu represents a physical and intellectual blending of the African and the French. He was a Western-educated African who returned to Africa as an explorer. His writings and research papers helped to change many of the misconceptions relating to Africa and its people. Unfortunately, present-day scholars have shown very little interest in this man and his pioneering work.

Like Paul Belloni Du Chaillu, Tippoo Tib was an African who decided to explore Africa. There are no other similarities in the lives of these two men. They had different motivations and different objectives. Tippoo Tib was an adventurer and a tradesman. He crossed the path of the Europeans when they were attempting to colonize East and Central Africa, and he exposed the fact that their mission was far from being *Christian*. The standard work on this fascinating East African personality is the book *Tippoo Tib* by Dr. Heinrich Brode, published in 1907. Parts of this book were republished in 1966 by the East African Literature Bureau, with additional notes by W. H. Whitely.

Behanzin Hossu Bowelle—called "The King Shark"—was the last of the great kings of Dahomey. His opposition to French rule and his colorful supporting female army make him a fascinating personality to behold but not an easy one to write about. Most of the books about him are in French and strongly partial to the French colonial point of view. The few exceptions are *A Mission to Gelele, King of Dahome* (1864) by Richard F. Burton and *Dahomey, An Ancient West African Kingdom* (1938) by Melville J. Herskovits. There is no straightforward, easy-to-read literature on King Behanzin and his country, Dahomey.

The life of Samuel Adjai Crowther is a good example of an African's attempt to find a solution to the problem of the slave trade and the worst aspects of the colonial system. He thought there was a Christian solution and he devoted the greater part of his life to work in this field. In many ways he is one of the makers of modern Nigeria. Short biographies of this great African churchman have been published in a number of books. His fellow countryman, Dr. Kenneth O. Dike, has written a good short account of his life and work in the pamphlet *Origins of the Niger Mission 1841-1891* (1957).

Samory Touré, grandfather of Sékou Touré, President of the Republic of Guinea, was a thorn in the side of the French while they were attempting to consolidate their empire in West and equatorial Africa. He is a national hero of this country. There are still people alive who fought in his wars against the French. There is no full-length biography of Samory in English. The best short biographies of him can be found in the following books: *African Heroes and Heroines* by Carter G. Woodson (1939) and *Protest and Power in Black Africa* edited by Robert I. Rotberg and Ali A. Mazrui (1970).

Rabah Zobeir was a former slave trader who gave up this evil business and became a nationalist. He emerged in the Sudan when the Mahdi Wars for the liberation of this country were starting. In general, he stood in opposition to all the colonial powers in Africa. Though information about his life and campaigns against the Europeans is scattered throughout a large number of books, research papers, and monographs, there is no one book that treats his life in depth and detail.

The uniqueness of Morocco is that it has never been completely Arab, Berber, or what is referred to as "Black African." For well over a thousand years it has been a blend of all of these ethnic elements. The Africans from the south, on different occasions, have been slaves in and rulers of Morocco. Bu-Ahmed was a darkskinned African and the last of the many black rulers who held power over Morocco before the French established their rule. Information about the life and times of Bu-Ahmed can be found in the early chapters of the following books: *Morocco, Old Land, New Nation* by Mark I. Cohen and Lorna Hohn (1966) and *Morocco* by Nevill Barbour (1965).

After the defeat of the Matabeles and the death of Lobenguela in 1893, the rebellious Zulus brooded over their lost glory and remained comparatively peaceful until immediately after the Boer

War. The Zulus who lived in and around Natal resented the postwar taxes that had been imposed upon them. Two small groups within the Zulus—the Zondis, led by the young king, Bambaata, and the Cubes, led by the old king, Siganarda—refused to pay the taxes and rebelled against British authority. This was the last Zulu rebellion of any significance. The life stories of Bambaata, Siganarda, and Zinizulu, the Paramount King of the Zulus at the time of the rebellion, can be found in the following books: *History of the Zulu Rebellion* by J. Stuart (1906) *Natal Rebellion of 1906* by W. Basman (1913), and in a recent book, *Dinuzulu: The Death of the House of Shaka* by C. T. Binns (1968).

Menlik II was the last Ethiopian king to have won a military victory over a Western power. He was King of Ethiopia during the first Italian-Ethiopian War and he personally led the Ethiopian army in this encounter. The most up-to-date short biography of Menelik II is in the book *Leadership in Eastern Africa,* edited by Norman R. Bennett (1968).

During the tumultuous years of transition in South Africa following the death of Chaka, when the Basuto king, Moshesh, was struggling to make a nation out of the frightened and scattered groups of Africans who were trying to escape from the crossfires of conflicts between the Zulus, the Boers, and the English, a son was born to an undistinguished King of the Bamangwato people of Bechuanaland. This son was destined to become the savior of his people and nation. He was also a great South African Christian and one of the most highly regarded persons in South African history. His name was Khama. In the book *Khama, King of the Bamangwato* (1931) the British writer Julian Mackford proves to be his most faithful biographer. Other books on his life are: *Three Great African Chiefs* by Edwin Lloyd (1895) and *The Bechuanaland Protectorate* by A. Sillery (1952).

General Alfred A. Dodds helped to win and secure the French colonial empire, and during the last years of his life was forgotten by the French whom he had served so well. By America's racial standards he was a "Negro." By his own standards he was a loyal Frenchman, just and foremost. He never denied his African blood and he never flaunted it. His life was rich enough to have been the subject for a number of books, but so far none has appeared.

The best-known Ashanti king in this century was Kwaka Dua III, better known as King Prempeh. His rise and tragic decline marked the end of the Ashanti people's years of war and glory. Like his distant relative, Osei Tutu, his life related to the legend of the Golden Stool. He was unjustifiably exiled for a period of nearly thirty years. He lived through these years of insult to his royal pride and breeding and returned to Ghana, still an Ashanti king, made wiser by his ordeal. The books about his life and his troubles with the British are numerous. The two most informative recent books on his life are *A Political History of Ghana 1850-1928* by David Kimble (1963) and *Ashanti under the Prempeh 1888-1935* by William Tordoff (1965).

Hadj Thami El-Glaoui, the famous Pasha of Marrakesh in Morocco, died in January, 1956, after the settlement of his dispute with the King of Morocco, Mohammed V. The last phase of his rich and colorful life still bears on current events. He was the last of the powerful black rulers of southern Morocco. The first full-length biography of Glaoui, *Lords of the Atlas* by Gavin Maxwell, was published in 1966.

Isaac Wallace-Johnson was the father of the West African trade union movement. He was active in West African politics until his death a few years ago. He was one of the conveners of the fifth Pan-African Congress in Manchester, England, in 1945. Aside from a number of articles in more than a dozen magazines, there is no adequate biography of Isaac Wallace-Johnson.

Haile Salassie's greatest achievement is that he managed to hold the Empire of Ethiopia together during its most troubled years. He had to flee his country as the second Italian-Ethiopian War was ending and his ancient nation was facing one of the few defeats in its history. He returned to Ethiopia in the midst of World War II and has been the head of state since then. He is also the titular head of the church of Ethiopia. The guiding hand of Haile Selassie brought the ancient Empire of Ethiopia into the modern world. The best up-to-date history of Ethiopia and the reign of Haile Selassie is the book *Ethiopia: A Political History* by Richard Greenfield (1965).

J. H. C.

Abraha

EMPEROR OF ETHIOPIA WHOSE ADOPTION OF
CHRISTIANITY CHANGED THE FACE OF THE WORLD
(c. A.D. 350)

FEW MEN have had greater influence on world history than Abraha, Emperor of Ethiopia, even though he lived 1600 years ago. His decision to change the religion of his country from paganism to Christianity probably changed the fate of white Western civilization. But for this, Europe might now be Moslem instead of Christian. When Islam was sweeping through all North Africa and southern Asia, Ethiopia held firmly against it—for more than a thousand years Ethiopia was the Verdun, so to speak, of Christianity in the East. Had Islam been able to conquer her, it would have swept over all of East Africa and effected a junction with the Islamic powers in Central and West Africa, and the Christian powers, which were European and white, might not have been able to get a foothold in Africa at all. Furthermore, had there been no Ethiopian opposition, Islam in its invasion of Europe in the eighth century—it reached almost to the gates of Paris— would undoubtedly have been more powerful and might have been able to conquer all of Western Europe. In any case, had not Ethiopia been Christian, the conquest of Africa by the white Christian powers would have been enormously more difficult.

Abraha's conversion came as the result of an accident. In A.D. 330 a number of Phoenicians who were en route to India were shipwrecked off the coast of Ethiopia, among them the two young sons of the leader, Merobius. The Ethiopians, who were then at war with Rome, killed all save the two lads. These were presented to the king, Ameda, who took them into his household.

One of them, Frumentius, became tutor to Abraha, the crown prince, whom he won over to Christianity. After making other converts, Frumentius returned to Constantinople where he was received by the emperor, Constantine the Great, who was so impressed by his story that he aided him. St. Athanasius, head of the church, made him a bishop. Returning to Ethiopia with his aides, Frumentius established the church, with Abraha, who was now king, giving him full support. Abraha also adopted for his empire the name "Ethiopia" from the Bible. Previously his titles had been: "King of the Axumites, Homerites, and Sabaens; ruler of Raiden, Zeilah, Tigre, Belljas, Kaens, King of Kings; Son of the Invincible God, Mars." His sway extended from the Nile eastwards to the Red Sea, and from the southern borders of Egypt to Zeilah on the Indian Ocean.

One of Abraha's first steps was the erection of a magnificent temple which became a center for Christian pilgrimage until its destruction by the Mohammedans 1200 years later.

Having established Christianity in his own land, Abraha became eager for its dissemination through Arabia and especially Yemen, the traditional land of his forebears, one of whom had been the famed Queen of Sheba.

Yemen at that time included much of what is now the Hedjaz. Its inhabitants, who claimed descent from Ishmael, son of Abraham and the Egyptian slave woman Hagar, were of mixed black and white ancestry, and were pagans and fire worshippers. Their holy city was Mecca, where there was a splendid *kaaba*, or temple, which, it is said, was built by Abraham and Ishmael. The other inhabitants of Yemen were Jews who had migrated there after the destruction of Jerusalem by Titus in A.D. 70.

Invading Yemen with a large army, Abraha defeated the Arabians and captured Mecca after a two months' siege. In this conquest of southern Arabia he succeeded where Rome had failed. Having sown the seeds of Christianity there, Abraha returned to his capital, Axum, laden with plunder. The cause of his departure is unknown, but his planting of Christianity there was later to cause worldwide repercussions.

Associated with Abraha in the government was his brother

Eisebaha. L. J. Morie calls Abraha "the Clovis of Ethiopia, achieving less glory than Clovis but possessing more goodness and gentleness." "Chroniclers," he adds, "celebrate with high praise the grandeur and the virtues of the two beloved brothers who were always friends and equals without being rivals."

REFERENCES

Morie, L. J., *Histoire de l'Ethiopie*, 2 vols. Paris, 1904.
Budge, E. A. W., *History of Ethiopia*, 2 vols. London, 1928.

ADDITIONAL REFERENCES

Davidson, Basil, *A History of East and Central Africa*, p. 14. Garden City, N.Y., Doubleday and Company, Inc., 1969.
———, *The Lost Cities of Africa*, p. 218. Boston and Toronto, Little, Brown and Company, 1959.
Doresse, Jean, *Ethiopia*, trans. by Elsa Coult, pp. 32, 64, 84. New York, Frederick Ungar Publishing Company, 1959.
Greenfield, Richard, *Ethiopia*, p. 25. New York, Washington, and London, Frederick A. Praeger, 1965.
Huggins, Willis N., *An Introduction to African Civilizations*, p. 71. New York, Avon House, 1937.
Jones, A. H. M., and Monroe, Elizabeth, *A History of Ethiopia*, pp. 29, 30, 72. Oxford, Clarendon Press, 1955.

Abraha Al-Arsham

❧❧

EMPEROR OF YEMEN AND ETHIOPIA WHO
STARTED A THOUSAND YEARS' WORLD WAR
(d. A.D. 569)

TWO CENTURIES after Abraha's invasion of Arabia there occurred as a result of it another epoch in world history under another Ethiopian ruler of the same name.

This Abraha, who is styled emperor of Yemen and Ethiopia, started a war that lasted for more than a thousand years and raged across the Old World from France to Japan.

When Abraha came on the scene, the Jews, now the dominant power in Yemen, were persecuting the Christians, who had multiplied in number since the establishment of their faith in Yemen by the first Abraha.

The Jewish ruler, Dhu Nowas, had burnt the Christian church at Zhafar, desecrated the bones of St. Paul of Zhafar, the patron saint of the Yemenite Christians, by throwing them into the roadway, and had had put to death 20,000 Christian faithful by burning them alive in a cavern transformed into a furnace.

The despairing Christians sent a mission to Justinian, the Roman emperor at Constantinople, begging him to come to the rescue. Justinian, moved by the horrible recitals but remembering previous Roman defeats in Arabia, feared to risk another expedition. He therefore wrote to the Patriarch, or head of the Coptic Church at Alexandria, asking his advice. The latter suggested an appeal to St. Elesbaan, Emperor of Ethiopia.

Justinian accordingly sent his envoys to St. Elesbaan, who received the Romans in state. Mounted on a gold chariot with four wheels and scythes of gold, drawn by four elephants, the emperor received his visitors. On his nude and dusky torso glittered ornaments of pure gold and rare gems; his arms were ringed with heavy gold and jeweled bracelets; his head was swathed in a turban of fine linen fastened by a golden brooch; and in his hand he held a richly ornamented buckler and two spears.

St. Elesbaan promised to aid the Christians in Yemen. Assembling an army of 70,000 warriors, he put it in command of Abraha, his leading general, who had risen to that high post from slavery.

Crossing the Red Sea with a fleet of 150 ships, Abraha arrived off the coast of Yemen. Dhu Nowas awaited his landing with a large army. A great battle was fought on the beach, the account of which reads like Julius Caesar's landing on the coast of Britain. Abraha was victorious: 26,000 Jews were killed, and the triumphant Ethiopians captured Zhafar, taking among the prisoners Dhu Nowas' favorite wife. Dhu Nowas rallied his forces and gave battle again, but wounded in the hand and faced with total defeat, he threw himself from a cliff into the sea.

As master of Yemen, Abraha put to death all the ministers of the Jewish king, seized the wealth of the country, and rebuilt the church of Zhafar.

For some unknown reason Abraha aroused the displeasure of St. Elesbaan, who appointed a Christian Arab named Aryat to replace him as governor of Yemen. Abraha gathered an army and marched to attack Aryat. When the two forces met, Aryat challenged Abraha to single combat to avoid bloodshed and to preserve Ethiopian power in Yemen unimpaired.

Abraha accepted the challenge. The two met in a fierce duel. Abraha received a wide gash across the eyebrows. The flow of blood blinded him and he was forced to yield. Shortly afterward, however, a slave of Abraha's stabbed Aryat in the back, killing him, and Abraha again seized power. The slash across the forehead brought him the name of "Al-Arsham," or Scarface.

Under his rule Yemen prospered. His merchants traded with India, Ceylon, and Siam, and with Greece and other European countries. Being overzealous for the spread of Christianity, he built a splendid temple at Sanaa in order to attract the multitude of pilgrims who passed through his country to go to the temple at Mecca. The Roman emperor contributed the marble for Abraha's temple. Further to induce the pilgrims not to go to Mecca, he gave them special concessions.

The Arabians, construing this as an attack on their faith and their trade, protested, and one of them from Kanana, to show his contempt, deposited his excrement on the altar of Abraha's temple.

Abraha considered this an act of war and swore to demolish the temple at Mecca. With an army of 40,000 men, cavalry, and armored elephants, he marched against the city. Before he could reach it, however, disaster overtook him. Thousands of his men were killed by a sandstorm in the desert. Smallpox also broke out in his army. However, he did reach Mecca sufficiently strong to intimidate the defenders of the city and persuade them to open the gates of the city to him.

Mounted on his magnificent white elephant, "Mahmoud the Praiseworthy," with its trappings of silk and gold, Abraha went to receive the city's submission in person, but as the elephant was passing under the archway of the city's gates it stood still and nothing could induce it to budge. Perhaps it was ill or nervous. Arab writers say that it knelt there rather than pass.

At this, a roar of joy went up from the Arabians. They saw in it a sign from God that their sacred city should be preserved. Rushing at the Ethiopians, they attacked them with such frenzy that the elephants stampeded and soon the rout of the Ethiopians was complete. Abraha returned to Sanaa where he died of smallpox.

The refusal of Abraha's elephant to enter Mecca so struck the imagination of the Arabs that they have called the period "The Era of the Elephant" and place above it in importance only the birth of Mohammed, which it is regarded as having foreshadowed since both occurred the same year, A.D. 569.

According to Arabian historians, God himself attacked the forces of Abraha. They say that he sent thousands of little birds from the sea each with a stone on which was graven the name of an Ethiopian soldier to bombard the enemy; that Abraha rotted away and his limbs fell apart—all of which is, of course, a poetic rendering of the sandstorm and the plague of smallpox.

The event as related by Mohammed in the 105th chapter of the Koran:

> Do you not know how God treated the conductors of the
>   elephants?
> Did he not turn their own perfidy against them?
> He sent myriads of birds soaring over their heads
> Who threw down upon them stones graven with the
>   celestial vengeance,
> The infidels were cut down like corn by the reapers.

The Mohammedans later used Abraha's attack on their city as a justification not only for an attack on the Ethiopians in Yemen but also for their campaign against the Christians in Ethiopia and North Africa. Thirty-three years after the death of Abraha the Ethiopians were driven back across the Red Sea, and Christianity's brief day in Arabia was over.

Gibbon emphasizes the universal significance of Abraha's defeat in his *Decline and Fall of the Roman Empire,* thus: "If a Christian power had been maintained in Arabia, Mohamet must have been crushed in his cradle and Abyssinia would have prevented a revolution which has changed the civil and religious state of the world."

REFERENCES

St. Elesbaan, the Ethiopian emperor who sent Abraha to the rescue of the Yemenite Christians, was for centuries the patron saint of the Negro Catholics of Spain and Portugal, according to Abbé Gregoire.

Masudi, Arab historian (d. A.D. 956), says the Abyssinian invaders were "Negroes." *Prairies d'Or*, Vol. III, pp. 161, 173; see also Chap. 43. Barbier de Meynard, 1861.

In 1763 the ruler of Yemen was a Negro, according to Niebuhr, who saw him. His mother was a Negro slave who seized the throne on his behalf and had him proclaimed sultan with the title of El-Mahdi. His brothers, of whom he had twenty, Niebuhr says, "were as black as ebony, flat-nosed, and thick-lipped." (*Travels in Arabia*, p. 103. London, 1811.) For still other Ethiopian slave rulers see Kammerer, A., *La Mer Rouge*; *L'Abyssinie*, Vol. I, p. 162.

Nicholson, R. A., *Literary History of the Arabs*, pp. 26–29. Cambridge, 1910.

Syed, Ameer Ali, *Life and Teachings of Mohammed*. London, 1891.

Muir, William, *Life of Mohamet*. London, 1894.

Sale, G., *Al-Koran*, p. 501. London, 1784.

Harris, W. B., *Yemen*, pp. 317–321. Edinburgh, 1843.

Baring-Gould, *Lives of the Saints*, Vol. XII, pp. 659–668.

Kafur the Magnificent

❦

NO STORY ever told of hardships overcome, of the rise from the depths of degradation to the heights of power, excels, or perhaps even equals, that of Kafur Al-Ikshidi. The obstacles he overcame were so great that his triumphs make those of Cinderella sound commonplace.

First of all, he was black—"a deep shiny black"—and while blackness was not a major handicap in the East, in Kafur's case it was because he was also an alien with an alien religion and an alien tongue.

His very name, Kafur, was a product of scoffing and ridicule; it means "camphor" and is equivalent to the nickname of "Snowball" for a very black man.

He was also as fat and ugly as a walrus, and waddled around like one with splay feet and fallen arches. In his earlier days crowds of mocking youngsters followed him down the street.

Al-Muttanabi, greatest of Arab poets described him thus: "A Negro whose lip is half as large as himself, and whom they style the moon of darkness." In the same breath Al-Muttanabi calls him "a hippopotamus."

Furthermore, Kafur was not only a total stranger to the advanced culture of Egypt, but he was also illiterate.

Truly these were obstacles enough to block aspirations to even the most commonplace career, but there was yet another, and the worst of all: Kafur was a eunuch. Destined for the harem at an early age, his virility had been extirpated by the surgeon's knife.

But within Kafur there burned the eternal spirit of the chainless mind. He showed this when he was being driven in shame through the streets of Cairo for the first time chained to another slave. When the latter, hungry and tired, was passing a bakery and saw the tempting display of food, he said his greatest wish was to get work in that place and never have to feel hunger anymore. Kafur, equally hungry, said, "Nothing less than being master of this great city would ever satisfy me."

Sent for sale to the market, Kafur was bought by Ibn-Abbas, but the latter, pressed for money, soon sent him back to the slave block, where stripped, and as fat and pudgy as only eunuchs can be, his ugliness was the butt of the market wits. Prince Mejan, head of the sultan's household, was riding by with his brilliant entourage, and hearing the laughter, rode up to see the cause of it. At the sight of Kafur he too laughed. "By Allah," he said, "that Zeng [Negro] really takes the prize for ugliness."

But little did magnificent Prince Mejan know that he was laughing at his future master! A thought struck him—that ill-favored creature placed among the beauties of the harem would make a most diverting contrast. "How much?" he asked.

Ibn-Abbas, shrewdly appraising the handsomely garbed prince, demanded a hundred pieces of gold. The prince tossed him eighteen. Ibn-Abbas shrugged his shoulders at first but finally pocketed the coins, satisfied with what he felt was a good bargain.

Kafur's good nature and his ungainly appearance did much to relieve the boredom of the harem beauties and he became popular with them. As for the others in the palace, they considered him a nobody. Save one, and that was the sultan. One day when an elephant passed under the palace windows all the attendants rushed to look at it except Kafur, who preferred to remain with his master. Al-Ikshidi did not forget that. Nor did he overlook the fact that Kafur was spending his spare time in study.

But just when his future seemed most promising Kafur got an infection which caused his dismissal from the court and he sank lower and lower until he became a street beggar. This was the hardest period of his life. "In after life," says De Haas, "he never forgot that begging one day from a vendor of warm food he was rewarded with a blow that knocked him insensible. He recalled the incident, not in anger, but as the low water-mark of his experiences. Another incident of these beggar days that influenced him was that an astrologer prophesied that he would one day become master of Egypt and the adjacent lands."

When he was cured he again came to the sultan's notice, who restored him to favor until he became the second most powerful figure in Egypt, even though he had capable rivals in the palace, the principal ones being two fellow slaves, Fatik Al-Manjin, a Greek, who later became a king surnamed "the Great," and Yakub Ibn-Killis, a Mohammedanized Jew, who afterwards was King of Egypt.

Kafur's rise now surpassed the wildest dreams. As Baron Mac-Guckin de Slane says, "The poor Negro eunuch whose prominent belly, splay feet and perforated lower lip had furnished such subjects of laughter for his fellow slaves, had become the master of an empire." It is true that he was not yet on the throne, but as regent he was the virtual ruler, the new sultan, Abdul Amyr, still being a child.

Kafur planned to have the young sultan crowned at Cairo. While en route from Damascus with his charge he learned that Sauf Eddaulah, Emir of Aleppo, an old foe of the Ikshidis and one of the greatest warriors of the time, had revolted and seized Damascus.

It was then that Kafur displayed unsuspected military genius. Returning immediately with an army, he defeated the renowned Eddaulah and forced him to flee to Greece. Eddaulah returned with a powerful army which Kafur again defeated, killing Eddaulah. Then Kafur led a successful punitive expedition into Greece. There were other revolts to be quelled too, and when his former ruler, the King of Nubin, rebelled, Kafur marched into his country and routed his army.

Under Kafur's guidance Egypt became stronger than at any time since Cleopatra. Abdul Amyr, the young sultan, did not live long, and Ikshidi's second son, Ali, was named to succeed him with Kafur as regent. When Ali died, Kafur put the next heir aside and seized the throne in his own name.

In the meantime he had been ruling with such wisdom and

kindliness that his ugliness was quite forgotten. A patron of knowledge and art, he built libraries, schools, and parks, and for himself a magnificent palace. With handsome gifts and subsidies, he attracted writers, poets, astronomers, mathematicians, and philosophers to his court until for brilliance and learning it was second in the East only to that of the Caliph at Bagdad, his nominal overlord. Ibn-Khallikan (1211-1282), says in his famous *Biographical Dictionary,* "Kafur loved the society of learned and virtuous men, and treated them with marked honor."

According to *Biographie Universelle,* "Slavery and multilation, far from having degraded the soul of Kafur, caused rather to shine forth his genius. . . . This man, coming from the lowest depths of degradation, had all the virtues of a great king."

There was one, however, who could not forgive Kafur his once lowly position, and that was his former slave companion, Fatik Al-Manjin, the Greek. Before the coming of Kafur he had been the king's favorite. Rather than ride in Kafur's train after the death of Ikshidi, the haughty Greek returned to his native land. Years later Kafur had him in his power and could have taken his life, but his spirit was above revenge.

Kafur was quick to recognize merit and to advance those possessing it. Among those he rewarded was Yakub Ibn-Killis, the Jew already mentioned, whom he admitted into his privy council and who rose to such a position in Kafur's favor that all the chamberlains and nobles stood up when he entered the council chamber.

Kings, princes, nobles bowed before Kafur and took pains not to offend him. Ibn-Khallikan tells of a certain very wealthy noble named Tabataba who was in the habit of sending gifts of sweetmeats to his friends. Kafur was especially favored; to him he would dispatch two vases of the choicest delicacies every other day, together with a cake that was folded up in a napkin and carefully sealed.

An enemy of the nobleman wrote to Kafur telling him that while the gift of the sweetmeats was proper, the cake was intended as a thrust at Kafur's post. Hearing of this and fearing a plot to ruin him, Tabataba galloped to Kafur's palace to assure Kafur that the cake had been baked by his own daughter as a tribute of purely religious motive and not out of a feeling of superiority.

"If, however," continued the nobleman, "Your Majesty wishes it discontinued, I shall do so."

"By no means," replied Kafur. "From this time on, I shall eat no other." Calling his chamberlain, Kafur bade him fetch a magnificent necklace, which was sent off by a slave to Tabataba's daughter.

The most noted figure at Kafur's court was the celebrated poet Al-Muttanabi. Enticed by Kafur from the court of King Handan of Greece by rich presents and the promise of the government of Sidon, he was made poet laureate—a very necessary adjunct to rulership then. Poems of praise, after being recited at court, were taught to the people, and thus helped maintain the sovereign's popularity.

Muttanabi's verses in praise of Kafur are of such skill, beauty, and adroitness that they are among the most remarkable that have been produced in any land.

At court gatherings he would recite:

Whether I wish or not to praise Kafur, his noble qualities dictate to me and I must write. When a man leaves his family behind and visits Kafur, he finds himself at home again. [To be hospitable is a virtue of the highest order in the East.]

Praise bestowed on other men is falsehood mixed with truth, but that which thou receivest is pure from alloy. When I obtain proofs of thy friendship I despise wealth and look on all other men as dust. Were it not for thee, I had always been a traveler, every day changing towns and companions. For me thou art the world; to that world I am attached, and were I to leave thee, I would return. . . .

You out-rival the sun each time it rises by merely showing your face, shining and black. The skin is but a garment and the whiteness of a soul is worth more than that of a robe. Who, then, will aid the white kings to change their skins to the color and the appearance of Kafur, the great general?

But Muttanabi, like most professional flatterers, was a cynic. He despised Kafur for his blackness and for his humble origin, and Kafur was level-headed enough to see this. Muttanabi admitted this, once saying:

When I went into Kafur's presence with the intention of reciting verses, he always laughed on seeing me and smiling in my face, but he listened attentively when I said "Opinions might differ but not regarding thee. Thou art without a rival and a lion where other kings are mere wolves." Nay, in this comparison if the word "wolves" was not pointed out, and the reader took it for "flies," he would make no mistake.

This compliment is exceedingly clever. In Arabic the words "flies" and "wolves" look so much alike that a hurried reader may easily mistake one for the other.

Al-Muttanabi's hypocritical homage, however, reached its height in a passage wherein he describes Kafur's horses and Kafur's voyage to Egypt. He said, "They went to Kafur and neglected all other men; for he who seeks the sea despises the rivulets. They bore us to the dark pupil of the eye of the age and left behind them the white and its corners."

In this he alludes to Kafur's color, which he declares to be inseparable from his merit. To show the worthlessness of other men in comparison, and white men in particular, he likens them to the whites and the corners of the eye, in which the sense of sight does not exist. Kafur, on the other hand, he compares to the "dark pupil"—the center of vision.

Years passed but the government promised Muttanabi by Kafur was not forthcoming and Muttanabi grew weaker and weaker in his adulations and finally left the court. Still hopeful, he returned a year later, and when Kafur still showed no signs of keeping his promise, Muttanabi showed his true self at last. In verses that were as vitriolic as they were formerly honeyed he excoriated and ridiculed Kafur, taking care, however, to be safe out of Kafur's reach. He sang in this new vein:

Who could teach noble sentiments to this castrated Negro? his white masters or his ancestors who were hunted like beasts; or his ears bleeding under the hands of the coppersmiths; or the price set upon his head when none would give two oboles to purchase him?

But so it is! The best of the whites are incapable of honor or noble deed. How, then, can any be expected of a black eunuch?

A Negro whose lip is half as large as himself and whom they style the moon of darkness. When I praised that hippopotamus . . . it was not so much to praise him as to satirize the human race.

When Kafur was reproached for not having kept his word, he replied, "My good people, I saw the liberty he took in his verses and his haughty spirit. Would he who claimed the gift of prophecy after Mohamet not be capable of claiming a share in the empire with Kafur? This reflection alone should suffice."

Kafur died in A.D. 967 after a rule of twenty-two years. With him ended the Ikshidi dynasty.

He was buried in Lesser Karafa where, says Ibn-Khallikan, "His tomb is a well-known object." Khallikan adds, "Public prayers were offered up for him as a sovereign from all the pulpits of Mecca, Hedjaz, Egypt, and the cities of Syria, including Damascus, Aleppo, Antioch, Tarsus, and Al Mississa."

Kafur's rule is remembered to this day for its magnanimity, mildness, and justice. According to *Biographie Universelle:*

The following instance will throw some light on the nobility of his nature: A Greek [Fatik Al-Menjin], formerly his companion in slavery and his rival, whose talents and whose hatred had offended him, had left Kafur's court with much noise; but the care of his health had brought him back. Kafur could easily have rid himself of him, but he preferred to regain his friendship by kindness. What is more astonishing, he permitted, he even wished, that the praises of this old favorite of his master should be celebrated not only while alive but beyond the tomb by the famous poet, Al-Muttanabi.

It was wisdom of this sort that held the empire together. Kafur's death was followed by a great revolt not only in Egypt but throughout the whole Mohammedan empire.

Kafur is a significant figure in the East in that he was the forerunner of a long dynasty of slave kings, the Mamelukes, some of whom were black, and who ruled until defeated by Napoleon.

Al-Muttanabi's verses, whatever their spirit, helped greatly to perpetuate the memory of Kafur. Known as the *Kafur-iyat,* they are still extant.

REFERENCES

Kafur of Egypt must not be confused with Kafur of Bombay, India, another Negro who was also remarkable for the deep blackness of his skin and his skill as a commander. Kafur of Bombay, who was also a eunuch, was as handsome and shapely as Kafur of Egypt was squat and ugly. (See "Malik Ambar.")

Ibn Khallikan. *Biographical Dictionary*, trans. MacGuckin de Slane, Vol. II, p. 524 *et seq.* Paris, 1842.

Rapoport, *History of Egypt*, Vol. II, p. 369. London, 1904.

Blachère, *Un Poète Arabe: Al-Motanabbi*, pp. 189–216. Paris, 1935.

Haas, Jacob de, *History of Palestine*, pp. 168–170. 1934.

Encyclopedia of Islam (see "Kafur.")

Sacy, S. de, *Chrestomathie Arabe*, Vol. II, pp. 137–156. Paris, 1826.

ADDITIONAL REFERENCES

Brockelmann, Carl, *History of the Islamic Peoples*, trans. by Joel Carmichael and Moshe Perl Mann, pp. 154, 159. New York, Capricorn Books, 1960.

Du Bois, W. E. B., *The World and Africa*, pp. 187–188. New York, International Publishers, 1965.

Yusuf I

SULTAN OF AFRICA AND
CONQUEROR OF THE CHAMPIONS OF CHRISTENDOM
(c. 1080)

FOR RAPIDITY of rise from insignificance to the height of power, history affords no more striking example than the Almoravids, a Negro Mohammedan people, under their leader, Yusuf ben Tachfin.

In this respect they were not excelled even by the Macedonians under Alexander the Great. Originating in what became French West Africa, chiefly around Timbuctoo, Upper Senegal, the seat of many another great Negro civilization, these people traversed the vast distance into Morocco, made that the center of their empire, and then crossed into Europe where they became the foremost power in the eleventh century A.D.

F. Ossendowski says, "In the expanses of Senegal arose a powerful dynasty of sultans, the Almoravides, who struggled against Gau, subdued Morocco and Spain and by the sword of the magnificent Yusuf ibn Tashfin, left after them a proud memory in the form of Arab-Negro mulattoes."

These African blacks, with a vastly inferior force, broke the power of white Christendom and defeated its best commanders. Among those who fell under the fury of their onslaught was Rodrigo Díaz de Bivar, better known as the Cid, the most renowned white champion of the time, and the foremost character in Spanish literature.

216

The beginnings of the Almoravid Empire were far less auspicious than those of the Macedonian. An Almoravid, Yahya, returning as a pilgrim from Mecca with advanced ideas, founded a new religious sect. In less than half a century this sect had become the most powerful in Northwest Africa.

Their first commander was Abu Bekr, a conqueror of repute; his second in command was Yusuf ben Tachfin. Tall, handsome, dashing, of agreeable and fascinating manners, generous and with a reputation for valor, the swarthy Yusuf was the best beloved person in the empire. In the gratification of his personal ambitions, however, he was, like most great men, thoroughly unscrupulous.

Abu Bekr loved and trusted Yusuf. When he left on an expedition to distant Tunis, he placed Yusuf in command. The latter, however, soon started to supplant his chief by winning over the army with presents of money, expensive garments, horses, suits of armor, and Christian captives and slaves dressed in costly silk.

He next won Abu Bekr's favorite wife, Zeinab, a woman of remarkable intelligence, rare energy, and great beauty. Abu Bekr had captured her from another king and her wise counsel had aided greatly in his rise to power. On the other hand, it may have been Zeinab who won Yusuf, as she had long admired the handsome usurper. The marabouts, or chief priests, finding reasons why Yusuf should be proclaimed ruler, with Zeinab as queen, seated him on Abu Bekr's throne.

Yusuf's first step was to build a capital worthy of himself, with splendid homes, a magnificent palace, and beautiful gardens. To inspire the laborers, he himself worked as a hod-carrier. The city he built, Marrakesh, or Morocco City, is still the native capital of Morocco.

At last Abu Bekr, successful in his expedition against Tunis, started to return and dispatched envoys to Yusuf to notify him, but even the envoys were bought off, and Abu Bekr, realizing that all was lost, retired into the Sudan and died there fighting in 1088.

Yusuf continued his conquests until his empire stretched from Senegal in the south to the Atlantic on the west, and included Algeria and Tunis, an area larger than Western Europe.

At that time, across the waters of the Mediterranean in Spain ruled the original Moors, a people composed of all shades from time immemorial. Three centuries before, A.D. 711, under their leader Tarik they had crossed the Straits of Gibraltar, defeated the Goths, built the great fortress Gebel-Tarik, named in honor of their commander, and made themselves masters of Spain.

Their power increasing, they crossed the Pyrenees and conquered southern France, giving this backward region one of the finest cultures Europe has had. Draper says that while the Moorish kings of Spain were living in magnificent palaces the kings of England, France, and Germany had homes "little better than stables—chimneyless, windowless and with a hole in the roof for the smoke to escape."

In the tenth century the Christians of the peninsula, who were chiefly of North European descent, under their leader Charles Martel defeated the Moors with great loss at Tours in northern France and slowly pushed them back into Spain, where the Christian king, Alphonso VI, defeated them in successive battles and overran their territory as far as Tarifa in the extreme south. Spurring his horse into the sea, Alphonso had claimed the last tip of Spain for the Cross.

The Moors, who still held out in their cities to the east and west, now looked to Yusuf as the champion of Islam. Some of them, however, fearing that he would remain as ruler if he came, hesitated. But Motamid, the wise and brave ruler of Seville, said, "If it is the will of Allah that I should be deprived of my kingdom and become the slave of a foreigner, I would rather be a cameldriver in Africa than a swineherd in Seville."

This striking argument broke down all objections to Yusuf. To punish a Moslem captive the Christians would sometimes make him a swineherd, the deadliest of all insults.

Yusuf promptly accepted the overtures, promising to leave as soon as the Christians were beaten. He was nearly eighty years old at the time, but thanks to a life free from vice and indulgence, and an inherently robust constitution, he was vigorous in mind and body.

He crossed the straits with an army of 15,000 men who were armed chiefly with swords and poniards, and several thousands of whom were mounted on camels and horses. The pick of his army consisted of 6,000 Senegalese, jet black and of unmixed descent, who were mounted on white Arab chargers as fleet as the wind. Utterly fearless, and knowing every trick of warfare, these picked horsemen were considered invincible.

All the Moorish leaders, the kings of Seville, Granada, Badajoz, and Almeria, came to welcome Yusuf, giving him presents so rich that his desert warriors reared amid warfare and self-denial marveled.

Yusuf, in his turn, held a review of his troops which greatly astonished the Moors. "Now," said Yusuf to his delighted hosts, "lead us to the enemies of our faith."

The Moorish kings, who had been able to raise only 10,000 men, put themselves under Yusuf's command. All marched northward in search of the Christians.

Alphonso VI, going north, rallied 70,000 Christians to his banner, among whom were thousands of French knights, the flower of Christendom, glittering from head to foot in splendid armor, attracted by plunder and the desire to uphold their faith.

The two armies faced each other at Zalacca, in October, 1086. Victory seemed certain for the Christians. Not only did they outnumber the Moors and the Almoravids three to one; not only were they better and more heavily armed, but they were more united. Almost every Christian warrior was a tried veteran who had taken part in many a bloody fray. Alphonso, who had beaten the Moslems in almost every encounter, felt certain of victory.

"The advantage," says Clarke, "seemed to lie with the Christians who were nearly three times as numerous. Moreover, a large part of Yusuf's army was made up of Andalusians [Spanish Moors]—men who were accustomed to be worsted in almost every encounter with the hardier Christians."

Everything seemed against Yusuf. While the Christians were united under a single leader and by a common cause, the Moorish kings were not only jealous of him, but of each other and were quarreling for precedence even in the face of the enemy. The formidable hosts of the Christians for a time disconcerted Yusuf too, and made him long for the legions he had left behind in

Morocco. "I never dreamed," he said, "that the pigs were so strong."

He had no other alternative, however, but to show a bold front. Sending a messenger to Alphonso, he audaciously offered him the choice of conversion to Islam; of paying tribute; or the sword. Alphonso retorted with biting courtesy. "Islam has always paid tribute to me." Yusuf replied, "What will happen, you'll see."

Negotiations having failed, the next procedure was to fix a day for the battle. Yusuf courteously offered Alphonso the first choice. Alphonso replied, "Tomorrow [Friday] is your holy day, the day after is that of the Jews, and Sunday is ours. We give you battle on Monday."

The following day Yusuf, accepting Alphonso's word, prepared to leave with his men for prayer. But Motamid, who had been fighting the Christians for years, was uneasy. "I fear," he said, "that the pigs mean to surprise us. If this battle is lost, all is lost. You go to pray. I will stay behind."

Yusuf went and Motamid's worst fears were realized.

Soon after Yusuf left there was a movement in the Christian camp, and Alphonso's forces came charging down on him. Rallying his men, Motamid hurried off a messenger to Yusuf, and resisted valiantly despite the desertion of a large number of his men, who, accustomed to defeat by the Christians, fled at the first onslaught. Motamid, greatly outnumbered, fought courageously. Three horses were killed under him. Bleeding from several wounds, he fought valiantly, expecting succor from Yusuf at any moment.

Yusuf came not! Had he deserted to the enemy? But when all seemed lost, a body of Yusuf's men arrived and helped stem the Christian tide.

Where was Yusuf? On hearing of the Chrisitan treachery, he decided to beat them at their game. Stealing behind the mountains, he crept upon the rear of their camp, and descending on the guards, killed them before they could give the warning, and set the Christian tents ablaze.

Alphonso was now in an awful position. Attacked in front and rear, his men were crowded into such a narrow space that their very numbers were a disadvantage. The horses, frightened by the camels and the flames, became ungovernable and plunged, unseating their riders and throwing further disorder into the ranks. Those Christians who could extricate themselves fought with valor, taking and retaking the Moslem positions only to lose them again.

Throughout all the day the battle raged savagely. The Moorish soldiers who had fled at the first Christian attack, returned, giving fresh ardor to the combat. Night was coming. Yusuf, who in spite of his seventy-nine years, had been everywhere in the thickest of the fight, felt with the instinct of the born general that the decisive moment had come. Three thousand of his invincible black horsemen on their white chargers had been kept fresh in reserve. Now he unleashed them. With blood-curdling yells, they swept down on the Christians, passing through their ranks with fearful carnage. The white hosts, panic-stricken, wavered, broke, and fled. The rout became a massacre. Alfonso, stabbed in the thigh by a black horseman, ran away with 150 of his men.

Night alone saved the Christians from annihilation. Some 35,000 of them, or half of their force, were killed, wounded, or captured. It is said that it was not the darkness but the eagerness for loot that alone saved the Christian survivors and prevented Alphonso's capture.

The call to prayer next morning was made from a tower built of thousands of heads of the Christians who had been slain. The wealth that fell to the victors was enormous. True to his promise, Yusuf returned soon afterward to Africa.

The Christian power, however, had not been crushed. Soon after Yusuf's departure, Alphonso rallied and defeated the Moors repeatedly. Another and more formidable foe had risen in the person of the Cid, a guerrilla chief and the greatest figure of Christian Spain.

Again an appeal was sent to Yusuf. This time he feigned refusal for three years. When he returned, he meant to make himself master of Spain; therefore, he wanted the Moorish population to appreciate his worth to the full. At last, Motamid himself came to Marrakesh to plead with him.

Yusuf replied, "Motamid, you had but to send me a letter written in your own hand and I would have come."

Yusuf returned and was again victorious. The Cid alone held out. But he too finally fell at Cuenca. Five years after his second campaign, Yusuf was master of all but a small portion of the peninsula.

In the interim he had been winning the hearts of the Moorish people. Several of the Andalusian kings too, deciding that they would rather have him as their overlord than Alphonso, began to plot in his favor, among them being Moutassim, King of Merida.

Most of the cultured Andalusians considered the Almoravids crude and vulgar and wished them away. They ridiculed the illiterate Yusuf who could not express himself in fluent Arabic. One day Motamid, who was now very eager that Yusuf should leave, exclaimed impatiently in Moutassim's presence, "These people in their country lived miserably, having scarcely anything to eat. We brought them here to keep them from starving. Now that they are full, just see them!"

Moutassim reported at once to Yusuf, who made Motamid a prisoner and sent him into exile.

To his counsellors, Yusuf said, "To deliver the Peninsula from the Christians is our only goal. But when I see the soft, effeminate ways of the Moslem princes, their lack of ardor for war, their internal dissensions, their love of ease, with no desire save to drink, to listen to songs and to pass the time in amusement, I am determined to stay until every Christian pig has been taken."

One after the other Yusuf absorbed the Moorish kingdoms—Granada, Malaga, Cordova, Carmona. From Abdullah, King of Granada, he took an immense treasure, consisting of heaps of precious stones, tapestry, the finest silk hangings, gold and silver plate, weapons of marvelous workmanship, bracelets and a string of 400 pearls, each pearl being valued at 100 pieces of gold.

In all these regions he abolished exorbitant taxes, placing them instead on those Jews and Christians who refused to accept Islam. The cost of living, which had been high before, became cheap. The people rejoiced and every Friday Yusuf's name was proclaimed from tens of thousands of mosques throughout his empire. Thirteen kings in Europe and Africa acknowledged him as their overlord.

He befriended science, encouraged learning, and did his best to restrain the fanaticism and bigotry of his priests. When war was on he waged it fiercely, but in times of peace he was merciful and refused to sign the death warrant of even an enemy.

Thus the Sultan of Africa, as he is sometimes called, died in 1108, at the age of 101, enjoying to the last the full of his facilities.

REFERENCES

The *Roudh el Kartas*, a Moorish work of 1326, gives the following description of Yusuf: "Brown color; middle height; thin, little beard; soft voice; black eyes; straight nose; lock of Mohammed falling on the top of his ear; eye-brows joined; wooly hair." (Trans. by A. Beaumier, *Histoire du Maghreb*, p. 190.) He was a member of the Masufah tribe, which lived on the northern border of the Sudan in what is now French West Africa.

Yusuf's empire, like Alexander's, did not long survive his death. He was succeeded by his frizzly-haired son Ali, whose mother was a beautiful white captive called Fadhel-Hassen (Perfection of Beauty). To Ali he left 7,500,000 pounds of silver, 125,000 pounds of gold, and a great quantity of jewels.

Ali soon afterwards defeated Alphonso in battle. Among the slain was Alphonso's favorite son, Sancho, by a Moorish wife. The loss of this son broke the aged king's heart and hastened his death. But as the years passed, the Almoravids, under new leaders, were defeated by the Christians, until the rise of another and more brilliant African people, the Almohads, who also made themselves masters of Spain.

The *Encyclopaedia Britannica* says, "The Almoravides were Berbers and largely mingled with pure Negroes." To this must be added the fact that the Berbers in Morocco, the Sahara, and all that region are themselves largely mixed with Negroes and are, on the whole, a mulatto people, race-mixing having gone on uninterruptedly between white and black in this region from the earliest times. What Donnet says of the Zanara Berbers is perhaps true, and has always been true, of all the Berbers who are living or have lived in this region, namely, "Their frequent alliances with Negro women have, particularly in the South, changed the color of their skins. A good many mulattoes and others are quite black without their exhibiting any of the physical characteristics of the pure Negroes."

The leaders of the Almoravids were the Lamtuna, or Veiled Horsemen, now known as the Touaregs. After centuries of intermixture the type became fixed, being neither Caucasian nor purely Negro.

Beaumier, A., *Histoire de Maghreb*, pp. 190–224. Paris, 1860.

Huart, *Histoires des Arabes*, 2 vols. Paris, 1912–13.

Clarke, H. B., *The Cid*. New York. 1897.

Ibn Khaldun, *Histoire des Berbères*, trans. by M. de Slane. Paris, 1925–34.

Bovill, E. W., *Caravans of the Old Sahara*. London, 1933.

Makkari, *History of the Mohammedan Dynasties in Spain*, trans. by Pascual de Gayangos, 2 vols. London, 1943.

Delafosse, M., *Haut—Senegal, Niger*, 2 vols. Paris, 1912.

Dozy, R., *Spanish Islam*, trans. by F. G. Stokes. London, 1913.

Ossendowski, F., *Slaves of the Sun*, pp. 44–45. 1928.

ADDITIONAL REFERENCES

Bovill, E. W., *The Golden Trade of the Moors*, pp. 75–78, 80, 84. London and New York, Oxford University Press, 1970.

Brockelmann, Carl, *History of the Islamic Peoples*, trans. by Joel Carmichael and Moshe Perl Mann, pp. 203, 205. New York, Capricorn Books, 1960.

De Graft-Johnson, J. C., *African Glory*, pp. 87–88. New York, Walker and Company, 1954.

Du Bois, W. E. B., *The World and Africa*, p. 205. New York, International Publishers, 1965.

Yakub Al-Mansur

※C※

GREATEST OF THE MOORISH RULERS OF SPAIN
(1149–1199)

YAKUB IBN YUSUF, better known as Al-Mansur, was the ablest and most powerful of the Moorish rulers who dominated Spain for 500 years. He was also one of the most enlightened, most just and magnanimous. His surname, Al-Mansur, means "The Invincible." This was no braggadocio. He defeated all his enemies and never lost a battle.

Like nearly all the rulers of Morocco he had a Negro strain. Not only was his father Yusuf of Negro ancestry, but his mother was an unmixed Negro woman, a slave, probably brought from Timbuctoo or Senegal. Ali Ibn-Abd Allah, celebrated Moorish historian, writing in 1326, says in his *Roudh el Kartas* (*History of the Rulers of Morocco*), "He was the son of a Negro woman who had been given to his father and he was born in the house of his grandfather, Abd el Mumen."

Mansur came to the throne when his father was killed while beseiging Santarém, Portugal, in 1184. He swore a great oath of revenge for his father's death but internal troubles with the Almoravids, the dynasty which his family, the Almohads, had ousted from the throne, detained him in Africa. At last having defeated the Almoravids and their allies, the Arabs, he gathered an army for the invasion of Spain and Portugal and in 1189, with 10,000 of his redoubtable cavalry and foot soldiers, he landed at

Algeciras, Spain. Marching on Santarém, the scene of his father's death, he destroyed it, and continuing to Lisbon, captured that city. Hearing that the Almoravids had taken advantage of his absence to rebel again, he returned to Africa laden with spoils and Christian captives, 3000 of whom were young women and children. At his coming, however, the leader of the rebels, Yahya, fled into the Sahara Desert.

The Christians of Spain, who were whites, mostly of Germanic descent, hearing of the new revolt in Africa, began an all-out attack on the Moorish kingdoms in Spain. Aided by the English Crusaders who were on their way to Palestine, they swept through Andalusia and other nearby regions, capturing Silves, Beja, Vera, and other towns. Mansur, on this, landed in Spain in 1191 and again defeated the Christians. Chaining them fifty by fifty, he took a great number of them to be sold into slavery in Africa.

On his return there, he was stricken with fever, and the Christians, thinking the time propitious, gathered an immense army, aided by the Crusaders, to drive the Moors out of the Peninsula once and for all. The three principal leaders were Alphonso IX, King of León, in supreme command; Alphonso III of Castile; and Sancho I of Portugal. The Christians, winning victory after victory, neared Algeciras on the Mediterranean.

Alphonso, feeling certain that Moorish rule was now at its end in Spain, sent a message of defiance to Mansur. "If it is too difficult for you to come to Spain," taunted Alphonso, "send me enough ships and I will come to Africa to beat you there."

Mansur sent back in hot haste, "We are coming to Spain! We are coming with an army that will teach you a lesson. We intend to chase you out of Spain, debased and humiliated."

Mansur sent his emissaries over his vast domains, which stretched from the Atlantic across the length of Africa to the borders of Egypt, to come to the succor of Islam. They came in vast numbers and were of all "races" and colors. In 1194 he sailed from Alcassar and landed at Algeciras, Spain.

Alphonso, with an army of 300,000, one of the vastest ever assembled up to that time, awaited him near the fortress of Alarcos on the plains of Zalacca, where in 1086, 108 years before, an Almoravid Negro ruler from Morocco, Yusuf ben Tachfin, had annihilated another immense Christian army under Alphonso VI. (See "Yusuf I, Sultan of Africa and Conqueror of the Champions of Christendom.") Mansur marched to Zalacca to meet Alphonso and lost no time in giving him battle.

Mansur, as did Yusuf before him, resorted to strategy. Feeling sure that Alphonso was going to direct his chief attack on that part of the Moorish army where the royal standards were (since that was where Mansur would be), he shifted another commander, his uncle, to that place and went off to another himself. He also placed a number of his men in a position to cut off the retreat of a possible Christian force coming toward the royal standards.

Alphonso did exactly what Mansur had suspected. Selecting 10,000 of the elite of his knights, he gave them the honor of drawing first blood and bringing Mansur a captive. Encased in their bright armor and mounted on mettlesome horses, lances set, they swept down on the Moors. But Mansur's men stood firm, and closing in on the Christian knights, hamstrung their horses and cut the riders to pieces. Alphonso gave the order for a general advance and his vast army swept down on the foe, the beat of his drums and the tramp of his men and horses shaking the ground like an earthquake. But again the Moors held their ground and fought back with incredible fury and fanaticism, shouting, "There is no other God but God and Mohammed is his Prophet! God alone is invincible!"

For hours the Christians tried to pierce their ranks in vain. They were pushed back and back until their retreat became an ignominious flight. Alphonso, wounded, fled to Toledo, while the surviving noblemen of his army took refuge in the fortress of Alarcos where Mansur besieged them and forced them to surrender.

The number of Christians slain was immense. The estimate varies. Some historians say 30,000; others as high as 146,000. Makkari, Arab historian, gives this latter figure. As for the spoils, he says that some authors say 158,000 tents; 80,000 horses; 100,000 mules; 400,000 asses; 60,000 suits of armor—"while the money and the jewels were beyond calculation." Mansur reserved 5 percent of the booty for himself and gave the rest to his men.

Going to Seville, Spain, Mansur made that his headquarters and

then swept northward capturing the principal Christian strongholds of Calatravas, Guadalajara, Madrid, Salamanca, and Toledo, where Alphonso and his family had taken refuge. Cutting off
all water and supplies from Toledo, he was about to destroy the
city when Alphonso's mother, wife, and children came to Mansur's lines to beg for mercy, tears in their eyes. Mansur, generous
always, not only granted their request but sent them back laden
with rich presents.

As for the 24,000 Christian prisoners he had captured at
Alarcos, he set them free also. Mansur declared on his death bed,
however, that this noble act had been one of the three mistakes of
his life, as the freed Christians had taken advantage of his kindness to keep up the fight against him.

With the greater part of Spain and Portugal in his power, he
yielded to the Christian pleas for a truce of ten years, and returning to Africa began to meditate on a project he had long in mind:
the invasion of Egypt. But before he could set his plans in motion
he died on March 20, 1199, at the age of fifty and in the fifteenth
year of his reign.

Mansur was not only a great organizer and a military genius but
a patron of the arts and a lover of justice. The chief virtue of a
king, he would say, was justice and a king who did not place it
first was like "a cloud that brings no rain." On coming to the
throne his first act was to distribute vast quantities of food to the
poor. "A rich man who does not practice charity," he said, "is like
a tree that bears no fruit." He also freed all who were unjustly
held in prison and reformed the laws to prevent others from being
so held. He gave larger salaries and pensions to the holy men and
began a vast public works program, rebuilding cities and erecting
mosques, schools, hospitals, and aqueducts. He built the city of
Rabat, now capital of Morocco; Alcassar, near Sallee; Mansura;
and other cities. He also built the famous Kasbah of Morocco as
well as the Giralda, one of the greatest monuments of Moorish
rule in Spain, at Seville. It was the impetus given by Mansur that
led to such immortal specimens of architecture as the Mosque at
Cordova, and the Alhambra and the Generalife at Granada.

Ali Ibn-Abd Allah, fourteenth-century historian, says of him,
"His reign was remarkable for the tranquility, the safety, the

abundance, and the prosperity that reigned everywhere. . . . His government was excellent; he increased the treasury; his power was exalted; his actions that of a most noble ruler; his religion was sincere and deep; and he was a great benefactor of Islam." *Biographie Universelle* says he was "the most magnificent and the most powerful of the Moslem rulers" since the caliphs of Bagdad. In fact, the great Saladin, Sultan of Egypt, Palestine, and Syria, appealed to him for aid against the Crusaders, whose alleged motive was to free "the tomb of Christ" from Islam.

Mansur was not only the most powerful ruler in the West—that is, of Africa, Europe, and eastern Asia—but in his time probably in the world. His kindgom stretched from the Atlantic along the Mediterranean to the borders of Egypt and included Mauretania, Morocco, Algeria, Tunis, Tripoli, the Balearic Islands, and most of Spain and Portugal.

One of Mansur's most noted sayings was, "Nothing exhales so sweet an odor as the dead body of an enemy, and especially a traitor."

Because of the great wealth he brought into Morocco and his patronage of the arts he is often called "The Golden." But to the common people, who adored him and repeated his sayings, he was known as "The Black Sultan."

REFERENCES

Sancho VII, the white King of Navarre, aspired to be Mansur's son-in-law. He came to Africa, hoping to marry his daughter, it seems on Mansur's promise. But the latter changed his mind.

At Mansur's court lived the famous Negro poet Al-Kanemi, who wrote of Mansur, "Well may his hajibs conceal him from my view; my reverence for him is such that I see his image on the curtain.

"My knowledge of his virtues prompts me to approach but fear and respect fix me to my place."

Mansur was succeeded by his son, Al-Nasser, who continued his conquests in northern Spain, but with Mansur's death not only did the Almohads decline but also Moorish power in Spain. Alphonso IX, after his defeat at Alarcos, had shaved his head and his beard, turned his cross upside down, and taken an oath not to approach a woman or ride a horse or other animal until the Moors were beaten. In 1212, thirteen years after Mansur's death, he had his revenge. Aided by the Crusaders, he decisively defeated the Moors at Las Navas de Tolosa, near Valencia, breaking their power and making possible their expulsion from Spain in 1609, four centuries later. In this battle, according to the Christian historians, the Africans had 180,000 dead while the Christians, as Alphonso said in his letter to Pope Innocent, had only 25 killed, thanks to divine intervention. (Power, G., *History of the Empire of the Mussulmans*, p. 211. 1815. Also *Biographie Universelle*, sketch of Alphonse IX.)

Mansur's chief architect was named Guever. There can be little doubt that some of the architects, astronomers, and scientists who created the marvelous Moorish civilization in Spain and rescued Europe from her Dark Ages were of Negro ancestry. In 1927 I saw Negroes of the blackest jet at work on the Mosque in Paris, laying the mosaic, etc.

The Moors of Spain were a very mixed people, white and black. Naturally, with so many of the Moorish rulers being wholly or partly of Negro ancestry, a dark skin was at no time a handicap. The Moors, like the Egyptians, drew most of their military strength from the more Negro part of Africa to the south and gave high rank to capable blacks. White women and black were intermingled in the harems of the emperors and the rich even as they are now.

Ali Ibn Abd Allah, *Roudh el Kartas*, trans. by A. de Beaumier, pp. 303–326. Paris. 1860.

Makkari, *Mohammedan Dynasties in Spain*, trans. by Pascual de Gayangos, Vol. I, pp. 31, 225, 327, Appendix iii; Vol. II, p. 319, Appendix lxii, lxv, cccxxi. London, 1843.

Ibn Khaldun, *Histoire des Berbères*, trans. by M. de Slane, pp. 205–216. Paris, 1927.

Chenier, *Recherches historiques sur les Maures*, Vol. III, pp. 275–280. 1787.

Conde, J., *Histoire des Arabes en Espagne*, Vol. II, pp. 430–446. 1825.

Luna, M. de, *Histoires des deux coquetes d'Espagne*, pp. 329–408. 1708. Personal details on the life of Mansur as told by Aben Susian, Moorish writer.

Diccionario Enciclopedia Hispano-Americano, 1887, see "Almanzor, Jacub Ben."

Biographie Universelle, see "Mansour."

Ibn Khallikan, *Biographical Dictionary*, trans. by Baron MacGuckin de Slane, Vol. IV, p. 323.

McCabe, Joseph, *The Splendour of Moorish Spain.* 1935.

There seem to be no portraits of the Moors. They were forbidden by their religion. But when shown in Christian coats-of-arms they were depicted as coal-black. (*Biblioteca de Escritores Aragoneses Aragon*, Seccion Historica 3, p. 110. 1878.)

ADDITIONAL REFERENCES

Brockelmann, Carl, *History of the Islamic Peoples*, trans. by Joel Carmichael and Moshe Perl Mann, p. 209. New York, Capricorn Books, 1960.

Abu Hassan Ali

"THE BLACK SULTAN" OF MOROCCO
(d. 1351)

ABU HASSAN ALI, "El Sultan Aswad" or "The Black Sultan," was the most famous of the Merinides rulers of Morocco.

He was renowned in the annals of the East for his ambition, courage, and the fortitude with which he bore his reverses, as well as for his patronage of art. Under him Moroccan art, architecture, and literature rose to the zenith of their splendor.

The Black Sultan came to the throne by ousting his brother. In 1330 he inflicted a crushing defeat upon the Christian King of Castile and captured Gibraltar. Ten years later he made himself master of the Mediterranean by destroying the Christian fleet commanded by the white admiral, Godfrey Tenorio.

Then began a long series of misfortunes. The kings of Castile and Portugal, allying themselves against him, defeated him. They took not only his treasures but also his wives. Driven from Europe, he returned to Africa, conquered Tunis and Algeria, and became so great a power in North Africa that the Mameluke sultans of Egypt looked to him as the protector of Western Islam.

While he was absent from Morocco, his subjects revolted under his son, Abu Fares, who seized the throne. With his army, the Black Sultan sailed from Tunis for Morocco, but a tempest in the Mediterranean wrecked his fleet. Thrown into the water with the dead tossing around him, he managed to save himself by clinging to a piece of wreckage, and finally drifted ashore near Algiers.

Undaunted, he gathered a large army and marched against his son. He was defeated but, not withstanding, he reached Fez and captured it. But he was unable to hold the city and was driven into the desert, where he assembled army after army, hurling them against his foes again and again, only to be beaten.

Stern, self-denying, and dynamic, the Black Sultan refused to yield to the pleasures that had softened so many of his predecessors, and was thus able to endure hardship and vicissitudes such as few monarchs have had to face. While at times he was subject to outbursts of extreme cruelty, he was nonetheless refined and possessed great nobility of spirit. His colleges, upon which he lavished all the beauties of Moroccan art, are monuments to his highly civilized taste and love of culture.

His favorite wife was a European named Shams-ed-Douha, or "The Morning Sun," and his tomb and hers, at Shella, are one of the architectural treasures of Morocco. Upon the eastern face of the Sultan's cenotaph is a wall of red stone carved with an inscription from the Koran with the exquisite ornament of the Alhambra —a page softened by the passing of time.

O'Connor says of him:

To the Sultan, Abu Hassan Ali, "The Black Sultan," are due the Merderseas of Es-Sahrij and El Mesbahiya (1331-48). He got his name like his dark skin from his mother, who was an Abyssinian Negress to whom in one of his inscriptions he paid a lofty tribute: "Her noble and saintly Highness! May God enlighten her tomb and sanctify her soul!" His reign following that of his father, Abu Said, who was unable to make wars of conquest in Spain, had turned to the maintenance of his power in Africa and had built three of the Merinide Merderseas, marked the height of the civilization associated with their name. Abu Hassan was man of many parts; he inscribed a copy of the Koran with his own hand and had it richly bound in leather and gold and sent to Mecca to be placed in the Mosque. He likewise sent copies to Medina and Jerusalem. He sought by the foundation of the Merderseas to strike the imagination of the Moslems of his capital and to show them what he could accomplish. He appealed to the civic pride of the East and conciliated the learned who at Fez have always been influential. His power and glory reached their height at the date of the foundation of the Mesbahiya for he subdued Central

Morocco and had made himself the most powerful sovereign in Western Islam. He sent rich gifts and entertained equal relations with the sultans of the east end of Africa. He married a daughter of the king of Tunis and upon the death of her father annexed his dominions to Morocco.

He died June 21, 1357, after a reign of twenty-one years.

The Black Sultan's son, Abu Fares, later grieved for his disloyalty and in remorse erected the Bu Ananija, a temple of learning, and left an endowment for its perpetual preservation. This edifice is still one of the most artistic and most sacred in Morocco.

REFERENCES

De Chenier, *Histoire du Maroc*, Vol. II, pp. 215–216, 278. Paris, 1788.
O'Connor, V. C., *A Vision of Morocco*, pp. 99–100. London, 1923.
Biographie Universell, see "Abou'l Hacan Ali."

ADDITIONAL REFERENCES

Boahen, Adu, *Topics in West African History*, p. 18. London, Longmans, Green and Company, Ltd., 1966.
Bovill, E. W., *The Golden Trade of the Moors*, pp. 91–92. London and New York, Oxford University Press, 1970.
Brockelmann, Carl, *History of the Islamic Peoples*, trans. by Joel Carmichael and Moshe Perl Mann, pp. 207, 214, 215. New York, Capricorn Books, 1960.
Huggins, Willis N., *An Introduction to African Civilization*, p. 107. New York, Avon House, 1937.
Trimingham, J. Spencer, *A History of Islam in West Africa*, pp. 70, 81. London, Oxford University Press, 1970.

Sonni Ali

FOUNDER OF THE EMPIRE OF TIMBUCTOO
(d. 1493)

OF THE SEVERAL NEGRO KINGDOMS that rose in West Africa between the eleventh and sixteenth centuries, the most notable was the Songhay, or Songhoi. This empire occupied the rich tract of land within the buckle of the majestic river Niger, whither centuries before its people had fled to escape the Mohammedan invasions from the northeast. At the height of its power it had expanded to stretch from the Atlantic Ocean across the vast width of Central Africa almost to the borders of the Anglo-Egyptian Sudan. In power and wealth it was the equal to any European country of that time.

Songhay had several flourishing cities, the principal being Jenny, which was strongly fortified and was one of the great commercial centers of Islam. Caravans came to it from all parts of the East, and Ibn Batuta, the celebrated traveler who visited it, tells of its grain, gold, cloth, cattle, salt markets, and of its vast wealth.

"It is very prosperous," he comments. "God has accorded all His favors to this city as a thing natural and innate. Everyone finds great profit in going to Jenny and in the acquisition of fortunes of which God alone can tell the sum."

Similarly, Félix Dubois says:

This accomplishment brings the greatest honor to the Negro race, and merits from this point of view all our attention. In the 16th century the Songhay land awoke. A marvellous growth of civilization mounted there in the heart of the Black Continent. And this civilization was not imposed by circumstances, nor by an invader, as is often the case even in our day. It was desired, called forth, introduced and propagated by a man of the Negro race.

This man was Sonni Ali, whose fame as a conqueror was outstanding in his time. Sonni Ali, whose real name was Ali Kolon, began as a common soldier in the army of Kankan Musa, Mandingo ruler of the Mellestine empire, into which, he had been impressed after the defeat and subjugation of his people, the Songhays, by Kankan Musa.

Forced even to fight his own people, Sonni Ali was overcome with rage at the cruelties of the Mellestine emperor and swore that one day he would take up arms to free them. As for the empire of Kankan Musa, it exceeded in wealth and magnificence anything he had ever imagined, and yet, common soldier that he was, he dared to feel that some day it should be his.

Kankan Musa, on a pilgrimage to Mecca, had displayed a lavish splendor never seen before in the African east. In addition to his foot soldiers, he had an escort of 60,000 mounted men. Preceding him were 500 slaves, each bearing a wand of gold weighing six pounds. Describing this pilgrimage, Houdas says:

In their annals the people of the East have told of the pilgrimage of this African monarch; they wondered at the power of his empire but did not speak of him as being good-hearted or generous. In spite of the vastness of his empire, he gave to the holy cities, Mecca and Medina, but 20,000 pieces of gold while Askia El-Hadj Mohammed [a later Songhay emperor] consecrated 100,000 pieces of gold to the same purpose.

Sonni Ali, together with his brother Selmar Nar, laid careful plans for escape. They carefully charted all the roads that led to Jenny, and whenever Kankan Musa went on expeditions they stole away and hid supplies of food, water, and arms along the way. Finally, after an exciting chase by the guards, they managed to escape.

Rallying his people around him, Sonni attacked Jenny, capturing it by storm on January 30, 1468. Impetuously, he took city after city until the forces of Kankan Musa had been driven entirely out of Songhay territory.

Then he directed his onslaughts against Kankan's vassals and did not rest until they were decimated. The Humburi, the Mossi, the Teska, the Ghana, the Bara, all came to acknowledge him as their lord.

Next he struck at Senhadja Nounon, where he captured the Negro queen, Bikoum Kabi. The Housas, the Senhadata, the Fulbes, the Dias, and the Peuhls capitulated, and marching to Lake Debo, he destroyed the strongly fortified city of Chiddo. After these victories the empire and the power of Kankan Musa collapsed.

Master of all the territory from Timbuctoo to the blue waters of the Atlantic, Sonni Ali now turned his attention to the affairs of his new empire. For a long time he had been galled at having to pay homage to the head of the Mohammedan religion at Mecca, the priests and learned men of which were influencing the people over his head. He wanted to be absolute master in his home, and decided to strike at the Church through its own representatives. He began by ordering their religious rites to be observed in a manner that bordered on derision. Instead of having prayers said five times a day as the Koran ruled, he postponed all the exercises until the evening, when instead of an elaborate ceremony, he made five brief gestures, saying after each, respectively, "This is the morning prayer; this is the midday prayer," and so on to the fifth, concluding with, "Now you may all go home since you know your prayers by heart." Thus a ritual that once took hours was reduced to a minute or two.

The priests, the learned men, and all who made a living by religion, including the faculty of the University of Sankore, plotted against Sonni Ali, whereupon he put to death every one of his enemies within reach, and warned others to cease meddling in political affairs. Es-Saadi, Songhay historian, dwells in detail on this period. In a measure, his enemies secured revenge, for the names they invented for Sonni Ali—"The Celebrated Infidel," "The Horrible Tyrant," "The Great Oppressor"—stuck.

Es-Saadi, one of the savants, wrote:

The master-tyrant, this celebrated scoundrel, Sonni Ali, whose name is spelt with an "o" after the "s" and an "i" after two "n's" was endowed with great military skill and inexhaustible energy. Wicked, libertine, unjust, oppressive man of blood, he persecuted the learned and pious personages and put so many of them to death that God only knows the number thereof.

Those learned men and priests who kept out of politics, however, were kindly treated and given land and money. After his death, El-Mamoun, the chief judge, said, "I speak only good of Sonni Ali. He treated me well."

Sonni Ali's temper was cyclonic. At times he would send to death even his most faithful followers, and then wish they were alive. His intimates, knowing this, would sometimes stay the execution and plead for the condemned when Sonni Ali had calmed down. One of these unfortunates was his favorite secretary, El-Kadr, who had brought Sonni Ali's wrath down upon him because of a slight contradiction. Later when a book arrived from a vassal king which no one at the court could read, Sonni Ali sighed for El-Kadr, who was then brought in alive. Overjoyed, Sonni Ali handsomely rewarded those who had saved him.

Another who escaped death this way was his favorite general, Abu Bekr, who succeeded him as Askia the Great.

After Sonni Ali had put down the priests, his insatiable desire for conquest and plunder led him again to the battlefield. Starting out, he conquered the territory eastward as far as the country of the Gomas, several hundred miles distant. Returning home, his booty-laden horse slipped and he fell into Koni River, was swept over the falls, and drowned. This was November 6, 1493. To preserve his body until Timbuctoo was reached, his son removed the intestines and placed it in honey.

Of Sonni Ali, Félix Dubois says:

He was a soldier only, and a true Negro soldier who marches from conquest to conquest, absorbing all the population by war without thinking to organize and create a durable work. He is a plunderer, most occupied with booty and prisoners than the tributes to be had. His lance travels from east to west, tracing the grandeur of the Songhay, unknown to him, it is true. But the task is being prepared for an organizer that is to come rapidly to lead the Songhays to the heights of splendor, power, and prosperity.

REFERENCES

For Bibliography see "Askia the Great, Builder of the Empire of Timbuctoo."

ADDITIONAL REFERENCES

Boahen, Adu, *Topics in West African History*, pp. 24–26. London, Longmans, Green and Company, Ltd., 1966.

Chu, Daniel, and Skinner, Elliott, *A Glorious Age in Africa*, pp. 87, 89–98, 100–103, 116. Garden City, N.Y., Zenith: Doubleday, 1965.

Davidson, Basil, *A History of West Africa*, pp. 69, 74,, 120–123, 184–191. Garden City, N.Y., Doubleday, 1965.

Du Bois, W. E. B., *The World and Africa*, p. 211. New York, International Publishers, 1965.

Fage, J. D., *A History of West Africa*, pp. 26–27, 38, 41. Cambridge, Cambridge University Press, 1969.

Flint, John E., *Nigeria and Ghana*, p. 52. Englewood Cliffs, N.J., Prentice-Hall, 1966.

Gailey, Harry A., *History of Africa*, pp. 70–71, 76. New York, Holt, Rinehart and Winston, Inc., 1970.

Hargreaves, John D., *West Africa: The Former French States*, pp. 23–24. Englewood Cliffs, N.J., Prentice-Hall, 1967.

Levtzion, Nehemiah, "The Long March of Islam in the Western Sudan," in *The Middle Age of African History*, Roland Oliver, ed., p. 16. London, Oxford University Press, 1967.

Shinnie, Margaret, *Ancient African Kingdom*, pp. 74, 76. New York and Toronto, New American Library, 1965.

Askia the Great

BUILDER OF THE EMPIRE OF TIMBUCTOO
(d. 1538)

SONNI ALI WAS SUCCEEDED by his son, Abu Kebr, but one far worthier than he felt entitled to the throne. This was Mohammed ben Abu Bekr, the favorite general of Sonni Ali. Claiming that the power was his by right of achievement, Mohammed attacked the new ruler a year later and defeated him at Anghoke in one of the bloodiest battles of history. Of the 150,000 men engaged on both sides, the majority were reported to have been killed or wounded.

Mohammed seized the throne, calling himself "The Prince of Believers" and "Caliph of the Mussulmans." But when one of the daughters of Sonni Ali heard the news, she cried out, "Askia" (Usurper) at which Mohammed in irony took "Askia" as his name.

Askia began by consolidating his vast empire and establishing harmony among the conflicting religious and political elements. For this task he was well fitted, as he had "a good heart, well-inspired, and was endowed with a generosity that God had placed naturally in him."

This praise came from the holy men. Instead of suppressing these as Sonni Ali had done, he took them under his wing, which further inspired them to denounce Sonni Ali as an infidel whose offspring was unfit for the throne. Nevertheless, Askia took adroit steps to keep the priests from meddling in the government.

To create a still closer union within the empire, he took wives from the daughters of his vassal chiefs, marrying his daughters and relatives to his subject chiefs in turn. He followed the same procedure in the case of high dignitaries, governors, and judges, until most of the prominent families of the empire were in some way related to him. The empire he divided into four parts, placing a viceroy over each.

To increase commerce he created a regular army with a reserve unit, which left the rest of the population free to trade and carry on agriculture during the time of war. To police the empire, he formed an army of cavalry which was equipped with lances, poisoned arrows, armor, and steel helmets. Some of these men came from as far north as the Barbary states. These cavalrymen were so many in number and rode so swiftly that it was said of them, "They flew off like a cloud of grasshoppers."

Along the mighty Niger River and its tributaries Askia had harbors constructed and canals dug. A merchant fleet and war fleet were built to facilitate commerce and protect it. He stationed the main body of his navy at Kabara, in the center of the Niger.

To his ports came ships from Portugal and the Mediterranean bringing goods in exchange for Songhay gold, copper, woods, and hides. Songhay ships traded with these lands in return, while Songhay caravans went to Cairo, Algiers, Morocco, and Bagdad. To reassure foreign merchants, he ordered the standardization of weights and measures. Thieves were punished with utmost severity, and the empire was so well policed that brigands disappeared and caravans came and went with security.

The youths of the land were sent to the Moslem universities of Europe, Asia, and North Africa, and savants regardless of color or religion were invited to reside at Timbuctoo, where they were handsomely subsidized and honored. Science and learning flourished and many scholars emerged whose names are given in the *Tarik-es-Sudan.*

Askia's subjects, too, were enlightened. At a time when the people of England cowered at the spectacle of a comet, the Songhay, thanks to their astronomers, knew one for what it really was.

Askia visited Caliph Motoweskel at Bagdad, spending several

weeks conversing with him and the learned men in this center of culture and opulence; upon his return to Timbuctoo he kept up a correspondence with the caliph for years.

Under the leadership of Askia, the Songhay Empire flourished until it became one of the richest of that period. Timbuctoo became the real center of the Mohammedan world, and was known as "The Queen of the Sudan," and "The Mecca of the Sudan."

With his empire firmly established, Askia resumed his attack on unbelievers, carrying the rule of Islam into new lands. He brought under his sway the kingdoms of the Yollofs and the Mossis as well as those of many minor kings and chiefs, till his realm extended beyond Lake Chad, and took six months to traverse from west to east.

As for his wealth, if we accept the account of his pilgrimage to Mecca as accurate, it must have been among the greatest of his time. In his retinue on that occasion were 1500 princes and chiefs of the empire and a vast army of cavaliers and foot soldiers; he is reported to have given 300,000 pieces of gold to Mecca, Medina, and other holy cities; at Medina he had a marvelous garden laid out in his memory; and he spent 100,000 pieces of gold among the Mecca merchants; at Bagdad he dazzled the caliph with his wealth, giving him presents surpassing in value those of all other rulers.

Says the *Tarik-es-Sudan*:

God favored Mohammed Askia. He assured him great conquests and covered him with his brilliant protection. This ruler took all the country from Kounta to the Atlantic Ocean on the west and his authority stretched from the frontier of the country of the Bindokas as far as Teghazza. All the people he subdued by the sword and by force, as one reads in the recitals of his expeditions. God accomplished all that this monarch desired so that Mohammed Askia was docilely obeyed in all the states and in his own palace. Everywhere throughout his vast empire peace reigned in abundance.

Askia's subjects worshipped him as a god. In the audience chamber no one approached him until he had first sprinkled dust on his head. Askia never spoke directly to an assembly, a herald repeated his words.

His retinue was preceded by tambours, trumpeters, and musicians. The trappings of his horse were the richest imaginable and the jewels on his person were worth an immense fortune. He invariably rode in the center of his processions, attendants holding the bridle and walking by his side.

Askia did not hesitate to put to death individuals or groups who threatened his power. Among those upon whom his wrath descended was a group of learned men, the Za-Bir-Benda, whom he enticed into the city of Sankore, the university center, and massacred. When his favorite brother, Omar-Konzagho, heard of it, he tearfully rebuked Askia for desiring the ruin of Sankore and the empire.

Askia replied, "On the contrary, I wish its prosperity. All these people I have executed would have made life difficult for the Songhay. There was no other way to deal with them."

But despite his power, wealth, and magnificence, a sword hung over Askia's head. He was losing his sight. In time his vision grew so dim that he appointed his brother Omar as his representative, pretending fear of the evil eye. Fortunately for him, he had always remained inaccessible to all except the most intimate members of his family and to visiting rulers, so his subjects did not know of his infirmity.

Even later when he became quite blind this was concealed for years with the help of his faithful secretary, Ali Folem. But at last the truth leaked out and one of his sons, Faria Mousa, revolted and forced Askia to abdicate in his favor. This was on September 27, 1529, after a glorious reign of thirty-six and a half years.

The usurper soon died and was succeeded by a brother, Benkan, who treated his father still more contemptibly, even taking possession of his palace and exiling him to an island in the Niger where he lived in a miserable hut.

One day a loyal son, Ismail, came to see him. Askia, feeling the muscular arm of Ismail, asked him how it was possible that one so strong permitted his aged father to be "eaten by mosquitoes and leapt on by frogs." When Ismail replied that he had no money to make war, Askia directed him to a spot where he had hidden a large sum of gold. Telling him the names of those who could be counted on for support, Askia dictated a plan of battle. Ismail was victorious and Askia returned to the palace, where he died in 1538.

Timbuctoo survived in splendor for the next fifty-two years. Wealth had softened its people, however, and when Emperor Mansour of Morocco sent his troops across the Sahara, they were able to plunder it. Two centuries later another Moorish invasion brought about its almost total destruction. Today only vestiges of its former glory remain, such as the Mosque of Kankan Musa and the tomb of Askia.

Félix Dubois, who visited Timbuctoo, says:

> Askia the Great made Timbuctoo one of the world's great centers of learning and commerce. The brilliance of the city was such that it still shines in the imagination after three centuries like a star which, though dead, continues to send its light toward us. Such was its splendor that in spite of its many vicissitudes after the death of Askia, the vitality of Timbuctoo is not extinguished.

REFERENCES

Ibn Batutu, *Travels in Asia and Africa*, pp. 318–344. London, 1929.

Ahmad Baba's *Chronicles*, trans. by Barth.

Abderrahman Sadi, *Tarik-es-Sudan*, trans. by Houdas. Paris, 1901.

Leo Africanus, Vol. III, Book VII. 1896.

Dubois, Félix, *Tombouctou la Mysterieuse*. Paris, 1897.

Cooley, W. D., *Negroland of the Arabs*. London, 1841.

Lugard, Lady, *A Tropical Dependency*. London, 1905.

Delefosse, M., *Negroes of Africa*. Washington, D.C., 1931.

Huart, *Histoire des Arabes*. Paris, 1912–13.

Castries, H., *La conquete du Soudan*, in *Hesperis*, Vol. III, pp. 433–488. 1923.

ADDITIONAL REFERENCES

Boahen, Adu, *Topics in West African History*, pp. 26–33. London, Longmans, Green and Company, Ltd., 1966.

Bovill, E. W., *The Golden Trade of the Moors*, pp. 137–142, 145, 147, 149–151, 154, 182, 227. London and New York, Oxford University Press, 1970.

Chu, Daniel, and Skinner, Elliott, *A Glorious Age in Africa*, pp. 103, 110. Garden City, N.Y., Zenith: Doubleday, 1965.

Clarke, John Henrik, "Askia Mohammed's Return from Mecca." *Negro History Journal*, (Feb., 1950), p. 106. Society for the Study of Negro Life and History, Washington, D.C.

Davidson, Basil, *A History of West Africa*, pp. 69, 113–114, 168–179. Garden City, N.Y., Doubleday, 1965.

———, *The Lost Cities of Africa*, pp. 93, 102–103, 117–118, 127, 282. Boston and Toronto, Little, Brown and Company, 1959.

De Graft-Johnson, J. C., *African Glory*, pp. 104–109. New York, Walker and Company, 1954.

Du Bois, W. E. B., *The World and Africa*, p. 211. New York, International Publishers, 1965.

Fage, J. D., *A History of West Africa*, pp. 27, 28. Cambridge, Cambridge University Press, 1969.

Gailey, Harry A., *History of Africa*, pp. 71–72, 80. New York, Holt, Rinehart and Winston, Inc., 1970.

Gollock, Georgia A., *Sons of Africa*, pp. 20–31. London, Student Christian Movement, 1928.

Hargreaves, John D., *West Africa: The Former French States*, pp. 23–24, 27. Englewood Cliffs, N.J., Prentice-Hall, 1967.

Huggins, Willis N., *An Introduction to African Civilizations*, pp. 124, 127. New York, Avon House, 1937.

Levtzion, Nehemiah, "The Long March of Islam in the Western Sudan," in *The Middle Age of African History*, Roland Oliver, ed., pp. 16–17. London, Oxford University Press, 1967.

Shinnie, Margaret, *Ancient African Kingdoms*, pp. 76, 78–81. New York and Toronto, New American Library, 1965.

Wiedner, Donald L., *A History of Africa South of the Sahara*, p. 36. New York, Vintage Books, 1962.

"Askia the Great." *Negro History Bull.*, Vol. I, No. 2 (Nov., 1937), pp. 7–8. Association for the Study of Negro Life and History, Washington, D.C.

Ann Zingha

Ann Zingha

AMAZON QUEEN OF MATAMBA, WEST AFRICA
(1582–1663)

NZINGHA, better known as Ann Zingha, renowned warrior queen of Matamba, was born about 1582, when the Portuguese were establishing trade settlements on the African coast and otherwise encroaching on native territory.

When Ann grew up she did not sit idly by watching the invaders at work. Extremely wroth, she led her army of fierce woman warriors, which she had assiduously trained, into action against them, and won battle after battle. But in the long run she lost since spears were hardly a match for firearms.

In 1622 her brother, the King of Angola, sent her to arrange a peace with the Portuguese viceroy at Loanda. A dwelling befitting her royal rank was prepared for her and she and her escort were received with due honors, which pleased her.

But when she entered the viceroy's audience chamber, Ann, who was quite temperamental, was indignant. She noticed that while a magnificent chair of state had been arranged for the viceroy, there was merely a cushion on the floor for her. The fact that the cushion was made of gold-embroidered velvet and had been put in the center of a handsome carpet did not placate her.

Though she felt that she had been slighted, she did not make a scene. Instead, she gave one of her attendants a meaningful look. The woman came over, knelt down on her hands and knees, and

Ann Zingha sat herself down on the woman's back and waited thus for the viceroy to appear.

If on his arrival he thought it strange for his honored guest to be seated in this way, he politely refrained from comment and began talking business. As a matter of fact, Ann Zingha did not appear at all ludicrous in her disadvantageous position. She acted with such spirit and dignity that the viceroy was impressed, and negotiations were terminated satisfactorily. Not given to bickering, Ann had refused outright an alliance with the Portuguese, one of the terms of which was the payment of an annual tribute to the King of Portugal. She persuaded the viceroy that this ought to be eliminated, emphasizing that the giving up of her Portuguese prisoners was concession enough.

When the audience was ended, the viceroy arose and conducted Ann Zingha from the room. Looking back, he saw to his astonishment that the attendant she had used as a throne had not moved an inch. When he mentioned this, Ann Zingha drew herself up haughtily and said, "It is not meet that the ambassadress of a great king should be served with the same seat twice. I have no further use for the woman."

The viceroy was so astonished at this that he quite forgot to thank her for the unusual, if somewhat shopworn, gift.

During her stay in Loanda Ann Zingha embraced Christianity. Whether she did this from inner conviction or as a matter of policy is not known. At any rate, she was baptized and adopted European customs. Not long after her return to Angola, her brother died and she seized the throne. To simplify matters, she disposed of her nephew by strangling him, or so it is said. If this was not in the true Christian spirit, neither was a similar deed committed by her famous contemporary, Elizabeth of England, who got rid of her rival, Mary Stuart, by having her head chopped off. Drastic methods were in the best tradition of the times.

No one who knew the Portuguese ever expected permanent peace as a result of the treaty between the viceroy and Ann Zingha. They were tricky customers, just like all the rest of the Europeans, and when you gave them a square inch, they took a square mile. They did not like to see Ann Zingha on the throne because she was independent and could not be hoodwinked or bluffed into paying tribute. So, deciding that it was better to have her out of the way sooner than later, they sent an army against her.

But allying herself with the Dutch and the native chiefs, she fought back in a war that dragged on for years. Her amazons were terrible in battle, and whenever the Portuguese saw them coming, they were struck with fear. Finally the Portuguese were victorious and offered to let her stay on the throne if she would pay annual tribute. Rather than submit to this extortion, she fled into the bush, and gathering another army, repelled the invaders for the next eighteen years, refusing even to consider any overtures.

With the somewhat dubious examples of Christian behavior provided by the Portuguese before her, Ann Zingha tempestuously dropped the faith she had embraced and had those of her people who clung to Christianity killed. Time and again the Christian missionaries among her captives tried to win her back to Christianity, but in vain. She held out as firm as a rock against their exhortations. But then her sister, of whom she was very fond, died. This, perhaps, and the mellowness of advancing age—she was now nearly seventy—softened her heart.

Acting upon a suggestion from the missionaries, she again declared herself a convert, and was restored to the throne by the Portuguese. To show that she was sincere, she set about reforming her people. She ordered the adoption of Christianity, abolished the sacrifice of captives and criminals, and prohibited polygamy. When this latter injunction offended her subjects, she set an example herself by marrying one of her courtiers, though she was seventy-six at the time.

She strictly observed her treaties with the Portuguese but could not be induced, even by her priests, to pay tribute or recognize the overlordship of the Portuguese. But when one of her chiefs took it in his head to attack some Portuguese in 1657, she went so far as to make war against him, and when he was captured, had him decapitated and sent his head to the viceroy.

During her last years she sent an emissary to the Pope asking for more missionaries for her kingdom. When the Pope's answer came, Ann Zingha appeared in church, amidst great pomp and pageantry, and had it read publicly. There was much celebrating, and at a festival attending this occasion, she staged a mock battle in which her woman warriors, dressed in full war regalia, were the star participants. Ann Zingha led them herself, and though she was past eighty, she displayed astonishing agility and skill and was superior to many of her youthful followers.

Ann Zingha died in 1663 at the age of eighty-one. Her body was shown to her mourning subjects arrayed in royal robes, her hands clasping a bow and arrow. When the time for burial came, she was clothed in the Capuchin habit, as she had requested, with a crucifix and rosary in her hands.

John Ogilby, an Englishman who lived at that time and wrote a good deal about the native rulers of Africa, said of her, "She is a cunning and prudent virago so much addicted to the use of arms that she hardly uses other exercise, and withal so generously valiant that she never hurt a Portuguese after quarter was given and commanded all her slaves and soldiers the like."

After her death Angola fell completely into the power of the Portuguese, in whose possession it still is.

REFERENCES

Chambers, W. R., "Intelligent Negroes." *Misc. of Useful and Entertaining Tracts*, No. 63. Edinburgh, 1841.

Ogilby, John, *Africa*, pp. 563–564. 1648.

Castilhon, J. L., *Zingha, Reine d'Angola*. 1769.

Cadornaga, Oliveira, *Historia geral de guerras angolanas*, Vol. II, pp. 91 *et seq.* 1902.

Battell, A., *Andrew Battell in Guinea*. Hakluyt's 2nd ser., Vol. VI.

ADDITIONAL REFERENCES

Davidson, Basil, *A History of East and Central Africa to the Late Nineteenth Century*, pp. 271–272. London, Longmans, Green and Company, Ltd., 1965.

Osei, G. K., *The Forgotten Great Africans, 3000 B.C. to 1959 A.D.*, pp. 18–19. London, G. K. Osei, 1965.

Polatnick, Florence T., and Saletan, Alberta L., *Shapers of Africa*, pp. 39–75. New York, Julian Messner, 1969.

Osei Tutu

FOUNDER OF THE ASHANTI NATION
(d. 1731)

OSEI TUTU was the most noted ruler of the Ashanti, a powerful, warlike, and highly disciplined people of West Africa, whose history goes back more than 2000 years. The Ashanti are said to be the descendants of those Ethiopians mentioned by Diodorus Siculus and Herodotus who were driven southward by a conquering Egyptian army.

It is believed that they traded with the Phoenicians long before the Christian era. They started trading with France in 1366 and with England in 1672. It is not improbable that Negroes from this region had been crossing over to America before Columbus.

Osei Tutu succeeded to the throne in 1697, upon the death of his uncle, Obiria Yebo. In his youth he had been shield-bearer to Boa, King of Denkera, an overlord of the Ashanti kings. But handsome and stalwart Osei Tuti had a love affair with the king's sister; she had a child by him, and he was forced to flee for his life. To this there was to be a tragic sequel years later.

Coming to the throne, Osei Tutu removed the seat of government to Coomassie, and together with his cousin, Bautin, a neighboring monarch, entered into an alliance for the conquest of their neighbors. He reorganized his army, modeling it after the way of ants on the march.

This alliance led indirectly to a war with Bosinante, King of

Denkera, a territory to the southwest—a war that was to shake all West Africa. As at Troy, the direct cause of the quarrel was a beautiful woman. Bosinante, ostensibly as a compliment, but really out of pride, sent a mission to Osei Tutu composed of his favorite wives. Richly clad and loaded down with jewels, they were accompanied by a magnificent escort of Bosinante's most stalwart warriors.

This royal delegation was received by Osei Tutu with all the honors and courtesy due its rank. He gave the queens rich presents and sent them safely back. In reciprocity, Osei Tutu sent Bosinante an embassy of his most beautiful wives, led by the chief queen, a woman of extraordinary beauty.

When this delegation arrived, Bosinante received its members with due respect, but fell in love at first sight with the beautiful chief queen. Bosinante was young and handsome, and the attraction was mutual.

On her return, Osei Tutu noticed that she was an expectant mother and swore that he would not rest until he had Bosinante's head. Bosinante offered him a large quantity of gold as the price of peace, but Osei Tutu was adamant. He began mobilizing his army, forgetting apparently that he had once been forced to flee from Denkera for a similar offense.

He ordered a great quantity of arms and ammunition from the Europeans. The Denkera, either through fear or negligence, made the fatal mistake of permitting his agents to transport these supplies through their country.

While Osei Tutu was in the midst of these preparations, Bosinante died. But Osei Tutu, determined upon conquest, led an army of 300,000 against Denkera. Aided by the Akim, another powerful tribe, the Denkera attacked the Ashanti but the allies were beaten in two great battles. Among the dead was Ntim, the Denkera king who was said to be Osei Tutu's son, born of the illicit union with King Boa's sister.

It took the Ashanti fifteen days to collect the spoils of the victory. According to Bosman, "One of the European officers who was sent after the battle as an embassy to the Ashanti king, saw the immense quantity of gold which he had reserved as his own share of the treasures from the Denkeras."

Much of this wealth had been derived from the sale of slaves to the New World. In addition, the Ashanti found among their booty the note by which the Dutch were obliged to pay tribute for the privilege of maintaining Elmina Castle.

Osei Tutu's vengeance went further. He dug up the body of Bosinante, stripped the flesh from the bones, and fed it to the serpents. The skull and thighbones he brought back as trophies for his palace, where Dupuis saw them a century later. Dupuis says that even then, the Ashanti, on their sacred feast days, execrated these relics.

As for the Akim, allies of the Denkera, they lost 30,000 of their men in battle. After his victory Osei Tutu invaded their territory and levied an enormous indemnity upon them as well as an annual tribute.

Osei Tutu next conquered all the neighboring tribes, clans, and villages, uniting them with his kingdom. His own people he ruled with such impartiality and generosity that he became a favorite with them.

When the Akim failed to pay their tribute of 4000 ounces of gold, Osei Tutu decided to annex their territory, and sent a large army against them in 1731. Intending to catch up with this army later, he went to visit the sepulchers of his forefathers at Bantama and to pay his respects to the tutelary diety. He was accompanied by his favorite wives, many of his children, and the flower of the nobility.

Having gone through the customary ceremonies, Osei Tutu started for Denkera territory with a handful of soldiers. He felt quite secure, as his army had already passed that way. But the Akim, learning of his plans, sent a strong detachment of men to ambush him.

Unsuspecting, Osei Tutu came along. Just as the royal party was about to cross the Prah River at Coromantee, the Akim opened fire. Osei Tutu was wounded in the side at the first volley. Springing from his litter, he was rallying his men when a second ball pierced his throat and he fell dead, plunging face downward into the river. Taking advantage of the confusion, the Akim charged, killing the whole party of 300, including 60 wives of the king and his nobles.

The loss of their beloved ruler prostrated the Ashanti, and their vengeance upon the Akim was devastating. They burned their city to the ground, killing every living thing in it. As in biblical days, not only the prisoners were sacrificed, but also the sheep, fowls, and dogs.

Osei Tutu's body was never found but his memory did not perish. He died on a Saturday and in commemoration his people instituted their most sacred oath after the sad event—Coromantee Miminda (Coromantee Saturday). The oath taken on this day was considered so solemn and binding that it was hardly ever mentioned by name, being spoken of as "the great oath of the dreadful day," and even then in a whisper.

They surnamed Osei Tutu "the Great." Dupuis says of the high esteem in which his people held him, "To the excellence of this monarch the Ashanti still revert with a national satisfaction. They say he was Good, as well as Great, for in his reign justice was ever on the alert and the claims of his subjects were listened to without distinction of rank or title."

REFERENCES

Dupuis, Joseph, *Journal of a Residence in Ashanti*, pp. 229–232. London, 1824.

Beecham, John, *Ashanti and the Gold Coast*. London, 1841.

Claridge, W. W., *History of the Gold Coast*, pp. 193–199. London, 1915.

ADDITIONAL REFERENCES

Boahen, Adu, *Topics in West African History*, pp. 70, 73–76, 78. London, Longmans, Green and Company, Ltd., 1966.

Davidson, Basil, *et al.*, *A History of West Africa 1000–1800*, pp. 222–226. London, Longmans, Green and Company, Ltd., 1969.

Du Bois, W. E. B., *The World and Africa*, p. 161. New York, International Publishers, 1965.

Fage, J. D., *A History of West Africa*, p. 108. Cambridge, Cambridge University Press, 1969.

Flint, John E., *Nigeria and Ghana*, pp. 89–93. Englewood Cliffs, N.J., Prentice-Hall, 1966.

Fuller, Sir Francis, *A Vanished Dynasty Ashanti*, pp. 8–24. London, Frank Cass and Company, Ltd., 1921 and 1968.

Gailey, Harry A., *History of Africa*, p. 94. New York, Holt, Rinehart, and Winston, Inc., 1970.

Gollock, Georgina A., *Sons of Africa*, pp. 32–49. London, Student Christian Movement, 1928.

Kimble, David, *A Political History of Ghana, 1850–1928*, pp. 265–266. Oxford, Clarendon Press, 1963.

Kyeretwie, K. O. Bonsu, *Ashanti Heroes*, pp. 1–13. Accra, Waterville Publishing House; London, Oxford University Press, 1964.

Metcalfe, G. E., *Maclean of the Gold Coast*, p. 36. London, Oxford University Press, 1962.

Omer-Cooper, J. D., *et al.*, *The Making of Modern Africa*, Vol. I, p. 18. London, Longmans, Green and Company, Ltd., 1968.

Reindorf, Rev. Carl Christian, *The History of the Gold Coast and Ashanti*, pp. 48–71. Accra, Ghana University Press, 1966.

Shinnie, Margaret, *Ancient African Kingdoms*, p. 110. New York and Toronto, New American Library, 1965.

Tordoff, William, *Ashanti under the Prempehs*, pp. 3–6, 14, 32, 284, 325. London, Ibadan and Accra, Oxford University Press, 1965.

Ward, W. E. B., *A History of the Gold Coast*, London, Allen and Company, 1948.

Mulai Ismael

Mulai Ismael

MOST EXTRAORDINARY RULER
OF THE EIGHTEENTH CENTURY
(1647–1727)

THE ANCESTRY of the Sultan Mulai Ismael is so extraordinary as compared with not only that of other rulers, but of the average individual, that it upsets all current notions of esthetics and eugenics and gives the despisers of plain and lowly women something over which to rack their brains.

The mother of this perhaps most remarkable and dynamic ruler of the eighteenth century was a full-blooded Negro slave, which, of course, was not uncommon in Islamic lands, especially Egypt, Arabia, Algeria, Morocco, and Spain. But whereas Negro women usually were chosen for their beauty or their charm of personality, Mulai Ismael's mother had been selected for her repulsiveness.

It was in this manner that Mulai Ismael came to be born: His father, Mulai Sherif, King of Tafilalet, had been captured by Omar, King of Sillec, and thrown into prison. Bored by the long confinement, the captive wrote to Omar, "You might at least send me some feminine company." Omar said to his chamberlain, "Pick out the blackest and most hideous Negro slave you can find and send her to him." This was done and of that union two sons were born, Rachid and Mulai Ismael, both of whom, in turn, became sultans of Morocco.

Mulai Ismael's path to the throne was not easy. On the death of his brother Rachid, he was forced to fight his nephew, Achmet.

The contest between them was long and bloody, Mulai Ismael finally defeating Achmet in a great artillery battle and capturing him.

This, however, led to another war which lasted for twenty-four years, most of which was spent by Mulai Ismael in the field. Finally he secured peace by defeating his Turkish opposers in a battle in which he had sent 10,000 heads of the slain, including that of the Turkish commander, to his capital at Fez. Mulai Ismael also conquered the formidable Berbers of the Atlas.

As to the white Christian powers, he pushed them entirely out of Northwest Africa. He defeated the English at Tangier and Fort Charles, and broke the hold of Spain on Africa. Crushing the Spaniards at Larache, he drove them across the straits. Moroccan ships plundered the vessels and the coasts of Spain, France, and England, bringing back tens of thousands of white Christian captives, who were held for ransom at from $1000 to $15,000 each. Collections at Christian churches for the ransoming of white slaves became a feature of the times. This, incidentally, was happening at the same time that Europe was raiding Africa for black slaves. Among Mulai Ismael's slaves was Alexander Selkirk, hero of *Robinson Crusoe*.

Many of the Moors were also taken as slaves to Europe. Attempts were made at exchange, but Mulai Ismael was as eager to hold his white slaves because of their modern knowledge as Louis XIV and the other white rulers were to hold the Moroccans for their artistry and their seamanship.

Zealous for the spread of his faith, Mulai Ismael considered it as holy to attack the Christians as the latter did to wage the wars of the Crusades and to uphold Christ. He even sent frequent missions to the European rulers, among them Louis XIV of France and James I of England, urging them to embrace Islam.

With all of his enemies within and without defeated, Mulai Ismael devoted himself to internal affairs. He began by increasing the number of the Bokhara, a corps of fighting men which he founded early in his reign, composed entirely of full-blooded Negroes from the Sudan.

These blacks, 150,000 strong, lived with their wives in beautiful villages built for them by Mulai Ismael. At sixteen their male children were drafted into the army and the girls were taught cooking, housekeeping, and music, and were married to the officers with a dowry. All relations between these blacks and the natives were discouraged. Differing in language and traditions, they had, moreover, nothing in common. Battalions of the Bokhara were stationed in the most strategic posts in the empire and their officers were given positions of the highest trust. One of them, Empsael, was grand admiral and prime minister. In battle they were regarded as invincible. They were fanatically loyal, and with them Mulai Ismael felt as secure as the Caesars with their Pretorian Guard.

Added to this was a picked corps of 10,000 white Christian warriors, captured or born in captivity, which he commanded himself. With an iron hand he established a justice and an orderliness that became proverbial. "Everywhere," says Ezziani, a Mohammedan historian, "the country enjoyed the most complete security. A Jew or a woman could go from Oudjda to Oued-Noun free from all molestation. Abundance reigned everywhere; cereals, food, vegetables, cattle were sold at a low price. In all the Maghreb one found neither thief nor brigand."

Articles dropped accidentally remained where they fell. Once a man reported to the police that he had seen a large bag of walnuts on the road. Mulai Ismael, hearing of the incident, sent for him. "And how did you know that the bag contained walnuts," he demanded.

"I kicked it, Your Majesty."

"Give him one hundred lashes," ordered Mulai Ismael sternly. "Since it was not his, he had no right to touch it, even with his foot."

The common people loved him, the rich he taxed heavily. Each morning the butchers, bakers, and other dealers in food had to bring samples of their products to the nearest police station to prove that the quality was good and that the price was not exorbitant.

Mulai Ismael aspired to restore the ancient glories of Morocco. She had once been the world's leading empire and had dominated southwestern Europe. Under the Almohads, the Moroccan-Spanish power had extended from the Atlantic to the borders of Egypt and had included Spain and parts of France. Moroccan art, architecture, science, literature, embroidery, copper-wood, and leatherwork were world-famed. The stables of the Moroccan rulers were once finer than the palaces of the kings of England, France, and Germany. Morocco, though on the decline, was still a world power and Mulai Ismael wished to make her supreme.

Moreover, he had to find work for his great army of soldiers and slaves to keep them from plotting against him. "When you have rats in a basket," he said, "the only way to keep them from gnawing through is to keep the basket shaking."

He built the great city of Meknes, or Mequinez, which still stands. On the works were employed, among others, 25,000 white European slaves—engineers, physicians, merchants, writers, noblemen, and others.

The glory of Meknes was the sultan's own palace, the Dar Kebra, with its marvelous gardens, parks, and fountains. It had forty reception rooms, twenty pavilions, and looked out on an artificial body of water on which vessels of the largest size could sail. In his stables, the most colossal ever built, were 12,000 Arabian horses, with a white and a black slave for each. A stream of water ran through each stall, for to the Moor a horse is the noblest animal on earth, and standing water is considered unclean. Mulai Ismael's own splendid charger, which had carried him through many a stern combat, was sacred. There was no criminal so vile who would not be pardoned could he but succeed in kissing the horse's hoof.

Mouette describes Mulai Ismael's favorite palace thus:

Its enclosure was formed of battlements: its doors encircled with superb columns of marble. In the interior there were 45 houses and two marvelous mosques. As one entered one saw vast covered galleries, overlooking richly ornamented courtyards, surrounded by colonnades, and with many spouting fountains. The walls of all these galleries were embellished with mosaics and Moorish inscriptions relating the principal deeds of arms of the imperial dynasty. The entire ground was paved with ceramics, and the roofs of green tile. In the vast gardens, watered by serpentine streams and running on, as it were, to infinity, grew all the year round flowers, fruits and perfume-bearing trees of every kind.

Because of his activity in building and the length of his reign, which was fifty-five years, Mulai Ismael is frequently called the "Moroccan Louis XIV." But the sultans of Morocco had a reputation as builders when both France and England were still in a savage state. In the western half of the Old World, Morocco is eclipsed in age only by Ethiopia and Egypt: When the empire of the Caesars was in its infancy, Morocco had been in existence at least a thousand years.

Mulai Ismael's favorite wife was Zidana, a full-blooded Negro woman who was a slave and remarkable for her beauty. Abbé Busnot, who had been sent by Louis XIV to Mulai Ismael to negotiate for the freedom of white French slaves, describes her as "very black and of a size and stature enormous. She was the slave of Mulai Rachid, his brother, and Mulai Ismael bought her for 60 ducats. One cannot understand why she seems to have such absolute power over the sultan, and turns him about as she wishes. As to the other wives in the harem, she dominates them completely."

The second wife was an Englishwoman who had been captured at the age of fifteen. The third was another black woman, Lela Coneta, who later raised her son, Mohamet Deby, to the throne.

As for his sons, Mulai Ismael found it much easier to deal with his subjects than with them. The heir to the throne, Mulai Zidan, son of Zidana, and Mulai Mohamet, son of the Englishwoman, quarrelled over the succession. When Mohamet rebelled, Zidan defeated and captured him and Ismael ordered the amputation of a foot and a hand of Mohamet, after which he did everything to save his life.

When Mohamet died, Mulai Ismael did penance and erected a lavish monument to his memory.

Later, when Zidan also rebelled, Mulai Ismael defeated him and captured him, and turned him over to his seven wives, who strangled him while he was drunk. His mother, Zidana, in revenge, had the wives sawn asunder while alive.

Others sons also rebelled and were beaten. On one occasion, Mulai Ismael offered to fight two of them, Mamoun and Mohamet, together, and was prevented from doing so only by the intervention of his generals.

Inured to war, and always fighting in the forefront of battle,

Mulai Ismael had the callousness of the born warrior. He was a cruel disciplinarian. When Tahar, one of his generals, lost an army during a snowstorm in the Atlas, he broke Tahar's arm with the butt of his pistol, and had him sown up in a raw bull's hide and dragged over the ground by wild horses.

The only European king he admired was Louis XIV. "The King of France," he said, "is the only monarch who knows how to reign like myself. The King of England is but a slave of Parliament." To show this admiration he demanded, through his envoys, the hand of the beautiful Princess de Conti, a daughter of Louis XIV, in marriage.

By Christian historians Mulai Ismael is placed in the same category with Nero, Henry VIII, Ivan the Terrible, and Pedro the Cruel. Most of these stories are based on the accounts told by Christian slaves to the Abbé Busnot. "Thirty-six thousand persons are said to have perished by his own hand, so fearful was his reputation for cruelty," says V. C. O'Connor. This would mean, however, that he killed an average of two persons with his own hands for every day of his reign! Pidon de St. Olon sets the number at 20,000.

Much of what the Christian slaves told about his cruelty was true. Those were barbarous days, when the bodies of stolen Negroes strewed the sealanes from Africa to America. It is also true that the Moorish captives, in the hands of the Christians, were as badly treated. In a letter dated April 23, 1682, addressed to Mulai Ismael, the Moroccan slaves in France said, "Never has there been practiced such torments in hell as these Christians inflict on us: hunger, nudity, curses against our holy religion and our prophets; contempt for our emperor and our nation; blows, chains weighing more than 100 pounds; excessive pain and labor are but a few of the everyday torments we suffer." The Moroccan slaves were chained to the Christian galleys and forced to labor there.

The number of Mulai Ismael's wives also differs in the accounts. O'Connor, a recent writer, sets the number at 4000; the Abbé Busnot, who met Mulai Ismael personally, gave 500 of all races and nationalities; O'Connor says he had 867 children, but Ezziani, historian of that time, says that he knew of only eight sons and twenty daughters.

Abbé Busnot describes Mulai Ismael thus:

He is of middle size; his face is long and thin; his beard, forked and white; his color, almost black with a white mark near the nose; his eyes are full of fire and his voice very strong; it seems that neither age nor anything else has diminished his courage, his force or his ability. He can leap over by a single bound anything on which he places his hand.

His mind is ever alert. He seems to read the thoughts of others, and his answer is always to the point. He is very shrewd; foresees danger and knows how to win his end against the cleverest, and is intrepid and courageous in time of danger. He is self-possessed and firm when misfortune occurs.

He rules by the terror of his name. When revolt threatens and all seems lost, then suddenly and sometimes without a blow, the principal rebels are captured and delivered over to torture.

. . . One cannot help but be astonished at the king who has ruled so long and by means that are quite contrary to politics . . . treating the Christians with barbarity; ruining the merchants with his avarice; toying with all the kings of Christendom; boasting of commanding all the nations of Europe and bending their rulers to his will; and amid all this reigning peacefully.

Georges Hardy, French historian, says of him, "He may be compared with the greatest kings in the history of France."

In spite of his enormous wealth, which was estimated at $750,-000,000, he lived simply. He ate rice, chicken, pigeon, and barley, simply prepared. Very devout and strict in observing the Koran, he drank only water. He dressed simply also, and hated display. All in all, this extraordinary son of the ugliest woman in the kingdom was a strange mixture of excellent qualities and amazing defects. He died in 1727, at the age of eighty, enjoying the use of all his faculties to the last.

His dynasty still occupies the throne of Morocco. The finest monument to his memory is the Bab Mansour, which bears the inscription, "The Asylum of the Weak and the Providence of the Needy; the King who is obeyed from Love and Respect."

REFERENCES

Busnot, D., *Histoire de Regne de Mouley Ismael*. Rouen, 1714.

Pidon de St. Olon, *Estat de Morocco*. Paris, 1694.

Al Lairfani, *Le Maroc, 1631–1812*, trans. by O. Houdas. Paris, 1866.

Windus, John, *A Journey to Mequinez*. London, 1725.

Du Chenier, *Histoire de Maroc*, Vol. III. 1788.

Braithwaite, J., *History of the Revolutions of Morocco*. London, 1729.

Colin, E. R., *Le Grand Ismail*. Paris, 1929.

Asia Magazine, May-July 1932. New York.

Le Dépêche Coloniale et Maritime, Sept. 16 and 17. Paris, 1931.

For other sources and details, see *Sex and Race*, Vol. I, Chap. 11.

ADDITIONAL REFERENCES

Bovill, E. W., *The Golden Trade of the Moors*, pp. 158, 193, 238. London and New York, Oxford University Press, 1970.

Clarke, John Henrik, "Mulai Ismael," in *African Heritage*. New York, African Heritage Publishing Company, 1959.

Omer-Cooper, J. D., *et al.*, *The Making of Modern Africa*, Vol. I, pp. 13, 100, 102. London, Longmans, Green and Company, Ltd., 1968.

Chaka

MIGHTY ZULU CONQUEROR AND DESPOT
(1786–1828)

CHAKA, Zulu monarch, is not a pleasant figure to contemplate. If but half of what is told of him is true, he might be ranked as the world's greatest despot. None of the world's great conquerors was as hard and unfeeling as he. He had the heart of a tiger, and his savagery was the more devastating because combined with it was the military skill of Caesar and Napoleon, the organizing genius of Alexander the Great, the stern discipline of Lycurgus, the inflexibility of Bismarck, and the destructive force of Attila.

These are seeming exaggerations; nevertheless, one can quote Rider Haggard to say:

He was one of the most remarkable men that ever filled a throne since the days of the Pharaohs. The invincible armies of this African Attila had swept north and south, east and west, and slaughtered more than a million human beings. Wherever his warriors went, the blood of men, women, and children was poured out without stay or stint. Indeed he reigned like a visible Death, the presiding genius of a saturnalia of slaughter.

Some historians call him "The Black Napoleon"—but this is as absurd as calling Napoleon "The White Chaka." It is true that Chaka began to rule the year after Napoleon was defeated at Waterloo, but the men used different tactics, fought with different weapons, and in entirely different spheres. Napoleon won his victories by cannon; Chaka by hand-to-hand conflict. Chaka had no rifles at his disposal; physically Chaka could have crushed "The Little Corporal" as a python would a lamb.

While Napoleon was beaten several times, Chaka suffered but one minor defeat. Napoleon was finally overcome by a combination of enemies; Chaka so thoroughly annihilated his foes that none was left to attack him.

Chaka was born in 1786. His father was Senzangakona, Zulu chieftain, his mother was named Nandi. His parents were blood relatives, and it was lucky for Senzangakona that he was a chief for otherwise this union with kindred was punishable with death.

Chaka was wild, wayward, and headstrong as a boy. He quarreled with everyone save his mother. The children of the Langeni, his mother's tribe, used to tease him about his crinkly ear and his short and stumpy phallus. Sometimes they poured hot porridge into his hand and forced hot collops down his throat. Later they were to regret it very much, for Chaka never forgot.

When Chaka was old enough to wear a loincloth he was put in his father's charge, but before long the two were quarreling. The cup was full when Chaka set his dog on his father's fat-tailed sheep, and consequently was expelled from the tribe and sent back to his mother. Nandi, quarrelsome and masculine herself, took him to his grandfather, and stayed too. In the course of more family strife, both were turned adrift. Ngendeyana, chief of the Ndedwini, by whom Nandi also had a child, took them both in, only to put them out in short order.

At the request of Chaka's father, a head man of the Mtetwas gave them a home. At last their wanderings were over. Their host, Ngomane, was kind to them. Chaka never forgot this, and when he became a mighty ruler, he showed his gratitude by appointing Ngomane second in command. It is said that the only persons Chaka ever loved were his mother and Ngomane.

Seven years after making his home with Ngomane Chaka was taken into the service of Dingiswayo, a famous Mtetwa chieftain. He was the tallest man in the army, standing well over six feet. The ugly duckling had become a swan. He was broad-shouldered, slim-waisted, and his frame was svelte and elegantly knit. In strength and daring he had no equal. In combats of wrestling and

Chaka

other matches he was wont to take on two of the strongest rivals at a time and down them both. He was also the best and most graceful dancer. Excelling in all that primitive men admired, he became the idol of his people.

One of Chaka's most talked-about exploits at this time was a combat with a huge madman who was terrorizing the district. He had robbed and killed a number of people, and when several soldiers were sent to take him in custody, he beat them off. Chaka attacked him singlehanded and in a terrific fight killed him.

Even his father, who had once cast him off, became one of his greatest admirers. The latter, on a visit to Dingiswayo, was honored by a tribal dance, and seeing one of the warriors whose fire and grace excelled all the others asked who he was. When told that it was his own son he was so delighted that he called him over and named him his heir despite the fact that he was not born of a union with one of his own wives.

Chaka was twenty-six when his father died. Another son, Sijuana, took his father's place, but Chaka ambushed and killed him while he was bathing. When another half-brother, Dingaan, came by, Chaka merely laughed at him and told him to go on his way. Later Dingaan was to become a powerful chief, and Chaka was to regret that he had only laughed. But now that he was chief, he felt secure.

When Chaka took over that chieftainship the Zulus were an insignificant tribe owning less than 100 square miles of land. His secret ambition was to make himself ruler of all blacks.

He started out with the material at hand. His first step was to segregate all married men between the ages of thirty and forty. He built a separate *kraal* for them which he called "Belebele," meaning Everlasting Plague. Chaka hated married men. Next he segregated the youths between seventeen and twenty, informing them that they were to remain bachelors. He subjected them to Spartan discipline. To inspire them with an example of bravery, he once sat down on a hornets' nest, scooped out the angry insects and beat them off without rising. He wanted strong men only.

N. Isaacs, an English traveler who knew Chaka well, said of these youths, "Their figures are the noblest that my eye has ever gazed upon; their movements the most graceful; and their attitude the proudest—standing like forms of monumental bronze."

Hailing their chief with a kind of fascist salute, they would say, "You mountain, you lion, you elephant, you that are black."

Chaka next revolutionized military tactics. It is claimed that he took his ideas from the whites. This may be true, but it seems more likely that they were the product of his own resourceful courage.

At that time it was the custom for an African warrior in battle to throw his spear and immediately advance or retreat according to the action of the enemy. Chaka considered this ineffective, if not cowardly. He ordered the spears that had hitherto been used to be scrapped, and had his blacksmiths forge long swords with short hafts. This type of weapon could not be thrown; it could be used only at close quarters. For protection he equipped each soldier with a shield of toughened cowhide his own height.

He also changed the attack formation, modeling it after the shape of a bull's horns. In the center were the main body and the reinforcements, while two forward flanks curved out to enclose the enemy.

Chaka was not ready for action. But before he commenced, he took several precautions. Certain that some of his relatives would try to usurp his place while he was gone, he caught as many of his half-brothers, uncles, aunts, and other relatives as he could lay hands on and killed them. Then he set out to settle old scores with the Langeni, who had been cruel to him when he was a boy. Invading their lands, he called the whole tribe together, and picking out those against whom he bore a grudge, had them all impaled on sharp stakes, set the stakes on fire, and left them to die in slow agony.

His next objective was Pangashe, chief of the Butelizi. When the two forces met, the Butelizi, confident in their old way of victory, threw their spears. But to their amazement Chaka's warriors caught the weapons on their shields, flung the same back, and charged down on them with blood curdling yells. Soon the Butelizi were in headlong flight.

Chaka took all their cattle and gave the young captive warriors the option of joining his army or death. His men then slaughtered the rest, except the young wives and virgins. As to Pangashe, he left him to die a slow death sitting upright on a sharp stake.

After wiping out several other smaller tribes, Chaka set out against Matwane, chief of the Ngwanemi, who was held to be invincible. To stimulate his courage, this ferocious chief had the habit of drinking the gall from the livers of the chiefs he had slain. When Matwane learned of Chaka's plans, he marched off to ally himself with Zwide, King of the Ndwande, whose territory lay beyond the Drakenberg Mountains.

After Dingiswayo, Zwide was the most powerful king in South Africa, and he, too, thirsted for supreme power. He welcomed Matwane and the two hatched a plan to eliminate Dingiswayo. Instead of attacking him openly, they enticed him into a hut and chopped off his head. Taking out his heart, liver, and other vital organs, Zwide boiled them and drained off the fat for a charm.

Chaka was beside himself over the death of his old master, and to make sure of its support, he annexed the whole tribe after killing the chief who had succeeded Dingiswayo.

Zwide, now ready, marched to meet Chaka. Fearing that the powerful Ngwanes might join Zwide's forces, Chaka attacked them, massacring some 30,000 of them. While in the vicinity, he annihilated the Tembas for good measure.

Zwide, on the march, induced many other chiefs to join him, but this did not help. The two finally met on the banks of the Mhlatuze River and a battle fought until the river ran red with blood and corpses were piled deep. It was Zwide who withdrew.

In the course of these campaigns Chaka had not neglected the organization of his army and kingdom. On the theory that the standard of physical fitness he desired could be attained only by curbing promiscuity between the sexes, he placed all the young unmarried girls in enclosures ten feet high, where they were reared under the strictest supervision. Any male caught within the stockades was killed.

Boys were drafted into the army at the age of thirteen. At seventeen, after rigorous disciplining and training, they were assigned to a regiment. None of these youths was allowed to speak to a girl. Their business, Chaka told them, was war, not love.

Men of a given class or age were compelled to marry mates picked out for them. Only warriors of extraordinary distinction were permitted to select their wives. Divorces were forbidden. Adulterers were thrown headlong from a cliff into the Umvelosi River to be devoured by crocodiles. Circumcision was forbidden. The interests of the nation came first, Chaka preached.

Chaka's reforms even affected cooking. He saw to it that his warriors were fed only the best, and the quality of the beer was ordered improved.

He imposed hard rules upon himself and lived up to them. He was practically abstinent sexually and never took a wife. He wanted no children, and once, when one of his few concubines presented a son to him saying that it was his, he killed the child with one blow of his fist and sent the mother to her death. When his white friend, Isaacs, told him of George III's advanced age and that the English king had but one wife, Chaka said to his people, "You see, King George is like me. He does not indulge in promiscuous intercourse with women. That accounts for his long life."

Chaka's whole being was concentrated on supremacy. Iron himself, he imposed his hardness on others. The warrior who showed the slightest fear was as good as dead. After each battle Chaka held a review, and as the warriors marched by he called out those of whom he had not had a good report. These were stabbed to death on the spot.

It was certain death for a beaten regiment to return. Chaka's motto was literally "Death or Victory." There was but one way for a Zulu soldier to march, he told his men, and that was forward. The families of disgraced soldiers were put to death with them. On occasion he would let a lion loose and expect his soldiers to kill him with their bare hands. He would have been an ideal god of war for the Greeks.

In the course of his conquests he defeated Pakatwaye, a chief who had called him a "silly jackass" in earlier days. Storming the mountain fortress of King Mshida of Pepetaland, he tossed the king and his men to death on the crags below.

Zwide, with a strengthened army, headed once again for Zululand. On the march to meet him, Chaka laid waste all the land over which Zwide would pass, and then withdrew. Zwide, who had left his base with only a day's rations in the expectation that he could forage cattle and food on the way, found himself without food. After four days, when Zwide's men were worn out from hunger, Chaka sent out his young bloods to attack them, and there was great slaughter and another victory.

The last obstacle in the way of his goal of achieving supremacy in South Africa was the still unsubjected territory of Zwide's people, the Ndwande. With an army of 30,000 he set out for Ndwandeland. As he approached, Zwide's people, some 40,000 men, women, and children, sought refuge in the mountains. With Chaka in hot pursuit, they made a stand on the plateau of a snow-covered mountain. The Zulus, coming to within a few feet of the Ndwandes, halted. A dramatic silence ensued while each warrior steeled himself for the coming conflict. Then Chaka gave the signal and the carnage commenced. When it was over, every single Ndwande had been tossed from the cliffs.

Chaka's nearest enemy was at least 600 miles distant now. Some tribes, fearing him, had fled further yet, thus coming into conflict with others. Hunger and cannibalism stalked in his wake. Some historians say that, directly and indirectly, he caused the death of over 2,000,000 persons.

In 1820, four years after he started out on his first campaign, and at the age of thirty-four, he had conquered a territory larger than France. A ring of desert land and devastated area protected it from invasion. His people had become immensely wealthy. The young men, the wives, the lands, the cattle of their victims were theirs. As for the handful of whites in South Africa at that time, they thought it best to be on friendly terms with Chaka.

"King George and I," Chaka would say to his white visitors, "are brothers. I have conquered all the blacks, and he has conquered all the whites."

When he strode onto the parade field, a Herculean figure, his warriors would salute him, "Bayede!" the equivalent of "Hail Caesar!" Then to the clashing of swords they would chant.:

> Thou has scattered all the nations;
> What remains now for thy forces to fight?
> Oh, what remains now for thy forces to fight?

Indeed, this was Chaka's most troublesome problem. He had a magnificent army of 100,000 strong, restless for battle, but no one to fight! To get rid of the surplus, he would incite one regiment to attack another.

With no outside enemies on which to fix their hate, his people began fighting among themselves. Foes among his own people sprang up like mushrooms. To preserve order he kept executioners by his side, and had people impaled or their hands chopped off for no reason but to create fear.

Defiance increased, however. His enemies grew bolder. Once, while he was dancing, someone struck at his heart with a dagger but succeeded only in wounding his arm. Thousands were put to death in retaliation. Even his pet monkey filled people with dread. Ngomane, his old friend and counsellor, and his mother sought in vain to stem the slaughter. When his mother died some 7000 persons were put to death. Chaka wept, and all whose eyes were dry, or who did not come to the royal city to mourn, were executed.

Nine years of this unbridled tyranny filled the people with desperation and they longed for his death. Dingaan, his half-brother, resolved to kill him at all costs. Plotting together with one of Chaka's domestics named Satam, Dingaan and his brother Mahlangana crept into Chaka's hut and stabbed him as he sat before the fire. They plunged the dagger into him again and again. Before he died, Chaka said, "What have I done to you! Oh, children of my father."

Chaka's body was flung into a corn pit where it was left to the vultures.

James Stuart, Assistant Secretary of Native African Affairs in South Africa, said of Chaka:

In his own unenviable career of unbridled ferocity, celerity and cunning, he stands alone and unrivalled; whilst among barbarians in strategy, tactics, and executive capacity he is again probably without a peer. He, in short, seems to have turned a page, albeit a dark one, that no mortal, white, yellow, brown or black, has ever before managed quite to turn. In that sense he is, I should say, at the head of all other despots. He shows what an able man in power can accomplish, once his passions and ambitions have free play and opportunity serves.

So long as the soldier and the conqueror are worshipped, Chaka deserves a certain kind of recognition. Monster that he was, he did some good for his people. By organizing them, he made it much more difficult for white men to seize their lands. His legacy of physical training gave the Zulu the finest physique in the world. Years later, when the English wanted to conquer the Zulus, they demanded that Zulu youths be permitted to marry.

Chaka had but one fear—that of old age. When he learned that in the land of the white man there was a "muti" for turning gray hair black, he wanted it, regardless of cost.

Chaka was the destructive force of an earthquake or a hurricane imprisoned in the soul of one man. Before such a spectacle one can but stand in awe and horror.

REFERENCES

Isaacs, N., *Travels and Adventures in Eastern Africa*. London, 1836.

Ferguson, W. S., "The Zulus and the Spartans" in *Harvard African Studies, Varia Africana*, Vol. II, pp. 197–234. Cambridge, 1918.

Bryant, A. T., *Olden Times in Zululand*. London, 1929.

Mafolo, T., *Chaka: An Historical Romance*. Oxford, 1931.

ADDITIONAL REFERENCES

Brett, B. L. W., *Makers of South Africa*, pp. 19–27. London, T. Nelson, 1944.

Dhlomo, Rolfes Reginald Raymond, *Ushaka*. Pietermaritzburg, Shuter and Shooter, 1958.

Du Bois, W. E. B., *The World and Africa*, pp. 31, 77, 96. New York, International Publishers, 1965.

Gollock, Georgina A., *Sons of Africa*, pp. 64–76. London, Student Christian Movement, 1928.

———, *Lives of Eminent Africans*. New York and London, Longmans, Green and Company, Ltd., 1928.

Mackeurtan, Harold Graham, *The Cradle Days of Natal*. London, Longmans, Green and Company, Ltd., 1930.

Mafolo, Thomas, *Chaka the Zulu*. London, Oxford University Press, 1949.

Marks, Shula, "The Rise of the Zulu Kingdom," in *The Middle Age of African History*, Roland Oliver, ed., pp. 86–91. London, Oxford University Press, 1967.

Mitchison, Naomi, *African Heroes*, pp. 81–104. London, Sydney and Toronto, The Bodley Head, 1968.

Morris, Donald R., *The Washing of the Spears*, pp. 40–67. New York, Simon and Schuster, 1965.

Niven, Sir Rex, *Nine Great Africans*, pp. 78–103. New York, Ray Publishing, Inc., 1964.

Omer-Cooper, J. D., *The Zulu Aftermath*, pp. 29–48. London, Longmans, Green and Company, Ltd., 1966.

——, et al., *The Making of Modern Africa*, Vol. I, pp. 213–217, 222, 236, 241, 243, 271. London, Longmans, Green and Company, Ltd., 1968.

Osei, G. K., *The Forgotten Great Africans, 3000 B.C. to 1959 A.D.*, pp. 31–35. London, G. K. Osei, 1965.

——, *Shaka the Great: King of the Zulus*. London, The African Publication Society, 1971.

Ridgway, Viola, *Stories from Zulu History*, pp. 35–95. Pietermaritzburg, Shuter and Shooter, 1946.

Ritter, E. A., *Shaka Zulu*. London, New York and Toronto, Longmans, Green and Company, Ltd., 1955.

Shooter, Joseph, *The Kafir of Natal and the Zulu Country*. London, E. Stanford, 1857.

Wiedner, Donald L., *A History of Africa South of the Sahara*, pp. 133–134, 146. New York, Vintage Books, 1962.

Woodson, Carter Godwin, *African Heroes and Heroines*, pp. 130–147. Washington, D.C., The Associated Publishers, 1939.

Moshesh

Moshesh

BASUTO KING, WARRIOR, AND STATESMAN
(1790–1870)

THE BASUTOS of South Africa enjoy the reputation of being the only dark-skinned people in the world to defeat a British army and get away with it. The credit is due to Moshesh, their king, one of the ablest generals and shrewdest statesmen of his time.

After defeating one of England's best generals in the field, he outwitted him in a match of intelligence that became a classic in diplomatic circles.

Whether in war or diplomacy, Moshesh was more than a match for any combination of his opponents, white or black. He played his white opponents one against the other and defeated them. As to the black allies of the white men, he ate them up as a leopard would a cat. No member of the darker races in the struggle for survival against the white man has covered himself with greater glory than Moshesh.

Born about 1790, the son of a captain in an insignificant tribe, Moshesh showed his genius for leadership at an early age. When Chaka, the Zulu king, was devastating South Africa, Moshesh's tribe fled to the Drakensberg Mountains, where they settled in an area unexcelled for hunting and for raising grain and cattle. They were joined by other fugitives from Chaka. Moshesh received these wrecks of the petty nations hospitably and built up the powerful Basuto kingdom.

Selecting a broad, flat tableland site 5000 feet above sea level, Moshesh established his capital there. Fortifying and strengthening it, he looked down from that height on his neighbors like a robber baron of the feudal ages.

Under his rule the Basutos became rich, healthy, and contented. Not even the Zulus excelled the Basutos in physique, bodily skill, and courage. Superb horsemen, they could gallop down steep inclines on their sure-footed ponies, or pick their way among enormous boulders and through mountain passes, without saddle or bridle. What the Indian was to North America, the Basuto was and is to South Africa.

Moshesh was not to enjoy his splendid isolation for long. The Boers of Cape Colony, pressed by the British, began their great trek of 1836, and coming into territory belonging to Moshesh or his subject tribes, founded the Orange Free State, now called Orange River Colony.

As to the ownership of the lands they were invading, the Boers gave it little or no thought. Were they not Christians and white men, and were not the Basutos only blacks and heathens?

Despite their artillery and rifles, the Boers soon began to feel the power of Moshesh. With his impetuous horsemen he would descend on their farms, driving off their cattle to increase his own herds. They simply could not reach him. When they came against him with their cannon, he would loosen an avalanche of rocks on their heads from the heights of his mountain fortress.

This continued until 1843 when the British found it in their interest to make a treaty of peace with Moshesh. The Boers, coming under British protection about this time, had the British governor-general, Sir Harry Smith, arrange one for them also.

To these arrangements Moshesh readily affixed his mark, but with the mental reservation that he was going to keep his word only as far as his own interests were served. The wily black monarch foresaw that the situation would develop into a three-cornered battle for supremacy—British against Boers, and British against Basutos. Moshesh knew that these two enemies were going to unite against him when it suited their purpose because they were white and he was black.

In fact, during the signing of the treaty with the British

Moshesh had seemed more amused than intimidated by Sir Harry Smith, who went through some incredible antics by way of impressing on the Basutos what would happen if the treaty were not made. One minute he snored and the next he wept—the snoring signifying the sleep of peace; the weeping, the loss of loved ones in war. Moshesh was by no means the simpleminded savage Sir Harry thought he was.

Contact with white men had taught Moshesh one important lesson, namely, that religion played an important role in their politics. So he decided that, as a matter of policy, it would be wise to introduce the white men's religion among his own people. Once they became Christians, he reasoned, the Boers and the British could not so easily justify hostilities against them.

Accordingly, Moshesh sent a white friend of his in Cape Colony 6000 head of cattle with instructions for him to dispatch missionaries to Basutoland. His orders were that these missionaries should be brought from as many white nations as possible, and before long there was a response from England, France, and Switzerland.

When the missionaries arrived, Moshesh established them in a settlement at the foot of his fortress and made his people follow their teachings. On the missionaries' recommendation, he ordered that no more alcohol be brought into his territory. Naturally, the missionaries sent home to their respective lands the most glowing reports about him, considerably strengthening his prestige in Europe. This so angered the Boers that they destroyed several of the Christian missions, which served further to strengthen the prestige of the Basuto chief in Europe.

Moshesh himself remained a pagan at heart, although he could quote the Bible as glibly as any of the white men who were hungering for his land. Toward the end of his life he shed even this veneer of Christianity.

Knowing that the white men, treaty or no treaty, meant to treat his people as they had other tribes, Moshesh decided to strike first. Soon after Sir Harry left, he attacked the Boers. Raiding them, he took 10,000 cattle and 2500 horses.

British and Boer now united against him as he had expected. The former sent an expedition commanded by Major Warden to attack Molitsane, one of his chiefs at Viervoct. The battle was fought on an extensive flat-topped mountain edged with perpendicular cliffs. The Basutos killed a number of their foes and drove the rest to the brink of the precipice, where a desperate struggle took place, the *assegai*, the battleaxe, and the rifle taking a fearful toll of life. Others were hurled to death on the awful crags below. British artillery, supported by the Cape Mounted Rifles and a large body of natives, came to the rescue, but also were defeated and forced to retreat.

After this victory Moshesh, who had been keeping the bulk of his warriors in check, unleashed them, harrying the farms and the flocks of the Boers with greater vigor than ever.

At last General Sir George Cathcart, governor of Cape Colony, with an army of 3000 picked white regulars and a large body of natives, started for Basutoland. On the way he induced all the native tribes hostile to Moshesh to join him. Reaching the borders of Basutoland, General Cathcart sent an ultimatum to Moshesh, demanding the immediate surrender of 10,000 head of cattle. Moshesh, whose quarrel was with the Boers rather than the English, sent a pacific reply and 3000 head of cattle, and requested time to get the rest together.

General Cathcart, with his expensive and highly trained army, was in no mood for delay and marched on Thaba Bosigo. When he neared it, he saw an enormous herd of cattle feeding on the mountainside. Dividing his force into three parts, he sent one unit to round up the cattle while he dispatched another unit along a road that led to the heights. He himself remained below with the third, never dreaming that the cattle, with its guard of old women, was a trap.

As a matter of fact the British soldiers had regarded the Basutoland campaign as something of a lark. Cathcart had taken no pains to learn the real Basuto strength. Moshesh had 10,000 of the finest horsemen on earth and an equal number of foot soldiers, well-trained. As Poultney Bigelow said, "The Basuto, before he enters the ranks, is a better fighting man than the average European soldier after three years of drilling, for as a recruit, he is always an accomplished horseman, an excellent marksman, and familiar with the duties of a scout."

The soldiers sent after the cattle succeeded in rounding up 4000 head and were driving them down the mountain through a narrow pass when 800 Basuto cavalry emerging, as it were, from nowhere attacked them. The British, caught among the stampeding cattle, were an easy mark for the Basuto lances.

Abandoning the cattle, the British fled pell-mell down the mountains until they reached Cathcart's unit, which was also being hard pressed. Swarms of Basuto cavalry swept down on the foe and were kept off only because their horses were frightened by flares of gunpowder ignited by the British artillery.

A great thunderstorm at this critical junction aided the British and permitted their retreat across the Caledon River, whither the Basutos did not follow them. Cathcart, to save his army from annihilation, had been forced to leave his wounded behind.

Though victorious, Moshesh was cool-headed enough to weigh the results of the battle. He knew that the "Great White Queen" possessed enormously greater resources than he and that she would never rest until he had been beaten. Accordingly, he took a step that later became the talk of diplomatic circles in Europe. He sent General Cathcart the strangest letter a victor has even sent a beaten foe. It read:

Midnight, Dec. 20, 1852

Your Excellency: This day you have fought against my people and taken much cattle. As the object for which you have come is to have compensation for the Boers, I beg you will be satisfied with what you have taken. I entreat peace from you. You have chastised. Let it be enough I pray you, and let me no longer be considered an enemy of the Queen. I will try all I can to keep my people in order in the future.

Your humble servant,
Moshesh

General Cathcart received this astonishing letter most gratefully. "It miraculously gave him a loop-hole of escape," says Sir Godfrey Lagden. "He, too, had been deceived in the strength of the enemy," says Theal, "and he dreaded a war with a tribe so highly organized and so well armed and with such strong natural fortresses. In his opinion, there was nothing to be gained by such a war that could outweigh its difficulties and cost, so he eagerly availed himself of the opening from a grave difficulty which Moshesh's letter afforded. It gave him the privilege of using the language of a conqueror and in such language he declared he was satisfied with the number of cattle."

How many cattle had the British general captured? Only 1500.

At home, Moshesh followed up his victory with equal astuteness. No sooner was Cathcart out of sight than he sent couriers to all the neighboring chiefs announcing a mighty black victory over the soldiers of the Great Queen, a fact that the general's hasty departure seemed to confirm.

Moshesh became a greater figure than ever. "From this time on," says Bigelow, "the career of Moshesh in South Africa, was, in its way, almost as brilliant as that of Napoleon after the battle of Austerlitz." His letter to the general, broadcast in Europe by the missionaries, was construed as a remarkable case of Christian forbearance.

With the British soldiers gone, Moshesh now moved against the native chiefs who had aided Cathcart. Among them was one of his old enemies, Sikonyela. Moshesh surprised him in his stronghold during a snowstorm and great was his vengeance against him.

Stronger now than ever, Moshesh renewed his attacks on the Boers with fortune favoring him in a way he had not expected. The British, in withdrawing from the Orange River Colony, had given back the Boers their independence, leaving them to fight it out alone.

When the Boers invaded Basutoland again they were beaten back, each time with heavy loss. The few paths that led up to Moshesh's fortress on Thaba Bosigo were so well guarded that the Boers stormed them in vain. Moshesh finally sent a raiding party to attack their homes while they were attacking him and that brought him peace for a few years.

At intervals for the next twelve years the war went on, with both sides almost at the point of exhaustion. Two of the leading Boer commanders, Senekal and Wepener, were killed.

It is worthy of note that the Boers who were unsuccessful against Moshesh soon afterward defeated the British at Majuba Hill and won their independence. Moshesh had been forced to fight with spears and homemade gunpowder while the Boers always had the latest European weapons.

The war against the Boers continued until Moshesh was past eighty. Then, determined that the enemy should never get his territory, even after his death, he performed what was considered another stroke of diplomacy: he placed his people under the protection of the foe farther away and thus less able to pillage him directly—the British.

This step was made comparatively easy by the aid of his friends, the missionaries, as well as by the very high regard in which he was held by the English people. Happy in the thought that he had saved his people from the foe he had resisted successfully for twenty years, the brave old warrior went to his final rest in 1870.

Obituaries lauded him. Ambrose Pratt referred to him as "Moshesh, the Negro who broke Chaka, conquered and slew General Wepener and defeated Sir George Cathcart—Moshesh, the chief 'who was never conquered and died unbeaten.' "

Theal says:

Moshesh possessed abilities of a very high order as a military strategist, a diplomatist, an organizer of society, and a ruler of men. . . . All who submitted to him were treated alike no matter to what tribe they belonged, and as much assistance as possible was given to those who needed it. . . . Men of the tribes that had been recently destroying each other were induced to live side by side in friendship and peace. Thus a new community was forming under Moshesh, by far the ablest black ruler known in South Africa since the coming of the white man.

Lord Bryce, author of *The American Commonwealth*, says:

The Kaffir races have produced within the century three really remarkable men—men, who, like Toussaint L'Ouverture and Kamehameha I of Hawaii, will go down in history . . . Tchaka the Zulu, a warrior of extraordinary energy and ambition . . . Khama . . . and Moshesh.

Moshesh was several times engaged in war with the Orange River Boers and once had to withstand the attack of a strong British force led by the governor of Cape Colony. But tactful diplomacy made him a match for any European opponent and carried him through every political danger.

"The individual Negro most nearly entitled to be called great," says Bigelow, "in so far as history leaves any record—is Moshesh. . . . With trifling modifications of color and education, he would have been welcomed in diplomatic circles as an advanced opportunist of the Bismarckian school."

Sir Godfrey Lagden says:

It is impossible to recall the story of his life without admiration for the untiring energy of the man; simple by nature, toughened by rude association, contending for supremacy with other tribes and for life alternately with Dutch settlers or British, yet all the while staggering under the weight of intrigues, domestic and foreign, and worried perpetually by envoys from all parts, and correspondence hard for his untutored mind to grasp the meaning of. . . .

The gift of foresight was peculiarly his; it was because he experienced it so intelligently that British governors, one after another, challenged his bad faith and ingratitude for not following advice or orders which he knew for a certainty would prove fatal to national interests. If his besetting sin was crookedness, the times were crooked.

The *Encyclopaedia Britannica* says:

He . . . was endowed with intellectual gifts which place him on a level with Europeans and his lifework has left a permanent mark on South African history. In diplomacy he proved the equal of all black or white, with whom he had to deal, while he ruled with a large combination of vigor and moderation over the nation he had created.

Moshesh's presence of mind was equal to all occasions. When urged to attack cannibals who had eaten his grandparents, at a time when he could not spare men, he replied, "I must consider well before I disturb the grave of my ancestors." Again, when the Matabele, under the great chieftain, Moselikatze, had besieged his fortress and were returning to their homes beaten and hungry, Moshesh called them back and gave them food enough to take them home, thereby making friends of them.

Perhaps the most astonishing thing about Moshesh is that he could neither read nor write. Had he been born in Europe and had the educational advantages and the wide field of action of some of his white opponents, he might indeed have been another Napoleon or Bismarck. He possessed all the qualities that made these men great.

REFERENCES

Bigelow, P., *White Man's Africa*. London, 1898.
Bryce, Lord, *Impressions of South Africa*.
Lagden, Sir G., *The Basutos*, 2 vols. London, 1909.
Bryden, H. A., *History of South Africa*. London, 1904.
Pratt, A., *The Real South Africa*. London, 1913.
Theal, G. M., *History of the Boers*. London, 1888.

ADDITIONAL REFERENCES

Brett, B. L. W., *Makers of South Africa*, pp. 32–37. London, T. Nelson, 1944.

Casalis, Eugene, *Les Bassoutos*. Paris, Librairie de Ch. Meyrueis, 1859.

Ellenberger, D. Frederic, *History of the Basuto*. London, Caxton Publishing Company, 1912.

Gollock, Georgina A., *Sons of Africa*, pp. 77–92. London, Student Christian Movement, 1928.

Gollock, Georgina Anne, *Stories of Famous Africans*. London, Longmans, Green and Company, Ltd., 1937.

———, *Lives of Eminent Africans*, New York and London, Longmans, Green and Company, Ltd., 1928.

Omer-Cooper, J. D., *The Zulu Aftermath*, pp. 99–114, London, Longmans, Green and Company, Ltd., 1966.

———, et al., *The Making of Modern Africa*, Vol. I, pp. 221, 231, 238, 242–243, 245, 250, 255–259, 263. London, Longmans, Green and Company, Ltd., 1968.

Polatnick, Florence T., and Saletan, Alberta L., *Shapers of Africa*, pp. 108–146. New York, Messner, 1969.

Tylden, G., *A History of Thaba Bosiv*. Basutoland, Maseru, 1950.

Williams, J. Grenfell, *Moshesh: The Man on the Mountain*. London, Oxford University Press, 1950.

Woodson, Carter Godwin, *African Heroes and Heroines*, pp. 167–180. Washington, D.C., The Associated Publishers, 1939 and 1944.

Cetewayo

Cetewayo

ZULU KING WHO DEFEATED A BRITISH ARMY AND
KILLED THE PRINCE NAPOLEON
(d. 1884)

CETEWAYO, King of the Zulus, was the hero of the greatest little war that England ever had.

Armed only with spears and knives, his men inflicted on the British the most crushing defeat that England experienced at the hands of any portion of a dark race in modern times.

His victory at Isandlhwana was marked by one of the most terrifying slaughters in the annals of warfare.

In one skirmish he defeated and killed Prince Napoleon, heir to the French throne. It took England over $100,000,000 and her ablest general to cope with this Negro king.

Cetewayo had an amazing people as his subjects. Of all peoples, they possessed, and still possess, the finest and most perfect physiques.

A white American woman visiting Zululand while out walking met a Zulu. So great was the physical force he radiated that when he passed she said she felt as, if she had been overthrown by "a wave of power."

Once a missionary, in trying to frighten Cetewayo into accepting Christianity, told him of hell fire.

"Hell fire!" Cetewayo laughed scornfully. "Do you frighten me with hell fire? My soldiers would put it out. See!" He pointed to a grass fire which was burning over a considerable tract of land,

and calling to the officer commanding a regiment, he ordered, "Before you look at me again, eat up that fire." In an instant thousands, shouting their war cry, bounded toward the fire, leaping into it barefooted, and the fire was soon "eaten up" without regard to those who were maimed and permanently injured.

A warrior's outfit consisted of a shield of dried hide, two or three spears, and a short blade for stabbing. As to clothing, he wore only a loincloth.

Discipline was most rigid. There was only one penalty for disobedience or neglect of duty: death. A warrior knew he must conquer or die, for certain death awaited a beaten army. He who ran or showed a trace of fear in battle was instantly cut down by the man behind him.

According to Colonel Browne, who saw service against the Zulus, a Zulu warrior could march thirty miles a day, and if need be, fifty, and give battle at the end of the day.

The Bible and Greek mythology tell of giants whose tread shook the earth. When Cetewayo's army of 35,000 marched, the earth literally trembled.

Not since the days of ancient Sparta had the world seen a body of fighting men comparable in physique. And Cetewayo needed this army to protect his kingdom—the kingdom he had inherited from his granduncle, Chaka, himself a great conqueror and the founder of the Zulu nation.

The Boers, or Dutch settlers, were treacherously encroaching on his territory. Years before, to escape British persecution further south, they had migrated into his land and had been welcomed by his uncle, Dingaan. Later, they became so grasping that Dingaan was incited to massacre them.

British colonial politics did not view Cetewayo and his soldiers with a friendly eye. But as British policy was always to divide and conquer, he was allowed to keep his army—it could be used to frighten their rivals, the Boers.

Besides, the British thought they could easily handle Cetewayo. They felt sure that when the time came all that would be necessary would be to march into his territory with a few fieldpieces and machine guns, press a button or two, and presto! his army would disappear. But they took care to see that shotguns were kept out of his reach.

In time, the Boers surrendered their republic, leaving the British a free hand in South Africa except for Cetewayo, whose presence now took on a different aspect. From being a tool of British foreign policy, he was now a menace. The Boers, now British subjects, must be protected! Cetewayo must go!

Having no love for the British, but deciding to use them against Cetewayo, the Boers laid claim to a part of Cetewayo's territory and began to settle on it. Cetewayo drove them away. The British, called in as arbiters, decided in favor of Cetewayo, but seized the opportunity to scold him about affairs in his own kingdom.

For instance, he had banished the missionaries because they had been plotting against him and meddling in his national affairs. One of them had written a letter to the governor of Cape Colony, declaring that "only the utter destruction of the Zulus can secure peace in South Africa."

The British also made several demands, among them: that Zulu warriors be permitted to marry; that Cetewayo permit a British resident—a sort of official spy—to live in his capital; and, to crown all, that he disband his army.

Cetewayo was astounded at this ultimatum. It was as if a judge, after deciding in favor of the plaintiff, had proceeded to lecture him on his personal affairs—affairs that had not come before the court. Miss Sarah Frances Colenso, Cetewayo's defender among the whites, said that he was treated as if he were a child instead of the head of a nation.

There was but one alternative for Cetewayo. Rising from his throne to his magnificent six feet four of brawn, he flung his defiance at the white envoys: "Go back and tell the white men this and let them hear it well. Myself and every one of my men will die first. I give you until sunset to get out of my territory."

Early in January, 1879, the British, 12,000 strong, under Lord Chelmsford, invaded Zululand at three different points. On the 22nd, one of these columns, composed of 1000 whites and 2000 blacks, under Colonel Durnfold, fell in with a Zulu army of 10,000.

The Zulus, as was their custom, began by chanting their war

song—a song without words. It was wonderfully impressive and stirring as the waves of sound majestically rose and fell, then rose again in a weird, mournful strain, yet warlike in the extreme. This ended, the order to march was given, and the long black line swept steadily and terribly forward to encircle the foe. In the front were the young warriors, behind them, the veterans. The British, entrenching themselves behind their wagons, opened fire with their artillery and machine guns. The Zulus, armed only with spears, came rushing on, shouting their battle cry, while the guns mowed them down in rows like wheat in the path of a reaper.

But charging madly home to death or victory, the gallant black warriors pressed grimly on until they reached the barricade. Then, leaping over, they gave the enemy a taste of what fighting at close quarters and with equal weapons meant.

Next morning when Colonel Browne, one of the scouts, wandered on the scene, he beheld a sight such as few human beings have ever witnessed.

A vast silent field of dead! Six thousand five hundred warriors lay there! There were no wounded. The Zulus had killed the entire British force, all but forty-two, who escaped by swimming their horses down the stream.

"In their mad rush," says Browne, "the Zulus had killed everything, even the horses, dogs, and mules. There were heaps and heaps of Zulu dead; where the machine guns had mowed them down they lay in heaps."

In addition the Zulus had captured 40,000 cartridges and the rifles of the British.

Of the Zulus, 3500 lay dead, not to mention the wounded, who had been carried off.

A few days later Cetewayo again defeated the British at Rorke's Drift, and laid siege to Etshowe. He followed it with another victory at Inahalobane.

At the news of this defeat the whites in South Africa were in consternation. They saw themselves sharing the same awful fate. They cabled to England for aid, and the same week 15,000 soldiers under Lord Wolseley, with the latest equipment, left for the Cape. Among the volunteers was the Prince Napoleon, son and heir of the recently deposed Napoleon III of France.

In August, 1879, the British, strongly reinforced again, invaded Zululand. With a force of 15,000, Lord Chelmsford met Cetewayo and his 25,000 warriors at Ulundi. Strongly entrenched behind their ammunition carts and wagons, the British opened fire at a range of 1000 yards.

The Zulu heroes charged with their usual courage but it was impossible for them, ill-armed as they were, to pass the belt of fire that protected their foes. Against the machines, valor and bravery counted for naught. "A thrill of admiration passed through me," says Browne, "when I thought of the splendid courage of the savages who could advance to the charge suffering such awful punishment." Finally Cetewayo was forced to withdraw, leaving 5000 of his men dead.

A few days later, however, Cetewayo caused another surprise. One of his detachments defeated and killed Prince Napoleon, causing great excitement in Europe and extinguishing the hopes of the Napoleonic party in France.

Soon after this Cetewayo was captured and kept a prisoner for three years, during which time his country, missing his strong hand, fell into anarchy. Many kings arose, and the tribes were broken up.

At last even his enemies began to demand his return, and Cetewayo was granted his wish to go to England to present his case to Queen Victoria.

When he arrived in England he was accorded a reception such as few monarchs have received. The Zulu War had been very unpopular with the people at home. They felt that Cetewayo had only been protecting his land as any other patriot would have done.

This opinion was strengthened when they found that Cetewayo was not the man-eating savage his enemies had depicted him as, but a courteous, amiable, and smiling gentleman. Queen Victoria was so impressed with him that she personally promised to restore him to power.

In the words of Theal, a white South African:

He was received and treated as if he had been a beneficient and civilized ruler who had merely done his duty to his people by heroically endeavoring to protect them against an invading army. Great crowds assembled to hear him wherever he went, deputations from various societies waited on him; he was taken to see places of interest, far and near; in short, he was made the lion of the day, such as no white head of a third-rate state would have been.

As guest of the British government, he was provided with everything that could tend to his comfort, and he was fitted out with clothing in the greatest variety and of the most expensive kind. He appeared in London dressed as an English gentleman and what is wonderful, really, he conducted himself as though he had been accustomed all his life to wear a silk hat and kid gloves. Great as is the power of imitation of the ordinary African, Cetewayo certainly excelled all his countrymen in this wise.

Presents of the most incongruous kinds were showered on him, such as gold lockets and cashmere shawls . . . three wagon loads in all. . . . He would have been utterly spoiled if it had not been that his intense desire to return to Zululand overcame all other feelings and enabled him to keep his senses.

When questioned by the Prime Minister about his defeat, Cetewayo said, "Yes, we lost some very fine men. But what could all our courage do against you English? You stand still and only by turning around, make the bodies of our warriors fly in pieces— legs here, arms there, heads, everything. Whew! What could we do against that?"

Despite the Queen's promises, the home officials, on the demand of the South Africans, did little. Worse, when Cetewayo returned to Zululand, he found that his kingdom had been split into three parts, only one of which was restored to him.

Anxious to rebuild his nation, he made war on one of these chiefs, Usibepu, but the latter, aided by the whites, defeated him. On February 9, 1844, Cetewayo died, presumably of heart trouble.

Sir T. Shepstone, governor of Natal, one of his foes, speaks in the highest terms of his personal character and his indomitable courage. "He was remarkably frank and straightforward," he says, "with much force of character and a dignified manner."

Miss Colenso says, "Cetewayo's treatment reflected no credit on the name of England." One might add that the treatment of this fine and brave people and their continued exploitation in the mines of South Africa are a blot on white civilization.

It was not until years after Cetewayo's death that the home government was convinced that a grave injustice had been done him.

REFERENCES

Bryden, H. A., *History of South Africa*. London, 1904.

Fairbridge, *History of South Africa*.

Theal, G. M., *History of South Africa Since 1795*. London, 1908.

Stow, G. W., *The Native Races*. London, 1905.

Wilmot, A. H., *Story of South Africa*. London, 1901.

Colenso, F. E., *History of the Zulu War*. London, 1880.

———, *The Ruin of Zululand*. London, 1884.

Illustrated London News, Aug. 12, 1882.

Vijn, Cornelius, *Cetewayo's Dutchman*. London, 1880.

Gibson, J. Y., *Story of the Zulus*. London, 1911.

Haggard, R., *Cetewayo and His White Neighbors*. London, 1896.

Moodie, D. C. F., *Battles of the British, Boers and Zulus*. 1879.

Déléage, P., *Trois mois chez les Zoulous*. Paris, 1879. (On Prince Napoleon.)

ADDITIONAL REFERENCES

Brett, B. L. W., *Makers of South Africa*, pp. 27–32. London, T. Nelson, 1944.

Ducarne, Victor Eugene Georges, *Conterence sur les Zoulous et Leur Territoire*. Bruxelles, Imprimerie A. Cnophs, fils, 1879.

Dunn, John, *John Dunn, Cetywayo and the Three Generals*. Pietermantizburg, Natal Printing and Publishing and Company, 1886.

Farrer, James Anson, *Zululand and the Zulus*. London, Kerby and Endean, 1879.

Huggins, Willis N., *An Introduction to African Civilizations*, pp. 117, 121. New York, Avon House, 1937.

Ludlow, Sir Walter Robert, *Zululand and Cetewayo*. London, Simpkin, Marshell Company, 1882.

Marks, Shula, "Harriett Colenso and the Zulu 1874–1913." *Journal of African History*, Vol. IV, No. 3 (1963) pp. 403–411. London, Cambridge University Press.

Moodie, D. C. F., *Cetewayo and Three Generals*. Natal Printing and Publishing Company, 1886.

Osei, G. K., *The Forgotten Great Africans 3000 B.C. to 1959 A.D.*, pp. 36–38. London, G. K. Osei, 1965.

Woodson, Carter G., *African Heroes and Heroines*. Washington, D.C., The Associated Publishers, 1939 and 1944.

Mohammed Ahmed—the Mahdi

❧

CONQUEROR OF THE
GREAT ENGLISH GENERAL GORDON
(1848–1885)

THE MOSLEM who received the greatest veneration in our times is, without doubt, Mohammed Ahmed, "The Mahdi," or Messiah of the Sudan. His followers held him in such esteem that they fought for the water in which he bathed and scraped up the earth over which he walked, keeping it as sacred.

And well they might. It was he who freed them from sixty years of slavery and cruel taxation by the British and the Egyptians. He defeated every combined British and Egyptian army sent against him, which seemed nothing short of a miracle to his people.

Like Mohammed of old, the Mahdi had very humble beginnings. Born at Khanag, Dongola, Sudan, in 1848, the son of a poor carpenter, he started in life as a house boy in the home of a French merchant at Khartoum. Unusually bright, he could recite whole chapters of the Koran by heart when he was only twelve. He let escape no moment that could be used in study, and as he cleaned his master's house or shined his boots, he had his books by him. Unable at last, however, to tolerate any kind of occupation that did not contribute directly to his goal, he left his French master and arranged with his two brothers, who were as wretchedly poor as himself, to support him while he devoted himself to his studies.

At school he was the most brilliant pupil. But his zeal and

sincerity got him into trouble. He felt that while numbers of his people lived so wretchedly, others of them should not live luxuriously and wastefully. When his teacher, Mohammed Sherif, gave a feast in celebration of the circumcision of his son at which he was one of the guests, the Mahdi not only refused to touch a morsel of the food but upbraided Mohammed Sherif before all his guests. It was a shame, he said, that those present should be gorging themselves while others of the faith were starving. The guests, which included most of the leading citizens of the town, were horrified at the audacity of the penniless young man, and Mohammed Sherif, beside himself with rage, kicked him into the street. This incident made the Mahdi a marked man and it was only after much pleading that he was admitted into another school.

But it had another effect. It made him a hero among the poor of the town. That he had dared to rebuke the rich in their own homes electrified them. Even before that incident, however, they had been impressed with him, especially the women. He was so polite and would help them with their heavy water buckets. Soon it was being said that he was the long expected Messiah who would appear in the year 1300 of Islam, or A.D. 1881. That time was drawing near. Belief in his divine origin increased when it was known that his name was also Mohammed, and that like the Prophet's, his parents' names were Abdulah and Eminah.

The authorities, alarmed at the growing popularity of the Mahdi and the increased discontent among the Sudanese, tried to arrest him, but he escaped and with a few followers went up the Nile to an island 240 miles away where he established himself.

To this island now came pilgrims from all parts of the Sudan, who after listening to his fervent prayers would leave more convinced than ever that he was the promised Messiah who would free them from the "Turks," as they called all their oppressors, regardless of race or religion.

And so it went until the year 1300 of Islam arrived. On that New Year's Day the Madhi sent his messengers over the land to boldly announce that he was the Promised One. Purify your religion, he bade the people, and await the moment of revelation.

The authorities decided that it was time to act. But it would not do to arrest the Mahdi. Accordingly, Raouf Pasha, the governor-general, sent messengers to him, inviting him in most polite language to come to Khartoum to be examined in the Koran to see whether he was really the Expected One. If he so proved to be, all obedience would be given him.

The Madhi, seeing the trap, sent back to say, "By the grace of God and his Holy Prophet, I am master in the Sudan. Never shall I come to Khartoum to justify myself."

Raouf Pasha offered a large sum for him, dead or alive. The Mahdi retorted by calling a *jehad*, or holy war, in which he promised his followers four-fifths of all the wealth taken from the oppressors.

Raouf Pasha sent two separate companies of soldiers to seize the Mahdi, but when they neared his island, the commanders of the two companies fell out over which of them should seize the Mahdi first and thus get the reward. The quarrel broke into an open fight, and the Mahdi, waiting until both companies had been weakened sufficiently, fell upon them and scored a signal victory.

This was hailed as a miracle. The enemies who had come to kill the Mahdi had killed themselves. Verily, the Messiah had come!

From all over the land the people now flocked to him, bringing captured weapons. The Egyptians sent a large army against him. The Mahdi, ambushing it, wiped it out to a man. The miracle increased. That a poorly-armed mob should defeat a well-armed body of regular troops could only have been the work of Allah. The Mahdi's leaders declared that Allah had sent invisible angels to fight for them during the battle and that this divine aid would always be forthcoming as long as they served Allah faithfully.

From the hills and the plains, deserts and forests, the tribes rallied to the black flag of the Mahdi—tens of thousands of them, the Selem, Baggara, Risega, Homer, Dinka, Bongo, Madi, Bari. They came on horseback armed with rifles or lances, or with homemade spears. Some, the poorest of the poor, wore only filthy loincloths. But all, fanatically brave, had but one goal: Freedom or Paradise.

The Egytpians, recalling Raouf Pasha, sent another governor-general with a stronger army, but in battle after battle the Paradise-intoxicated hordes of the Mahdi swept all before them. The Mahdi himself, tall, powerfully built, with the features of a god cast in black bronze, dressed in flowing white, on a splendid white Arabian horse, led them on.

The victories continued. At Senaar, of 6000 Egyptians only 20 escaped alive; at Djebel-Gadir in June, 1882, two whole army corps were wiped out; at Seribah on July 11 of the same year, of an army of 6100 only 12 escaped. In October, he inflicted another defeat on an Egyptian force of 10,000.

Strong enough now to take the fight to the foe, he attacked the city of El Obeid, where he suffered a momentary repulse, but soon afterward captured it with great slaughter and much plunder. His followers, maddened by years of cruelty and injustice and wrought up to the highest pitch of religious fanaticism, showed no mercy to the foe.

The Mahdi's next goal was the city of Khartoum—the city he had once left as a fugitive. Capital of the Sudan, Khartoum was wealthy. It was the center to which caravans came from the interior as far away as Ethiopia. The slave trade also brought immense wealth into its treasury.

England, as overlord of Egypt, was now thoroughly alarmed. The Mahdi was setting an example that might be followed by all Africa. She sent an army of 10,000 men, armed with the latest weapons, under Sir William Hicks, a veteran of the Indian wars, to attack the Mahdi.

Arriving in Egypt in December, 1882, Hicks passed through the Suez Canal, landed with his army at the old slave port of Suakin on the Red Sea, and marched to attack the Mahdi. Crossing the Nubian Desert after frightful difficulties, heat, and thirst, he reached Berber and went up the Nile, defeating the hostile tribes as he went. His goal was Khartoum.

The Mahdi, who in the meantime had crushed the Egyptians at Abu Ahmed and El Dheheb, thus enormously increasing his prestige, on hearing of Hicks' approach divided his forces in two. Sending one portion to meet Hicks, he led the remainder toward Khartoum.

Hicks reached Khartoum first. Leaving 3000 of his men to guard the city, he set off to attack the Mahdi. But the latter retreated toward El Obeid, Hicks following. When Hicks reached that city, however, he found that the Mahdi had retreated into the desert. Hicks went after him but the Mahdi poisoned all the wells, leaving no water for man or beast. On the third day, when Hicks' force had been weakened by thirst, a spy of the Mahdi's, who had posed as a friend of the British, led Hicks and his army into a trap.

Hicks and his men, though greatly weakened, held out gallantly for several days but on November 3, 1883, the Mahdi swept down on them, wiping them out. Only one white soldier escaped. Hicks was found dead under heaps of slain. It was a dark day for England.

As for the force that the Mahdi had sent to Suakin, that also had been successful. Led by the Mahdi's ablest general, the renowned Osman Digna (said to be in reality a French mulatto named Georges Nisbet), it defeated the English general, Sir Samuel Baker. Osman Digna then marched on Suakin itself, but was beaten off by the English General Graham.

Other amazing successes for the Mahdi continued. He captured Berber, Dongola, Darfur, and the rich Equatorial Provinces.

Britain, realizing that she had a foe of the first rank to deal with, sent out her ablest man, General Charles George Gordon, the celebrated "Chinese" Gordon who had served in that region before and had an immense reputation there. A Christian, he was as firm in his faith as the Mahdi was in his.

Arriving at Khartoum, Gordon found the situation in the Sudan desperate. Seeing that it would take an immense force and much money to conquer, he decided to use diplomacy instead. There was but one man in all Africa capable of dealing with the situation: Zobeir Pasha, a mulatto adventurer and descendant of the Abbaside caliphs, who, in turn, were descended from the family of Mohammed. Zobeir (see "Rabah Zobeir") had first come into the Sudan as a slave dealer, had made himself master of the trade, and had somehow been able to ingratiate himself with the natives. Invited to Egypt on a pretext, he had been thrown into an Egyptian prison.

Gordon, despite his loathing for slavery, now asked for Zobeir, but there was such a great outcry in England against any dealing with this ex-slave trader that Mr. Gladstone, the Prime Minister, rejected Gordon's request. Thus Gordon was forced to deal directly with the Mahdi. Gordon now offered to make the Mahdi governor-general of a province. But the Mahdi ridiculed him. Why should he be a mere governor-general when the whole Sudan, except one or two places, was already his. In reply he urged Gordon to become a Moslem.

Gordon, seeing all was lost, sent the women and children out of the city. The Mahdi arrived with his army soon afterward and laid siege to the city.

It was one of the longest sieges in modern history. Months passed while the English parliament wrangled. The terrain was difficult and England feared losing another army. Finally an expedition of 25,000 men was dispatched under the famous Lord Wolseley (later field marshal) whose victory over the Egyptians at Tel-el-Kebir in 1882 had given mastery of Egypt to England.

Wolseley made his way up the Nile in 800 boats, hoping to reach Gordon before it was too late. At Abu Klea, he came upon a part of the Mahdi's forces, won a victory, and captured the wells, but he sustained heavy losses. Also, a few days later his second in command, General Stewart, was beaten and killed.

Weeks later a part of his expedition reached Omdurman, a few miles from Khartoum, but not before the English ships had been severely battered by the Krupp guns of the Moslems. Wolseley's success was an empty one—two days before (January 25, 1885) Khartoum had fallen with frightful slaughter.

After a siege of 321 days 25,000 of the Mahdi's fanatical troops had swarmed over the ramparts of the beleaguered city. When they reached the palace of the governor-general, Gordon had walked calmly out on the steps, where a giant Kordofan Negro ran him through with a spear, and an officer named Nisser decapitated him with his sword. Hundreds of soldiers stuck their spears into his body, after which it was flung up into a tree for all to see. His head was sent to the Mahdi, who, it is said, admired Gordon and hoped to win him over to Islam.

Wolseley, seeing that all was lost, retreated to Cairo with the remnants of his army.

The fall of Khartoum and Gordon's tragic end were a severe

blow to English pride. To make matters worse, another expedition composed of 11,000 English and Egyptians was defeated with great loss at that time by Osman Digna at Kassala.

Lord Wolseley, bent on revenge, asked for another opportunity to attack the Mahdi, and was given it. He returned with 13,000 white troops the same year but was beaten back. England thereupon withdrew from the Sudan, retaining only the port of Suakin, which could be defended with warships.

The Mahdi was now supreme master of a rich empire 1600 miles long and 700 miles wide. And he kept his word to his people. He not only set them free but made life easier for them. He had a communal house—the Beit-el-Mal—stocked to overflowing with food at which anyone could eat free. Grain was stacked so high that from afar it looked like mountains. Whole rooms were filled with gold, silver, and jewelry, and with English sovereigns and Maria Theresa dollars. All of this was for the people. There were no beggars anymore. Expensive brocade and costly silks had been cut up into garments for them.

Flushed with success, the Mahdi planned to extend his conquests. He would be another Mohammed. He would conquer all the adjoining regions; subdue the Christian part of Ethiopia; march into Egypt as thousands of years before Piankhy, King of Nubia, had done; convert the world to Islam; and establish the thousand years of universal peace at Mecca.

His amazing career had reached its end, however. Six months after Gordon's death he was stricken with typhoid fever. On June 22, 1885, the sixth day of his illness, he stumbled to his feet, and summoning his last strength, shouted the Islamic creed, "La illaha illallah Mohammed Rasul Allah," and fell dead. He was only thirty-seven.

His followers were frantic with grief. They mourned him for months and erected a magnificent tomb on the spot where he had died. This became so famous a shrine that for a time it superseded that of Mecca.

As for the Mahdi's personal character, reports are contradictory. Slatin Pasha, a white man whom he kept a prisoner for years, accused him of licentiousness and greed. Others, however, are equally emphatic that he lived abstemiously in spite of his enormous wealth. Dujarric says, "The accusations brought against the Mahdi in the hope of making him appear odious in the eyes of Europe, are without foundation."

L. J. Morie, says:

The Mahdi never assumed the manners of a sovereign; he did not wish even to accept from his followers the modest title of Emir of Kordofan, and still less that of Sultan of Khartoum. He retained, even at the height of his power, his humble clothing and his simple ways; and remained to his death the living model of the austere dervish, poor, devout and scrupulous; but while one is obliged to recognize in him great intellect, and political, warlike and moral qualities that are indisputable, one cannot but abhor the cold cruelty of which he gave so many examples when he caused to be butchered the unhappy wounded or the prisoners that fell into his power.

The Mahdi's program was universal equality for all men; universal law and religion; and the equal distribution of wealth. There were to be neither rich nor poor. All opponents of Islam were to be destroyed.

SEQUEL

The Mahdi was succeeded by his second in command, Abdulla the Khalifa, whose announced intentions were to carry out his master's program. He would first conquer Ethiopia, and then uniting the south and the east with Islam, would gather a mighty force and march on Egypt.

He sent Osman Digna against King John of Ethiopia. The latter was killed in battle but Osman Digna was beaten back. Later the Khalifa defeated Ethiopia in a big battle, but unable to follow it up, withdrew his forces.

For the next eleven years the Khalifa reigned undisturbed. His regime, however, lacked the cohesion and the spirit of devotion that the Mahdi had been able to infuse even into the tribes that had once been hostile to one another. Among those who quarreled with the Khalifa was Osman Digna, who was the abler general of the two.

In 1896 occurred an event which led to the doom of the Khalifa's empire even though it did not happen within his own borders. Menelik of Ethiopia had defeated the Italians decisively at Adowa, and Osman Digna, taking advantage of this, besieged the Italians at Kassala. It looked as if Italy would be pushed out of East Central Africa. And after Italy, why not also France and England?

England, alarmed at the success of the native Africans as well as by French designs on the Sudan, decided to attack the Khalifa. She had not forgotten, moreover, her humiliating defeat by the Mahdi.

Gathering the largest army she had put into the field since the Crimean War of the 1850s, she placed it under Lord Kitchener, who had already tasted defeat at the Mahdi's hands, and sent it to Egypt. This force, 23,000 strong, later to be reinforced by Egyptians, was armed with dumdum bullets (later outlawed) and lyddite, a newly-discovered explosive—the first high explosive ever to be used in warfare.

This huge force reached the Khalifa's territory on June 9, 1896. It had a convoy of gunboats for bombarding the river strongholds of the Khalifa.

The Khalifa summoned his warriors, and they came, 70,000 strong, armed only with guns and cannon that were no longer modern and spears and knives, but they were brave and fanatical to the last degree.

His skirmishers engaged the British in several battles, but they were unable to retard their advance and lost thousands of men. In the meantime the Khalifa, with the main body of his army, 40,000 men, awaited Kitchener at Omdurman, the city from which Wolseley had once been beaten back. He had only forty cannon with shells of thin brass casings, while the cartridges for his old-fashioned rifles were homemade. But his men were undaunted. They really preferred a sword to a gun. It was the weapon they knew best how to wield.

The two armies met on September 2, 1896. At the first sign of dawn the Khalifa gave the order to attack and his mighty, dark-skinned host in white robes surged forth with one great cry, "For God and the Prophet."

The spectacle was magnificent, sublime, and will thrill ages to come. With tens of thousands of swords in the air, catching the glint of the rising sun, they came fearlessly on, horse and foot, against the most terrific odds possible—the latest in technological warfare. Lyddite at that time was, in a measure, what the atom bomb now is—it permitted victory without ever coming to grips with the enemy.

E. M. Bennett, an English war correspondent, describes the opening of the battle thus:

Six-thirty A.M. The formidable mass advanced by a single movement in a vast line. A noise, enormous, confused, made up of the beating of the tambours and the war-cry of the barbarians, floated above and rolled over the plain.

Suddenly the English infantry opened fire; a terrible fire that for several seconds made the Mahdists hesitate; then the army anew marched resolutely under the hail of balls, which swept out entire files. As the mass advanced, the tumult increased; on the side of the English, they fired with a cold rage. Upon all the line is a rolling fire in the midst of which break at short and irregular intervals the discharge of the machine-guns. On the side of the Mahdi, the order is perfect but from the swarming of burnous and of flag, arise fierce clamors; at each discharge a great gap forms in the mass; the dervishes press their ranks, lance forward; scimitar high; advance under their banners which clack in the wind as thrown in advance by their furious cries and the gesture of their leaders.

During all that battle the British stayed comfortably outside the reach of the spears and obsolete rifles, mowing down the Mahdists, who charged to the very mouth of the cannon. They fell in such numbers that their white clothing and turbans covered the ground until it looked like snow. Yakub, the Khalifa's brother, with only 150 men, charged the whole 23,000 invaders in an exploit that eclipsed that of the famous Light Brigade.

Valor counted for naught against the machines. Some of the blacks, however, did succeed in reaching the British squares and breaking through, winning the admiration of Rudyard Kipling. Finally, after two hours of slaughter, Kitchener gave the order to charge and his men, comparatively fresh, swept the few surviving Mahdists from the field. Of their number, 27,000 lay on the field, 11,200 dead.

The Khalifa retreated, but only to gain breath. A few hours later he hurled another 20,000 men at the British, breaking into their squares again and again. But unable to make a stand against the withering fire of the machine guns, the dervishes were again defeated.

English war correspondents, without exception, went into rhapsodies over the valor of the blacks. Describing the final phase of the first battle, G. W. Steevens says:

Now began the fiercest fight of that fierce day. The Khalifa brought up his own black banner against his staunchest die-hards drove it into the earth and locked their ranks about it. . . . It was Victory or Paradise. . . .

No white troops would have faced the torrent of death for five minutes, but the Baggara and the blacks came on. The torrent swept into them and hurled them down in whole companies. You saw a rigid line gather itself and rush on evenly; then before a shrapnel or a maxim, the line suddenly quivered and stopped. The line was unbroken, but it was quite still. But other lines gathered it up again, and again, and yet again they went down and yet others rushed on. . . . It was the last day of Mahdism and the greatest. They could never get near and they refused to hold it. . . . It was not a battle but an execution.

Our men were perfect but the Dervishes were superb—beyond perfection. It was their largest, best and bravest army that ever fought against us for Mahdism, and it died worthily for the huge empire that Mahdism won and kept so long. Their riflemen, mangled by every kind of death-torment that men can devise, clung around the black flag and green, emptying their poor, rotten, home-made cartridges dauntlessly; their spearmen charged death at every minute hopelessly; their horses led each attack riding in the bullets till nothing was left but three horses, trotting up to our lines, heads down, as if saying: "For goodness sake, let us in out of this." Not one rush, or two, or ten—but rush on rush, company on company, never stopping though all their view that was unshaken was the bodies of the men who had rushed up before them. A dusky line got up and stormed forward; it bent, broke up, fell apart, and disappeared. Before the smoke had cleared another line was bending and storming forward in the same track. . . .

Now, under the black flag, in a ring of bodies, stood only three men facing the 3,000 of the Third Brigade. They folded their arms about the staff and gazed steadily forward. Two fell. The last dervish stood up, filled his chest; he shouted the name of God and hurled his spear. Then he stood still waiting. It took him full. He quivered, gave in at the knees, and toppled with his head in his arms and his face towards the legion of his conquerors.

Then came the second battle that day:

The black Jehadia stood firm in their trenches through the infernal minutes and never moved till those devilish white Turks and their black cousins came yelling, shooting, bayoneting, right on top of them. Many stayed where they were to die, only praying that they might kill one first. Those who ran, ran slowly, turning doggedly to fire. The wounded, as usual, took no quarter. They had to be killed, lest they kill. For an example of ferocious heroism, I cite a little, black, pot-bellied boy of ten or so. He was standing by his dead father and when the attackers came up, he picked up an elephant gun and fired. He missed and the kicking monster half-killed him, but he had done what he could.

The correspondent of *Le Temps* of Paris, said:

One must indeed render homage to the last efforts of soldiers who would have been worthy to serve under the standard of Saladin and to measure arms with Richard of the Lion Heart and the flower of Christian chivalry. In the final hand-to-hand clash were produced a host of brilliant tragic exploits which will be buried in history only through the fault of the poet and the historian.

Kitchener, victorious, proved to be very barbarous. He ordered the massacre of the 20,000 wounded on the field.

"Our native battalions," says Bennett, "were soon busily engaged in killing the wounded. . . . The whole formed a hideous picture not easy to forget. . . ."

Kitchener, in his own defense, said, "All was done as humanely as possible." He also bombarded the tomb of the Mahdi and took his bones and dumped them into the Nile. His explanation here was, "If the tomb of the Mahdi had been respected, it would have become the goal of fanatical pilgrimages and caused immense evil to the good government of the Sudan." Into the bargain, the Mahdi's head was packed in a kerosene tin and taken to Cairo, later to be used, it is said, as a tobacco container by Kitchener.

For his services Kitchener was officially presented with a gold sword and made a viscount—but throughout England people dubbed him "The Butcher of Omdurman." In Parliament William Redmond said that Kitchener would go down in history as the English general who made war on women and children.

Steevens is of the opinion that the Khalifa lost the battle of Omdurman only through bad generalship. Had he attacked Kitchener at night, he says, nothing could have saved the British.

The Khalifa kept up resistance for months and died in battle. Brave Osman Digna, one of the most persistent and redoubtable foes the English ever had in Africa, was proclaimed Mahdi, and continued the fight for years, sweeping down unawares on the British time and time again. Wounded in battle, he was captured and sent into exile, where he died in 1928.

The Mahdists are as fine an example of heroism and devotion as history provides. Even Kipling, the arch-imperialist, was inspired by their courage. He wrote:

So 'ere's to you, Fuzzy-Wuzzy, at your 'ome in the Soudan
You're a pore benighted heathen but a first-class fighting man
An' 'ere's to you, Fuzzy-Wuzzy, with your 'ayrick 'ead of 'air
You big, black, bounding beggar—for you broke a British square.

REFERENCES

The Mahdi's son, Sir Sayid Abderrahman El-Mahdi, resided at Khartoum. In his possession were his father's massive gold-handled sword, which is adorned with stars and half-moons in pearls and diamonds; his sheath of hammered gold set in the same fashion is a remarkable weapon of the time of Charles V. The Khalifa's son was aide-de-camp to the governor-general at Khartoum.

There is a tendency to deny that some of the peoples of Sudan are Negroes. Those farther north, of course, show less Negro strain than those to the south, but that there is Negro ancestry running through the entire native population is evident. The Kababish, for instance, are described as the "richest and most powerful tribe" in the Harvard-African Studies, which goes on to say that "the richest divisions, i.e., those possessing the most slaves, tend to contain the highest proportion of members with Negro or Negroid features." (*Varia Africana*, p. 107. Cambridge, 1898.)

Anglo-Egyptian Sudanese, even those as far north as the Egyptian border, show much more of the Negroid strain than the Afro-American, and this no one who has ever seen both can dispute.

Slatin, Pasha, *Fire and Sword in the Sudan*. New York, 1896.

Wingate, F. R., *Ten Years' Captivity in the Mahdi's Camp*. London, 1893.

Alford, H. S., and Sword, W. D., *The Egyptian Sudan*. London, 1898.

Steevens, G. W., *With Kitchener to Khartoum*. New York, 1898.

Burleigh, B., *Two Campaigns*. London, 1896.

Bermann, R. A., *The Mahdi of Allah*. New York, 1932.

Gordon, General C. G., *Journals*. Boston, 1885.

ADDITIONAL REFERENCES

Arkell, A. J., *A History of the Sudan to 1821*. London, The Athlone Press, University of London, 1961.

Atterbury, Anson P., *Islam in Africa*, pp. 104–107. New York, Negro Universities Press, 1899 and 1969.

Bennett, Ernest N., *The Downfall of the Dervishes*. London, Methuen and Company, 1898.

Beshir, Mohammed, *The Southern Sudan*. New York and Washington, D.C., Praeger, 1968.

Chaille-Long, Charles, *The Three Prophets: Chinese Gordon, Mohammed Ahmed (el Maahdi), Arabi Pasha*. New York, Appleton and Company, 1884.

Churchill, Winston S., *The River War*, 3rd ed. London, Eyre and Spottiswoode, 1899.

Collins, Robert O., and Tignor, Robert L., *Egypt and the Sudan*, Englewood Cliffs, N.J., Prentice-Hall, 1967.

————, *The Southern Sudan, 1883–1898*. New Haven, Conn., Yale University Press, 1962.

Du Bois, W. E. B., *The World and Africa*, p. 216. New York, International Publishers, 1965.

Farwell, Byron, *Prisoners of The Mahdi*. New York, Harper and Row, 1967.

Holt, P. M., *A Modern History of the Sudan*, pp. 75–89. New York, Grove Press, Inc., 1961.

Trimingham, J. Spencer, *Islam in the Sudan*, pp. 93–96. London, Oxford University Press, 1949.

Hill, Richard, *A Biographical Dictionary of the Sudan*. London, Frank Cass and Company, Ltd., 1967.

Holt, P. M., *The Mahdist State in the Sudan*. Oxford, The Clarendon Press, 1958.

Jackson, H. C., *The Fighting Sudanese*. New York, St. Martin's Press; London, Macmillan and Company, Ltd., 1954.

———, *Sudan Days and Ways*. New York, St. Martin's Press; London, Macmillan and Company, 1954.

El-Mahdi, Mandour, *A Short History of the Sudan*. London, Oxford University Press, 1965.

Moorehead, Alan, *The Blue Nile*, New York, Dell Publishers, 1962 and 1963.

———, *The White Nile*, pp. 199–349. New York, Harper and Brothers, 1960.

Oduho, Joseph, and W. M. Deng, *The Problem of the Southern Sudan*. London, Institute of Race Relations, Oxford University Press, 1963.

Ohrwalder, Joseph, *Ten Years' Captivity in The Mahdi's Camp*. London, S. Low, Marston and Company, 1892.

Omer-Cooper, J. D., *et al.*, *The Making of Modern Africa*, Vol. I, pp. 63–69, 79. London, Longmans, Green and Company, Ltd., 1968.

Al-Rahim, Muddathir A. B. D., *Imperialism and Nationalism in the Sudan*. Oxford, The Clarendon Press, 1969.

Theobald, A. B., *The Mahdiya*. London, Longmans, Green and Company, Ltd., 1951.

Wingate, Sir Francis Reginald, *Mahdiism and the Egyptian Sudan*. London, Cass, 1968.

Woodson, Carter G., *African Heroes and Heroines*, pp. 80–83, Washington, D.C., The Associated Publishers, 1939 and 1944.

Superintendent of Documents, U.S. Government Printing Office, *U.S. Army: Area Handbook for The Republic of the Sudan*. Washington, D.C., U.S. Government Printing Office, 1964.

Paul Belloni Du Chaillu

EXPLORER OF AFRICA AND BELOVED STORYTELLER
(1837–1903)

PAUL BELLONI DU CHAILLU, African traveler, discoverer of the gorilla, writer of children's stories, and one of the most talked of men of his time, was born on the island of Reunion off the east coast of Africa of a French father and a mulatto mother. The date of his birth is uncertain. It was probably 1837. Du Chaillu kept that, as well as the place of his birth and his ancestry, a secret, for reasons that will be seen.

Sent to Paris for his education, he later returned to Africa and began, like his father, to trade with the natives along the Gaboon River in West Africa. This venture ended in disaster. His canoe was upset, he was nearly drowned, and he lost his entire cargo of ebony and ivory. Deserted by his men, he stumbled upon an American mission four days later.

This misfortune was to be his making. The missionaries painted such an attractive picture of America for him that he decided to go there to make his fortune. With the money he had inherited from his father, he left for New York.

In America, realizing that it would be fatal should his true ancestry be known, he evaded mention of the place of his birth, leaving the inquisitive to make their own guesses. Fortunately for him, though his skin was dark and was burned even darker by the African sun and his face was Negroid, his hair was straight. He was further helped by his foreign accent, and as he spoke French, it was generally said he was from New Orleans. To this some added that he was of Indian extraction.

But he could not always escape suspicion. One night in midwinter some of the white men in the lodging house in which he lived decided to "teach him a lesson." They planned to surprise him in bed, tie him up in a blanket, toss him from hand to hand down four flights of stairs, and then down a steep incline into the icy waters of a lake. Du Chaillu, warned of this, went out and returned with a good supply of roast turkey, cake, pie, candy, and fruit. When his tormentors appeared, he invited them in courteously, and asked them to join him in supper. They ate and bothered him no more.

Du Chaillu's great ambition was to be a writer. He knew Africa and he felt sure he could thrill others by telling them of it. For instance, there was the gorilla—that creature too much like a beast to be a man, and too much like a man to be a beast. He had never seen one, it is true, but the natives had often told him wonderful tales about the animal.

He tried to interest the newspapers but the editors, sure that they knew what the public wanted, would not listen to him. Africa was then of little interest. The editor of the *New York Tribune* curtly told him that if he was so much interested in Africa, he ought to return there at once.

In his rounds Du Chaillu had noticed one thing, however. While the editors were not interested, the people with whom he talked were very much so. Accordingly, he planned a scientific expedition of his own, and began taking lessons in natural history. In October, 1865(?), he left for Africa, promising to send specimens to museums in Boston and Philadelphia.

Arriving in Africa, he was well received. The natives, remembering his father, brought him ivory, ebony, gold dust, and other merchandise. But he was now a scientist and no longer a trader. When he did not buy their goods but tried to get them to accompany him into the interior, they became suspicious. At that time ivory and ebony were passed from hand to hand through the lands of the various tribes until they reached the coast. In the passage each middleman took his share of the profit. Accordingly, it was believed that Du Chaillu in wishing to get into the interior meant to trade directly with the natives there, so they tried to discourage him from going by telling him of the great dangers—of the lions, leopards, snakes, elephants, and the cannibal tribes, all of which only served to excite him the more.

He started off. Most of the dangers against which he had been warned materialized. One night as he was about to get into bed, he found an eighteen-foot snake curled up in it. He encountered crafty savage kings and cannibals, but because he put on a bold front and never showed fear they let him proceed unmolested. Before setting out he had made three resolutions, namely, never to show fear, to appear unconcerned no matter what the danger, and never to yield to people of bad faith.

His goal, he ever reminded himself, was to find the gorilla— Njina, King of the Jungle—which no white man had ever seen. The largest specimens of anthropoid apes then known were the orangoutan and the chimpanzee. In 1847 an American missionary had told of an ape in the jungles larger than either of these two species, but the public, and even scientists, scoffed at the idea, even though there were two incomplete skeletons of the gorilla in museums.

Yet the scientists could hardly be blamed, as the tales about the gorilla taxed the imagination. Fabulous stories were told of his cunning and his preference for black women over the females of his own kind. As for his strength and ferocity, they were appalling. The two most dangerous animals in the world, it was said, were the crested lion of the Atlas Mountains and the gorilla, with the latter the worse of the two. Even the lion, it was said, avoided the gorilla.

The natives believed that the gorilla was inhabited by the spirits of the dead, and whenever they encountered one, they turned their eyes away. For a pregnant woman to see one was considered fatal to the unborn child. Du Chaillu heard that the great ape was in the habit of lying in wait on the trees over a pathway, seizing human beings as they passed and tearing them from limb to limb as easy as paper.

Du Chaillu pushed on dauntlessly into the unknown. When his followers begged him to turn back, he drove them on instead.

There were many hardships, including hunger. At first he refused to eat roasted snakes and monkeys. After the day's march he tried to still his hunger by drinking liquor. But finally he was forced to eat monkey to keep from starving, and he learned to like it.

At last he reached the land of the gorilla and saw the tracks of one. His encounter with one was to come sooner than he expected. The next day he heard a roar so unearthly that it seemed to freeze the marrow in his bones. Cautiously he crept forward and saw a never-to-be-forgotten sight—a hairy monster fully six feet tall with the body of a giant; great muscular arms; deep-sunken gray eyes, fiercely glaring; and a face more diabolic and terrible than he had ever seen in a nightmare. He stood almost petrified.

At the sight of the intruders the great ape ground his fangs fiercely, savagely twitched his face, beat his enormous fists on his chest till it resounded like an African drum, and screamed like a madman. Then with a look of unutterable hate he stalked, arms stretched wide open, toward the intruders. Du Chaillu and his men fired at him. He fell groaning and writhing like a wounded colossus. Soon he was skinned, and the natives, forgetting the sinister powers with which they had invested him, ate him ravenously.

Soon afterward Du Chaillu killed an ever larger one with a chest measurement of sixty-two inches. Then he pushed farther into the jungle—and more danger. He fell seriously ill with bush fever; the party narrowly escaped being devoured by a horde of great ants on the march; and he narrowly escaped being torn to pieces by a band of infuriated women whose sacred dance he had spied on.

After four years of these adventures, he was forced to quite because of swollen feet, and returned to America loaded with specimens.

With these he created such wonder that overnight he became the most widely talked of man in Europe and America. Learned societies showered invitations on him and leading scientific journals carried his articles. But he had not reckoned with those scientists who did not want their pet theories disturbed—nor with the objections of skeptical readers. After reading his description of the gorilla, many flatly declared that there was "no sech animal."

In vain he produced the skin and the skull of a gorilla and

declared that he had seen them with his own eyes. The skull, his enemies said, was that of a giant Negro. Finally, since the Bible had never said anything about gorillas, they did not exist. A live gorilla, perhaps, would have convinced them, but he had none.

The skin, however, could not be so easily explained away; however, they finally found a way to do so. Du Chaillu in one of his lectures told of having seen an animal, the *Potomogale volex*, and erroneously said it was a species of otter. This was only an academic slip but his enemies magnified it to grotesque proportions to picture him as ignorant and unreliable.

A fierce controversy now waged around Du Chaillu. Ministers of the gospel and their congregations called him an atheist, one who believed that men sprang from monkeys. And as much of what he related tended to shatter orthodox beliefs, the publishers of textbooks and Bibles, and their friends among the college professors, fought him bitterly. He was ridiculed, cartooned, and elected president of the Ananias Club.

However, the Royal Geographical Society, then the most powerful institution of its kind, took him seriously and invited him to England, where he was very warmly welcomed. He showed his specimens of the gorilla to British scientists, after which the British Museum bought them for a large sum and a publisher gave him a large price for his manuscripts. To add to his fame, and to fan the dispute even more, Sir Richard Burton, famed explorer of Africa and Asia, endorsed him.

His prestige increased, but feeling that his honor was still at stake, he decided to return to Africa and bring back a live gorilla. He sailed for that continent in 1864, but misfortune overtook him again. While in Africa he lost all of his scientific instruments, part of them by the capsizing of a boat and the remainder during an attack by the Ashangos. He did succeed, however, in capturing a female gorilla and her young, but she died shortly afterwards. He rushed the young one to England by one of his bearers, but it died on the ship. In time, however, he sent back enough skulls of Negroes and gorillas to prove that the two were unlike.

He remained in the jungle for two years, taking photographs and sending back specimens enough to silence the objections of his opposers and strengthen the confidence of his friends. When he returned to England, he brought many native novelties, among them a harp of vegetable strings.

His appearance before the Royal Geographical Society was a sensation. At a gathering composed of some of the most distinguished savants of Europe he related his thrilling adventures and told of the strange customs of the people he had been among. One unusually fascinating story described a tribe whose king-elect was beaten, spat upon, and generally ill-used by his people to show him that he was nothing without their sanction and good-will, all of which was borne cheerfully by the future ruler.

Among those present at this meeting was another noted traveler in Africa, Winwood Reade, who endorsed Du Chaillu highly. Henceforth, his position in the scientific world was assured. His word was accepted that the gorilla was one of the most savage of beasts, was taller than the average man, weighed sometimes more than 400 pounds, and was as strong as fifteen men.

His book of travels became the best seller of the day. Its style, vigorous and rapid, thrilled his readers. He next wrote books for children, such as *Wild Life under the Equator, Lost in the Jungles, My Apingi Kingdom, The Country of the Dwarfs*, and *A Journey to Ashango-Land*. Their popularity was amazing. Boys and girls over the English-speaking world read them eagerly, learning whole passages by heart. There were but few persons in the United States who did not know of Cousin Paul, or Ami Paul, as Du Chaillu was affectionately called.

Du Chaillu was good-natured, jolly, generous, and a favorite with the women although he never married. He was a lover of good food and wine, had an inexhaustible stock of anecdotes, and was so sociable that he became one of the most popular and beloved figures of his time. He had an air of almost wistful niceness about him, while his small, brilliant, piercing eyes—his most striking physical characteristic—gave him an impression of extraordinary alertness.

But good-hearted as he was there was one thing for which he never forgave anyone: prying into his ancestry. However, when he became so famous it was natural that people should inquire into his birth, and they began to search. In Paris, where some said he had been born, no record could be found. The same was true of the United States. No one could recall ever having seen him in his childhood. Proof that he wasn't born in America is that he became naturalized.

It was not until after his death that the secret came out. But so great was his popularity that had it been said he was of Negro ancestry it would have been generally regarded as an attempt to slander him. In fact, there are very few who know it or wish to believe it to this day.

Du Chaillu's wanderlust was incurable. But he had had enough of Africa. His next field of research was as cold as Africa was hot: Scandinavia. There he decided to gather material for a book on the Vikings, who were then believed to be the ancestors of the English-speaking peoples.

When he reached Sweden in 1871, he was received with a guard of honor and escorted to the king's palace. He also went to Norway, Lapland, and adjoining lands. In Copenhagen he spent five years making fresh, literal translations of old documents and another year in the museums, after which he set about writing his book. It was an enormous task. He worked on it fourteen to sixteen hours a day with three secretaries. The result was *Svar the Viking*, which had a good sale and added to his fame. In Philadelphia he was offered $500 for a single lecture—a large sum at that time.

On his return to America he lived in the Marlborough Hotel in New York, from which he made frequent trips abroad. A voyage across the Atlantic meant no more to him than a buggy ride to some others.

In 1899 his great friend Judge Daly died, leaving a big gap in his life. He was nearing seventy, but with his desire for travel still undimmed, he left for Russia to study the life of the peasants there. He felt, also, that one day commerce would develop between America and the East and that such a step would help.

Arriving in Russia in 1901, he was received as a hero. On April 30, 1903, he was striken with paralysis and died. His body was placed in a vault reserved for distinguished men of science, and was later shipped to New York, where it was interred in Woodlawn Cemetery on June 25 of that year.

Du Chaillu's renown rests on the fact that he contributed perhaps more than any other single individual to the opening up of Africa to Western civilization. Livingstone, it is true, had preceded him; however, he not only preceded Livingstone into the deep interior but his books publicized Africa as it had never been before. His work paved the way for Sir Henry M. Stanley and created a receptive public for the latter. Editors who had once laughed at him lived to regret it.

Du Chaillu traveled more than 8000 miles in Africa, killed and stuffed more than 2000 birds, gorillas, and other animals, and wrote hundreds of magazine articles and books. But above all he was human. Helen E. Smith, who knew him well, said:

His way was to live with the plain people, sharing their daily life, their sorrows and joys, their hardships and sacrifices. In this way, he learned the hearts of men, their most secret longings. His controlling traits were an inexhaustible energy and courage, a thirst for acquiring and communicating information, and a heart, big and warm with human sympathies.

REFERENCES

Edward Clodd, noted English writer on evolution, discussing the mystery of Du Chaillu's ancestry, says:

"No less secure place in the affections of our little group was held by Paul Belloni Du Chaillu, known as Paul. Like more than one eminent man, he invented more than one birthplace for himself. One day it was New York; another day it was Paris; while, according to the obituary notice of him in the *Herald*, May 1, 1903, it was New Orleans. The truth is, he was born on the island of Bourbon, or Reunion. His father was a Frenchman, clerk to a Gaboon trader, and his mother a mulatto. He was not much over twenty when bitten by the gad-fly, he started to travel through Equatorial Africa. Paul's diminutive stature, his Negroid face, and his swarthy complexion made him look somewhat akin to our simian relatives. Only those of his friends who survive, can enter fully into the drollery of the story of his appearance in a Baptist pulpit in the backwoods of America where he was on a lecturing tour." (*Memories*, p. 71. London, 1916.)

The case of Du Chaillu is precisely that of thousands of other foreigners—British West Indians, Cubans, South Americans, Egyptians, Jews, Greeks, and others of Negroid ancestry—who come to the

United States, and who because they speak with a foreign accent, are not regarded as Negroes—Negro, in America, being a caste system rather than a mere distinction of color.

The Book Buyer (Nov., 1889, p. 356) gives Du Chaillu's family tree dating back to his great-great-grandfather; the *Scientific American* (May, 1903, p. 355) gives his birthplace as New Orleans, though he was a naturalized citizen; *Encyclopaedia Britannica* says, "He was probably born in Paris . . ." and so on.

A biography of Du Chaillu by Michel Vaucaire (New York, Harper and Brothers, 1931) makes no mention of this passage from Clodd. Helen E. Smith's "Reminiscences of Paul Du Chaillu," *Independent*, Vol. 55, pp. 1146–1148 (1903) gives an intimate account of him but no hint of his real ancestry.

ADDITIONAL REFERENCES

Clodd, Edward, *Memories*, pp. 71–74. London, Chapman and Hall, 1916.

Du Chaillu, Paul Belloni, *My Apingi Kingdom*. New York, Harper, 1928.

————, *Lost in the Jungle*, New York and London, Harper and Brothers, 1869.

————, *King Mombo*. New York, Charles Scribner's Sons, 1902.

————, *A Journey to Ashango-Land*. New York, D. Appleton and Company, 1867.

————, *In African Forest and Jungle*. New York, Charles Scribner's Sons, 1903.

————, *Explorations and Adventures in Equatorial Africa*. London, J. Murray, 1861.

————, *Adventures in the Great Forest of Equatorial Africa* and *The Country of the Dwarfs*. London, J. Murray, 1892.

————, *The Country of the Dwarfs*. New York, Harper and Brothers, 1871.

Tippoo Tib

꧁꧂

VOLUMES HAVE BEEN WRITTEN about the exploration of Africa by
the European; little if anything of the black man's part in it. Yet
the greatest of all the African trailblazers was a Negro—Hamid
ibn Mohammed, better known as Tippoo Tib.

We are familiar with the adventures of Stanley, Livingstone,
Burton, Speke, Cameron; nevertheless, those of Tippoo Tib were
much more exciting. In the path that he blazed Stanley followed,
as did Livingstone and others.

"It is thanks to his support," says *La Grande Encyclopédie*,
"that Cameron, in 1874, and Stanley in 1876, and Wissman in
1882, could cross Africa."

Starting from the island of Zanzibar, his birthplace, Tippoo Tib
crossed Africa by way of Lake Tanganyika, up through the vast
stretch of what is now the Republic of the Congo. The journey
took him eleven years, during which he traversed territory no one
from the outer world had ever penetrated before. He fought his
way through the primeval forest, forced himself into the lands of
the tribes, and defeated chief after chief until he was master of a
territory as large as Western Europe.

He was by far the greatest of those who dominated in Central
Africa just before the seizure of that region by the white man.
Europeans who came into Africa were forced to reckon with him,

among them King Leopold of Belgium, who was glad to come to terms with him. As to wealth, he was one of the richest men in the world of his time.

Tippoo Tib was born in 1837 and was three parts Negro and one part Arab. (And an Arab can often be a Negro, but because he has the slightest trace of Arab ancestry he is considered an Arab.) His father was the son of an Arab merchant from Muscat; his mother and grandmother were both full-blooded Negro women. His father had been a trader in ivory, gold, gum, cattle, and slaves, chiefly the last. But neither he nor any of the Arab merchants had ever penetrated deeply into the African interior.

As a boy Tippoo Tib listened to his father's tales of the wealth that was waiting to be gathered there until he was seized by the desire to go himself. At sixteen he persuaded his father to take him on one of his expeditions, during which he distinguished himself. In bargaining, too, there was none so astute and suave as he. Was it necessary to fight? None excelled him in audacity and skill.

On the next expedition, as he was about to leave with his father, the latter was called back to Zanzibar and the command was given to another. Rejecting the idea of being a subordinate, Tippoo Tib, though only eighteen, got together 100 men and set off into the interior. Arriving at Lake Tanganyika, he crossed that great body of water in canoes he hollowed out from the trees of the primeval forest, and continued until he came to the territory of Temba, King of Tabora, a usurper.

Temba, on meeting Tippoo Tib, planned to provoke a quarrel with him, kill him, and take away his goods. But as the laws of hospitality demanded that no business should be discussed until the third day after a trader's arrival, Tippoo Tib heard of the plot. Siding with the followers of Mnyma, the rightful heir, he attacked Temba and killed him, and soon afterward returned to the coast laden with ivory, gold, cattle, and slaves.

Tippoo Tib soon started again on a second expedition, taking with him goods valued at $40,000 that had been furnished him by twenty creditors. (Getting credit was no easy matter, as traders had a habit of remaining in the interior to lead a life of luxury.)

On this trip he wandered into territory ravaged by famine but

Tippoo Tib

he turned this to advantage by getting bearers cheaply. When some of these porters ran off with his goods, he promptly made prisoners of their whole tribe until his property was returned.

Continuing, he came into the territory of Nsama, a powerful and bloodthirsty king, who had conquered all his neighbors, and whose cruelty and power had discouraged all other traders until now.

Nsama received him with a great show of hospitality and led him into a large hut where he showed him much gold and ivory. Then he attacked him. Tippoo Tib was struck in the shoulder by three arrows, but managed to fight his way out. Rallying his men, he attacked Nsama, and after four days of fighting, seized Nsama's kingdom.

This brought him much prestige, as Nsama had been regarded as invincible. Soon afterward he returned to Zanzibar where the story of his exploits had preceded him and where he was received as a guest by the sultan.

He was now twenty and rich. But money passed through his hands like water. Penniless again, he was forced to return to the forests.

This time he took goods valued at $80,000, the sultan himself being one of his creditors. Another of them was Taria, a shrewd and crafty merchant who had never been known to lend money without security before. "At the time," says Tippoo Tib, "I had neither a plantation nor a house in Zanzibar, or anywhere else in the world."

On this expedition many of his bearers died from disease. Coming into the territory of King Mishama, he was attacked by the latter but defeated him.

His next adventure was in Ugalia, where several of his men were killed at his side. After eight days of fighting, he defeated the king, Taka, and seized his land and wealth. Then he clashed with Lunda, King of Kasembe. Lunda had 20,000 warriors, some of whom were armed with Portuguese rifles, but Tippoo Tib, with his small force of Arabs, half-caste Arabs, civilized Negroes, and a few white men, armed with rifles, was again victorious.

Setting up another king in Lunda's place, Tippoo Tib continued along the Mweru River until he reached the capital of King

Mpueto, where the Congo flows into Lake Luapala. Mpueto, on hearing of the coming of the invincible stranger, sent him tribute.

Turning southward, Tippoo Tib came to the region of Lake Kassala to the south of what is now the Congo. Here he found two chiefs, Tambwe and Kassembe, who were fighting for supremacy. Playing one against the other he defeated them both.

Continuing, he penetrated into Shensiland where no Arab or white man had ever been before and where he found trading very advantageous. The natives did not know the value of ivory. After eating the elephant, they would throw the tusk away. For a string of beads worth a few cents he would get a tusk worth $50.

For the next nine years he worked his way in, entering virgin territory and becoming the uncrowned king of a vast land with untold wealth.

His exploits excited the greed of the Europeans, who were soon arriving on his heels. But they had to submit to him. Though he had neither press nor telegraph, he was master. Even the most powerful chiefs dared not offend him.

Stanley, Livingstone, Speke, Cameron, Glerrup, and all the great explorers were indebted to him. But for his aid they might have had to turn back. Stanley said in his autobiography, "Unless Tippoo Tib accepts my offer, the expedition will be broken up."

Later Stanley accused him of trickery, charging him with failure to live up to his contract. Tippoo Tib, he says, had promised him 600 bearers, but had given him only 400 in order to hinder him. Stanley had come to the rescue of Emin Pasha but he was also eager to get a large quantity of ivory to the coast, which was why he needed so many men. Moreover, Stanley was in the employ of Leopold of Belgium and was planning to oust Tippoo Tib and give his territory to Leopold after he had used Tippoo Tib.

Tippoo Tib strenuously denied retarding Stanley or any other white explorer. He said in an interview with Alfred J. Swann, resident commissioner of Nyasaland:

If I had wished to stop him [Stanley], I should not have played with the matter by sending 400 men instead of 600, as per contract. I should have killed him long ago. I do not simply hinder, I destroy. If I assist, it is at all costs.

Who helped Cameron, Speke, Livingstone? Who sent Glerrup from the Congo to Sweden? Who saved your life and those of all your party?

Without my help he [Stanley] could never have gone down the Congo, and no sooner did he reach Europe than he claimed all my territory. . . .

Tell Europe Stanley lies, and tell them also, if they love justice as you say, to compensate me for stealing my country."

Of this dispute, which became famous, Tippoo Tib said, "Stanley, in face of the difficulties of the march and the unwillingness of the carriers, lost his head completely and he himself made the proposal to diverge to the Congo."

Barttelot, also an explorer, thinks it was Stanley who broke faith. He said that Stanley told him he would as soon trust Tippoo Tib as "any white man."

Using Tippoo Tib's slave-trading activities as a justification, the European powers gave his territory to Leopold II of Belgium, whose minions were far more greedy and cruel. Tippoo Tib decided to fight, on which Leopold made him governor-general and commander-in-chief of the Congo and gave him Georges Steleman, a white Belgian, as secretary.

Tippoo Tib now fought the slave traders and ruled with success until the Arabs and the natives, who had opposed the coming of the white man, revolted under Raschid, his nephew, and Rumeliza, his lifelong friend. Rather than fight these old comrades, he gave up his post in 1890 and retired to Zanzibar to enjoy his wealth. His departure was followed by a massacre of the whites and a long war. He died in 1905 at the age of sixty-eight.

Tippoo Tib (the name means "whistling bullets" from the bullets that flew wherever he went) was a great instrument of evil. He brought immense suffering to the primitive people of Central Africa. When blamed for this by the white explorers, he would justify himself by pointing out what the whites themselves had done in capturing slaves for the New World. When accused of seizing the lands of the natives, he would point out how England had seized India, and when told that God opposed slavery, he would say that Abraham, Isaac, and Jacob of the Christian Bible had held slaves with the apparent approval of God. He could also have said that George Washington and Thomas Jefferson held slaves.

The white explorers spoke highly of him in certain other respects, however. Stanley says:

He was a tall, black-bearded man of Negroid aspect in the prime of life, straight and quick in his movements, a picture of energy and strength. He had a fine intelligent face with a nervous twitching of the eyes and gleaming white, perfectly formed teeth. He was attended by a large retinue of young Arabs whom he had led thousands of miles through Africa.

After regarding him for a few minutes, I came to the conclusion that this Arab was a remarkable man, the most remarkable man I had met among the Arabs.

Norden says:

Tipoo Tib, the son of an Arab half-breed and a full-blooded Negro woman, was in 1874 the most powerful figure in Central Africa. He had gone into the interior with an army of one hundred and had terrorized the blacks into crowning him king. Nyangwe was headquarters of his empire. So matters stood in Central Africa when Stanley was sent by the *New York Herald* to find Livingstone.

Haardt and Debreuil say:

Tippo Tib was a powerful sovereign. This adventurer, who was immensely rich and possessed considerable influence over the blacks, was a strange figure. In his obscure and inaccessible soul he united generosity and astuteness; hypocrisy with frankness. Stanley, as well as Cameron and Trivier, had to take him into account and to ask for his aid, which he granted. Thanks to this, they were able to succeed in their rash enterprises.

C. Eliot, consul-general at Zanzibar who knew him well, says, "His features were of the Negro type and produced a first impression that he was a low-caste hybrid, but this impression was quickly dispelled by his polite and dignified manner and his flow of speech."

F. D. Moore says he was

one of the strangest, most extraordinary figures of the nineteenth century.

The tale of this Negroid Arab, ignorant of scholarship even of his own kind, who by his dominant will and character and ruthless aggressiveness made himself the ruler of a hundred thousand square miles of terriroty, who commanded tens of thousands of savage ruffians armed with muzzle-loading guns of all dsecriptions, who held absolute power of life and death over a million human beings, who with serene detachment caused and witnessed a thousand crimes and agonies beyond the power of description that bits of ivory might be playthings and ornaments, already seems incredible. . . .

Tippoo Tib was both a gentleman and an inhuman monster. He was the soul of courtesy, kindliness and generosity and an incarnate fiend who dealt out cruel death as easily and naturally as other men breathed. He saved the lives of many white men; he murdered a hundred thousand miserable blacks. He sprinkled his spotless garments with Arab perfume and drenched his hands in human blood. . . .

Vale, Old Tippo Tib! Never will this world see your like again.

Alfred Swann, who also knew him well, says:

The first and by far the most important was the great Tippoo Tib. Although not of pure Arab descent, he was the most influential. His activity was astonishing. He possessed a frank, manly character enlivened by humor and he loved to play practical jokes upon his intimate friends. In business there was no beating about the bush; it was always take it or leave it; and in warfare "unconditional surrender" was the basis of his terms for all enemies who sued for peace.

His power was sung around most camp-fires from the East Coast to Stanley Pool on the Congo. His very name was sufficient to strike terror into the hearts of all who were liable to attack.

Speaking of his death, Swann adds:

It would have perhaps, been putting into practice that justice which I never ceased to hold before him as our standard if, when he died, some of our great geographical societies in Europe had acknowledged how much they were indebted to Tippoo Tib for allowing explorers to travel where he was in power, collecting valuable scientific data. As it was, all I noted was the announcement of the death of "the notorious slaver."

When the true history of the opening-up of Eastern and Central Africa comes to be written, Tippoo Tib, and not Henry M. Stanley, will be acclaimed the real pioneer. The history of travel contains no bolder figure than this son of Africa.

After Tippoo Tib withdrew from the Congo the minions of Leopold, King of the Belgians, in order to get the natives to produce rubber instituted a regime of horror and cruelty that overshadowed that of Tippoo Tib. Had Tippoo Tib had the foresight, he could have held onto his territory by placing his conquests under the protection of the sultan of Zanzibar, then a recognized ruler. Had he done this, says Dr. Heinrich Brode, he might have changed the whole political aspect of Africa.

REFERENCES

Brode, H., *Tippoo Tib*. London, 1907.
Janssens, D., and Cateaux, A., *Les Belges au Congo,* Vol. III, Anvers, 1912.
Hinde, S. L., *Fall of the Congo Arabs*. London, 1897.
Swann, A., *Fighting the Slave Hunters*. London, 1910.
Jameson, J. S., *Story of the Rear Column.*
Norden, *Fresh Tracks in the Belgian Congo*. London, 1924.
Barttelot, W. G., *Life of Edmund Musgrave Barttelot*, 3rd ed. 1890.
Moore, F. D., *Ivory: Scourge of Africa.* 1931.

ADDITIONAL REFERENCES

Atterbury, Anson P., *Islam in Africa*, pp. 65–67. New York, Negro Universities Press, 1899 and 1969.
Du Bois, W. E. B., *The World and Africa*, pp. 71–72, 77, 224. New York, International Publishers, 1965.
Mwenyewe, Kwa Maneno Yake, *Maisha Hamed Bin Muhammed El Murjebi yaani Tippu Tip*, trans. by W. H. Whitely. Kampala, Nairobi, and Dar es Salaam, East African Literature Bureau, 1958.
Omer-Cooper, J. D., *et al.*, *The Making of Modern Africa*, Vol. I, pp. 296, 299. London, Longmans, Green and Company, Ltd., 1968.
Wiedner, Donald L., *A History of Africa South of the Sahara*, pp. 172, 223. New York, Vintage Books, 1962.

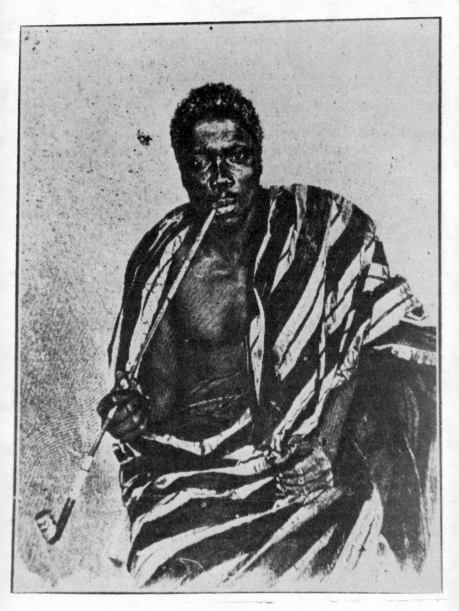

Behanzin

Behanzin Hossu Bowelle—
"The King Shark"

❧❧

AFRICAN POET-KING WHO DEFEATED FRANCE
FROM HIS THRONE OF GOLD
(1841–1906)

BEHANZIN, surnamed "Hossu Bowelle," or "The King Shark," was the most powerful of the West African kings in the closing years of the nineteenth century.

He was not what so often passes for a "king" in Africa, but a real monarch. He was descended in direct line from Tacodounon, who conquered Dahomey in 1610 and took the throne from the Houenous, whose ancestry, incidentally, went even further back.

In December, 1670, one of Behanzin's ancestors, Adanzan the First, visited Paris and was received with great ceremony at Versailles by the Grand Monarch himself.

The reason for this was the visit in October, 1626, of Admiral D'Elbee, to Dahomey, in the service of Louis XIII. The reigning monarch received the Frenchman with great deference and held fetes in his honor. He tendered him the highest possible honor by passing him his own cup to drink from, and presented France with a trading post on the coast. From then on trade flourished between the two nations.

The gift of this trading post was virtually responsible for the clash between King Behanzin and France over two centuries later.

Like his ancestors, Behanzin was absolute master of his kingdom. A nod of his head meant life or death for his subjects. His person was sacred. His common subjects saw him only at cere-

329

monials; only a few were permitted to see him do even the most ordinary things. If he wanted water while on the march, a screen was placed before him till he finished drinking it. When the water was passed to him, the soldiers would throw themselves prostrate on the ground, uttering "Ah-h-h," as if they were enjoying the drink with him. Not even his saliva was allowed to touch the ground.

Describing the veneration accorded to Dahomey kings, one writer says, "Dada! [King] we hear even yet the accents of veneration mixed with terror with which the old Dahomeyans pronounced the word. For them it symbolized the richness, grandeur and power of the fatherland. It epitomized the souvenirs of the glorious conquests of Dahomey."

Dahomey was wealthy. The elements of its success were its trade, its powerful army, and the courage of its soldiers, who were deemed invincible. The king, as the central authority, was supported by an efficient body of secret police.

The army contained 25,000 warriors, the pick of Behanzin's subjects. They were thoroughly trained and kept in trim by a system of gymnastics developed by the Dahomeyans themselves. They were divided into brigades and companies. Discipline was perfect. At the head of the Army was Agli-Agbo, the king's brother. Each warrior, on the march, had a servant to carry his weapons and his food.

But the most redoubtable part of Behanzin's army were 5000 female warriors, who were recruited from among the lustiest virgins in the kindgom and were sworn to chastity. They ranked above the men. The king sometimes picked his wives from among them, or gave them to his bravest warriors. When a man had an unruly wife he gave her to the king for his army.

The training of these amazons was rigorous indeed. One of their drills was charging barefoot into a construction of thorns. Boghero describes this extraordinary scene as follows:

Upon the ground reserved for the exercises, had been reared a mound, not of earth, but of very sharp thorns, about 50 yards long, 8 yards wide, and 7 feet high. At about 50 yards further, was another construction like a house, also thickly covered with thorns, the whole resembling a citadel.

All the women are at their posts in an attitude of combat, arms raised, swords in hand, massed in line of battle before the front of attack. The King rises and goes to the head of the columns. He addresses them, inflaming them, and at a given signal, they throw themselves with incredible fury upon the mass of thorns.

Descending as if beaten back, they return three times to the charge, each time so swiftly that the eye has difficulty in following them. They mount onto the construction of thorns with the same ease that a dancer moves on the stage, and yet it is with their bare feet that they have been trampling the sharp spines of the cactus.

Another of their exercises was killing a maddened bull with their bare hands. Some were injured in the attempt, but, invariably, by the end of this maneuver the bull would be dispatched.

"One should not be astonished after this," another writer adds, "to hear that these women fight with extreme bravery, exciting by their courage and their indomitable energy, the other troops that follow them. Like the men, they fought nude to the waist."

From infancy the Dahomeyan warrior was trained to despise death. The following is an account of the death of a Dahomeyan spy as told by an eyewitness:

Executioner: "You know, brother, I am going to cut." (Significant gesture at the neck.)

Spy: "Good."

The condemned man knelt and hung his head as if he were only going to have his hair cut. The executioner raised his weapon and said, "Are you ready?"

"Yes."

"Here comes," and the sword fell upon the neck of the poor devil, making only a deep wound. The blood spouted, the executioner becoming ferocious tried to saw off the head. Fatigued, streaming with sweat, he shouted to a comrade for his sword. In the meantime, the half-decapitated man, silent, stoical, uttered not even a groan.

Two hundred of the sturdiest women warriors and five hundred of the finest males formed the king's bodyguard.

The preferred weapons of the Dahomeyan warriors were short swords and knives, but some of them carried modern rifles, the use of which they had been taught by European instructors. The army also had six Krupp guns and a few fieldpieces.

Behanzin's policy was to keep all white persons out of the interior of his kingdom and exceptions were made in rare cases only. These were permitted to bring with them no sextants, surveying instruments, or cameras. The customs service was strict, and visitors had to carry about with them a special passport consisting of a palm almond wrapped in a special kind of leaf. Fear of the king's wrath and the vigilance of his secret police prevented the corruption of the country's officials. Theft or crime of any kind was rare.

Explorers and others who visited Dahomey were received as guests of Behanzin. Every courtesy was shown them, but they were virtually prisoners. Guides and domestics received strict orders as to what was not to be shown and with whom the visitors were not to speak.

Behanzin had ordered this because he had noted with increasing anger the intrusion of the European into neighboring kingdoms, as, for instance, Ashanti, where they appeared first as traders, missionaries, and visitors, and then as conquerors. They had gobbled up everything. He alone was left, and he meant to remain master in the land of his ancestors.

Behanzin was tall, well built, strong, and impetuous, but dignified. Unlike his rival, King Toffa, nominal ruler of the neighboring protectorate of Porto-Novo, and unlike his own rich subjects, he dressed simply. In the manner of the senators of ancient Greece and Rome, he wore a long strip of silk around his body and draped across his bare shoulders. His only affectation was a long pipe of exquisite craftsmanship, which he puffed nonchalantly most of the time.

He was also a poet. His verses and war chants are said to be the finest ever produced in Dahomey.

It is difficult to say what started the war with France in 1892. Dahomeyans say that Africa had been divided into spheres of influence by the European powers, and that their country had been awarded to France, which sought a pretext for conquest. Others declare that France attempted to force the opening-up of the interior to commerce. Others charge it to the fear and jealously of King Toffa, who had a difficult role to play between the rival British and French interests.

In any case, Behanzin had been getting too strong for the neighboring French colonies. Germany had been supplying him with modern rifles, and five Germans held high rank in his army. In 1890 he had defeated a French expedition and made France pay him for the use of Cotonou port. Stronger now, he felt that he could repeat the performance.

Whatever the cause, war began when Behanzin declared the treaty he had made with France null and void. This treaty was an outgrowth of one that had been made in 1868 by his father, Gli-Gli, who had ceded Cotonou to France. By virtue of a subsequent agreement made in 1890, France had agreed to pay 20,000 francs in gold annually for the use of this port.

Behanzin, it is charged, deliberately turned his back on attempts at amicable settlement. When the French envoys arrived at his palace of Dioxene with presents from M. Eitenne, secretary of colonies, it is reported he brushed the presents aside, saying contemptuously, "We have cases full of that in Dahomey."

When told of the workings of the system of government in France, it is said that he took his pipe from his mouth and laughed loud and long, saying that he much preferred his own, which was quicker and more original.

"Dahomey," he asserted, "has never ceded Cotonou to France, and if the French do not get out at once, I will drive them out myself."

War began. In the first few engagements Behanzin was victorious. France, realizing that she had a difficult enemy to cope with, selected her best colonial fighter, Colonel A. A. Dodds, a Senegalese mulatto, and sent him against Behanzin.

Behanzin defied Dodds. To a letter demanding submission, he replied:

France wishes war. Let her know that I am stronger and more determined than my father. I have never done anything to France that she should make war on me. I have never gone to France either to take the wives or daughters of the French. If they wish to take the seacoast, I will cut down all the palm trees. I will poison them. If they have not what to eat, let them go elsewhere. Every other nation, German, English, Portuguese, can come into my kingdom. But the French, I will drive them away. I am the friend of the whites; ready to receive them when they wish to come to see me, but prompt to make war whenever they wish.

Behanzin and his warriors fought bravely, but they proved no match for the well-armed forces of the French, except in hand-to-hand combat. At Atchoupa, during a fierce storm, a force estimated at 7000 warriors and 200 amazons hurled itself at the French. The women fought with supreme courage, preferring death to retreat. Clinging to the legs of the French troops, they brought them to earth and poignarded them.

Describing the battle, an eyewitness said:

The Dahomeyans showed a tenacity and bravery unheard of. But their dash was broken by the discipline and the marksmanship of the Senegalese sharpshooters. The entrance to the fort bore witness of the rage with which the Dahomeyans fought. . . . It was heaped with the corpses of men and women warriors.

At Djebe and Kana the amazons charged the machine guns, falling dead at the very feet of the French gunners. But again it was the old story of primitive man with his bravery and persistence against the machine. A few days later Dodds captured Dioxene, Behanzin's largest palace.

Behanzin now sought peace, the more so as two of his neighbors, the Egbas and the Gesus, had joined the French. He sent three envoys to Colonel Dodds, offering an indemnity of $5,000,-000 and free trade at the port of Cotonou. As a peace token, he sent cattle, gold, and two silver hands of superb Dahomeyan work, asking Dodds to take one of the hands and cross it with his own in a sign of friendship.

Dodds, in return, sent biscuits and conserves, saying that he was willing to make peace on condition that Behanzin permit him to hoist the French flag at Abomey, his capital.

Behanzin promptly refused. After a stiff battle, the French captured Abomey, or rather its ruins. Behanzin had fired the town, destroying his palace with all its wonderful art treasures.

His throne of beaten gold was undamaged, however. Later this was presented to King Toffa, in recognition of his loyalty.

With Behanzin in flight, Dodds named Behanzin's brother, Agli-Agbo, king and told the Dahomeyans that henceforth they were under the protection of France.

Soon afterward Dodds sailed for France. But hardly had he arrived when Behanzin was again on the warpath. Returning, he defeated Behanzin. On January 24, 1894, with the last remnants of his army gone, Behanzin walked coolly into the French camp, his long pipe in his mouth, and gave himself up.

He was given a glass of rum—"which he drank as an ordinary mortal would"—was bustled off to the coast, and thence to France. Later he was exiled to Martinique.

For many years he vainly sought permission to return to his native land. Finally he was permitted to live in Algeria. He passed away at Bleda in 1906, at the age of sixty-five.

In 1928 his son, Prince Ouanilo Behanzin, removed his body to Dahomey, the prince himself dying on the return trip to France.

REFERENCES

For bibliography see "Alfred A. Dodds."

ADDITIONAL REFERENCES

Boahen, Adu, *Topics in West African History*, pp. 85, 87, 133. London, Longmans, Green and Company, Ltd., 1966.

Burton, Richard F., *A Mission to Gelele, King of Dahome*. London, Tylston and Edwards, 1864.

Fage, J. D., *A History of West Africa*, p. 166. Cambridge, Cambridge University Press, 1969.

Hargreaves, John D., *West Africa: The Former French States*, p. 153. Englewood Cliffs, N.J., Prentice-Hall, 1967.

Herskovits, Melville J., *Dahomey*. London, H.M. Stationary Office, 1920.

———, *Dahomey, An Ancient West African Kingdom*. New York, J. J. Augustin, 1938.

Woodson, Carter G., *African Heroes and Heroines*. Washington, D.C., The Associated Publishers, 1939.

"Behanzin, Last King of Dahomey." *Negro Hist. Bull.*, p. 8 (Nov., 1937). Washington, D.C., Association for the Study of Negro Life History.

Samuel Adjai Crowther

Samuel Adjai Crowther

❧❦

EXPLORER, AFRICAN EDUCATOR, AND
BISHOP OF THE BRITISH REALM
(1806–1892)

SAMUEL ADJAI CROWTHER, foe of the slave trade and the liquor traffic in Africa and pioneer of civilization in the basin of the Niger, was the first Negro on record to be ordained a bishop of the United Church of Great Britain and Ireland.

Crowther was born in West Africa about 1806, and belonged to the Yoruba, one of the oldest and most advanced of the tribes of Africa. His father, who was a bale, or duke, was wealthy, having made his fortune by the weaving of a certain fabric of his own design.

Adjai—he was so named because he was born with his face to the ground—showed spirit and enthusiasm from his earliest years. He was only ten years old when he rescued a family from a blaze which destroyed his home, plunging through the flames to do so.

He started on his own as a breeder of poultry and cultivator of African yams, walking seven miles each morning to his fields. He was successful and prosperous. The town in which he lived had 12,000 inhabitants and was protected by stockades and a force of 3000 fighting men. One morning as he was about to leave for his farm, he heard a great uproar. Rushing out he found that a battle was in progress with an army of slave raiders. Victorious, the attackers seized him, his mother, and his brothers and took them

337

to the coast where Adjai was torn away from his mother and sold. In riveted chains, he and a group of others were put aboard a Portuguese ship, the *Esperanza Feliz*, for transport to America.

In the filthy hold where he and his fellows were packed, young Adjai suffered frightfully from nausea and seasickness. On the third day out, sounds of a commotion on deck came to him in the hold and soon afterward uniformed men came below and marched him and the other terrified captives out.

Adjai thought his end had come. But the newcomers were English sailors, whose ship, the *Myrmidon*, had captured the Portuguese vessel. It was not easy to reassure the slaves that they were really saved, and Adjai when taken aboard the warship was alarmed when his glance fell on a side of newly-shaved pork glistening white in the sunlight. It looked so much like the color of his captors that he felt sure he had fallen among cannibals. Years later when he met the captain of the same warship under altogether different circumstances, both laughed heartily at the incident.

Adjai was taken to Sierra Leone and placed in a missionary school, where he was baptized and given the name of Crowther. From there he was sent to England for further training and upon graduation he was sent back to Sierre Leone to teach. His salary was only $5 a month, but he was grateful.

In those days Sierra Leone was very unhealthful for Europeans. It was known as "the white man's grave." Many missionaries had succumbed to its fevers. The Church Missionary Society decided, therefore, that if West Africa was ever to be won over to Christianity, it would have to be largely through native missionaries. Crowther seemed to them to be promising material in every way.

Like a true missionary, Crowther was self-sacrificing. Upon his return from England he had brought back with him many luxuries, among them white stockings, clothes, and a fine mattress that had been a gift from his English friends. When the head missionary, Haensal, a white man, advised him to part with these possessions and live the simpler life of the native in order to gain converts more readily, Crowther gave them up without a murmur. To his thirst for classical knowledge, the young missionary added a keen desire to know all the native tongues.

The most enthusiastic reports of his conduct were sent to England by his superior, and his salary was increased to $10 a month. Soon afterward he married a native woman named Susan Thompson.

Crowther was particularly grieved by the slave trade and the whiskey traffic—the two great curses of Africa—and fought them where he could. In 1838 he saw slavery and slave trading formally abolished—but in the interior of the continent both went on as actively as ever.

Queen Victoria, determined to end this, sent the First Royal Niger Expedition to explore the basin of the Niger. The party consisted of 150 Europeans and only one Negro official—Crowther.

Not all the white men were equal to the task. Jungle diseases struck the party. First three white missionaries and three doctors died. In two months forty-two of the whites were dead while the remaining 108 had been stricken and more or less seriously incapacitated. The bulk of the work fell on Crowther, who alone remained well. Thanks largely to him the expedition did not return empty-handed. Instead it brought back valuable knowledge of native life and languages; of more effective methods for combating slave dealers, and of building up legitimate trade. It also demonstrated that Africa's own sons were best fitted, physically and psychologically, for doing missionary work.

Crowther won high praise for his work. He was recalled to England to complete his studies, after which he was regularly ordained. His first sermon, which was preached to a white congregation at Northrup Church, was warmly praised by Sir Thomas Fowell Buxton, noted abolitionist, and others who had journeyed especially to hear him.

Upon his return to Sierra Leone Crowther was joyously received by his fellow blacks, who were proud to see one of their number a regular ordained minister. Then, to crown all, he was unexpectedly reunited with his mother, from whom he had been separated for twenty years and whom he had thought dead.

In 1851 he was again called to England, this time to discuss the slave question with Queen Victoria herself. Arriving at Windsor Castle, he was ushered into a magnificent drawing room, and when a handsomely dressed lady wearing a long train entered, Crowther, thinking it was the Queen, stood up. But it was only one of her maids-of-honor, who had come to escort him to an upper drawing room. There Prince Albert, the Queen's husband, the Prince of Wales, and other members of the royal family awaited him.

Prince Albert, with maps of Africa spread out before him, plied Crowther with questions which Crowther respectfully answered. But as he went on to tell of the slave traffic, the bringing in of rum, and the injustices done his people, he was swept away by emotion. Almost forgetting the rank of his auditors, he did not spare their feelings. "It is the people in England," he said, "who are to blame for sending out rum which destroys the natives physically and morally, increasing the death rate frightfully and arousing the worst instincts in them. Liquor is far worse than the idols we used to worship."

At times, out of respect, he checked himself, but his royal hearers, who listened breathlessly, urged him to go on. Then, as it got dark, the Prince Consort said, "Will Your Majesty kindly bring us that candle from the mantelpiece?" It was only then that Crowther knew that the Queen had been present. He had seen the stout and plainly dressed woman enter but had taken no special notice of her. Fearing that his outspokenness might have offended his sovereign, he apologized, but she assured him that she would not have had him speak otherwise. She agreed with him that Lagos was serving as the center of the slave traffic and said that warships should be sent there to stop it.

The Prime Minister, who was present, told of Crowther's translation of parts of the Bible into the Yoruba language, and at the Queen's request he recited the Lord's prayer in that language.

In addresses at the University of Cambridge and to leading organizations in England he stirred his hearers with his earnestness, his scholarly manner, and his wide and authentic knowledge of Africa. Knowing that he would interest the majority of his hearers more by presenting Africa as a commercial proposition, he told of its wealth in ivory, gold, palm oil, lumber, and pointed out that the present exports, which did not exceed two million pounds sterling, could easily be increased ten times if this commerce were protected till it had gained a foothold.

The result was that the British government sent another expedition up the Niger. Again the Europeans suffered heavily in loss of lives and again Crowther won added honor, the more so as it was this expedition that broke the back of the West African slave trade. In doing this he was aided by the native chiefs, who were so won by his sincerity that some of them became Christians.

In 1864 he was again called to England, this time for an unusual honor—to be made a bishop of the Anglican Church. Some objected on the grounds that this was too great an honor for a black man—nevertheless, on June 29, 1864, in the historic Cathedral of Canterbury, he was ordained with the title: His Lordship, Bishop of the Niger.

Special trains were run from London and elsewhere for the occasion, and the cathedral was filled to overflowing. Among those who stood near Crowther on the occasion was the former captain of the *Myrmidon*, now Admiral Sir H. Leeke.

Crowther returned to his work. The years that followed, however, were to be the hardest and most trying of his career. War broke out once more in Dahomey. The slave traders were inciting the native chiefs to rebellion. Deprived of their revenues, the chiefs yielded readily in the hope that the sale of their subjects would start again. Christian natives were persecuted.

Crowther went boldly into the midst of all this, in the name of Christ. On one occasion he was kidnapped by Aboko, a cruel and treacherous chief, who held him for a ransom of $5000. White men sent to free him were killed by poisoned arrows. Crowther finally escaped.

He also succeeded in stopping several native customs, one of which was the killing of twins and the banishment of their mother. He ended this by preaching sermons from Genesis XXV: 24: "And the Lord said to her: Two nations are in thy womb." No home, he told them, could ever be looked on as having a full share of heavenly blessings unless it had twins.

Everywhere he opposed the witch doctors and the means by which they kept the people in terror. To show that Christ was superior he would walk boldly into their Ju-ju huts, seize the most sacred idol there, and break it to pieces before a horrified audience!

He also believed in "the gospel of the plough," and introduced modern agricultural methods. Kindly, unobtrusive, upright, even his enemies liked him.

But his diocese was too vast. It stretched a full thousand miles up the Niger. Age and overwork were beginning to tell on him, and his vigilance relaxed. Some of his native assistants, lacking his moral stamina, broke their religious oaths.

Conditions went from bad to worse. Some of his missionaries, both white and colored, were guilty of grave religious misconduct, others grew lax and negligent, while some of the native members who were pledged to one wife returned to the African custom of taking several. For this Crowther was being blamed in England.

Religious leaders there did not seem to realize that it was as difficult to make European ways work in Africa as it would have been to make African ones work in England. Both represented thousands of years of evolution. They could not understand that polygamy was as much a part of African life as monogamy, adultery, and prostitution were a part of European; and that the best the new ways would be able to accomplish for some time to come was a slight modification in the existing customs; in short, you cannot change the habits of a people overnight.

At last came a horrible murder followed by a report from a body of missionaries that Christianity on the Niger had sunk to a low level. The central missionary body in London sent out a commission of inquiry which found that many of the charges made were true. Some of Crowther's assistants were discharged. As to Crowther, he was absolved from all blame. It was acknowledged that to "his labors, life and unique personality the work on the Niger had owed its very existence," that "his stainless name was associated with every step of its advancement," and that "when the storm of trial came and it seemed as if shipwreck was inevitable, his courage and loyalty were not counted on in vain."

Page, his biographer says:

Amid circumstances of almost unexampled difficulty, in the face of discouragements, he went steadily on his way with indomitable perseverance in a holy cause. . . . He lived in an atmosphere of suspicion and scandal, yet no tongue, however malicious, of black man or white man, ventured to whisper reproach against his personal reputation.

Knowing that the charges against some of his native assistants were not true, Crowther defended these individuals. Under the strain and deep distress the whole situation had caused him, his health gave way, and he died at Lagos on January 9, 1892, at the age of eighty-six, after nearly sixty years of continuous labor.

Before his death the Royal Geographical Society presented him with a splendid gold watch in recognition of his services to science. In 1932 a costly stained-glass window was unveiled in his memory in the Cathedral Church of Christ at Lagos.

REFERENCES

Page, Jesse, *The Black Bishop*. London, 1900.

Crowther, Samuel, *Journal of an Expedition up the Niger*. London, 1854.

Encyclopaedia Britannica, see "Crowther."

ADDITIONAL REFERENCES

Dike, K. Onwuka, *Origins of the Niger Mission 1841–1891*. Ibadan, Nigeria, Ibadan University Press, pamphlet, 1957.

Fage, J. D., *A History of West Africa*, pp. 129, 200. Cambridge, Cambridge University Press, 1969.

Gollock, Georgina Anne, *Lives of Eminent Africans*. New York and London, Longmans, Green and Company, Inc., 1928.

July, Robert W., *The Origins of Modern African Thought*, pp. 177–195. New York and Washington, D.C., Frederick A. Praeger, 1967.

Polatnick, Florence T., and Saletan, Alberta L., *Shapers of Africa*, pp. 76–107. New York, Julius Messner, 1969.

Niven, Sir Rex, *Nine Great Africans*, pp. 130–148. New York, Roy Publishers, Inc., 1964.

Walters, Jane G., *African Triumph*. London, George Allen and Unwin, Ltd., 1965.

Eminent Nigerians of the 19th Century, pp. 49–58. Series of studies originally broadcast by the Nigerian Broadcasting Corp., Cambridge, Cambridge University Press, 1960.

Samory

"THE NAPOLEON OF THE SUDAN"
(1830–1900)

SAMORY TOURÉ, West African conqueror, defied the power of France for eighteen years with such skill that the French commanders, among whom were Marshals Joffre and Gallieni, dubbed him "The Black Napoleon of the Sudan." Again and again he defeated France's best men and compelled them to make treaties with him.

Samory was born at Bissandugu in the Niger Valley in 1830. Like many another great man, he began life in the humblest circumstances, being the son of a poor black merchant and a female slave. The upward turn of his fortunes came out of adversity. One day a neighboring king, Sori Bourama, swooped down on his tribe, killed many, and captured, among others, Samory's mother. Unable to pay her ransom, Samory freed her by taking her place.

But Samory, a giant in ambition though only thirteen, decided not to remain a slave. Five years later he escaped and killed his pursuers. Going to Bitike Souane, King of Toron, he offered him his services. The latter, struck by Samory's splendid physique, his martial bearing, and his skill at throwing a spear made him a member of his bodyguard. From this post he rose to be counsellor, thanks to his knowledge of Arabic, and finally to be second in the tribe.

Samory had become the idol of the soldiers, but because the

344

king was jealous of him he returned to his native Bissandugu, where he was made chief of his tribe. With this taste of power, his ambitious soul yearned for more. Making war on the neighboring chiefs, he killed them all and annexed their lands.

Continuing his march northeastwardly along the banks of the Niger, he seized all the region east of Sierra Leone to the buckle of the Niger, and well up into the upper Niger—a territory of 100,000 square miles or more.

Among Samory's victims was his former benefactor, the King of Toron. Like Genghis Khan, Napoleon, and Hitler, Samory permitted no thoughts of past favors to stand in his way.

He was now the most powerful native ruler in West Africa. Rejecting the title of king or sultan, he called himself "Samory, son of Lafla, African of the Negro Race, Prince of Believers." A firm Mohammedan, he gave the conquered the alternative of accepting the Koran or death.

With visions of the period when great black emperors, like Kankan Moussa, Sonni Ali, and Askia the Great ruled in Timbuctoo, he aimed at making all West Africa into a single nation. But unknown to him, his empire had changed hands. England, Belgium, Germany, and Portugal, sitting in conference, had awarded it to France.

Samory heard the news while besieging the town of Keniera, Upper Niger, in 1881. A black sergeant in French uniform came to him with an order from the French commander to discontinue the siege. Amazed at the man's impertinence, Samory held him for torture. The sergeant, escaping, found his way back to camp. The prestige of France had to be upheld, and a war began that lasted for fourteen years.

When the French reached Keniera, Samory had already captured it and was awaiting them in a strategic position.

The battle lasted a week. In the first three days the French, armed with the latest artillery, were victorious. But when their ammunition was exhausted, Samory, who had only a few modern rifles, attacked them with spears and won. For the next five years the war went on with alternating success. France's ambition was to maintain a straight overland route from the French Congo through her North African possessions to France. Samory, swooping down on the caravans, made this impossible. France finally arranged a treaty with him in 1886. He gave his favorite son, Karamook, as hostage. The latter was taken to Paris.

Another treaty followed in 1887, by which Samory gave up all the territory on the left bank of the Niger. No sooner was it ceded, however, than the French began to fortify the right bank of the river, and Samory, his suspicions aroused, incited the native chiefs to rebel until war broke out again in 1891. The French, attacking him in force, defeated ally after ally of his until they reached him at Kekouner, where he awaited them with his army of 40,000 men, of whom 10,000 were armed with rifles, 2000 were cavalry, and the remainder had only spears. He had also two small cannon.

The French, with machine guns, drove him from his capital, Bissandugu, but taking to the woods, he resisted so successfully for the next fifteen days that the French offered to make a treaty with him.

By this agreement he was permitted to continue his conquests toward the south, and he went there to build up a new empire. Sometime later a French expedition, under Captain Marchand, narrowly escaped capture at his hands.

Samory, however, was never reconciled to seeing white men on on territory that he felt was his, and once more he descended on the caravans. Again France declared war on him, and again after a fierce struggle—his spears against the cannon of the French—he was forced to retreat with his army of 28,000 men. He took along 120,000 women, children, and captives, and 20,000 head of cattle.

France now decided to wipe out his power once and for all. She pressed the fight, and throughout the next year the struggle went on, with Samory retreating the greater part of the time.

But in retreat he showed his skill. One of his opponents, Commandant de Lartigue, says, "One cannot help but admire from a military point of view his precision, the minute care with which he conducted this retreat, and with what zeal his orders were executed by his generals." France, hoping to discourage him, had sent back his son Karamook, after showing him a review of the French army, to advise him to surrender, but Samory chained the youth in a hut giving him just enough food to keep him alive.

Unbeaten in spirit, Samory, with a vigor that would have been astonishing in a much younger man, organized tribe after tribe, strengthening all the strategic points of their territory. He also won to his cause the surviving princes of Sikasso and Amadou Sékou, fugitive King of Segu.

Cut off by the French and British forces to the south of the Sudan and thus deprived of his base of supplies, Samory conceived the audacious project of crossing the north of Liberia to Sierra Leone, where he hoped to secure arms and ammunition to continue the struggle. On the way he pillaged in order to feed his large army, causing intense suffering among the tribes through whose territory he passed.

But age and a life of war were beginning to tell on his once robust constitution. No longer could he be everywhere to assure the success of his plans, while the French were becoming more and more entrenched in his country.

He had domestic troubles, also. His son, Saranké Mory, was enamored of the favorite of his 300 wives and Samory had surprised them in adultery. Rather than be punished, Saranké Mory fled, taking a large part of Samory's troops with him.

A few days later, September 29, 1898, Samory, as was his daily custom, retired a little distance from his tent, alone and unarmed, to read the Koran and to pray. While he was thus engaged a black scout in the French army and a white sergeant crept upon him and held him. Overhearing his cries, his men rushed to his rescue, but as the two armies stood facing each other, Samory, worn with fifty years of warfare and wishing to avoid useless slaughter, bade his men yield. He was taken to the small island of Njolo in the Congo where he died June 2, 1900, of tuberculosis at the age of seventy.

La Grande Encyclopédie says of him:

Samory, great Negro potentate, who disputed for a long time with France for possession of the Sudan. . . .

Handsome, of splendid height, very intelligent, very cunning and extremely brave. . . .

Unhappily for him, he crossed the path of France from the Senegal to the Niger when France wished to ascend the great river towards its source and to descend towards Timbuctoo. The war between us and him started in 1881-2 and ended in 1898. . . . He struggled very cleverly against Borgin-Debordes, Combes, Hubert, Archinbaud, Bonnier, and others.

Like most great military leaders, Samory relied almost as much on strategy as on force. He had a method of frightening the native enemy that was highly original. During a battle he had his orchestra 100 pieces, composed of drums, cornets, flutes, fifes, whistles, and tom-toms, make a din that sounded like the shouting of victorious warriors and the groans and cries of the dying and defeated. This never failed to dishearten the enemy, who often could not see all that their own men were doing in the woods.

Samory's comparison to Napoleon is fitting. In ability, and also in his rise and his fall, Samory resembled the great Corsican. Both died on a little island surrounded by the wreck of their courts. Napoleon, it is true, rose to greater heights, but had Napoleon been born in Samory's place, and had he been forced to use spears and antiquated rifles against modern artillery, the world would have heard no more about him than it did about Samory.

REFERENCES

Lartigue, *La Prise de Samory*. Lille, 1910.

Arlabosse, *Une Phase de la lutte contre Samory*, pp. 189–192. *Revue d'Histoire de Colonies Françaises*, Sept.–Oct., 1932, pp. 385–432; Nov.–Dec., 467–514.

Mohammed Sanfa, *Notice sur Samory*. Marseille, 1888.

Mevil, *Samory*. Paris, 1931.

Labouret, H., *Les Bandes de Samori, L'Afrique Française Renseignements Coloniaux*, pp. 341–355. 1925.

Gaffarel, P., "Samory," *Mémoire de la Soc. Bourguignonne de Géographie et d'Histoire*, Vol. XV, pp. 226–282. Dijon.

Mangin, *Gen. Revue des Deux Mondes*, May 15, 1931.

Petit, M., *Les Colonies Françaises*, Vol. I, p. 705. Paris, 1902.

Hanotaux, G., *Histoire des Colonies Françaises*, Vol. IV, pp. 200–229. Paris, 1931.

L'Illustration, Sept. 17, Nov. 26, 1892; Oct. 22, Dec. 31, 1898.

ADDITIONAL REFERENCES

Atterbury, Anson P., *Islam in Africa*, pp. 102, 104. New York, Negro Universities Press, 1899 and 1969.

Boahen, Adu, *Topics in West African History*, pp. 46, 133. London, Longmans, Green and Company, Ltd., 1966.

Claridge, W. W., *A History of the Gold Coast and Ashanti*. London, Frank Cass and Company, 1915.

Fage, J. D., *An Introduction to the History of West Africa*. New York, Cambridge University Press, 1957.

————, *A History of West Africa*, pp. 157–158, 166, 169. Cambridge, Cambridge University Press, 1969.

Hargreaves, John D., *West Africa: The Former French States*, pp. 102–105, 111. Englewood Cliffs, N.J., Prentice-Hall, 1967.

Omer-Cooper, J. D., *et al.*, *The Making of Modern Africa*, Vol. I, pp. 170–172. London, Longmans, Green and Company, Ltd., 1968.

Trimingham, J. Spencer, *A History of Islam in West Africa*, pp. 165, 185, 187–93. London, Oxford University Press, 1970.

Woodson, Carter G., *African Heroes and Heroines*. Washington, D.C., The Associated Publishers, 1939 and 1944.

Samory Touré. New York, Nommo Associates, Inc., 1963.

Rabah Zobeir

※※

AFRICA'S WARLIKE CHAMPION AGAINST
EUROPEAN DOMINATION

(d. 1900)

THE CAREER of Sultan Rabah Zobeir affords proof that innate ability is conditioned by neither "race" nor birth and that given a favorable environment those who possess it will rise above those who do not no matter what opportunities the others might have.

Born among a primitive and entirely illiterate people in the heart of the Sudan and held as a slave with his mother, Rabah Zobeir fought his way to liberty and carved for himself an immense empire in the richest region of Central Africa.

Old kingdoms crumpled under the tread of his well-trained cavalry. These lands he later ruled with such statesmanship that European administrators in Africa used him as their model. He built cities, had an army over which he exercised Roman discipline, and forced the head of the mightiest secret organization in Africa and the East to obey him.

A most uncompromising foe of European expansion in Africa, Rabah made colonial interests in England, France, Germany, and Belgium fear him. For thirty years he ruled, defeating able white commanders and exacting a heavy toll in lives from the French.

Rabah's first contact with civilization was about 1860 when he was captured at Bahr el Ghazal on the Upper Nile and sold as a slave in Egypt. Soon afterward a Frenchwoman, Mademoiselle Tinné, who was going on an expedition up the Nile, hired his master, Zobeir, as a guide and the latter took Rabah with him.

On her return to Egypt Mademoiselle Tinné gave her guns and the remainder of her ammunition to Zobeir, who gathered a number of other adventurers and went up the Nile to Rabah's former home to hunt slaves, taking Rabah along.

Zobeir established himself as a slave trader and prospered so greatly that he proclaimed a kingdom of his own. At that time (1872) Egypt was engaged in conquering the Sudan, and made war on Zobeir. The latter, however, defeated the Egyptians and peace was concluded by virtue of which Zobeir was made a viceroy. Much of Zobeir's success was due to Rabah, who, by this time, had risen to second in command.

Zobeir, as viceroy, was invited to Cairo for a celebration in his honor. But there he was made prisoner by the English general, "Chinese" Gordon. Zobeir's son, Suleyman, thereupon once more attacked the Egyptians, but Suleyman, beaten in battle, was promised his life if he surrendered. He did and was executed.

A similar invitation had been extended to Rabah, but being more cautious, he declined. When the Egyptians came to seize him, he rallied 700 of his countrymen around him and dashed off with them into the desert on fleet Arab horses.

For the fugitives there was but one way of making a living: plundering. At that time (1879) there were several Negro kingdoms in Central Africa, south of the Sahara, that did considerable trade with Europe, such as Wadai, Baghirmi, and Bornu.

The last, lying in the fertile region around Lake Chad, was the richest, oldest, and most important. Over 75,000 square miles in extent, it had been founded in the ninth century and had reached a fairly high state of civilization when most European nations were still in a relatively primitive state. When the Europeans were still using bows and arrows, the Bornuese, according to some historians, were using gunpowder.

From these Central African kingdoms went out gold, ivory, skins, leather, ostrich feathers, and slaves; into them came silks, watches, and other products of European manufacture. Commerce was by caravan through the Sahara Desert to Tripoli and the sea. Rabah and his band of plunderers began to operate along this route and soon became wealthy. Rabah now decided to have a kingdom of his own and planned to annex the above-mentioned Negro kingdom. For a beginning, he selected Mohammed Senussi II, the head of a secret organization whose influence extended across Africa from the Atlantic Ocean to the Indian Ocean and even into Turkey and Arabia, whose aim was to keep Europeans out of Africa. It was especially powerful in Senegal, Nigeria, and Western Ethiopia. Attacking Senussi II in his stronghold in the Sahara with a thousand picked horsemen, he gave him the alternative of death or an alliance. Senussi chose the latter and gave his daughter, Hadjia, to Fad-el-Allah, Rabah's son and heir.

To test Senussi and to alienate him from the French, he ordered him to attack and massacre a French expedition led by Commander Crampel, Senussi did this, turning over the captured arms and ammunition to Rabah.

Rabah next decided to annex the Wadai Kingdom. He had only a thousand horsemen but these were superbly drilled, well disciplined, and inured to hardship. Uncontaminated by dissipation, each was worth ten of the enemy.

Attacking the Wadai, he swept through their large army as fire through paper. His next mark was Sultan Gourang of the Baghirmi. Charging that Gourang had welcomed the French, Rabah laid siege to his capital, Mainhaffa, captured it, and took 30,000 slaves. Reorganizing Gourang's kingdom, he replaced him on the throne as his vassal.

He next attacked the warlike Sakara and annexed their country; then he cast his eyes on Bornu, which had an army of 80,000 men, and outnumbered his own force twenty to one.

The Bornuese, well provided with the comforts of life, loved ease. After a long period of peace, their once great military powers had atrophied. Nearly all the important commands in their army were held by former captives, while most of the soldiers were slaves. Public affairs also interested them little, their chief concern being trade. Their two largest towns, Kuka and Diloa, had markets to which came tens of thousands of people from the surrounding countries.

Their ruler, Sultan Haschem, had four palaces and was quiet and easygoing, preferring the company of his 400 wives and his books, and tinkering with his watches (of which he had several hundred), which had been given to him by Arab traders and European visitors.

Rabah, to reach Bornu, had to pass the territory of Sultan Salah. Sending a rich present to Salah, he offered him an alliance, and when Salah came to talk with him, he seized him. This so frightened Salah's people that they surrendered their capital, Leogane, without firing a shot.

Seeing the threat to his country, Sultan Haschem sent an army of 15,000 men against Rabah, which the latter routed with only 2000 of his cavalry after a fierce three-hour battle. On this Haschem wanted to surrender but his nephew, Kiara, killed him, and taking command, attacked Rabah and defeated him. Rabah, in a great rage, sentenced his own generals, including his son, to receive 100 lashes, after which he ordered an attack. The Bornuese, taken by surprise this time, were utterly routed and surrendered their capital.

Rabah's victories, especially over the Senussi, alarmed England, France, Belgium, Germany, and other European powers who had territory adjoining his. France sent an expedition under Commander Bretonnet against him but Rabah, meeting the latter at Togbao in 1899, defeated and killed him and captured all his arms and ammunition. Turning south, Rabah defeated a German expedition in similar style, both victories enhancing his prestige greatly.

The French now conspired with the Baghirmi, Rabah's vassals, and gave them arms to attack Rabah, but he marched against them, killed their king, Gourang, and 3000 of his men, and seized all his wives and his portable proverty.

Having conquered an empire larger than France and Germany combined, Rabah now set himself the task of consolidating it. Reorganizing Bornu, he established a military dictatorship, rebuilt the towns, and encouraged commerce. Of the old town of Dikoa, which he remodeled, Colonel Gentil, a French commander says:

This second city is really very beautiful. Reconstructed entirely by Rabah, who made it his capital, Dikoa is without a doubt one of the most elegant centers, as well as the most populous, of Central Africa. The palaces of Rabah, Niebe, and Fad-el-Allah are especially distinguished by their grand appearance."

Of Rabah's palace he says:

With the carpets covering the floor, the seats, the rich cushions, and the bed with its costly coverings, the apartments had an air of distinction. I had the impression of being in some old manor of the Middle Ages.

I brought from Dikoa the impression of something great, of an intensity of life, and a movement of population such as I had not seen before in Africa.

In the years that followed, Rabah continued to repulse the French, killing, among others, Commander DeBahagle. France prepared another expedition against him to which *Le Temps* of Paris objected editorially: "It is necessary to remember that we are going to meet Rabah and not Rabah us. He is in his own empire and is defending himself."

Another expedition commanded by Colonel Gentil, composed largely of Senegalese sharpshooters, invaded Rabah's territory. Rabah fortified himself on a hill, cut away the trees and brush to allow the play of his fieldpieces, and awaited the French. When both met in October, 1899, Rabah won a complete victory, although the Senegalese performed feats of prodigious valor. Colonel Gentil retreated into French territory, where he joined his force with that of two other expeditions—Violet and Chanoine.

Rabah now invaded German territory in Tanganyika and feeling certain of victory left most of his cavalry to guard Bornu. The French, learning of this, thought it favorable to attack him now, and after asking the Germans for permission to attack him in their territory, went after him with a superior force.

The two met at Kussuri, where Rabah had fortified himself on a hill. The French fired thousands of shells into his position, but Rabah held them off until his ammunition gave out, then he sallied out with his men to give battle to the death.

A terrible slaughter followed. The French commander, Lamy, was killed. Rabah, wounded, withdrew into the bushes but a deserter from his own army who was fighting with the French saw him there, and recognizing him, killed him, cut off his head, and took it to Colonel Gentil.

Gentil, who admired Rabah's bravery and skill, was touched at the sight. He wrote, "This man, whose bloody head was lying at my feet, was very brave, and from the manner in which he defended himself, deserved to have had his life spared."

When Gentil entered Bornu later he was full of admiration for the government that Rabah had instituted. "It shows me," he said, "that in the work of organization I am going to undertake, I will do well to be inspired by the methods of Rabah."

Rabah had the reputation of being cruel and austere. It is said that one day, seeing an amulet around the neck of one of his wives who was asleep, he cut the thread, and opening the amulet, found an undecipherable inscription inside. Taking it to one of his learned men, he bade him read it. The latter, knowing that the woman was one of Rabah's favorite wives, replied flatteringly, "Your majesty, it means good for both you and her. By this charm she holds your love."

Rabah replied wrathfully, "What! Do you mean that seeking to have power over me is good for me?" And he ordered both the learned man and his wife put to death.

Rabah lived and dressed simply. Dujarric, in the story of his life, described him as

very tall, raw-boned and dry, endowed with Herculean force and possessing all the characteristic traits of the great African conquerors; remarkable intelligence, great political ability, indomitable will, and a courage that stood all tests. . . . A born ruler of men, he held great sway over his soldiers and his people. His qualities as an organizer were especially revealed after his conquest of the Baghirmi. . . .

Rabah can best be compared to one of those great barbarian chiefs who, in the early Middle Ages, swept in torrents over Europe.

Mezieres says of him, "He was the most remarkable adversary of French influence in Africa and intimidated the natives over a vast area from rallying to support us."

REFERENCES

The *Encyclopaedia Britannica,* 1942 (see "Rabah"), describes Rabah as "half Arab, half Negro," but he was Sudanese by birth, and Arab only by culture, that is, if we can call the Egyptian environment in which Rabah was once a slave, Arab. Moreover, "Arab" and "Negro" have similar ethnic meanings as "American" and "English." An Arab may be a white man or an unmixed Negro. Maurice Delafosse, an authority on Negro culture, says he was "Sudanese."

After Rabah's death, the fight was carried on by his son, Fad-el-Allah, who died two years after him.

Visscher, Hans, *Across the Sahara*, p. 132. London, 1910.

Dujarric, G., *La Vie de Sultan Rabah*. Paris, 1902.

Gentil, E., *La Chute de L'Empire de Rabah*. Paris, 1902.

Revue de Paris, 1895.

Schweinfurth, G., *The Heart of Africa*, 2 vols. London, 1873.

Slatin, Pasha, *Fire and Sword in the Sudan*. London, 1896.

Hanotaux, G., *Histoire des Colonies Françaises*, Vol. IV, pp. 450–479. Paris, 1931.

Oppenheim, M. A., *Rabah und das Tschadseegebiet*. Berlin, 1902.

"Rabah, sa defaite, son empire." *Revue Française de l'Etranger et des Colonies*, Vol. XXV, pp. 133–142. Paris, 1900.

ADDITIONAL REFERENCES

Atterbury, Anson P., *Islam in Africa*, p. 58. New York, Negro Universities Press, 1899 and 1969.

Cook, Arthur, *Africa: Past and Present*, p. 214. Totowa, N.J., Littlefield, Adams, and Company, 1969.

Farewell, Byron, *Prisoners of The Mahdi*. New York, Harper and Row, 1967.

Hargreaves, John D., *West Africa: The Former French States*, p. 111. Englewood Cliffs, N.J., Prentice-Hall, 1967.

Trimingham, J. Spencer, *Islam in the Sudan*, pp. 91–92, 94–95. London, Oxford University Press, 1949.

Bu-Ahmed

IRON CHANCELLOR OF MOROCCO
(d. 1900)

SI AHMED BEN MUSA, better known as Bu-Ahmed, was the last
great ruler of Morocco. Seizing power, he kept off for twenty years
the wolves of Christendom who were baying at the flanks of the
dying Moorish empire.

Bu-Ahmed was a slave, a Negro almost unmixed, born in the
palace of the sultans. He grew up with the heir to the throne,
Mulai Hassan, to whom he was devoted body and soul. When
Mulai Hassan became sultan, the attachment continued and Bu-
Ahmed was made court chamberlain, confidant, and finally sultan
in all but name.

Bu-Ahmed came into absolute power in 1894, when the sultan,
on a visit to the interior, fell ill and died at Tadla. His last request
of Bu-Ahmed was that his youngest son, Abdul Aziz, then only
thirteen, be placed on the throne.

This was a very difficult task. In the cities of Rabat, Fez, and
Marrakesh, there were any number of expectant heirs, chief of
whom was Mulai Hafid, the sultan's eldest son. Bu-Ahmed knew
that the moment it was known the sultan was dead, the claimants
would be in ferment. His only hope was to keep the death a secret
until he reached Rabat.

But to reach Rabat would take five days of fast travel. He
therefore dispatched his swiftest and most trusted horsemen there

to proclaim Abdul Aziz sultan while he remained with the body.

Giving orders to return at once, he made it appear as if the sultan were only indisposed. He had the state palanquin taken into the royal enclosure and then brought out with the accustomed ceremony as if the sultan were still alive. At nights, on the march, the royal tent was pitched, the band played, meals were served and papers were taken in to be signed.

For three days this went on. Then the secret could be kept no longer: the decomposition of the body in the warm climate had told all. By this time, however, Bu-Ahmed's most trusted aides, by riding day and night, had reached Rabat.

Bu-Ahmed now installed himself as regent, in which he had the full support of the young sultan's mother, Lalla Reqia, a white Circassian slave of great beauty, intelligence, and strength of character. Others, high in power, opposed him, however. Among these were the Jamai brothers, members of the Maghzen aristocracy, who had a traditional claim to high employment and honors; as well as Si Mohammed Soreir, Minister of War, and Haj Amaati, the grand vizier, or prime minister. Both were noblemen and as such were strongly supported by the aristocratic element.

They were other obstacles too. To be acknowledged regent it was necessary to win recognition at Fez, the center of Moroccan learning. New heads of government would go there to present themselves to the aristocratic Fezzans. These latter, Bu-Ahmed knew, considered him an upstart, a nobody.

He nevertheless started off thither with the young sultan. Deciding that his best course was to steal a march on his foes, he planned to make them come to him instead. Accordingly, when he reached Meknes, he halted and had the sultan sign an order summoning Haj Amaati, the prime minister, to his presence.

Haj Amaati arrived with a splendid white-robed guard of honor, rode proudly through the gates, and was ushered into the royal presence. Beside the young sultan stood the corpulent Bu-Ahmed.

Prostrating himself, Haj Amaati waited for the sultan to speak. The youth, in a frightened voice, asked him a question involving Haj Amaati's honesty. When Haj Amaati hesitated, Bu-Amed, who had prompted the question, launched into a torrent of accusations against Haj Amaati, charging him with treason, avarice, and extortion, and without giving him an opportunity to reply, asked the sultan's permission to arrest him. The sultan nodded and Bu-Ahmed's eager guards pinioned him. The prime minister, who a few minutes before had arrived in such pomp, was dragged from the royal presence pleading and disheveled. The arrest of his brother, another of Bu-Ahmed's rivals, followed immediately. Both were thrown into dungeons where they remained ten years.

When the party reached Fez the opposition was so thoroughly cowed that Bu-Ahmed had no trouble, especially as he had the support of Mulai Omar, half-brother of the sultan and one of the most powerful men of the city, who held the title of caliph. Mulai Omar himself was a dark mulatto, his mother having been an unmixed Negro slave.

Bu-Ahmed was now in complete control; the young sultan did as he advised. When revolt broke out in a distant part of the kingdom, Bu-Ahmed marched against the rebel leader, Taber ben Suleiman, defeated him, and brought him back in a cage and exhibited him in the marketplace where he was spat on by the populace. When Mulai Mohammed, the sultan's brother, also revolted, Bu-Ahmed defeated him, and contrary to all precedent, took him from the religious shrine in which he had taken refuge and threw him into prison.

There were other troubles too, external ones. The European powers coveted Morocco. But Bu-Ahmed, who had been reared in the midst of palace intrigue, was the incarnation of craftiness. He was more than a match for his foes, white and colored. He not only kept the Europeans at bay and held the rebellious Berber clans in check, but managed at the same time to give Morocco the most stable government it had had in years. Commerce thrived, finances were placed in order, and the country grew prosperous. A keen lover of art, Bu-Ahmed also fostered learning. He sent promising youths to be educated in Europe. Calling in his architects, he gave orders for the building of a palace such as Morocco had never seen before.

For the next five years he devoted himself to its building, supervising almost every detail. Even when he fell mortally ill, he continued with iron nerve to drive the workmen on. When he grew worse and the doctors told him that an oxygen tank was necessary to save his life, he dispatched a ship to Europe for it.

But even this could not save him. He died in 1900, and his death marked the end this last of the great Moslem empires.

His passing was the signal for civil war, anarchy, and massacre. Abdul Aziz was driven from the throne by his brother, Hafiz, who, unable to maintain order, called in the French, a step which so angered the rebels that they slaughtered the French residents. As a result, France sent warships which bombarded Casablanca, killing thousands of natives. A French protectorate was declared and in 1906 this Negroid empire which had lasted more than 1700 years and had held world supremacy more than once was partitioned between France and Spain. Bu-Ahmed's marvelous palace became the residence of the French governor-general.

Walter B. Harris, the British ambassador, who knew Bu-Ahmed well, gives the following description of him:

Bu Ahmed was a slave; a little fat man with short legs; an enormous stomach that gave him a rolling movement, with a dark skin that told of his origin and a keen piercing look that was eloquent in its power. He was of the breed of the Sultan's Black Guard.

De Amicis, who was a guest of Bu-Ahmed's in the latter's palace, says of him:

He is the minister of ministers, the soul of the government, the mind which embraces and moves all things all over the empire and after the Sultan the most famous man in Morocco. . . .

What a strange figure! A man about sixty, a dark mulatto, of middle height with an immense oblong head, two fiery eyes of a most astute expression, a great flat nose, two rows of big teeth and an immeasurable chin; yet, in spite of these hideous features an affable smile, an expression of benignity, and voice and manners of the utmost courtesy.

Harris describes Bu-Ahmed's palace thus:

The Bahiya—that is to say, The Effulgence, as the palace is called— consists of a succession of handsome court yards, one planted with cypress, orange, lemon, and the others with fruit-trees and flowers, leading one out into the other. These courts are surrounded by arcades to which the great rooms open. Everywhere are fountains and tanks of water. The palace must cover many acres of land. . . . On a recent visit to Marrakeesch, I was able to wander over it at leisure. . . . I had seen it years before, or rather a portion of it—for I had twice been entertained at dinner by its owner, Bu Ahmed. I recall now one of those evenings; the hot-jasmine scented air of the courts, for it was late spring and the great dinner served in one of the saloons while a native band discoursed anything but soft music outside and Bu Ahmed, himself—short, dark and of unprepossessing appearance, but none the less an excellent host. . . .

Into this palace with its rich coloring and many arches Bu-Ahmed had gathered a marvelous collection of treasures—priceless Oriental carpets of rarest and softest weave; pink and green standards that had been carried before some sultan or great prince; and saddles of crimson silk with silver-gilt stirrups. The most remarkable feature of the building was the sunlit Court of Honor, 90 feet long by 150 feet wide, paved with marble and green tiles.

Edith Wharton says:

Bu Ahmed was evidently an artist and an archaeologist. His ambition was to create a Palace of Beauty such as the Moors had built in the prime of Arab art, and he brought to Marrakeesch skilled artificers from Fez, the last surviving masters of the mystery of chiselled plaster and ceramic mosaics and honeycombing of gilded cedar. . . . It remains the loveliest and most fantastic of Moroccan palaces.

REFERENCES

According to Harris, Sultan Mauli Hassan was also a Negro. He says, "In complexion he is very dark, black blood showing very plainly in his thick lips, though this does not prevent his being an exceedingly handsome man." (*Land of an African Sultan*, p. 196, 1889.)

In Morocco, which is in reality a mulatto land, there has been little or no prejudice against unmixed Negroes from the Sudan. De Amicis says:

"The Moors not only seek them [the Negro women from this region] eagerly as concubines but marry them as frequently as white women from which comes the great number of mulattoes of all shades who are seen in the streets of Morocco.

"What strange chances! The poor Negro of ten years old, sold in the confines of the Sudan for a sack of sugar and a piece of cloth, may—and the case can be cited—discuss thirty years afterward as Minister of Morocco, a treaty of commerce with the English ambassador; and still more possibly, the black baby born in a filthy den, and exchanged in the shades of an oasis for a skin of brandy, may come to be covered with gems and fragrant with perfumes and clasped in the arms of a Sultan."

J. Stirling, *The Races of Morocco*, says similarly, "The Sultan, himself, though Sheryf, that is to say, the descendant of the Prophet, is pretty nearly as dark as his Bokhara Guards, and this complexion is likely to show itself for some generations as His Sheryfian Majesty's predilection for dark-colored wives is well-known."

"There are many Negroes in Morocco, both slaves and free men, and intermarriage of the females with the fair Moors produces a mixed race" (*Anthropol. Review*, Vol. VIII, pp. clxix–clxxiii. 1870.)

Wharton, Edith, *In Morocco*. London, 1920.

Harris, W. B., *Morocco That Was*, p. 33. Edinburgh, 1921.

O'Connor, V. C. Scott, *Vision of Morocco*. London, 1923.

McKenzie, Donald, *Khalifate of the West*. London, 1911.

Amicis, E. de, *Morocco, Its People and Places*, pp. 212–213, 296. 1882.

Bambaata

GALLANT AFRICAN CHIEF WHO
DEFIED THE WHITE RULERS OF SOUTH AFRICA
(1865–1906)

WHEN THE HISTORY of the African Negro comes to be written, it will be found that he fought as bravely and as gallantly to protect his homeland as the Britons, Gauls, Belgians, or any other primitive people we admire.

The American Indian and his white friends point with pride to King Philip, Geronimo and Sitting Bull. The Negro has his Cetewayo, Lobeguela, and Mosilekatze to be proud of. Just as Sitting Bull wiped out an entire American expedition sent against him, so Cetewayo, Zulu leader, annihilated an entire British force at Isandlhwana.

Of these primitive patriots Bambaata of Zululand was one of the greatest. Head of a lowly tribe, the Zondi, he led his people in one of the greatest black revolts against white supremacy. He made such resourceful use of his environment, and showed such bravery and daring withal, that it is no exaggeration to class him with Washington and other great white patriots. Even as they did the best with what tools nature had given them, so did Bambaata.

Bambaata's daring stands out all the more when we recall that he and his men matched their spears and clubs against modern rifles and cannon. If the charge of the Six Hundred at Balaclava was sublime madness, what, then, must be said of Bambaata and his men who charged machine guns with only spears? Death was certain in the face of such odds.

Bambaata was born in 1865. As a boy, he was headstrong and fond of fighting. In this he was like all Zulus. The Zulu takes great pride in his warlike prowess; his martial ardor and courage are world-famous—he is a born soldier. In skill at throwing a spear and in daring, Bambaata excelled his fellows. His pride of race was passionate.

As he grew to manhood, he viewed with intense resentment the presence of white exploiters in the land of his fathers. Gathering about him the bolder spirits of his tribe, he led repeated raids on Boer farms, seizing much cattle. He continued these raids until England defeated the Boers and took all of South Africa. The Boer War had lasted three years, and the British colonists, finding themselves heavily in debt, decided that the black natives should shoulder part of that war debt. Accordingly, a poll tax of $5 was imposed upon every male native. This was in addition to the regular hut tax of $15, and the dog tax.

Bambaata's tribe numbered 5500 and they lived in 1142 huts. When he heard of the new tax, he decided that not only was he not going to pay that tax, but for that matter, no tax at all. He and his people had been getting along well before the white men, these self-invited guests, had come along.

Other chiefs sympathized with Bambaata but they advised their people to pay. Some of them had revolted before and had seen the power of the white man's rifle—the *ubainbai*, as they called it, "the stick that kills from afar." There was one exception, however: Chief Sigananda, who, although ninety-six, had not cooled one bit in his hatred for the whites. Sixty-nine years before he had been one of the leaders in the historic massacre of the whites in Natal by Chief Dingaan. Sigananda had five taxable sons, and he could not see why they should pay taxes for merely living on land that his people had owned for centuries. This old "savage" felt, like Thomas Jefferson, that taxation without representation was tyranny to be fought to the death. He sided openly with Bambaata.

When Bambaata refused to pay, he was summoned to headquarters. He ignored the order. The government ordered him deposed and named another, Magwababa, in his place. When the white policemen came to seize Bambaata, he threatened to kill them. A force of 170 white men and a troop of native soldiers were sent after him. He fled into Zululand there to see his paramount chief, Dinizulu.

Dinizulu was wary. He sympathized strongly with Bambaata, but he had revolted once before and in 1889 had been exiled, like Napoleon, to St. Helena, and was now back on his good behavior. Promising secretly to help Bambaata, he gave him his ablest general, Cakijana, and sent him away. The two went secretly through Natal and Zululand stirring up the natives.

At this time three unusual incidents occurred that the two, clever propagandists that they were, turned to good account. The first was the withdrawal of troops sent from the British Isles by the home government, following a plan of retrenchment; the second was a phenomenon such as no South African, white or black, had ever witnessed before—whole fields of corn in Zululand, Bechuanaland, and elsewhere suddenly appeared as if they had been oiled and glittered weirdly in the sunshine. The third was a hailstorm of unusual severity, accompanied by terrific thunder, that swept over all South Africa.

The interpretations placed on these incidents were as follows: The first, that the Great White Chief, Edward VII, was displeased with the manner in which his children, the natives, were being treated and had withdrawn his support. The second was held to be a sign that Dinizulu had an important message to give all black people, namely that: "Deliverance is at hand." (The real explanation of the phenomenon was simple: the aphis, a harmless insect, had crawled over the corn, glossing it after the manner of the snail.) The third was regarded as a sign that the king of Basutoland, who in popular lore was master of the thunder, had sent the storm to show his displeasure at the conduct of the whites.

A message, said the propagandists, had come out of the storm. This was that all pigs should be killed (Zulus, like Moslems, regard pigs as unclean and rear them only for white consumption); that all objects of European manufacture, particularly those used for preparing food, should be destroyed, guns alone excepted; and that all should return to native ways. Those failing to comply were going to feel the effects of an even worse storm, the prophets threatened.

But Bambaata faced one great and almost insurmountable obstacle. This was the fear of older Zulus of firearms. They were dauntless where spears and war clubs were concerned—but not before death-spitting machine guns. The white man had but to stay out of range of their spears, press a trigger, and the blacks would fall in heaps, all their bravery and valor going for naught. No, miracles notwithstanding, one had to think twice.

To add to Bambaata's difficulties, voracious white ants had eaten off the stocks of most of the rifles he had cached in the hills. These rifles had been looted from the whites, and the whites had seen to it that getting others was impossible.

But Bambaata was resourceful. He told his people that a famous witch doctor had risen from the dead and had given Dinizulu a *muti* (charm) that would turn white men's bullets into water. News spread from kraal to kraal that Unkulunkulu (God) had at last hearkened to the prayers of his people.

Gathering his tribesmen, he seated them in a semicircle and bade the witch doctors appear. They came in with a special charm that had been prepared from the hearts, tongues, and livers of captured white men.

A cow was led in. With great ceremony it was anointed with the charm. Calling eight riflemen, Bambaata then bade them shoot it. The rifles spat forth their fire—but the animal was unhurt.

The tribesmen marveled. Truly a miracle!

Another cow was brought in. Again the riflemen were lined up and ordered to fire. But this time the animal dropped dead.

"See," cried out Bambaata in triumph, "no *muti* was put on it. There was no protecting power."

Certainly that seemed convincing enough. But Bambaata wasn't finished. He called for volunteers to be shot at. None answered. Leaping into the open, he ordered the witch doctors to sprinkle him with the charm and then bade the men reload and shoot at him.

Again eight rifles spat fire. But marvel of marvels, when the smoke cleared, there stood Bambaata, smiling and unhurt.

But that was not all. Bambaata felt it was necessary not only to inspire his men but to awe them also. He ordered a prisoner, one of his own men who had been giving information to the enemy, to be brought out. The man, bound hand and foot, was sprinkled with the *muti* and Bambaata impressively gave the order to fire. But although he was almost singed by the exploding powder, he remained unhurt.

A groan of dismay came from the warriors. The *muti* also protected traitors!

Then Bambaata raised his hand for silence. Striding forth, he leveled his spear. The next instant it whizzed through the air and the traitor fell, pierced through the heart.

Turning to the astonished group, Bambaata said, "Go tell what you have seen. And say, too, that while the *muti* will protect the faithful, it will not save traitors."

The explanation? Blank cartridges!

At last Bambaata was ready to strike. Returning to his tribe he ousted his successor and killed or put to flight the government forces. Several hundred soldiers were sent after him, but ambushing them, he killed many and set the others to flight.

The news of this victory, magnified as in true civilized style, flew over the land. Everyone felt, too, that Bambaata's *muti* had worked. Not a single native had been killed.

Another force of whites arrived a few days later and bombarded Bambaata's village from a distance of several thousand yards, but again he succeeded in ambushing his foes and putting them to flight.

Seeing that they had no mean opponent, the whites declared martial law and sent an army of 5000 men under General Sir Donald McKenzie against him. But even against this force he scored some success because the enemy could not reach him. Most of his fighting was done from ambush. The native soldiers of the whites wore strips of white and black cloth to distinguish them from the other blacks. Bambaata, putting strips on his own spies, had sent them among the whites to learn their plans.

After these successes, twenty other chiefs joined Bambaata. Others, more cautious, waited for a more decisive turn of events.

But as the conservative chiefs had foreseen, Bambaata hadn't a chance. He had less than twenty rifles, and what were spears against the latest model machine guns in the hands of men who had just won the great Boer War?

In every engagement—at Nkandbla, Otimati, Peyana, Insize, McCrae's Store, Mome Gorge—the black men fought like heroes of old. Like their American brothers at Carrizal, they charged practically unarmed into the maw of certain death—courageous to the last.

Bambaata himself was killed at Mome Gorge while making his way alone up a river. He was unarmed, and a native soldier, spying him, jumped upon him from behind a tree and plunged his spear into his back. The soldier tried to draw out the weapon for another blow, but it had been bent and he could not, whereupon another black soldier came to his aid. But Bambaata, seizing hold of the latter's spear, attacked them both, and though badly wounded, was getting the better part of the struggle when a third native ran up and putting his rifle to Bambaata's head, fired.

Soon after Bambaata's death the rebellion collapsed. Of the 12,000 blacks who took part, 2300 were killed and 4700 were taken prisoner. Among the latter was aged Sigananda, who died a few days after his capture, defiant to the last.

The rebellion lasted nine months (July, 1905, to April, 1906) and cost the government $5,000,000. Of the 11,000 white men engaged, 60 were killed and several hundred wounded. A considerable number of the 6000 native soldiers also lost their lives.

Some of the insurgents were sentenced to long terms in prison. Twenty-five of the leaders were exiled to St. Helena. Dinizula, paramount chief of the Zulus, who was accused of complicity, was given four years.

As for valiant Bambaata, his followers refused to believe him dead although the government publicly exhibited his head. His wife did not go into mourning, and this was taken as proof that he was still alive.

REFERENCES

Stuart, J., *History of the Zulu Rebellion, 1906*. London, 1913.
Bosman, W., *Natal Rebellion of 1906*. London, 1907.
Great Britain. Colonial Office. Natal. Correspondence relating to Native Disturbances in Natal. 1906. Also, further correspondence, etc.

Cd. 2905, 3207 (1906); Cd. 3247, 3563 (1908); Cd. 3888, 3998, 4401, 4403, 4404, 4195, 4328 (1908).

ADDITIONAL REFERENCES

Binns, C. T., *Dinuzulu*, pp. 201–207. London, Longmans, Green and Company, Ltd., 1968.

Lugg, H. C., *Historic Natal and Zululand*. Union of South Africa, Shuter and Shooter Company, 1949.

Marks, Shula, "Harriett Colenso and the Zulus 1874–1913." *Journal of African History*, pp. 403–411. London, Cambridge University Press, 1963.

Menelik II

"KING OF KINGS,
EVER VICTORIOUS LION OF JUDAH"
(d. 1923)

IF TRIUMPH against great odds entitles a ruler to be called great, Menelik II was one of the foremost figures of a century that includes Napoleon. Few monarchs faced greater difficulties than he did. He was beset by leading European powers greedy for his kingdom; harassed by rebellious chieftains of his own land; and worried by family dissensions.

Menelik belonged to a very ancient family. According to such records as we have, his pedigree was older than that of any other ruler of his time. Indeed, it towered over theirs as a California redwood over an oak. Of course, this will be doubted by some, but these will find it very difficult to disprove.

The oldest royal family in Europe was the Bourbon, which dates back to the ninth century A.D. The next is the English, which goes back to William the Conqueror, who was born in 1028, the illegitimate son of the Duke of Normandy and a tanner's daughter. Menelik, however, traced his descent from Menelik I, son of Solomon and the Queen of Sheba, or back to 930 B.C. Between Menelik I and Menelik II stretched 2793 years. But that is not all. Solomon's lineage is traced in the Bible to Adam, which for those who accept the legend would give Menelik nearly 6000 years of recorded ancestry. Thus if lineage makes for aristocracy, Menelik could have been called the most aristocratic monarch then living.

One indisputable fact is that when the book of Genesis was written, even granting that it was written by Moses (which it was not), Ethiopia was already a very ancient kingdom. Already in 750 B.C., when Greece and Rome were still in their infancy, one of Menelik's ancestors, Piankhy, had conquered Egypt.

Twice in its long history Menelik's line had been dethroned, first in A.D. 950 by the Falashas, or Negro Jews, and then again in 1855, by Kassai (King Theodore), a man of humble birth. Both times the dynasty reasserted itself with remarkable vitality.

Theodore had seized the throne on the death of Menelik's father, and his victory over this usurper shows that in him there was something far superior to mere blue blood.

Menelik's troubles began when he was eleven years old, at which time he had to flee to escape death at the hands of Theodore. The loyal element crowned him at Shoa with the ancient title "Elect of God, Emperor, King of Kings of Ethiopia, Sultan of the Nile, Ever Victorious Lion of Judah." With Theodore firmly in power, however, this was only an empty gesture and Menelik had to take to the wilds to escape capture. From time to time he attacked Theodore but was always beaten.

When matters seemed at their worst the English invaded Ethiopia to avenge some missionaries who had been killed by Theodore, who to escape capture killed himself. John, Theodore's son, then seized the throne, and Menelik, failing to oust him, made an agreement with him whereby he would be made John's heir, and John's son, Ras Area, would be Menelik's heir. To cement the treaty Menelik married his daughter, Zeodita, to Ras Area. But not long afterward Menelik was rid of both rivals. Ras Area died and John was killed in battle with the dervishes.

Emperor at last, Menelik, eager to restore the prestige and ancient glory of Ethiopia, dropped his real name, Sahaba Mariem, and took that of the son of the Queen of Sheba. But his troubles with the succession were by no means over. John's illegitimate son, Ras Mangascha, rebelled and made an alliance with the British, through whose aid he hoped to get the throne. Backed with British arms and money, Mangascha warred with Menelik for the next eight years.

There were other enemies too. Certain other European powers, anxious for a share of Menelik's land, backed the Egyptians, who came down from the north led by European officers and armed with European guns. Menelik, however, defeated these in 1875 and again in 1876.

The next attack was by the dervishes, who had driven England out of the Sudan and wanted to seize the headwaters of the Blue Nile. Again, in three campaigns, 1885, 1888, and 1889, Menelik defeated them and drove them out of his country.

His next enemy was Italy, who had ambitions of becoming a great colonial power like England and France and thought Ethiopia with its fine, rich uplands admirably suited to her purpose.

This was not Italy's first attempt. In 1869, much to England's chagrin, she had occupied the Ethiopian port of Assab on the Red Sea. Invading the interior, the Italians had been met by John, who was then emperor, and decisively defeated at Dogali. But the Italians returned the following year with 25,000 well-armed men of whom 12,000 were white. John was fighting the dervishes at the time and the Italians entrenched themselves. England, too, was having trouble with the Egyptians and thus agreed to let the Italians remain.

Menelik, unable to expel the Italians because of his fight with Mangascha, who, as it was said, was being backed by Britain, and also because of his fight with the dervishes, now decided to play one white power against the other, and called on Italy for aid, promising her a strip of territory. With this Italian aid, he defeated Mangascha.

Italy now asked for a treaty and Menelik made one with her in 1889. By its terms Italy was awarded Asmara and was pledged to pay Menelik $1,000,000.

For a time all went well. Menelik, now at peace, turned his attention to the improvement of his country. Some of his reforms were viewed with suspicion by the whites, however. One of these was his postal system. When he had postage stamps printed with his own likeness both England and Italy objected. They felt that this showed too much independence on his part.

The breach widened when Menelik made a treaty with other powers such as Austria, Russia, and France. Italy declared that by the terms of her treaty, Menelik was not free to do that. He had promised, she claimed, to use Italian diplomacy in dealing with other nations.

Menelik insisted that he had made no such promise, and pointed to the word *itchalloutchal* in Article 17 of his copy of the treaty. This, he maintained, meant "may, if he pleases" (use Italian diplomacy), and both Ethiopian and Oriental scholars backed him. The Italians contended that the word meant "must."

Eager for an understanding, Menelik wrote the Italian king, Humbert:

I realize that the Amharic text and the Italian version of this Article 17 are not the same. I have stipulated that Ethiopian affairs could be treated by Italian diplomacy on my invitation but I have never promised to have it done by Italy alone.

Your Majesty ought to understand that no independent power could ever make such a concession. If you have at heart the honor of your ally, you will hasten to rectify the error in the interpretation of Article 17, and to bring this rectification to the knowledge of the European power to whom you have communicated this badly translated article.

The Italian envoy, aware of what it would mean to Italian prestige if his nation yielded to this black, and as he considered it, barbaric, people, replied, "This, King Humbert will never do. It would wound the dignity and pride of the Italian people."

Menelik retorted, "If you have your dignity, we have ours, too."

Empress Taitu, his wife, added, "You wish to make us your pupils, but this will never happen."

Menelik repudiated the treaty and returned a loan he had taken from Italy with three times the stipulated interest. Italy's reply was to march into Menelik's territory and support Mangascha and other chiefs opposed to Menelik.

Menelik's next step was proof of his great statesmanship. Sending messengers through all the land, he called upon Ethiopians, friendly and hostile, to meet him at Boromeda. They came in great numbers, and addressing them in stirring language, he bade them unite to drive out the common foe.

"We cannot," he said, "permit our integrity as a Christian and civilized nation to be questioned, nor the right to govern our empire in absolute independence. We cannot, as long as we preserve our indomitable spirit backed by our warriors.

"The Emperor of Ethiopia is a descendant of a dynasty that is 3000 years old—a dynasty that during all that time has never submitted to an outsider. Ethiopia has never been conquered and she never shall be.

"We will call no one to our defense. We are capable of protecting ourselves. Ethiopia will stretch forth her hands only to God!"

The response to his appeal was overwhelming. Every chief swore fidelity. His old foe Mangascha pleaded for the privilege of being the first to attack the enemy. Ethiopia was united!

Menelik now withdrew to the interior to assemble his army, while a small force under Mangascha marched toward the coast to meet the Italians. This move was necessary, as Menelik had no standing army. At the call to arms, the Ethiopian would pick up his spear or gun, take his wife and his donkey, and set out. Liberty-loving, he had as little use for discipline as the New England farmer who fought the British.

In the first encounter the Italians, commanded by General Baratieri, were apparently successful over Mangascha. Mangascha's orders were to retreat and draw the Italians in after him. The Italian premier, Count Crispi, confident of victory, demanded $4,000,000 to carry on the war and sent 5000 more men to Ethiopia.

Crispi, not knowing of Menelik's ruse, interpreted the increasing penetration of Ethiopia as a sign of victory, which he jubilantly announced to his people. By this time he had resolved on nothing less than the annexation of Ethiopia.

In November, 1895, he sent out an additional 15,000 men. England, France, Russia, and Austria protested in vain. As if in answer, the defiant Crispi seized three Ethiopian princes who were studying engineering in Switzerland, despite Swiss protests.

Mangascha, in the meantime, continued to play his game of strategic retreat and continued to lead the Italians toward Menelik, who was lying in wait with 120,000 warriors.

At Delsa the Italian commander, General Baratieri, catching up with Mangascha, won another illusory victory, news of which was telegraphed, greatly magnified, to Italy.

It was time now for Menelik to take over the show, and he did. On December 7, 1895, the Italian vanguard of 5000 men under Colonel Toselli was killed to a man by a force under Ras Makonnen, Menelik's nephew and the father of Haile Selassie. This victory brought the Ethiopians a huge quantity of arms, ammunition, and supplies.

Ras Makonnen's next move was to march on the Italian stronghold of Makalle, which he captured in forty-one days. The commander, Major Galliano, offered a large sum for his men to be freed and permitted to rejoin the main body of the Italian army. Menelik accepted. He had an end in view far greater than the ransom money. In fact, what he did then revealed rare strategy. He insisted that his own men escort the Italians back to their lines. When this had been done, he so maneuvered his men as to give the impression that he was leaving that neighborhood for another Italian post, Addigrat. But after going a little way toward this place, he changed his direction abruptly and marched on Adowa where the main body of the Italian army was, and in such a manner as to reach it from the rear.

In the meantime the Italian scouts were completely fooled. The movement of the Ethiopian troops escorting the Italian captives back to their lines served as a screen for Menelik's advance. Before the Italian commander, General Baratieri, knew it, he was surrounded. His only hope was to try to break through back to the coast, but dubious of success, he tried to come to terms with Menelik, who demanded $12,000,000, the surrender of all his arms, and the complete evacuation of Ethiopian territory.

Negotiations went on for the next five weeks, Menelik growing stronger all the time. The Italians, with 20,521 men, were outnumbered four to one by Menelik. However, against their sixty-four modern cannon, Menelik had only forty, mostly of obsolete type.

Baratieri, in this precarious position, telegraphed Prime Minister Crispi saying that if he were attacked the very best he would be able to do was to hold off Menelik until relief came. Crispi, faced with a political crisis at home and knowing that only a victory could save him, sent Baratieri a stinging reply. He said that Baratieri was suffering from "military rheumatism." His ultimatum was, "Give me a victory, or out you go."

On the night of February 29, 1896, Baratieri, taking advantage of the moonlight and the fact that the next day was a major feast for the Ethiopians, advanced.

Warned by his scouts, Menelik went into action, although a third of his men were away for the holiday. Utilizing mountain passes unknown to the enemy, he crept up on them and surrounded them almost entirely.

At 6:30 the next morning the Italians opened battle. Their mountain guns played havoc with the massed Ethiopians. But Menelik, bringing up his modern quick-firers, retaliated with vigor. Then he gave an order for simultaneous advance on all fronts, and the Ethiopians, sweeping down, pressed the Italians into such a closely packed mass that they could not use their guns. Many of their cannon were found after the fight unfired.

Thereafter the battle was a massacre. The Ethiopians speared the foe like sheep. By 3:00 P.M. the Italians were in full flight, leaving behind them 12,000 dead.

The Ethiopians did not pursue them but the fugitives were harassed by the black subjects of Italy, who took advantage of the defeat to get revenge. Among the slain were two Italian generals, Dabormida and Arimondi. Albertone, a third, was captured alive with 7000 men. Menelik's loss was between 6000 and 8000 dead. The entire Italian army supplies, including the cannon and 4,000,000 cartridges, fell to Menelik.

The battle of Adowa made a great impression on the world at large. At last an African nation had decisively beaten a European invader. In Italy the effect was terrible. Crispi was mobbed in Parliament and thrown out of office; riots broke out over the country; and soldiers mutinied rather than go to Ethiopia.

General Balciderra, who succeeded Baratieri, estimated that it would take an army of 250,000 five years to conquer Ethiopia at a cost of $1 billion. With this bleak estimate, there was nothing for Italy to do but pay a stiff price for the ransom of her soldiers and acknowledge the absolute independence of Ethiopia.

The news of the victory traveled with astonishing rapidity over the continent and encouraged its oppressed inhabitants. As Castonnet des Fosses said at the time:

The white man is no longer considered a superior being. He has lost his prestige. It is known that he is not invincible and the natives have ceased to fear him. That is why one cannot insist too much upon the importance of the battle of Adowa. It is an event which is for Africa, the beginning of a new day.

After this victory there was a rather undignified scramble of world powers to make treaties with Menelik.

Menelik's personal conduct was as commendable as his military genius was praiseworthy. He lived simply. On one occasion, during a famine, he worked as a common laborer, tilling the soil. When a cattle disease so depleted the herds that only the wealthy could buy meat, he ate no beef but shared the lot of the poorest. "Why should I" said Menelik, "when my people are in want?" A French writer of the time said that he knew of no European ruler who would have done that.

Menelik always exacted from Europeans the formal respect due him as a ruler. When Prince Henri of Orléans, a member of French royalty, appeared before him attired in hunting togs, "Menelik publicly rebuked him, asking, 'Who is this person who does not know how to appear before a king?' "

But Menelik was not haughty. He had great pity for the sufferings of others. Once a letter to an Italian prisoner fell into his hands. It was from the man's mother, and told of her despair at not knowing what had become of her son. Menelik had the man released, ransom-free, and after giving him a handsome present, sent him off ot his mother.

Dr. Vitalien, a West Indian Negro and Menelik's private physician, said of him:

At the height of his activity, he often devoted more than fifteen hours a day to the administration of his empire, examining all the affairs, however trivial, that came to his attention. Sometimes during the same morning he would receive the diplomats, who would discuss foreign affairs; the governors of the provinces, with whom he would converse on politics and the administration of the interior; the engineers, with whom he would talk over mechanics and construction; the doctors, who spoke on prophylaxy and hygiene; the chief of Stores and Supplies, who submitted to him samples of velvet, silk, or showed him some new model of fire-arms; the governor of the palace, who spoke about the ordinary duties of the palace, or of taxes to be paid in kind, or of firewood. By a sort of intellectual gymnastics, he passed from one subject to another, treating each with great ease and competence.

His goodness and his benevolence were proverbial. All classes, rich and poor, were permitted to approach him with familiarity, calling him "Djanhoiy," and sure of his sympathy and help. When he died on December 12, 1923, his people regarded his passing as a great calamity.

He was a clever diplomat, an able warrior, an adroit sovereign, a good workman, very intelligent, very refined and instructed, curious at all times about the progress of new science, accessible to new ideas, with a character gentle, good and opposed to flattery; sometimes weak, but with a stubbornness that nothing could break, and crossed by crises of terrible anger. All who have approached him have recognized in him a highminded, noble and affectionate man.

In physique Menelik was imposing. According to Sir E. A. Wallis Budge:

He was stoutly built and about six feet in height. His skin was very dark; his features were somewhat heavy; and his face was pitted with smallpox. He had a good broad forehead and very bright, intelligent eyes; he had a large, strong mouth, very good teeth, and the chin of a determined man. He wore a mustache and a short, curly beard. His expression was good, and when lighted up by his pleasant smile, his face was very attractive. . . . His manners were dignified and kindly, and his gracious courtesy endeared him to all people; his speech was simple and direct.

Briefly stated: Menelik united Ethiopia; set up courts of justice; regulated custom duties and taxes; admitted railways and telegraphs; started a postal system. He checked slavery and reformed ist abuses; he prohibited the custom of mutilating prisoners. His name was potent, to some synonymous with that of God; years after his death it was still invoked in taking the most sacred of oaths. It is interesting to note that in 1873 he helped France pay her war debt to Germany.

Menelik took great pride in being an African. Blanchot says:

The Negro blood was predominant in him as it is in many Abyssinian chiefs, and the Europeans at his court, even those whom he admitted to a certain intimacy with him, were permitted to remain only on condition that they were willing to accept a sort of subordination and to Abyssinize themselves.

REFERENCES

Selassie, G., *Chronique du Regne de Menelik*, 2 vols. Paris, 1930.

Budge, E. A. W., *Ethiopia and the Ethiopians*, Vol. II. London, 1928.

Merab, *Impressions d'Ethiopie*. Paris, 1921.

Blanchot, L. L., *Geographie*, Dec. 1902.

Rogers, J. A., *The Real Facts about Ethiopia*, rev. ed. New York, 1936.

ADDITIONAL REFERENCES

Amero, Constant, *Le Négus Menelik et l'Abyssinie Nouvelle*. Paris, J. LeFort, 1897.

Berkeley, George Fitz-Hardinge, *The Campaign of Adowa and the Rise of Menelik*. London, Constable, 1935.

Del Boca, Angelo, *The Ethiopian War 1935–1941*, trans. by P. D. Cummins. Chicago and London, The University of Chicago Press, 1965.

Du Bois, W. E. B., *The World and Africa*, pp. 23, 116. New York, International Publishers, 1965.

Greenfield, Richard, *Ethiopia*, pp. 96–137. New York, Washington, D.C., and London, Frederick A. Praeger, 1965.

Holt, P. M., *A Modern History of the Sudan*, pp. 102–103, 114. New York, Grove Press, Inc., 1961.

Huggins, Willis N., *An Introduction to African Civilizations*, pp. 11, 31, 51, 80. New York, Avon House, 1937.

Mantegazza, Vico, *Menelik, l'Italia e l'Ethiopia*. Milan, Libreria Editrice Milanese, 1910.

Marcus, Harold G., "The End of the Reign of Menelik II." *Journal of African History*, Vol. XI, No. 4, pp. 571–589. London and New York, Cambridge University Press.

Monfreid, Henri de, *Menelik tel quil fut*. Paris, Grasset, 1954.

Niven, Sir Rex, *Nine Great Africans*, pp. 41–57. New York, Roy Publishers, Inc., 1964.

Omer-Cooper, J. D., *et al.*, *The Making of Modern Africa*, Vol. 1, pp. 69, 78–84. London, Longmans, Green and Company, Ltd., 1968.

Orléans, Henri Philippe Marie, Prince d', *Une Visite à l'Empereur Menelick*. Paris, Dentu, 1898.

Pankhurst, Richard, "Menelik and the Foundation of Addis Ababa." *Journal of African History*, Vol. II, No. 1, pp. 103–117. Cambridge, Cambridge University Press, 1961.

Khama

❦

THE GOOD KING OF BECHUANALAND
(1828–1932)

KHAMA OF BECHUANALAND is one of the noblest figures of history. His life is striking proof that among so-called savages are to be found individuals as innately humane and "civilized" as in the most cultured societies.

Invested, like other African rulers, with absolute power, Khama preached and lived democracy; born a heathen and converted to Christianity, he practiced rules and virtues that white rulers about him, despite their 1500 years of Christian tradition, flouted, or feared to observe.

His domestic troubles were many, so many that they seemed endless; yet he bore them with rare fortitude and self-sacrifice. More than once he gave up his rights rather than cause bloodshed among his own people.

That did not mean he was spineless. When necessary he could be as firm as the firmest, a fact that invaders of his country, white or black, knew only too well. He welcomed white people, but when any of them abused his hospitality or tried to debauch his people, he would check them in no uncertain words.

He was born in 1828, the eldest son and heir of Sekhomi, chief of the Bamangwato, a branch of the Bantu peoples, and overlord of a large part of northern South Africa. Under Khama, this territory, known as Bechuanaland, was to become larger yet. Bechuanaland is bigger than Texas, and includes the Lake Ngami region with its rich pasture and game lands.

Khama's troubles began when as a youth he embraced Christianity and cast off the religious rites of his tribe. This greatly angered his father, who was the most greatly feared sorcerer for a thousand miles around.

Father and son also disagreed on matters of policy. Sekhomi welcomed the white traders who sold whiskey; Khama strongly objected to them.

Sekhomi was cruel, also. He had killed one of his own brothers. Khama, on the other hand, was gentle and opposed bloodshed. He never scolded but tried to influence others by good example.

These differences finally caused an open break between father and son. Rather than give up his adopted faith, Khama gave up his rights to the succession and left Shoshong, his father's capital. But it wasn't for long. The people clamored for him and his father begged him to come back. They soon quarreled again, however, Sekhomi, years before had bought for Khama, with many head of cattle, the daughter of a powerful chief, and now he wished Khama to marry her. Khama, already married to a Christian girl of the tribe, refused.

"As a Christian," he said, "I cannot take another wife. But give me the hardest task you can think of instead, and I will perform it. Send me alone to hunt the elephant or the lion, and I will gladly do it to show my obedience."

When Khama would not yield, Sekhomi, infuriated, sent for his brother, Macheng, and offered to make him his heir if he would kill Khama. But Macheng, whom Sekhomi had once tried to kill, suspected a trick and refused.

Some of Khama's people lost patience with him, too. They could not understand why a young man who possessed all the physical qualities that primitive men hold dear should be so gentle. He stood six feet five inches, was the strongest among his people and the fleetest of foot. A daring hunter and a superb horseman, he would attack even lions singlehanded.

Admiration for him increased when he beat off Lobenguela, the most powerful of the neighboring kings. The latter, coveting Sekhomi's land, had gathered an army of several thousand and

Khama

was coming to take it. Sekhomi, who had been relying on his fame as a witch doctor, kept but a small army. Unprepared, therefore, to meet an invader, he called his witch doctors together, put the witch pots on the fire, and began casting spells on the approaching enemy.

Khama, hearing of this, went into the hut where the pots were boiling and kicked them over. "It is time to fight," he said, "not for worthless nonsense."

Calling the younger tribesmen around him, he sallied out to meet Lobenguela with only a few hundred men. Under his bold leadership his men fought so well that Lobenguela withdrew and out of respect for Khama never attacked him again.

After this exploit Khama could easily have ousted his father but instead suffered the old man with infinite patience, showing him the respect due a father. But this was lost on the unregenerate Sekhomi. To make matters worse, another of his sons, Khamana, became a Christian.

This meant that at the great festival of the year, the initiation ceremony of the youths who had attained manhood, Sekhomi, instead of marching proudly with his sons at his side in the procession, had to go alone because Khama and Khamana refused to take part in the ancient rites, considering them heathen and degraded. Sekhomi decided that Khama must die.

That night while Khama was asleep in his hut Sekhomi led a number of his warriors to it and bade them fire into it. They refused, and when Sekhomi himself attempted to fire his double-barreled rifle into it, one of them knocked it upward and the shots went wild.

Sekhomi, seeing that his authority was at an end, ran away that night. He knew, moreover, that according to tribal law his eldest son now had a right to kill him. However, Khama, ever the forgiving, sent messengers to tell him he could return in safety.

Sekhomi did return and was quiet for a while. But his opposition to Christianity and white men's ways soon got the better of him again. By fear of his magic he assembled several hundred of the tribesmen to drive out Khama, but Khama, instead of giving battle, left quietly. He went off to the mountains accompanied by Khamana and all the Christians of the tribe. Sekhomi attacked him there and was beaten off.

The people, tiring again of Sekhomi, clamored for Khama, and Sekhomi begged him to return. Though he could not forgive Khama for his "white" heart, he was really proud of him. Khama returned again and with all kindliness tried to win Sekhomi over to Christ.

But Sekhomi grew more obstinate with advancing age. When his son Macheng came to visit him he abdicated in Macheng's favor, after the latter promised to kill Khama. Once more Khama left. "Henceforth," he said, "my kingdom shall consist only of my guns, my horses, cattle and wagons. I take them and go, never to return."

But no sooner had Khama left that Sekhomi discovered his error. Macheng was a tyrant like himself and he had to run for his life, leaving everything he had behind. Macheng tried to poison Sekhomi's family in order to strengthen his power. Its members were saved from death only because a white trader suspected Macheng. When Macheng had asked for strychnine, the trader had given him marking ink.

Under Macheng, the tribes fell into anarchy. Khama, though he was being severely tried, refused to use force and pardoned his enemies the seventy times seven prescribed by his faith. At this point a relative of Khama, Secheng, chief of the Bakwena, angry at Macheng, attacked him, captured him, and ordered him to be shot. But Khama interceded for him and he was set free but driven from the tribe. He died soon afterward from drink.

Khama was now paramount chief. But his troubles were not over. His Christian brother, Khamana, mistaking Khama's kindliness for weakness, plotted against him—with Sekhomi, ever the ingrate, egging him on.

Once again Khama left, and going to Serowe seventy miles away, built his own town. With him came more than a half of the tribe, among whom were most of the leading men.

Again there was trouble in Sekhomi's tribe and Khamana sent messengers begging Khama to come back. This time Khama replied sternly, "When I was with you my presence was soreness to your eyes. You treated me as a dog in my own courtyard and before my own people; therefore I refuse to sit in the same town with you and Sekhomi. Those who prefer to stay with you, let them stay; and those who wish to come to me, let them come."

Under Sekhomi and Khamana conditions in Shoshhong grew so intolerable that the people begged Khama to return and restore order. He did, and this time made his father and brother prisoners.

Firmly in power at last, Khama began by driving out all the witch doctors and attacking tribal superstitions. His people worshipped a little gazelle known as the duiker, which was held so sacred that even its dung was preserved. To show that the animal had no magical powers Khama ate duiker steak and wore sandals of duiker leather. He put a stop to the rain-making ceremonies and the circumcision of boys and girls. Also he substituted Christian services for pagan rites at planting time and harvest.

His next object of attack was intoxicating drinks, which had largely been responsible for his father's behavior. He banished the rum and whiskey traders from his territory, and even prevented the building of a railroad through it, thereby sacrificing a fortune, because he knew that white men would have liquor at the stations, in which case it would have been impossible to keep it from his people.

"Strong drink," he would say, "is the only enemy on earth I fear. I fear Lobenguela less than I fear brandy. I fought Lobenguela and drove him back. He never gives me a sleepless night. But to fight against drink is to fight against demons and not men. I fear the white man's drink more than the assegais of the Matebele which kill men's bodies. Drink puts devils into men and destroys their souls and bodies."

Since alcohol degraded men, Khama maintained that its prohibition came within the sphere of governmental action. He even tried to abolish the strong Kaffir beer that his tribe had been drinking for centuries, but when his brother Radiclani thought this was too drastic and threatened revolt, he yielded.

Though only selected white men were permitted into his territory, bootlegging went on, until one day the bootleggers challenged him openly by drinking liquor in a public square. Khama saw all but he kept his temper and allowed several days to pass before he sent for the offenders. Addressing them with implacable calm, he said, "I am black but I am chief in my own country. When you white men rule it, then you may do as you like. At present I rule and I shall maintain my laws which you insult and despise. . . . You do so because you despise black men in your hearts. If you despise us, what do you want here in the country God has given us? Go back to your own country. . . . Take everything you have. Strip the iron roofs off your houses. Take all that is yours. I want no one but friends in my land. . . . I am trying to lead my people to act according to that word of God which we have received from you white people, and you show them an example of wickedness such as we never knew. . . . Go! Take your cattle and never come back again."

When they apologized, he replied, "My people need pity more than yours."

Khama built schools, improved agriculture, inaugurated scientific cattle breeding, and made his kingdom a model for the rest of South Africa. He established a mounted police corps and theft became a thing unknown. White traders passing through his territory no longer found it necessary to set a watch over their goods at night.

He cared for the aged and the infirm, and took all the weaker tribes under his protection. His treatment of the Makalala, a tribe so low that both whites and natives called them "dogs without soul," was so magnanimous that English ministers and editors held it up as a rare example of Christian conduct. To give this tribe equality with his, he married one of his own daughters to the Makalala chief. This was equal to the governor-general at Cape Town, to show his sympathy with the white working-class, giving his daughter in marriage to a white street sweeper.

In 1895, when the pressure of the whiskey traders and the railroad companies became too strong, Khama went to England to see Queen Victoria about them. The English people lionized him, treated him with the honors due a king, and confirmed his right go keep out alcohol and the railway. On July 22, 1922, his people celebrated his golden jubilee with great festivities. Present were many leading white officials from England and Cape Town.

In these happy circumstances he lived hale and hearty for another ten years, then he contracted pneumonia as the result of a cold caught in a rainstorm while horseback riding and died on February 21, 1932, at the age of 104.

In 1925 a monument was erected to him at Serowe. Proof of

the high regard of the English for him was that the Prince of Wales (later Edward VIII, and then the Duke of Windsor) journeyed a thousand miles from Cape Town to unveil it.

The monument bears the words: "Righteousness exalteth a nation."

REFERENCES

Bryden, H. A., *History of South Africa, 1652–1903*. Edinburgh, 1904.

Harris, John, *Khama, the Great African Chief*. London, 1923.

Hole, H. M., *Passing of the Black Kings*. 1932.

ADDITIONAL REFERENCES

Davies, Horton, *Great South African Christians*. Cape Town and New York, Oxford University Press, 1951.

Gollock, Georgina Anne, *Lives of Eminent Africans*. New York and London, Longmans, Green and Company, Inc., 1928.

———, *Sons of Africa*, pp. 93–110. London, Student Christian Movement, 1928.

Hepburn, James D., *Twenty Years in Khama's Country*. London, 1920. Republished by Frank Cass Ltd., London, 1967.

Huggins, Willis N., *An Introduction to African Civilizations*, pp. 11, 14. New York, Avon House, 1937.

Knight-Bruce, G. W. H., *Memories of Mashonaland*. London, Edward Arnold Company, 1885.

Lloyd, Edwin, *Three Great African Chiefs*. London, T. Fisher Unwin, 1895.

Mockford, Julian, *Khama: King of the Bamangwato*. London, Jonathan Cape, 1931.

Sillery, A., *The Bechuanaland Protectorate*. London, Oxford University Press, 1952.

Woodson, Carter, G., *African Heroes and Heroines*, pp. 181–189. Washington, D. C., The Associated Publishers, 1939 and 1944.

Alfred A. Dodds

❧❧

FRENCH GENERAL AND EMPIRE BUILDER
(1842–1922)

GENERAL ALFRED AMÉDÉE DODDS, France's outstanding soldier in
the period immediately preceding World War I, was born in Senegal, French West Africa, February 6, 1842. His grandfather, of
English descent, was born in the colony of Gambia, where he
married the daughter of a Frenchman and a woman of the Peuhl
tribe.

His father, Emery Dodds, a son of this union, married Mlle.
Billaud, daughter of a Frenchman and a Senegalese woman. General Dodds was thus of mixed ancestry on both sides of his family.

He entered the military academy at St. Cyr and was graduated
at the head of his class when twenty-one years of age. Six years
later he took part in the Franco-Prussian War, attaining the rank
of captain. At Bazeilles, where he was wounded, he was decorated
on the battlefield with the Legion of Honor for valor.

In the course of this war, so disastrous for France, he was
captured at Sedan and taken into Germany, but escaping, he re-
joined his company. Recaptured, he escaped into Switzerland
where he was interned. Escaping once more, he reached Paris in
time to aid in the defense of that city.

The end of the war did not mean the end of military life for
him. He put down revolts in Madagascar; led expeditions against

African chiefs in West Africa, among whom was the prophet Abu Bekr, ally of Samory; he won Senegal for France; put down revolts in Indo-China; wiped out the Tonkin pirates, and commanded the troops in Senegal for twenty years more.

In Senegal he married a woman of Negro ancestry. In 1891, after having participated in twenty-one wars, he was recalled to France, given command of a regiment, and made a commander of the Legion of Honor.

The following year war broke out in Dahomey. The Dahomeyans, armed with the latest weapons and secretly aided by Germany, defeated the French in battle after battle until France realized she had a difficult situation on her hands. Moreover, campaigning in Dahomey with its steaming jungles without roads, broiling sun, and little water fit to drink, was not easy. There was but one man capable of handling the situation: Dodds.

On May 5, 1892, he left Bordeaux with several companies of white marines, a company of artillery, and a battalion of black sharpshooters. Stopping at Senegal, he picked up other battalions of Senegalese sharpshooters and thousands of native bearers.

Arriving off the Dahomey coast, he blockaded it with his warships and prevented the landing of a ship filled with arms and ammunition for Behanzin. Then he called upon Behanzin to surrender. The latter replied in terms of hot defiance and dared Dodds to come and take him. Dodds bombared the Dahomeyan coast, and landing a few days later, captured and burned the town of Cotonou. Starting into the interior, he took the towns of Zobo and Takou.

Early on the morning of September 19 a part of the Dahomeyan army hurled itself with terrific fury against the French. Opening the attack with a volley from their repeaters, they rushed in with their swords and knives, shouting their battle cry of "Koia! Koia! Dahomey!"

Another commander might have been taken by surprise—but General Dodds, knowing that it was the habit of the African warrior to attack early in the morning, was ready. His men received the enemy with shot and bayonet. The Dahomeyans, beaten back, returned with incredible eagerness, but the French, bringing their artillery and machine guns into action, forced them to retreat, leaving heaps of dead.

It was evident that it was going to take a stiff fight to reach Abomey, Behanzin's capital. A few days later heavy fighting took place at Dogba. Here General Dodds, who always fought beside his men, saw one of them killed at his side.

So far the French had encountered only detachments of Behanzin's army. The main portion was ahead with the king at Allada. On the march, General Dodds lost many of his men. The Dahomeyans shot down the French from the tops of palm trees or crawled up through the bushes to snipe at them.

At Puguessa Dodds came up against the main portion of the Dahomeyan army, 10,000 strong with ten fieldpieces, and commanded by the king in person. After three hours of terrific combat, the Dahomeyans were forced to retreat before the withering fire of French artillery and machine guns. The battle was noted for the valor displayed by the enemy amazon warriors, who fought their way to within ten yards of the French squares.

Four of the five German captains in the Dahomeyan army were taken prisoner and executed immediately.

Soon afterward Dodds captured Dioxene, and Behanzin consented to make peace. He sent three envoys with presents and a promise to pay a large indemnity. Dodds demanded, in addition, that the French flag be raised over Abomey, Behanzin's capital. When Behanzin refused, the fight was renewed, and after a furious battle Dodds captured Abomey, or rather what was left of it, for the king had set fire to it.

Dodds put Behanzin's brother Agli-Agbo on the throne, and with order restored, left for France. No sooner had he arrived there than word came that Behanzin was again at war. Returning, Dodds defeated and captured him on January 24, 1892.

For his exploits General Dodds was made a grand officer of the Legion of Honor, and the press and the nation sang his praises. His popularity was so great that he might easily have made himself military dictator of France. As the *New York Tribune* said:

When he returned to France after the conquest of Dahomey and of other West African kingdoms, which he added to the colonial empire of France, the entire nation, irrespective of party or politics, turned out to welcome him and to such an extent did he become an object of popular enthusiasm that there is no doubt that he might easily have established himself in the role of a military dictator had it not been for his loyalty to the republic.

Soon afterward, he was appointed inspector-general of the marines, and after a tour of France, was given command of the 20th Army Corps. Later he was made inspector-general of all colonial troops and named a member of the superior War Council.

When war threatened in Indo-China he was sent there as commander-in-chief. During the Boxer uprising in China in 1900 he served for a short time as commander-in-chief of the allied army of English, French, German, American, and Japanese troops. On his return to France he was awarded the Grand Cross of the Legion of Honor and the Médaille Militaire, France's two highest decorations.

In 1912, having reached the age limit, he retired from the army, but returned in 1914 to become a member of the Supreme War Council in the First World War. Later, with the advent of the new heroes of that war, he was forgotten, though he had done more than any one to consolidate France's great colonial empire. He bore neglect patiently, but when he was not invited to take part in the victory parade of July 14, 1919, he could not refrain from saying, "They have forgotten me a little too much."

He died on July 18, 1922. *Aux Écoutes,* a French journal, said, "For many persons, General Dodds has been dead a long time. Few men with the reputation he had have been able to grow old in such forgetfulness. The war, evidently, brought many competitors to his fame."

He was interred with great ceremony in the presence of Marshals Foch, Joffre, and Pétain.

Dodds was tall, with large shoulders and a well-developed body. He had a powerful head and his features were regular and adorned with a luxuriant black mustache. His complexion was darker than that of the average mulatto owing to exposure to tropical suns. Every inch a soldier, he was very popular with his men, both white and black. His success was due in no small measure to his kindness and consideration for them.

REFERENCES

The accident of birth played a great part in the fortunes of Dodds. Had he been born, like his father, in a British colony and joined the British army, the highest rank that it would have been possible for him, as a Negro, to attain would have been sergeant-major.

As regards the United States, the *New York Tribune* said, "General Dodds would not have been permitted to drink at the same bar with white men here and in many states of the Union would not be permitted to ride in the same car."

Desplantes, F., *Le Général Dodds*. Rouen, 1894.

Grandin, L., *A L'assaut au pays des noirs*, 2 vols. Paris, 1895.

Blanchard, J. R., *Au Dahomey.*

Larousse, *Mensuel*, pp. 923–924, Oct., 1922.

New York Tribune, Apr. 17, 1910.

ADDITIONAL REFERENCES

Hargreaves, John D. *West Africa: The Former French States*, p. 109. Englewood Cliffs, N.J., Prentice-Hall, 1967.

Prempeh of the Golden Stool

❧

KING OF THE ASHANTI
(d. 1931)

AT THE DAWN of the twentieth century the leading topic was King Prempeh and the Golden Stool. A party of distinguished Britishers was beleaguered in the depths of the African jungle; an expedition was rushing to their relief; the world awaited tensely news of their fate.

All because of King Prempeh and the Golden Stool—or more accurately, perhaps, the Golden Stool and King Prempeh. When Britain demanded Prempeh, his people gave him up without a murmur, but when a British governor merely expressed a wish to sit on the Golden Stool, they rose up in wild defiance, with the result that England had another little war on her hands.

King Prempeh's people, the Ashanti, occupied most of the fabulously wealthy territory called the Gold Coast, which, as everybody knows, has become the synonym for wealthy residential districts the world over. Gold literally flowed in its streams. The rivers were full of it and left deposits of it along their banks. After rains, gold dust could be found washed free in the streets. Gold and the slave trade attracted the first Europeans.

The Ashanti ranked among the richest peoples in Africa. Thomas Bowdich, who came to make a treaty for England, said in his report:

The chiefs, as did their superior captains and attendants, wore

Ashanti cloths of extravagant price made from the costly foreign silks which had been unravelled to weave them . . . and massive gold necklaces, intricately wrought.

Some wore necklaces reaching to the navel, entirely of aggry beads; a band of gold and beads encircled the knees from which several strings of the same depended; small circles of gold, like guineas, rings, and casts of animals were strung around their ankles . . . and rude lumps of rock-gold hung from their left wrists, which were so heavily laden as to be supported on the heads of the handsomest boys.

Gold and silver pipes and canes dazzled the eyes. Wolves' and rams' heads, large as life, cast in gold were suspended from the gold-handled swords which were held about them in great numbers.

The Ashanti were a proud people, and not without reason. For two centuries they had not only dominated their neighbors but had successfully coped with Europeans. Both the British and the Dutch paid them heavily for trading privileges, and military expeditions sent against them came to naught.

Systematic attempts to conquer the Ashanti started in 1823, when a British expedition commanded by Sir Charles MacCarthy was killed to a man. A gold cast of Sir Charles' skull was used as a goblet by King Kwaka, while the skull itself was hung up as a trophy in the fetish house.

For the next four years the British persisted, but the best they could do was get a treaty by virtue of which they, and not the Ashanti, paid the rent. "The white man," said King Kwaka, laughing somewhat contemptuously, "brings many cannon to the bush but the bush is stronger than the cannon."

By 1873 this black nation had overrun the whole of the Gold Coast, even forcing out the Dutch. That year an Ashanti army of 45,000 fighters laid siege to Elmina, a fortified town and castle seven miles from the coast. They were led by King Kofi Kali Kali, distinguished both as a warrior and a spendthrift. His favorite sport was to toss gold nuggets among his wives and watch them scramble for them. (Ashanti kings, incidentally, held the world record for the number of wives they kept. Tradition exacted that they maintain 3333—it is not known if some went over this number.)

But the same year also brought Ashanti their first serious

check, this when the Fanti, with whom King Kofi was at war, called in their allies, the British. Lord Wolseley, with an army of 3000 European soldiers, regiments of West Indians and African soldiers, the Fanti, and their native allies marched on Coomassie, the Ashanti capital. The Ashanti fought with traditional valor, but the long-distance cannon beat them, and Lord Wolseley entered King Kofi's capital and burned it to the ground.

King Kofi was forced to sign a treaty whereby he pledged to pay 50,000 ounces of gold and to keep the road by which the conquerors had come open and in good condition.

No sooner had the British withdrawn, however, than the Ashanti regained the upper hand. They paid a small part of the idemnity only; as to the road, it reverted to nature in short order.

The situation was much the same in 1896, when we come to King Prempeh and the Golden Stool. Prempeh, or Kwaka Dua III, had come to the throne at the age of sixteen and was now twenty. He had inherited it, as was the custom, from the female line. His family had been ruling since 1635.

The young king did not have an easy task ahead. The English invasion had more or less disrupted the country, and the native tribes, who had taken to fighting among themselves, were difficult to curb. Into the bargain, the British were again interfering in native affairs.

As Sir F. C. Fuller puts it:

The government policy of non-interference in Ashanti affairs so long adhered to by the Coast authorities had now been definitely abandoned; but the interference was all directed against, instead of in support of the central power. This rendered Prempeh's task all the more difficult and gradually discouraged and embittered him and the court party. Prempeh, only 16, was beset by gravest difficulties.

W. W. Claridge, another English writer, said similarly:

England's policy toward Ashanti since 1874, had signally failed in both respects [in advancing civilization and promoting the welfare of the Africans]. The destruction of the central controlling authority in Kumassi and the weakness of the government in declining all further responsibility and refusing to interfere for the preservation of order had caused years of civil war during which the suffering and loss of life must have been immeasurably greater than that attending the occasional wars of united Ashanti while the naturally evolved civilization and arts of the country had been neglected and fallen into decay.

Notwithstanding, Prempeh did his best to establish cordial relations with the British. He wrote a friendly letter to the Prime Minister saying that he hoped Her Majesty's government would give him all assistance and good advice for the good government of his kindgom. He added, "I believe if there is any grievance, Her Majesty's government will assist me in this important matter. I wish Her Majesty's Government a Merry Christmas and a Happy New Year."

But the British rejected his overtures and drew up plans to annex his territory. Other European nations were grabbing adjacent territory, and England was determined to get supremacy of the Gold Coast. The best they offered Prempeh was a proposal to make Ashanti a protectorate.

In response, the young monarch sent the following reply—a reply that is remarkable, indeed, for its tact and firmness:

The suggestion that Ashanti under its present state, should come and enjoy the protection of Her Majesty, the Queen and Empress of India, I may say, is a matter of very serious consideration, and I am happy to say that we have arrived at the conclusion that the kingdom of Ashanti will never commit itself to any such policy. Ashanti must remain independent as of old, and at the same time friendly with all white men. I do not write this with a boastful spirit but in the clear sense of its meaning. Ashanti is an independent kingdom and is always with the white man. I thank Her Majesty's Government for the good wishes entertained for Ashanti; I appreciate to the fullest its kindness.

The British, thereupon, replied that the Ashanti had not lived up to the treaty of 1874; that they had not paid the indemnity nor kept the road open. Furthermore, they accused the Ashanti of practicing the rite of human sacrifice.

To this Ashanti scholars replied, "Might not an African who saw a criminal being shot, guillotined, or electrocuted after a religious ceremony ask what was the difference between his land and those of the Christians?"

They pointed out that the object of killing captives and animals was for protection, as in civilized lands. According to Sir Francis Fuller and others, who lived in Ashanti, reports of human sacrifice were greatly exaggerated.

But British sanctimony and practical considerations carried the day, and before long a large army, reinforced by the Fanti, was on its way to Coomassie.

King Prempeh offered no resistance whatsoever, receiving Governor Maxwell, Colonel Scott, leader of the expedition, and his staff, in his palace. General Baden-Powell, hero of the Boer War, who took part in the expedition, described the scene as follows:

And there sits Prempeh, looking very bored as three scarlet-clad dwarfs dance before him amid the dense crowd of sword-bearers, court-criers, fly-catchers, and other officials. He looks a regal figure on a lofty throne with a huge velvet umbrella standing over him, upon his head a black and gold tiara, and on his neck and arms, large golden beads and nuggets of gold.

Hoping to preserve the independence of his kingdom, Prempeh offered to pay a huge indemnity. "I am willing to pay," he said, "and beg His Majesty's Government to take a first installment. It is usual for a man before meals to take something to whet his appetite. If the governor takes an installment that will whet his appetite, he will look the keener for the remainder."

But this offer was to no avail. The English had come for nothing less than the whole of Prempeh's kingdom. The governor demanded absolute submission and ordered Prempeh to appear on the parade ground at six o'clock for formal surrender.

Prempeh, however, kept him waiting, and did not arrive until eight with his court. The governor, Colonel Scott, and his aide were seated on a platform, waiting. The chiefs were compelled to come up, one by one, and lay down their swords. Then the governor, apparently determined to humble Ashanti pride thoroughly, ordered the king and his mother to kiss the feet of himself and Colonel Scott.

Rising, the king took off his crown and his slippers as ordered, came forward with the queen mother, whose dainty feet were always bare. They approached slowly, and bending down clasped with their hands and partly embraced the legs and booted feet of the governor. Then they quietly returned to their seats.

At the sight of this supreme indignity to mother and son, whose slightest word had once meant life or death, King Prempeh's subjects stood aghast.

A heavy fine was imposed upon Prempeh, and he, his father, mother, and uncles were taken into custody, pending payment. They were imprisoned in Elmina Castle, which for some 200 years had witnessed white men paying rent to Ashanti kings. Later King Prempeh was deported to Sierra Leone and thence to the lonely Seychelles Islands, off the East African coast. But the British were to pay for humiliating the black monarch.

Why, it may be asked, did the powerful Ashanti army surrender without so much as throwing a single spear? That brings us to the extremely romantic, but nonetheless true story of the Golden Stool.

This stool was a masterpiece of African art. Carved out of a solid block of teak, it was studded with golden nails and hung with golden ornaments on which African goldsmiths had lavished their skill. Among these ornaments was a cast of the skull of Adinkera, King of the Fanti.

This latter king had had the temerity to have a copy of the Golden Stool made for himself, which brought Ashanti wrath down upon him. He was defeated and killed by King Bonsu, who stripped the gold from the imitation stool and had it melted down and cast into the shape of his rival's skull. Every monarch since Osei Tutu had added an ornament to the sacred stool, and in the course of centuries it had become extremely valuable.

According to Ashanti tradition, the Golden Stool had descended from the skies, having been conjured thence by a celebrated magician, servant of Onyame, god of the sky, who had commanded the wizard to make the Ashanti a powerful nation. One day, in the presence of a great multitude, the Stool dropped from a great black cloud and floated slowly down until it came to rest on the knees of the king.

It was firmly believed to be the fountainhead of health, wealth, courage, and strength and to be immutably linked to the destiny of the nation. What the Ark of the Covenant was to the Jews, the Golden Stool was to the Ashanti.

So sacred was it regarded that not even the king himself dared sit on it. When its power was invoked at ceremonials, the king would go through the motions of sitting on it three times, after which he would mount the chair of state, resting only his hand upon it. In processions it was carried ahead of him under a special canopy and had a retinue larger than his. It was housed in a special building which was guarded day and night by two chiefs. Over it was a covering of finely-spun gold.

On the coming of the English, the Stool had been carefully hidden away, its guardians taking a vow never to disclose its whereabouts. The Ashanti felt secure as long as the Stool was in their midst, which explains why they surrendered their king so readily. They did not wish to endanger their precious relic by a war of which the outcome seemed uncertain.

The English, however, wanted the Stool in order to be able to break fully the spirit of the Ashanti. It would be placed in the British Museum along with other African art objects. They threatened, coaxed, and pleaded in vain. Not even the large rewards they offered had any effect.

Four years passed. Ashanti was quiet. Not even the war of Samory against the French at the border seemed to disturb it.

Then came the news that drove consternation and dismay into the hearts of the natives: a lame boy named Esumi had come to Accra and offered to lead Sir Frederick Hodgson, the governor, to the hiding place. An armed expedition started out. But the baleful glances of his countrymen were too much for Esumi, and terror-stricken, he led the searchers to another spot. When the soldiers dug, they found nothing.

After this failure Sir Frederick decided to go to Coomassie himself, taking Lady Hodgson and his staff. Calling the Ashanti chiefs together, Sir Frederick promised them British friendship and protection, saying that in return he expected loyalty. Finally he came to the subject of the Golden Stool. "What," he said, "must I do to the man, whoever he is, who has failed to give the Queen, who is the paramount power in this country, the Golden Stool to which she is entitled?

"Where is the Golden Stool? Why am I not sitting on the Golden Stool at this moment? I am a representative of the paramount power, why have you not relegated to me this chair? Why did you not take the opportunity of my coming to Coomassie to bring the Golden Stool and give it to me to sit on?"

If Sir Frederick intended this as a peace talk, it certainly had the opposite effect. A horrified silence fell upon his hearers. The Ashanti could hardly believe their own ears. What! Give this intruder their most sacred emblem to sit on—this symbol of all their past glory, this holy object which contained the spirit of their dead kings from Osei Tutu to Kwaka Dua II?

Verily, this was the crowning insult. That night the chiefs assembled in Opuku's tent and drank fetish that they would submit no longer to British rule. Much later Governor Hodgson denied ever having asked for the Golden Stool to sit on. Newspaper correspondents, however, insisted that he had—not only figuratively, but also literally.

At any rate, the damage was done. A few days later wild whoops and yells announced that the Ashanti rebellion was on. Governor Hodgson, his wife, and others of their party found themselves besieged in Coomassie, Prempeh's ex-capital.

They were terror-stricken, and well they might have been. Tens of thousands of frenzied Ashanti warriors surrounded the fort, chanting:

The governor came to Coomassie on a peace palaver,
He demanded money from us and sent white men to bring him the
    Stool of Gold.
Instead of money the governor shall have white men's heads.
The Golden Stool shall be well washed in white men's blood.

Then they stormed the fort. Again and again they charged, only to be driven back by the withering cannon fire and sharpshooting from within. Captain Armitage, one of the besieged, describes the scene as follows:

The picture which was presented from the verandah of the Residency that night beggars description. The blazing houses in the cantonment and the Fanti and Cape Coast lines, some of which the rebels had fired, cast a lurid light on the surging mass of humanity clustering around the fort walls, from which arose the wailing of women and the pitiful crying of little children, who wept with their mothers out of sympathy not knowing the danger realized by their elders.

Behind all towered the black wall of the forest which surrounds

Coomassie, from which were borne the triumphant shouts of the rebels, who had at last caged the white man within the narrow limits of the fort. It was a night never to be forgotten.

Governor Hodgson tried to get word through to Accra but it was weeks before he succeeded. The first week in May he announced that he could hold out but eight or ten days longer. By May 31, relief had not yet come and provisions had almost run out.

Kobina Cheri, who was in command of the Ashanti, demanded the return of King Prempeh and the abolishment of forced labor as peace terms.

Day and night Ashanti tom-toms, male and female, as they are called, beat out their messages from camp to camp.

> First Camp: Do you hear the Buffalo moving in the forest?
> Second Camp: We hear him.
> First Camp: We are like the Buffalo in strength and bravery.
> Second Camp: We are like him, too.

Four months passed and the garrison held grimly on. The Europeans ate their parrots, dogs, monkeys, and domestic pets of all sorts. Rats fetched two and a half dollars each. Now and then friendly natives smuggled in food—but not enough.

Surrender seemed inevitable, when news came that General Sir James Wilcocks was fighting his way through the forest with an expedition. Except for its white officers, this army was composed of West African natives.

In a battle at the fort General Wilcocks defeated the rebels. Among those who fell was their dashing leader, Kobina Cheri. Wounded, he was taken prisoner and hanged the next day in the marketplace as an object lesson. To the last he was a rebel, urging his men, who had been brought to see him die, not to give up.

The war went on for several months more, the Ashanti fighting valorously, sometimes charging to within ten feet of the blazing guns that mowed them down. Peace was restored a year later.

And what about the Golden Stool? Its subsequent history, even as told in the language of official documents, reads like a romance.

For twenty-four years nothing was heard of it. Its guardians were vigilant and faithful to their trust. They could not be bribed. On one occasion its hiding place was nearly discovered by accident. This happened in the course of laying a government road, the bed of which was to run right over the spot where the Stool lay buried between two huge sheets of brass. Laborers were near the spot when the dismayed custodian arrived and frightened them away by telling them that the spirit of smallpox was buried there. That night the surviving guardian, aided by a friend, took it to the home of a third Ashanti. A solemn oath never to surrender the Golden Stool was again taken.

For four years nothing more was heard of it, then it burst into startling prominence again. There were rumors that it had been discovered at last. An old crone who had once seen the Stool identified two of its ornaments, the Golden Bells and the Golden Fetters, in the window of a pawnshop.

Inquiry revealed that a native goldsmith named Kujo Ruko had melted down several of the ornaments, having bought them cheaply from another native, named Yogo. It developed that the guardians of the Stool were robbers.

Ashanti indignation flared up with characteristic vigor. Only the protection of British soldiers saved the robbers from being torn to pieces of angry mobs. All Ashanti went into mourning.

The two culprits were handed over to a native tribunal and promptly sentenced to death—but as a result of British intervention the penalty was commuted to life imprisonment and exile.

The hiding place of what is left of the Golden Stool remains a mystery to this day. King Prempeh was permitted to return to Ashanti in 1925 after taking an oath of allegiance to Great Britain. His people welcomed him back and he regained his former prestige. He kept his word to the English, and spent the rest of his life laboring to improve the lot of his people. He died in May, 1931, respected and beloved by white and black alike. If he knew the secret of the Golden Stool at the time of his death, he never betrayed it.

REFERENCES

What we call "fetish" in the case of the primitive is closely related to what we call "religion" in the civilized. In fact, civilized customs and religions are, to a greater or lesser extent, but inheritances of the past.

Baden-Powell, R. S., *Downfall of Prempeh*. London, 1896.

Fuller, F. C., *A Vanished Destiny*. London, 1921.

Kemp, D., *Nine Years on the Gold Coast*.

Hall, W. M., *Great Drama of Kumasi*. 1939.

Illustrated London News, Mar. 14, 1896, p. 344.

Reindorf, C., *History of the Gold Coast and Ashanti*. 1895.

ADDITIONAL REFERENCES

Barnes, Leonard, *Empire or Democracy*. London, Victor Gollancz, Ltd., 1839.

Boahen, Adu, *Topics in West African History*, pp. 128–129. London, Longmans, Green and Company, Ltd., 1966.

De Graft-Johnson, J. C., *African Glory*, pp. 181–182. New York, Walker and Company, 1954.

Du Bois, W. E. B., *The World and Africa*, p. 36. New York, International Publishers, 1965.

Eastman, Albert E. Wilson, "Prempeh, the Last Ashanti King." *Negro History Bulletin*, pp. 19–22. Washington, D.C., Association for the Study of Negro Life and History.

Fage, J. D., *A History of West Africa*, pp. 168, 185. Cambridge, Cambridge University Press, 1969.

Flint, John E., *Nigeria and Ghana*, pp. 138–139, 155–156. Englewood Cliffs, N.J., Prentice-Hall, 1966.

Kimble, David, *A Political History of Ghana 1850–1928*, pp. 75, 153, 264, 272, 280–294, 295–300, 315–321, 479–485. Oxford, The Clarendon Press, 1963.

Ward, W. E. F., *A History of the Gold Coast*. London, Allen and Unwin Company, 1848.

Glaoui Pasha

"THE BLACK PANTHER" OF MOROCCO
(1893–1956)

HADJ THAMI EL-GLAOUI, Pasha of Marrakesh and Lord of the Atlas, was head of a Berber clan that has been in power in Morocco for more than a thousand years.

Until his death on January 23, 1956, the Pasha of Marrakesh, who was the ruler of Southern Marrakesh, was called many high-sounding names, and he literally deserved most of them. Among his other titles were: "Lord of the Atlas," "The Black Sultan," and "The Gazelle of the Sus" (the Sus being the rich fertile valley below Marrakesh over which he provided).

The Pasha, who was the most powerful figure in Morroco during his lifetime, possessed the highest decorations and orders bestowed by the French government, which considered him a valuable ally. He wore the Croix de Guerre, the Grand Cross of the Legion of Honor, and the Médaille Militaire, a decoration reserved for generals. On his visits to France he received honors equal to that of a royal visitor. For instance, during the International Colonial Exposition of 1931, he led the grand march of the ball with Miss Universe.

The prince began life humbly: his father was a salt merchant and his mother a Negro slave. Ability and force of character brought him to the fore.

V. C. Scott O'Connor, an English writer who was a guest in his palace, gives a vivid and intimate picture of him.

Glaoui sits there in his place unlike any one that one has ever known, with his large liquid eyes in their deep recesses, small aquiline nose, narrow chin, high cheek bones, a thin pointed beard, lips a little thick, delicate fingers and hands, a small soft wrist; traces of his Negro blood clearly written in the shadows under his eyes and in the dark color of his skin. He has somewhat the air of a scholar, even (if his lips did not forbid it) of an ascetic; he is gentle in his manner, has a low musical voice, laughs now and then in a subdued way, tells a good story and takes his share in the talk. His manner has not the grand air of the Arab; the stately reserve of the true Oriental, or the bluff style of an old warrior, or a Rajput Chief. No, this man is altogether exceptional. His military qualities and ardor in battle, for which he is known throughout the Atlas, are concealed behind a pensive and intellectual brow; the stern and cruel temper of a Berber chieftain—he must have sent many a man, enemy, rival, friend, to his death—behind an air that is almost gentle and deprecatory. The immense power he wields and is possessed of—he has never less than 12,000 men under arms in the Atlas—make no sign of their existence here. His iron hand is veiled under the glove of hospitality.

The Pasha, for all his frail physique, is a man of immense energy; he rides far and fast and exults in battle; yet he glides over the marble floor of his palace to wait with a fine courtesy upon his guests, offering to one a more convenient chair, to another a light for his cheroot. The French call him "La Panthère Noire." A Florentine of the Renaissance might have recognized in him a man and a brother. Rome in her later hours might have found for him a distinguished place. Like many Orientals, he is a collector of exquisite books, and many illuminated pages—the wreck of old Moorish libraries—have passed through his hands. Stories by the hundreds circulate about him. He has played the great game of the French in Morocco and has risen through the vicissitudes of the time to power. Some will tell you that though the head of the tribe of the Glaoui, his father once sold salt for a living and was no one at all; that his mother was a Negro slave. Others, that his methods of finance combine the dark practices of the Middle Ages with those that are most advanced in our present days of grace. In London and Paris, he has brokers who attend to his orders in the Stock Exchange; at the capital of the Protectorate he owns a sumptuous hotel for the accommodation of travellers from Europe and the United States; but at Marrakeech and in the recesses of the Atlas, he turns the screws of power in the ways that are better understood in the East. The profiteer feels the weight of his courtly hand. He is invited to dinner with the Pasha; he is received with

Glaoui Pasha

distinction; he is embraced by My Lord. Course after course of the most tastily cooked food passes before him and all is well. Then the Pasha gravely intimates, confides to his friend, the depletion of his fortunes; the expenses to which he is put on behalf of the State; the necessity for a loan. He whispers a sum that must sound formidable in Hassanis. The guest is heartbroken over the Pasha's misfortunes; for he also has suffered from the same blows of Fate. They part company; but the next day or the next, mules carrying the appointed burden enter the court of the Pasha's palace. This loan has no limit of time, it is soon forgotten.

But sometimes all is not well. Then misfortunes begin to overtake our profiteer; he retires for a solace to his country house or embarks upon a journey. But travel in Morocco has still its dangers; and one day there comes the sad news that he is dead.

In the mountains, the Pasha's methods are less ceremonious. At Telouet, holding a great pass across the Atlas, is the castle of the Glaoui; a grandiose and imposing place full of dungeons, where people live forgotten or die unknown to the world; and no man can cross that snow-driven pass that links the oasis of the Sahara with the Western Ocean without the knowledge and sanction of its Lord. Even the great Sultan, Mulai-el-Hassan, approached it with anxiety.

A crowd of attendants now advance like a flight of birds with a brass bowl and flagons of water and balls of transparent soap. The towels are perfumed. Then a low round table of soft wood is placed in our midst and the good Moorish bread is distributed from a basket. Soup of an excellent quality follows in little bowls, and after it a succession of dishes; the pastella, a vast circular pastry, delicately flavored, containing within its folds—its mille feuille—morsels of meat and poultry, of eggs and pistachios, and sprinkled over with a faint powder of sugar and cinnamon. The pastella comes from Spain —bestilla they call it here—and upon each such a dish might Abder-Rahman have feasted in Cordova in the days of his prime. The triumphs of the Pasha's women is followed by wild duck stuffed tightly with a delicately perfumed and flavored rice, and so admirably cooked that though all the bones of the ducks have been removed, they retain their original form.

Chickens follow, cooked in diverse ways, with olives and celery and strips of lemon; and after these joints of mutton baked crisp; and all in their turn so good and tender that fingers suffice to pull them to pieces. That is one of the merits of Moorish cookery. The traditional Couscous imported by the Barbary pirates from Provence, and now become the common dish of every Moorish home, makes way for a caramel, a compliment to the Bashadour.

P. Turnbull, another writer, who has lived among the Moroccans, says:

By far the most interesting of the Berber notables of today is Hadj Thami El Glaoui, Pasha of Marrakech, a real figure of romantic mediaeval fiction.

In appearance he is the very personification of the name given to him by a French journalist—the Black Panther.

He is tall and sparely built. His dusky features are aquiline and despite the fact that he is over sixty years of age his gaze is as keen as one of his mountain eagles. There is something feline in his movement. It is though he glides rather than walks. There is a feline impersonality in the coldness of his eyes and his mirthless smile as he passes swiftly by in one of his many luxurious cars. . . .

It is difficult to realize that the calm suave Oriental who walks in his lovely gardens quietly discussing politics and finance, who plays golf on his private course amid the palm trees, watches the dancing at Mamounia, and yearly takes the waters at Aix and Vichy, is the same man who has led his Berber warriors in a hundred battles in blazing sun or bitter cold, who is, in truth, more at home in the saddle of a plunging Barb war-horse than the cushions of his Rolls-Royce, and who could tell, did he wish, a thousand tales of raids, vendetta, bloodshed, torture and intrigue.

El-Glaoui's attitude toward world affairs is reflected in an interview given to Henry J. Taylor, Scripps-Howard staff writer and published in the *New York World-Telegram*, January 6, 1944:

America got some friendly caution and straight-from-the-shoulder advice today from Hadj Thami El Glaoui, the Pasha of Marrakech and potentate of this vital Atlantic section of the Moslem world. He gave it in terms of basic Moslem viewpoints regarding events on this fiery globe, which contains more Mohammedans than Christians and at a time when so many eyes are looking toward the East.

The talk was plain, but the circumstances were somewhat more formal.

In receiving me El Glaoui, as he is called everywhere in Islam, was granting the first interview given by any Moroccan pasha to any United Nations or Axis publications since the outbreak of the war.

The palace is in the restricted Medina section of the beautiful, mountain-rimmed city of Marrakech. I was escorted to El Glaoui who, as is customary, stood with his retinue in full Arab raiment and fingered a large bunch of keys.

Following the salutations, he directed the chamberlain to open a huge mosaic door to the reception apartments. I was motioned to enter alone, and the pasha himself locked the door from the inside.

We went into a sunlit garden like something out of the Arabian Nights, with rows of beautiful fruit-bearing trees shading a brilliantly tiled pool. Next we entered the potentate's personal apartments, removed our shoes and reclined on magnificent low divans beside a table laden with sweet mint tea and honey cakes. My host now was ready to talk.

At the time of the American landing in North Africa El Glaoui had wholeheartedly urged French and Arab co-operation with us, and I now asked why he had done this. Speaking in low, musical Eastern tones, in perfect French and with some English, El Glaoui told me that his impressions had been thoroughly bad of earlier visits paid him by Dr. Fritz Grobba, the "Colonel Lawrence" of Germany, and by George Werner von Hentig, chief of the Arab bureau of the German Foreign Office.

"Superficially the Germans' contacts with the Moslem world have been excellent," he explained. "But basically the Germans never have understood the Moslem world in its roots any more than they have understood America.

"The Germans are provincial Europeans. That is why they always make bad guesses, proceed half way, then fail. Notice the parallel between their traditional expectations that America will stay out of war, and their traditional expectations that the Arabs will revolt.

"Both are hopeful major policies of Germany, long pre-dating Hitler and consistently followed by him—for Hitler is the complete German traditionalist in foreign policy. And notice that both of these hopes still fail, at vast cost to the Germans."

For contrast, I asked the Pasha about Moslem reaction to America's current policies overseas. He answered: "I am sorry to say it is already plain that while America's policies are completely different in spirit and intention than Germany's, America must proceed with great caution—a caution not evidenced so far—or she will fall heir to the same deep-rooted antagonism and unending conflicts which the Germans would have encountered if their plans had prevailed.

"For example, Americans want to do everything quickly, so they are likely to do it badly. This mistaken speed will embroil your country in the same suspicions, resistances and resentments as though her purposes were bad. Strange as it may seem to far-off American policy-

makers, the fact is that the Moslem world does not want the wondrous American world or the incredible American way of life.

"We want the world of the Koran. There are devotional fragments
in the Koran which represent sustained theological, social and political doctrines for the Islamic areas, and nothing can be done peacefully in matters of individual freedom or prosperity which does not
remain within the limits of the faith expressed by the Mohammedan
Bible."

Referring to American radio campaigns suggesting a new day everywhere and undertaking to implant American concepts globally, El
Glaoui said: "If it does not seem impertinent coming from what I
realize you regard as a backward people, my view is that in these
current, world-wide guarantees, America either must omit the Moslem
world, which is the largest bloc, or else it must take over the responsibility of French, British, Belgian, Portuguese and Spanish positions
throughout the Moslem world.

"The radio talk from distant America is contrary to the actual
performance of America's allies, and such a position is obviously
untenable if not dangerous in the extreme.

"America either must assume the bewildering economic, social and
military responsibilities inherent in her dramatic words or else permit
others to do the best they can on the spot—including the French here
and the British elsewhere.

"American policy today stirs up everything and settles nothing. The
result is that it creates a void opening the way to new tyrannies
instead of new freedoms. At the bottom of America's attitude is the
assumption that all the world wishes to be American. And this assumption is false."

Near the end of his life Glaoui Pasha made several political
moves that, on reflection, were not to the best interest of Morocco.
He supported the French in their deportation of King Mohammed
V. The rise of Moroccan nationalism and the aggregation for the
return of the Moroccan King soon made him have some second
thoughts about matter. Soon he let it be known that he respected
the new political climate developing in Morocco. In addition to
supporting the aspirations for independence, he too demanded the
return of King Mohammed V. On January 23, 1956, Si Hadji
Thami El-Glaoui, the Pasha of Marrakesh, died of cancer. In his
lifetime he had become one of the most remarkable figures in the
history of Africa.

REFERENCES

O'Connor, V. C. S., *A Vision of Morocco*, pp. 296–300. London, 1923.
Turnbull, P., *Black Barbary*, pp. 48–51. London, 1939.
National Geographic, Mar., 1932, pp. 300–302.

ADDITIONAL REFERENCES

Gunther, John, *Inside Africa.* New York, Harpers, 1955.
Maxwell, Gavin, *Lords of the Atlas*, pp. 153–268. New York, E. P. Dutton and Company, Inc., 1966.
Mellor, F. H., *The True Morocco.* Casablanca, Argus, 1952.
True Magazine, Nov., 1955.
The Middle East Journal, Winter, 1953.
Reporter, Aug. 13, 1954.
Current Biography, Sept., 1954.

Isaac Wallace-Johnson

※※

AFRICA'S INDOMITABLE LABOR LEADER
(1895–1965)

Isaac Wallace-Johnson (Akku'nna Jaja), who was Africa's foremost labor leader, was born in Wilberforce, Sierra Leone, West Africa, the son of Odieka Jaja, a leading political and religious figure of Sierra Leone, and brother of the African king, Jack Jaja, a celebrated warrior and trader, who was deported by the British, it is said, not so much for his warlike activities as for his skill as a trader.

He was educated at the village school of Wilberforce and later at the Centenary Tabernacle school at Freetown, the capital, where he was regarded as the most positive and determined pupil. An able student and athlete, he was chosen leader by his fellow students.

At eighteen he entered the service of the Sierra Leone government as an outdoor officer of the customs department at a salary of $5 weekly. Considering this too small, he organized the other outdoor officers and eight months later led them in a strike for better wages, for which he was dismissed. However, a year later, in 1915, due to the shortage of labor caused by the first World War, he and his comrades were reinstated. Again he demanded higher wages and better working conditions. He was transferred to the Carrier Corps where he rendered valuable services as record and confidential clerk to the officer commanding the Royal Army Service Corps.

Demobilized in 1920, he served with the United Africa Company, a private concern, but again entered the government service as senior assistant clerk and typist in the town clerk's office at Freetown, rising soon afterward to the position of chief clerk of the Water-works Department.

Deciding that he and his fellow employees in this department were being underpaid, he organized them with a view to getting shorter hours, more pay, and a pension for long service. As a result, he was discharged.

Unable to get work either in private or government employ because of his record as an organizer, he finally became a seaman, and in the next five years he visited Europe, Asia, and other parts of Africa. During his spare time he published a small periodical, known as *The Seafarer*, urging seamen to demand better wages and working conditions. Nearly all of his slender earnings went into this magazine.

In 1931, while in Nigeria, he decided to devote himself henceforth to labor organizing and founded the Nigerian Workers Union, the first labor union in that British colony. He met great opposition from both white employers and conservative blacks, but he continued, undaunted by threats, and the same year was invited to attend the World Labor Conference at Moscow, where he was well received and where he studied at the People's University.

Two years later he returned to Nigeria, where he became an even more marked man to the authorities, and became allied with Herbert Macaulay, civil engineer and noted African political leader. A member of the International Negro Committee, Wallace-Johnson wrote for the *Negro Worker* but was forced to use pen names such as W. Daniels (under which name he had gone to Moscow) and Abdul Mohammed Afric. He was also editor of the *Nigerian Daily Telegraph*, and during his editorship the office was raided seven times and his poems, articles, and books exposing the bad treatment of Africans were seized.

Forced out of Nigeria by continual persecution and blocking of his activities by the authorities, he went to the neighboring colony of Gold Coast in 1933. At Accra he soon made his presence felt and with two faithful associates, Bankole Awooner Renner and Wuta Ofei, organized the West Coast Youth League. In the women's work he was ably assisted by Mary Lokko, head of the Ethiopian Ladies' League and Ethiopia Relief Fund. At the same time he also wrote for the *Gold Coast Spectator* and the *African Morning Post*.

In May, 1936, during the Italo-Ethiopian War, an article of his in the latter paper caused his arrest and prosecution for seditious libel. It was entitled "Has the African a God?" and asked whether the God being preached to Africans was not really an instrument for the furthering of white exploitation. It said, in part:

Personally, I believe the European has a God in whom he believes and whom he is representing in his churches all over Africa. He believes in the god whose name is Deceit. He believes in the god whose law is "Ye strong, you must weaken still further the weak." Ye "civilized" Europeans you must "civilize" the "barbarious" Africans with machine-guns. Ye "Christian" Europeans you must "Christianize" the "pagan" Africans with bombs, poison gases, etc.

Wallace-Johnson fought the case vigorously from one court to another. Finally he was convicted, two of his judges, Africans, declaring him not guilty, the third, white, finding him guilty. The white judge, whose vote was, of course, decisive, sentenced him to a fine of £50 ($250) or three months' imprisonment. Wallace paid the fine and took his case to the African Court of Appeals where he again lost. He next appealed to the Privy Council in England but the members of that distinguished body, headed by the Lord Chancellor, Lord Caldecott, rendered a most curious decision. They declared that they found the words of the article clear and unambiguous and entirely free of sedition either in act or content but they upheld the conviction on the ground that Wallace-Johnson was convicted under the Gold Coast Criminal Code, which held that such an attack on religion reflected on the government of the colony. In short, this highest court in the British Empire declared that there was one law for England and Scotland and another for Gold Coast natives, though all were under the same king, and that any native who made an utterance that the authorities decided would bring them hatred and contempt was a criminal.

While in England fighting his case, Wallace-Johnson used much of his time to organize the International Service Bureau and the Pan-African Federation for the purpose of disseminating information to all African peoples and also to get members of the British Parliament interested in the welfare of African workers. In this he was ably assisted by George Padmore, noted Negro socialist.

The activities of these two bodies at once brought colonial affairs to the forefront of British politics and when Wallace-Johnson returned to West Africa the same year he was arrested at Sierra Leone and his magazine, *The African Sentinel*, confiscated as subversive. His pamphlet, *Africa and the World*, was also seized by the comptroller of customs. The magazine contained parliamentary debates on oppressive conditions in Africa. Wallace-Johnson brought suit to recover his property but lost even though the comptroller of customs admitted his incompetence as an expert on what was seditious.

While detained in Sierra Leone, Wallace-Johnson organized the West African Youth League and the All Seamen's Union for better working conditions for all workers in the colony. He also founded the *African Standard* as the official organ of the Youth League, which gained considerable popularity and became the leading nationalist newspaper in Sierra Leone and the most widely distributed weekly paper in West Africa in the 1930s.

In the meantime, the authorities were leaving no stone unturned to silence him and stop his union activities. He was declared inimical to the welfare of the colony under the Defense Regulations and several unsuccessful attempts were made to imprison him. Finally on September 3, 1939, a few days after England declared war on Germany, he was arrested by order of Sir Douglas Jardine, governor of the colony, and thrown into an internment camp along with the German residents of the colony. He was barred from seeing everyone, including his lawyer.

The charge was criminal libel. In the previous August he had published an article in the *African Standard* entitled "Who Killed Foni?" An African of that name had been tied to a post in the Sherbro district by a white district commissioner who had gone there to collect taxes and had met with some opposition. Foni died while tied to the post and Wallace-Johnson declared that the official who had ordered him tied was responsible for his death. Inquiries conducted in the colony as well as by the secretary of state for the colonies in London bore out the truth of his charge but he was convicted nevertheless and sentenced to a year's hard labor at the Central Prison, Pademba Road, Freetown. While in prison, he won the high esteem of the officials there and with spirit unbroken wrote poems which were published under the title *Prison in the Muse* and had a large circulation. Conditions in the prison were shocking and he wrote letters to the authorities reporting them. The eventual result was an investigation which resulted in the transfer of the warden.

On March 19, 1942, after having served a total of two years and seven months in prison and the internment camp, he was exiled to the mosquito-infested island of Bonthe. He was accompanied by his wife, Enith Downes, a West Indian whom he had met in London, and several faithful comrades.

While in exile, he continued his activities among the Sherbro natives, organizing the workers into the Sherbro Amalgamated Union as well as teaching the children and the adults to read and write. He was so beloved by the people of Sherbro that when an order for his release finally came from London they heard it with regret even though they rejoiced at his victory.

On his return to Freetown, he was elected by a majority vote to attend the World Trade Union Congress in London in February, 1945. He was hailed as a hero there and feted and greatly publicized by the labor and liberal newspapers of the United Kingdom. His addresses pleading for greater support for trade unionism in Africa were enthusiastically received and help was promised by the Conference. He was also elected a member of the Post War Reconstructionist Committee.

Elected unanimously as a delegate to the World Federation of Trade Unions Congress, which was held in Paris in September, 1945, he made a similar impression there and was elected to the Executive Committee of the WFTU.

Undaunted by threats, persecution, imprisonment, he returned to West Africa the same year and resumed his activities on a greater scale. In June, 1946, despite all attempts of the authorities to block him, he left for London on his way to Moscow to attend the Executive Council of the World Federation of Trade Unions, of which he was a member, but in London he was prevented from leaving for Moscow by the British government.

The independence explosion that started in 1957, in the Gold Coast, which was renamed Ghana, brought the work of Isaac Wallace-Johnson again to public attention. Dr. Kwame Nkrumah, George Padmore, and others who remembered him as one of the organizers of the great Pan-African Congress of 1945, in Manchester, England, made use of his service in developing new approaches to trade unionism in present-day Africa. He continued in his work until his death in May, 1965.

Thanks to his unselfish and untiring efforts the African laboring class, one of the most badly treated in the world, has a new vision. It is awakening to a realization of its immense strength. Wallace-Johnson indeed awakened Africa to a new day. No longer is it being so easily trampled on by ruthless imperialist exploiters.

Haile Selassie

HAILE SELASSIE I, King of Kings of Ethiopia, last of the independent sovereigns of Africa, was born on July 17, 1891, reckoned by the Western calendar, and in 1883, according to the Ethiopian one. His father was Ras Makonnen, a nephew of Menelik, who distinguished himself in the victorious war against Italy in 1896.

Haile Selassie was an extraordinarily bright youth and showed great promise of statesmanship at an early age. At fourteen he was named governor of Garamoulata, which post he relinquished upon the death of his father in order to reside at the court of Menelik.

There he continued his studies under Ethiopian and European tutors. Then Menelik appointed him governor of Basso, which post he filled with such competence that he was made administrator of Harrar, the most important province of Ethiopia, while still in his teens.

At this time he nearly lost his life. While crossing Lake Arumüya with a party of seven, his boat capsized. He managed to swim ashore, but all the others were drowned.

As a result of political intrigue he was removed from Harrar and sent to the distant province of Caffa, but thanks to his skill and integrity, he was soon restored to Menelik's favor.

On Menelik's death, Lidj Yassu, Menelik's grandson, came to

the throne. Lidj Yassu's father, Ras Michael, was a Mohammedan, and Lidj Yassu showed Islamic sympathies. He took several wives, wore the fez, and sided with the "Mad" Mullah, a
Mohammedan prophet, who had driven the British from all of
Somaliland save the coastal region.

For 1600 years Ethiopia's policy had been a Christian one, and
as the King of England pledges himself to maintain Protestantism,
so the Emperor of Ethiopia swears to uphold Christianity. By
his observance of Mohammedan customs, Lidj Yassu not only
committed a breach of faith but violated Ethiopian law.

During World War I Lidj Yassu sided with Germany and tried
to effect a union of Christian and Mohammedan against England
and her allies. Since Ethiopia is of strategic importance to Britain,
the maintenance of Christianity in Ethiopia and her friendliness to
England are of vital political significance to Great Britain. Lidj's
efforts, while very laudable from a patriotic viewpoint, were rash,
as they threatened to increase British hostility and intrigue and
expose the country to an attack by the united forces of England
and France. Therefore, the Abuna, or head of the Ethiopian
church, and the Ethiopian leaders deposed Lidj Yassu, putting in
his place Zaiditu, or Judith, a daughter of Menelik. Haile Selassie
(then Ras Tafari) was named heir to the throne and regent.

Lidj Yassu's father, Ras Michael, gathered a large army and
marched against the forces of the Christians. In a great battle
fought at Sagalle on October 27, 1916, Ras Michael was totally
defeated. Haile Selassie, who was one of the Christian commanders, distinguished himself by his skillful generalship and his valor.

When Lidj Yassu raised another army in 1921, Haile Selassie
marched against him, captured him, and held him prisoner.

In 1923 Haile Selassie showed his ability as a statesman by
maneuvering himself into the League of Nations in the face of
opposition from England, Australia, Holland, Norway, and Lithu-
ania, but with the support of France, Italy, Portugal, Belgium, and
the Latin American nations. Thereafter, none of the European
powers could attack Ethiopia without breaking the covenant of
the League. At the time, Haile Selassie's move seemed a very wise
one.

In 1924 he toured Europe with an impressive retinue of thirty rases and chiefs with their respective retinues. Some of these were his enemies who were secretly plotting to dethrone him, and he took them along to keep his eye on them.

In England he was received by King George at Buckingham Palace and Cambridge University conferred the degree of LL.D. on him. King Albert of Belgium, Victory Emmanuel of Italy, the President of France, and other rulers received him with due honors. Victor Emmanuel bestowed on him the Collar of the Annunziata, Italy's highest distinction, which made the recipient a "cousin" of the King of Italy.

On his return to Ethiopia he launched a program for modernizing the ancient empire. He introduced the telephone and the airship, built a wireless station, and sent promising Ethiopian youths to be trained in France, Germany, England, and the United States, looking forward to the day when the great natural resources of Ethiopia would be developed by his own mechanics, engineers, and scientists. To insure the success of these efforts, he himself worked from sixteen to eighteen hours a day—a great feat in a hot climate. Haile Selassie knew that in order to win the sympathy and good will of the world, he must nullify the charge that he was permitting rich territory fit for "white" habitation to remain in a backward state.

He also took steps to reform the old patriarchal system of government, and remodeled the police and army organizations.

All this was done under great opposition from the Empress Zaiditu and her party. His opponents held that the old customs were good enough, hoping that by preserving these, the European influence, which has proved so disastrous to the freedom of all African peoples, might be curbed. Haile Selassie, on the other hand, thought it might be possible to adopt beneficial European customs and inventions, and at the same time keep European influence within bounds. Perhaps he would have preferred a minimum of this. As he once said, "We need European progress only because we are surrounded by it. That is at once a benefit and a misfortune."

In 1928, in recognition of his services, the leaders of Ethiopia appointed Haile Selassie negus, or king, and he was crowned in October of that year. Nominal power still remained in the hands of Empress Zaiditu. The same year he concluded a treaty of perpetual peace with Italy.

In 1930 Ras Guksa, husband of the empress, revolted. Haile Selassie marched against him and defeated him, Ras Guksa being among the slain.

The tragic news of her husband's death proved so great a shock to Zaiditu that she died. Haile Selassie succeeded to the throne and was crowned amid great ceremonies and festivities at Addis Ababa on November 2, 1930. Among those present at the coronation were the Duke of Gloucester, son of George V; the Duke of Udine, nephew of Victor Emmanuel of Italy; and Marshal Franchet d'Esperev of France.

But the accession of the throne by no means gave Haile Selassie a free hand to carry out his reforms. He had, first of all, to contend with the powerful rases, or rulers of provinces, who were even more jealous of their power than the various states of the American Union have been of theirs. Some of the chiefs were subjects only in name, and were actually hostile to the central authority. Lack of roads and communications made it impossible for the emperor to check them on short notice. Wild tribesmen profited by this situation too, and they invaded the territory of adjoining nations, bringing reproach on the central government and necessitating the payment of indemnities.

Another domestic obstacle was the swarming Ethiopian clergy, which was very powerful and as opposed to science, innovation, and modern methods, particularly medical science, as were their European brethren in the Middle Ages.

Haile Selassie also had to contend with incessant foreign intrigue for economic control and even seizure of his country that went on not only abroad but in Ethiopia itself.

His economic difficulties were tremendous. Ethiopia, although rich in natural resources, was in the stage of primitive agriculture. Her coinage was unstable, and being based on silver, was of trifling value in the purchase of modern implements in the gold countries. Furthermore, reforms are usually financed by foreign loans, but Ethiopian policy was not to borrow abroad. Haile Selassie felt that the first step toward losing his independence would be to borrow money from Europe or America. Thus the lack of money to carry out his reforms was his greatest handicap.

Yet, while working under these and other disadvantages, he was able to institute a parliament and modern court system, build roads, hospitals, and schools, and install electric lighting in the streets. He improved commercial and international relations, all the while steering a diplomatic course between the opposing factions and religions in his own land.

His daily duties were many and complete. He received the diplomats of various nations; attended to minute details affecting the government and the army; gave orders and personally inspected the erection of an important building or the installation of machinery; and served as chief justice of the empire. Each subject, however lowly, had the right of direct appeal to the emperor, a privilege which Haile Selassie scrupulously observed.

With all of these duties, he managed to keep an almost housewifely eye on details. Passing along the highway in his red Rolls-Royce, it was not at all uncommon for him to stop, get out, and show the Gouragi road workers how to perform their job best, and sometimes he would lift a stone himself and put it where it belonged, by way of illustration. He has truly been the guiding spirit of his nation, providing the rare example of a monarch who is really the greatest in his land not only in name but also in worth, ability, and vision.

As one writer said:

The weight of the whole empire rested upon the shoulders of this quiet but iron-hearted little sovereign. Night and day he was beset by a thousand different problems and a thousand different worries and perplexities. Even while he ate, he transacted state business. Even while he slept, he had no respite.

His secretary slept at the foot of his majesty's bed, ready at a moment to take the Emperor's orders in the event His Majesty awoke and thought about something he had forgotten during the day. Under terrific strain he struggled to transform his medieval empire into a modern state.

It was amazing how he managed all this for he has always been frail in appearance. Like Napoleon and Gandhi, he is small, being about five feet tall and weighing but one hundred and ten pounds.

Haile Selassie's outstanding achievement was his fight against slavery, which existed in Ethiopia from time immemorial. He began by freeing all the slaves in his palace, after which he made laws or the gradual emancipation of the remainder of the slaves in the empire. He provided free education and clothing for the children of slaves and ex-slaves, together with appointment to government posts, depending upon individual ability; he founded an antislavery society and an antislavery court; and made slave raiding punishable by death. In 1935 he issued a proclamation wiping out slavery forever.

In all his reforms Haile Selassie had to proceed slowly. He could not change the psychology of his people or educate them overnight. King Amanuallah of Afghanistan, who tried to hasten progress in his land, was forced out by a revolution. Haile Selassie's difficulties were increased by the anti-European attitude of his people. They knew that the Europeans were forever scheming to take away their land as they had already seized the rest of Africa.

War with Italy broke out in 1935 as the result of Mussolini's ambition to seize Ethiopia. Haile Selassie fought beside his men, enduring with them incredible hardships. His people, most of them primitive and illiterate, found themselves opposed by a European power armed with the latest and deadliest instruments of war. Against such weapons they had for the most part guns that had been discarded decades ago by Europe. Against Italy's large fleet of fighter planes and bombers Ethiopia had four small passenger planes, all unarmed.

In spite of this the Ethiopians were winning, thanks to the mountainous nature of their country, their knowledge of the terrain, and their valor, when the Italians resorted to wholesale slaughter by mustard gas showered down from planes.

Haile Selassie stayed on with his men until April 30, 1936, when the capture of his capital and the railway seemed imminent, then he yielded to the entreaties of his chiefs to go to Europe and place his nation's cause before the League of Nations.

There were those who thought that Haile Selassie should have remained with his people, but events have shown, as they did in the case of General MacArthur, who left his men at Corregidor, that his going was the wiser course.

Haile Selassie described the atrocity in his appeal to the League of Nations in 1936. He said:

It was at the time when the operations for the encircling of Makalle were taking place that the Italian command, fearing rout, followed the procedure which it is now my duty to denounce to the world. Special sprayers were installed on board aircraft so that they could vaporize, over vast areas of territory a fine, death-dealing rain. Groups of nine, fifteen, eighteen aircraft followed one another so that the fog issuing from them formed a continuous sheet. It was thus that, as far as the end of January, 1936, soldiers, women, children, cattle, rivers, lakes and pastures were drenched continually with this deadly rain. In order to kill off systematically all living creatures; in order the more surely to poison waters and pastures, the Italian command made its aircraft to pass over and over again. That was its chief method of warfare.

The very refinement of barbarism consisted in carrying ravage and terror into the most densely populated parts of the territory—the points farthest removed from the scene of hostilities. The object was to scatter fear and death over a great part of the Ethiopian territory.

These fearful tactics succeeded. Men and animals succumbed. The deadly rain that fell from the aircraft made all those whom it touched fly shrieking with pain. All those who drank the poisoned water or ate the infected food also succumbed in dreadful suffering. In tens of thousands the victims of Italian mustard gas fell. It is in order to denounce to the civilized world the tortures inflicted upon the Ethiopian people that I resolved to come to Geneva.

Haile Selassie's efforts at the League were fruitless. In vain he warned the representatives of the fifty-two nations assembled that international morality, or what there was of it, had broken down; that the life of no small nation was henceforth safe; that the Fascist ruthlessness that had engulfed him might one day engulf them. God and history, he told them, would remember their verdict. But hopes of trade with Italy stifled whatever conscience the larger nations had. They voted to withdraw the sanctions that had been imposed against Italy at the beginning of the war.

Later they sided, one by one, with the Fascist monster, and recognized the so-called conquest of Ethiopia as an accomplished fact. But many of them were to be in line for similar treatment. Poland and France, among the first to recognize Mussolini, were the first to taste the cruelty of Mussolini's partner, Hitler. France, the great accomplice of Mussolini against Ethiopia, remained four years under the Nazi heel. Wilhelmina, Queen of Holland, who was later to cry so loudly against the destruction of her country and the rape of her own people, had been among the most ardent advocates of recognizing the Italian rape of Ethiopia as lawful. Other Fascist recognizers to fall under the Nazi heel were Greece, Czechoslovakia, Belgium, Norway, and Denmark. England, which had so supinely appeased Mussolini, even to the giving over to him moneys that Haile Selassie had deposited years before in London as advance payment for cables and wireless service, saw her cities destroyed by bombs and robots even as Ethiopia's humble towns and villages, and the flower of her manhood killed in North Africa and France. Even Russia, the last to recognize Mussolini (November 26, 1940), did not escape. Fascist attack against her was the most terrible of all. Her eastern territories were devastated; her fine new cities reduced to rubble; and tens of millions of her men, women, and children killed, raped, and wounded.

But retribution did not end there. The Fascist nations, too, had their day of reckoning. Spain was torn with three years of civil war, her cities ruined, and hundreds of thousands of her people killed. Italy, weakened and almost bankrupt by the war against Haile Selassie, was dragged by Mussolini into the Second World War which left her prostrate with no hope of recovery as a great nation, while Mussolini was killed and hung up like a slaughtered hog for his people to shoot at and revile. Hitler, Mussolini's partner in crime who brought such ruin, suffering, and death to his own country that it is beyond human power to describe, killed himself. Perhaps never before in the history of the world had an attack on one small nation brought such accumulated evil on the attackers and their friends, real and opportunistic.

After his failure at Geneva, Haile Selassie remained an exile in Bath, England. As Mr. Tafari, he occupied a rambling gray stone Georgian house on a hilltop overlooking the fashionable town. The house was cold and draughty in the winter and was more than most of his household could bear. Colds were frequent and many left for the warmer weather of Palestine.

The Emperor's funds ran low. He had sold most of his silver

and family jewels to aid the Ethiopian refugees. He wrote his memoirs but the English publishers refused them. He made trips to Geneva in further vain appeals to the League of Nations. But he did not despair. In his broadcast to America he said, "Never shall I cease to hope and still I have faith in the ultimate triumph of international justice." Sustained by this belief, he laid plans for his return.

And that day was not far away. The League by its treatment of Ethiopia had committed suicide; international law and morality had returned to the rule of tooth and claw; and on September 1, 1939, fascism and so-called democracy came to death-grips. In June, 1940, France fell, and Italy, the nation she had helped seize Ethiopia, stabbed her in the back. Winston Churchill, in a speech proclaiming how much England had loved Ethiopia and the enmity she bore Italy because of that, declared Haile Selassie once more the legal ruler of his country.

On July 22, 1940, Haile Selassie arrived in Egypt. Donning the uniform of an Ethiopian general, he flew to Khartoum in the Sudan, where, meeting with his chiefs from Ethiopia, he laid plans with the British for the driving out of the Italians. Once again, he fought gallantly beside his people, and victorious this time, he entered Addis Ababa in triumph, May 6, 1941, after five years of exile.

One of his first acts was the setting up of a strong central government, made easier now by the hard lessons that those chiefs who had insisted on individual power had learned under Italian rule. The result was that when he opened his new parliament, November 4, 1942, and told his people that democracy was their only hope for progress, he found his chiefs far more ready to cooperate.

In disposition, Haile Selassie is firm. His people call him Arko (The Vise) because he holds to that which he believes is right. In March, 1935, when Mussolini demanded a diplomatic apology, an indemnity, and the saluting of the Italian flag at Addis Ababa over the Walwal incident, Haile Selassie sent him a flat refusal. In doing so, he took the unprecedented course of giving out his reply to the press before he notified Italy, thus giving Mussolini no chance to distort the truth.

When Bernard Shaw suggested to Haile Selassie that he yield to Italy and let Ethiopia become a protectorate, he replied, "I would rather kill myself, like Emperor Theodore sixty years ago, than become a puppet prince under the Italians.

"I would be unworthy of my great ancestors, beginning with Solomon, if I submitted to Italian vassalage. Nor can I, as sovereign of the oldest empire in the world, which had its beginning before the Flood, accept a British protectorate or an Anglo-French regime.

"We cannot cut up Ethiopia like a cake, handing sugared parts to this country and that country just to win their smiles and satisfy their sweet tooth.

"Would England or any other sovereign nation give up territory so willingly? No! I have taken an oath to the memory of the great Menelik to defend the empire until God calls me unto Him."

In manner Haile Selassie is pleasing and most affable, yet full of natural dignity. His face radiates intelligence, kindliness, good nature, and immense reserves of power. He smiles frequently. A true Christian, he has always observed the noblest injunctions of his faith. When a man who had tried to assassinate him was sentenced to death, Haile Selassie not only declined to sign the warrant, but forgave him. He also abolished public hangings; mutilation of habitual thieves; and endeavored to substitute for the old Mosaic law, by which a murderer is handed over to the victim's next of kin, modern justice. But it is also said that he never forgets an enemy.

Nearly everyone who has come in contact with him has been impressed by his personality. Karl von Weigand, a newspaper correspondent writing in *Cosmopolitan* magazine (March, 1936), said, "I know of no king or emperor who surpassed him in natural dignity, graciousness, refinement and ease. I have seen a number of white monarchs who do not even approach him in those qualities, or perhaps even in intelligence."

His character stands out in striking relief against that of Mussolini's. The latter glorified war. His method of settling with a rival was to threaten him, and if that failed, kill him. Haile Selassie, on the other hand, favors peace. His method of removing rivals is by reasoning and conciliation. He said in 1935, "We shall do all we can to avoid a war unworthy of civilization. We hope that right and justice shall always prevail over force." Mussolini said, "War becomes a man as motherhood becomes a woman. I maintain that peace is a negative virtue. It is only in war that one is revealed in a fitting light."

Born to autocratic power, Haile Selassie voluntarily relinquished it and endeavored to make Ethiopia a democracy. Mussolini, reared under a constitutional monarchy, and once a socialist himself, was more despotic than a sultan or a czar.

Haile Selassie belongs to the oldest family in the world, royal or otherwise. He is descended from King Ori, 4470 B.C. He can name all the rulers, his ancestors, who came after Ori. Despite his super-aristocratic lineage and the fact that he was invested with power more absolute than Mussolini was able to seize, he is modest, quiet, unassuming, affable, and utterly without pretension. Mussolini, on the other hand, was the descendant of a family that had been peasants for three centuries. His father was a blacksmith. He himself was a poor schoolmaster, who through ruthlessness as well as ability rose to supreme power in his native land. While it is character, not birth, that is important, and while servants who rise to power sometimes makes able and considerate masters, Mussolini exhibited all the odious traits of the servant who has risen to authority as mentioned in the Bible. He was a strutter, a poseur, a braggart. His patriotism was cheap because every move and gesture of his was spurious and calculated to impress the rabble. Like every parvenu, he was perpetually showing off. As Abdullah, King of Transjordania, said, "Mussolini's manner of speaking and the way he appears in photographs make me imagine him to be a cheap comedian." Mussolini was so theatrical that one felt it would be possible to lift him from the balcony of the Palazzio Venezia, and without any rehearsal whatsoever, put him on the grand opera stage of La Scala at Milan, and let the show go on. With his gesticulating and eyerolling alone, he could have made a fortune on the American stage as a clown.

Haile Selassie, on the other hand, is all that a true aristocrat should be. In his every move he is a gentleman, and he stands forth as a wise leader, a statesman not only of brains, but of heart. As such he is a ruler in the best sense of the word.

In his address to Parliament on July 18, 1935, he said, "We

have always believed that a government ennobles, not debases itself, when it voluntarily submits a quarrel to the judgment, perhaps the condemnation, of a qualified impartial international body."

Here is a model for all statesmen. With such an attitude prevailing the world over, wars would be no more. Thousands of years ago Ethiopia gave to the world the first ideal of right and wrong, the first morality. Now Haile Selassie again points the way to interracial and international amity and brotherhood, the true goal of civilization. He places right above politics.

In personal appearance Haile Selassie is equally prepossessing. His exquisitely chiseled features reflect refinement, culture, amiability, and intellectual sagacity. No picture of him has ever been able to capture the essence of his spirit. So far as a general impression of him is concerned, he has been truly described as a "black edition of the pictured Christ."

His beard and curly hair provide unmistakable proof of his African ancestry. In color he is a lightish black-brown and considerably darker than the published pictures of him. In the United States he would be immediately taken for an Afro-American.

In his family life Haile Selassie differs from most Eastern and African monarchs. He has only one wife and no concubines. In 1912 he married Weyzero Menen who bore him five children. The empress is a great-granddaughter of Menelik and a niece of the deposed emperor, Lidj Yassu.

Of Haile Selassie it may almost be said, "Behold the perfect man."

ADDITIONAL REFERENCES

Del Boca, Angelo, *The Ethiopian War 1935–1941*, trans. by P. D. Cummins. Chicago and London, The University of Chicago Press, 1965.

Greenfield, Richard, *Ethiopia*, pp. 200–203. New York, Washington, D.C., and London, Frederick A. Praeger, 1965.

Huggins, Willis N., *An Introduction to African Civilizations*, pp. 49, 85, 100. New York, Avon House, 1937.

Italiaander, Rolf, *The New Leaders of Africa*, pp. 55–63. Trans. by James McGovern. Englewood Cliffs, N.J., Prentice-Hall, 1961.

Sanford, Christine (Lush), *Ethiopia under Haile Selassie*. London, J. M. Dent and Sons, Ltd., 1946.

Talbot, David Abner, *Haile Selassie I*, The Hague, W. P. Van Stockum, 1955.